WHAT TEACHERS NEED TO KNOW

WHAT TEACHERS NEED TO KNOW

TOPICS IN DIVERSITY AND INCLUSION

Edited by
Matthew Etherington

Foreword by E. J. Boyce

WIPF & STOCK · Eugene, Oregon

WHAT TEACHERS NEED TO KNOW
Topics in Diversity and Inclusion

Copyright © 2017 Matthew Etherington. All rights reserved. Except for brief quotations in critical publications or reviews, no part of this book may be reproduced in any manner without prior written permission from the publisher. Write: Permissions, Wipf and Stock Publishers, 199 W. 8th Ave., Suite 3, Eugene, OR 97401.

Wipf & Stock
An Imprint of Wipf and Stock Publishers
199 W. 8th Ave., Suite 3
Eugene, OR 97401

www.wipfandstock.com

PAPERBACK ISBN: 978-1-4982-8907-8
HARDCOVER ISBN: 978-1-4982-8909-2
EBOOK ISBN: 978-1-4982-8908-5

Manufactured in the U.S.A.   MARCH 30, 2017

This book is dedicated to Susanna Pamela and Joanna Daisy—
from whom I have learned so very much.

Contents

Contributors | ix
Foreword by E. J. Boyce | xvii
Introduction: Education for All by Matthew Etherington | xix

Part One: Ethics

1. Family Pedagogy: (Re)claiming a Topic of Inclusion for Teacher Education—Sherick Hughes | 3
2. A Role for Teachers and Teacher Education in Developing Inclusive Practice—Martyn Rouse | 19
3. Achieving Culturally Sensitive Education with Faith-Informed Discourse—Jonathan Anuik | 36
4. Toward an Ecologically Informed Paradigm in Thinking about Educational Reforms—Chet Bowers | 51
5. Self-Worth and Meaning-Oriented Education—Eva Maria Waibel | 66
6. Uncritical Critical Thinking in Teaching and Learning: Smashing Down "Old" Ways of Thinking—Matthew Etherington | 82
7. Universities, Higher Education, and Ideological Diversity: Insights from Moral Foundations Theory—James Dalziel | 100

Part Two: Inclusion and Teacher Management

8. The Benefits of Choice in Education: A Canadian Perspective—Peter J. Froese | 121
9. Full Inclusion and Learners with Exceptional Needs: Educational Ideology vs. Practical Pedagogy—Ken Pudlas | 141
10. Building Resilience in Children in Relation to Bullying, Discipline, and Classroom Management—Lucinda Spaulding | 161
11. Education and Mental Health: A Parent Perspective—Karen Copeland | 181

12 Between Strangers and Friends: Toward a Theory of Hospitality, Reciprocity, and Respect for Difference in "Special Needs" Education—Bruce Shelvey | 197

13 The Teacher's Authority—Ken Badley | 216

Part Three: Worldview and Story

14 Worldview Inclusion in Public Schooling—John Valk | 233

15 What Teachers Need to Know about Tolerance—Matthew Etherington | 249

16 Experience, Education, and Story: A Transcultural Teacher Narrative—Edward R. Howe | 271

17 Considering the Nature of Science and Religion in Science Education—Adam Forsyth | 285

18 Epistemology, Religion, and the Politics of Inclusion in Ontario Public Education—Leo Van Arragon | 301

19 The Reconception of Story in Children's Picture Books: Will Any Story Do?—Christina Belcher | 320

20 Inclusion and Playing in the In-Between—Cynthia à Beckett | 338

General Index | 351

Contributors

Dr. Jonathan Anuik is an assistant professor in the Educational Policy Studies department at the University of Alberta in Edmonton, Alberta. His research interests are First Nations, Métis, and Inuit education policy and history and the pedagogy of history of education in Canadian teacher education.

Dr. Leo Van Arragon received his PhD at the University of Ottawa in 2015. His research on the regulation of religion in public education systems was conducted in the religious studies department and the Religion and Diversity Project. The title of his thesis is, "We Educate, They Indoctrinate: Religion and the Politics of Togetherness in Ontario Public Education." He coedited a book titled, *Issues in Religion and Education: Whose Religion?* (Brill, 2015), which includes his chapter titled, "Religion and Education in Ontario Public Education: Contested Borders and Uneasy Truces." He has presented numerous papers at Canadian and international conferences on religion and education. His doctoral research follows a thirty-seven-year career as a professional educator in privately funded Calvinist day schools in Ontario, working as a teacher, principal, and curriculum developer, and in political advocacy.

Dr. Ken Badley currently teaches foundations of education at Mount Royal University in Calgary, Alberta. He has taught in secondary, undergraduate, and graduate settings in Canada and the United States, as well as working with teachers in Kenya on seven occasions. He serves on the editorial board of the *New Educational Review* and as book review editor for the *International Journal of Christianity and Education*. Recent publications include *Voices from the Past: Wisdom for the Future of Christian Higher Education* (2016, with Patrick Allen), *Faith and Learning: A Guide for Faculty* (2014, with Patrick Allen), and *Educational Foundations in Canada*, with Jodi

Nickel and Allen Edmonds (2014). Ken lives in Calgary, Alberta, with his wife K. Jo-Ann Badley.

Dr. Cynthia à Beckett (DipKT, GradDipEdSt, BA (Hons) PhD) is a senior lecturer in early childhood education at the University of Notre Dame Australia–Sydney campus. She is an experienced teacher and academic in early childhood education with research interests in the sociology of childhood, young children and families, and the topic of play. She has published and presented her work both nationally and internationally. She is currently coediting a book with Sandra Lynch and Deborah Pike that provides new perspectives about play entitled *Multidisciplinary Perspectives on Play from Birth and Beyond*. In 2013 she was appointed to the board of SDN Children's Services, a high profile, community based organization that provides quality early childhood education and care in New South Wales, Australia.

Dr. Christina Belcher received her PhD in the Philosophy of Education from Monash University in Australia in 2012. Her dissertation was titled, "Worldview in Christian Higher Education: A Multidimensional Investigation into Experience, Narrative and Conceptions of Worldview." Christina is currently a full professor of education at Redeemer University College, where she is chair of the Department of Education. She has previously worked in higher education in Australia, New Zealand, and Canada, and writes widely on topics of children's literature, literacy, worldview, culture, higher education, and interdisciplinary collaboration. She has publications in academic journals and has contributed chapters in books on topics of literacy, higher education, children's literature, and worldview.

Dr. Chet Bowers (PhD from the University of California) has been invited to speak at thirty-nine foreign and forty-two American universities, and has written twenty books on the cultural and linguistic roots of the ecological crisis—as well as four books on how the digital revolution is undermining local democracy and the intergenerational knowledge of the cultural commons that will become more important as the ecological crisis deepens. His latest book, *Reforming Higher Education in an Era of Ecological Crisis and Digital Insecurities*, is now in press. His focus on language issues largely ignored across the disciplines, the failure to question the abstract and ethnocentric ideas of western philosophers, and the colonizing nature of the scientism that underlies the digital revolution represent the unaddressed issues of this era. What is in doubt is whether educational reformers can escape from the conceptual hold of their mentors who reinforced the cultural myths of earlier eras.

Karen Copeland lives in Abbotsford, British Columbia. She has two children and has extensive experience navigating school, health, and ministry mental health (children and youth) systems to obtain the services her family needs and deserves. Karen is the founder of Champions for Community Mental Wellness, an online resource where she shares personal experiences, mental health and wellness resources, tip sheets, and more. She strongly believes in the importance of honoring the champions who come into our lives to support us on our journey. Karen is passionate about the amazing things that can happen when youth and families are fully included and valued in all aspects of service systems.

Dr. James Dalziel is dean of education at Morling College and is a professor at the University of Divinity. James' interests including educational technology, learning design, Christian education, and moral values in education. James was previously professor of learning technology at Macquarie University from 2003 to 2015, and before this a lecturer in psychology at the University of Sydney. He has led numerous projects in e-learning and e-research, including the development of the LAMS (Learning Activity Management System) learning design system, and has an extensive record of refereed publication and presentation. James is a member of the Academic Board of the Australian College of Theology, and a research fellow at the Excellence Centre at Pacific Hills Christian School.

Dr. Matthew Etherington achieved his PhD from Macquarie University in Sydney, Australia, while completing doctoral research at the Ontario Institute for Studies in Education. He is presently an associate professor in the School of Education at Trinity Western University, British Columbia. Matthew is the director of the Institute of Indigenous Issues and Perspectives. His primary interests are in epistemological inclusion in education, and Aboriginal pedagogy, outcomes, assessment, and philosophy. Matthew has published two books, *Changing Careers to Become a Teacher: A Study of Mature Age Preservice Teachers in Career Transition* and *Foundations of Education: A Christian Vision* (editor and author). He writes on a diverse range of topics in education and spirituality using a philosophical lens for analysis.

CONTRIBUTORS

Adam Forsyth is a PhD candidate in the School of Education at the University of Queensland, Australia. His thesis is titled *Student Thinking About Science and Religion: The Influence of Religious View on Secondary School Students' Understandings of the Nature of Science*. Adam has previously completed a Master of Educational Studies at UQ, also under the supervision of Dr. Nichols, with a focus on using the history and philosophy of science in science education. Prior to this, Adam completed a PhD in Environmental Science at the Queensland University of Technology; he also holds bachelor degrees in applied science and education. Adam has taught science and mathematics in secondary schools in Australia and the United Kingdom for the past twenty years.

Dr. Peter Froese has been involved in public and independent school education for over thirty years. He began his career in public schools in British Columbia, where he was employed as a teacher, vice principal, and principal for twenty-two years. Four of those years were spent with the Canadian Department of National Defense in Lahr, Germany, where Peter administered a middle school. Peter was the superintendent of one of the largest independent schools in British Columbia prior to being appointed the executive director of the Federation of Independent School Associations in British Columbia. This not-for-profit organization has a voluntary membership of almost three hundred independent schools, representing 93 percent of the eighty-one thousand students attending independent schools in BC. In 2015–16, 13 percent of the overall K–12 student enrollment in BC attended an independent school. He is also the vice chairperson of the BC Council for International Education and an advisory board member for City University in Vancouver.

Dr. Edward R. Howe is an assistant professor of curriculum studies in the Faculty of Education and Social Work at Thompson Rivers University. Prior to that he worked for more than a decade in Japanese higher education. He obtained his MA in Educational Studies (Sociology) from the University of British Columbia, and a PhD in Curriculum, Teaching, and Learning (Comparative and International Education) from the Ontario Institute for Studies in Education of the University of Toronto. Dr. Howe's main research interests are teacher education and comparative and international education, with a focus on East Asia. His research blends narrative inquiry and reflexive ethnography through "comparative ethnographic narrative" as a means to better understand teacher acculturation and other educational phenomena. Recent publications include internationalization of higher education, transcultural teacher education, and narrative pedagogies. Dr. Howe's teaching focuses on social justice issues, global citizenship education, transformational learning, and educational leadership.

Dr. Sherick Hughes (MA, MPA, PhD) is an associate professor in the School of Education at the University of North Carolina at Chapel Hill. He is the founder/director of the Interpretive Research Suite and Bruce A. Carter Qualitative Thought Lab, and founder/codirector of the Graduate Certificate in Qualitative Studies. Hughes' research, teaching, and service involve: (1) critical race studies and black education, (2) social context of urban and rural schooling, (3) interdisciplinary foundations of education, and (4) qualitative methodology in education. Hughes has over fifty single- and coauthored manuscripts accepted for publication, and his books on nuanced black family pedagogy after *Brown* and the evolving significance of race earned 2007 and 2014 Critics' Choice Book Awards from the American Educational Studies Association. Hughes was the 2016 recipient of a prestigious Distinguished Scholar Award from the American Educational Research Association.

Dr. Kenneth A. Pudlas earned his EdD in Educational Psychology and Special Education, MA in Educational Psychology and Special Education, Diploma in Education of the Deaf, and EdB in Elementary Education. He is a full professor at Trinity Western University where he teaches in the School of Education. He is also the director of the Master of Arts in Educational Studies: Special Education, and he teaches graduate courses in special education, oversees thesis research, and capstone projects. Previously, he was on faculty at the University of British Columbia and the University of Wisconsin–Milwaukee. Prior to entering higher education, he taught deaf and hard-of-hearing students in public schools where he was an innovative pioneer in what has now become known as inclusion. He has spoken at national and international conferences, serves on the editorial boards of several journals, and is the president-elect of the International Christian Community for Teacher Education (https://www.iccte.org). Dr. Pudlas was born in Vancouver, and spent most of his life in British Columbia. He currently resides in Langley, British Columbia, with his wife. They have four adult children, miss their eldest, a son, and enjoy a dozen grandchildren.

Professor Emeritus Martyn Rouse was professorial chair of Social and Educational Inclusion at the University of Aberdeen and director of the Inclusive Practice Project, which was designed to reform teacher education so that teachers might be better prepared to work in the diverse schools of today. Previously, he was a senior lecturer in the Faculty of Education, University of Cambridge. He has undertaken research and development work on inclusion for national agencies in the UK. His international involvement includes work for several European agencies: the OECD, UNESCO, and UNICEF. He has worked for the Soros Open Society Foundation in Central Asia, and on inclusion and curriculum development in other countries of the former Soviet Union. Current work includes a European Commission project on inclusion indicators in the Republic of Georgia. He has published widely on teacher education, inclusion, and additional support needs. His coauthored book *Achievement and Inclusion in Schools* was winner of the NASEN/Times Education Supplement Academic Book of the Year 2008 (second edition forthcoming). With Kate Lapham, he is coeditor of *Learning to See Invisible Children: Inclusion of Children with Disabilities in Central Asia*, published in 2013 by the Open Society Foundation and Central European University Press, which has been translated into Russian.

Dr. Bruce Shelvey is an associate professor of history at Trinity Western University in Langley, British Columbia. He has been thinking and teaching on the topic of historical difference and theorizing about the function of history in identity formation for the past fifteen years. Much of the inspiration for his work on persons of difference comes from his own personal experiences and from conversations he has had with his life partner, Debi Jo, who is a high school teacher. He aspires to be an advocate, coach, and mentor for individuals with exceptionalities.

Dr. Lucinda S. Spaulding earned her PhD in Special Education and Educational Psychology, MEd in Special Education, and BS in Elementary Education. She is an associate professor at Liberty University where she teaches advanced research courses and chairs dissertations in the Doctor of Education program. Prior to serving in higher education, she taught general and special education in urban schools in New York and Virginia, and spent a year teaching English in Japan. Dr. Spaulding is the vice president of the Virginia Council for Exceptional Children and serves as coeditor of the association's journal. She has published and presented extensively on factors related to doctoral attrition and persistence, resilience in children and youth, specific learning disabilities and best practices, and the history of special education. Dr. Spaulding was born and raised in Ottawa, Ontario, and currently resides in Forest, Virginia, with her husband and three children.

Dr. John Valk graduated from the University of Toronto with a PhD in Religious Studies with a dissertation entitled "Religion and the Schools: The Case of Utrecht." He is currently professor of worldview studies at Renaissance College, University of New Brunswick. His teaching, research, and writing focus on worldviews: worldviews and education, worldviews and leadership, worldviews and religion, and more. He has presented academic papers at various national and international conferences, and has published in various academic journals and books. His latest book is entitled, *An Islamic Worldview: Religion in a Modern, Democratic and Secular State* (2016), written with colleagues at Ankara University in Turkey. His next book, *Worldviews In and Around Us: A Framework Journey into Knowing Self and Others*, is in progress. He is also visiting professor at the Protestant University of Darmstadt, Germany, where he teaches worldviews and inclusive education.

Dr. Eva Maria Waibel, born in Dornbirn, Austria, was a primary and secondary teacher, then studied educational psychology in Innsbruck, where she also finished her PhD followed by an education as a psychotherapist in logotherapy and existential analysis in Vienna. Since then she has worked in teacher education at different universities in Austria and Switzerland with the main topic of existential education: www.eva-maria-waibel.at. She has published extensively in German. In English, *The Impact of Existential Pedagogics on Teachers and Educators: A Qualitative Study* (together with Heidi Siller) is in press.

Foreword
E. J. Boyce

THE CONCEPT OF INCLUSION, politically and socially, has become in many societies an important point of discussion, consideration, and practice. In educational terms, the concept of inclusion has been through both peaks and valleys but is now commonly regarded as being for the common good.

Throughout the world, as this book reflects through its authors and topics, the importance of critical thinking in education is obvious. The importance of critical awareness from many different perspectives allows there to be an inclusiveness within the pages of this book.

Of making many books there is no end, but this particular book promotes through its pages the inclusiveness that comes from diversity, so that uniformity is not obvious although it is also true that unity is not reached. The concept of freedom through choice and building of resilience in learners are considered separately and yet provide a complementarity of understanding that reinforces the importance and value of inclusion. Although this book is not an ongoing story it allows the reader to go beyond a cultural norm and to engage in assessment of the construct of inclusion across a wide range of disciplines and practical examples.

Our understanding and practice of inclusion in the culture of teaching and learning communities is dependent on our basic assumptions, presuppositions, and beliefs. These foundational aspects of our thinking and our beliefs system determine significantly the reasons for inclusion and the ways in which inclusion operates in any community setting. Our experiences and our values also contribute to the viewpoints that we hold. The baggage that we bring to a given point of time in given circumstances, the context of which we find ourselves as teachers and learners, and the goals and purposes that we hold all contribute the praxis by which we operate.

What Teachers Need to Know: Topics of Inclusion represents a resource that will allow for reflection, alternative ways of thinking and acting, and increases the dialogue between theoreticians and practitioners who are seeking best practices in communities of learning.

Introduction

Education for All

Matthew Etherington

THIS BOOK IS ABOUT topics of inclusion. The term *inclusion* is understood in its basic anthropological sense in that it refers to the human presence of being, doing, thinking, and valuing for which human beings assign meaning and purpose. Human beings do not just exist in the world in private but live, move, and breathe in the public domain and build up particular, diverse, and varying ways of acting and interacting, shaping artifacts, telling stories, building dwellings, inventing names, and so on.[1]

The Education for All (EFA) initiative from the United Nations reports that we still have a long way to go with inclusion in education. There are currently fifty-eight million children out of school globally and around one hundred million children who do not complete primary education.[2] The United Nations reports that inequality in education has actually increased, with the poorest and most disadvantaged shouldering the heaviest burden.[3] Although for some countries the concern is about basic access to an education, in well-schooled Western countries, the focus is more about "ensuring meaningful participation in a system where achievement and success is available for all."[4]

Education has a basic function to the sustaining of society—to pass on to the next generation the values of the culture, information, and traditional roles,[5] and to also reflect and accommodate the diversity of the communities being served.[6] Yet this is not always successful and in diverse Western societies *the* culture is increasingly becoming many cultures. Diversity, therefore, includes all aspects on which people differ from each other and

1. Smith, *Learning from the Stranger*, 6.
2. See "Fixing the Broken Promise."
3. "Education for All 2000–2015: Achievements and Challenges."
4. Rouse, "Developing Inclusive Practice," 3.
5. Fant, *Liberal Arts*, 23.
6. McIsaac and Moody, *Diversity and Inclusion*.

is a topic that is becoming more important at the core of public debates and policy-making.

Some examples of diversity recognition occurs when K–12 schools and institutes of higher education are located on Indigenous lands, they acknowledge and pay respect to the traditional custodians of the land. In addition, they are responsible to consult with Indigenous leaders and teachers to create culturally sensitive and inclusive curriculum. In many religious and faith-based schools, the inclusion of Indigenous languages and musical instruments, acceptance of traditional rituals which were once considered to be anti-Christian,[7] and the acknowledged coexistence of Aboriginal and Western Christian ideas about spiritual existence are now part of school life. Unfortunately, although progress has been made, there are still systemic inequalities (i.e., governance, attitude) in Western education that undermine an authentic Indigenous presence. In addition, when schools of learning are located in multi-faith and multicultural regions they are responsible for including into the curriculum a diversity of values and perspectives mirrored by the surrounding cultures. Although cultural pluralism is the reality, especially in the West, concerns over heightened ethnic group identity, separatism, and fragmentation of society is also a reality for those who believe that cultural pluralism is dangerous to Western education and societies.[8]

With crafted policies outlining the importance of diversity in the classroom, some schools and institutes of higher education are well on their way to an inclusive practice of teaching and learning, while others have only just begun. Although schools include the importance of diversity in educational policy, generally speaking, they struggle with diversity and inclusion as a reality. Moreover, although well intended, "our current practices of inclusion too often are sentimental and sloppy thinking."[9] Of course, just mentioning the words "diversity" and "inclusion" in a policy or curriculum document doesn't mean you have done it. There has to be some evidence that it is actually being done.

As Western society becomes increasingly diverse in terms of people's identity and epistemology,[10] there is one common question that all educators will have to negotiate sooner rather than later—as diversity of identity

---

7. McDonald, *Blood, Bones, and Spirit*.

8. Bennett, *Comprehensive Multicultural Education*, 15.

9. Westerhoff, *Good Fences*, 28.

10. Epistemological diversity is the way a person explains, claims, or interprets reality which includes ideas, values, and interpretations. For more, see Ruitenberg and Phillips, *Education, Culture and Epistemological Diversity*, 15. Identity diversity is when people identify themselves with particular nations, cities, neighborhoods, or communities, a specific social class, subculture, ethnicity, religion, gender, and so forth.

and thought increases, how should teaching and learning change? This is a critical question for ongoing conversations with numerous stakeholders because epistemological screening and ignoring or denying differences is unsustainable and unethical as we passage together into the twenty-first century of learning.

Educational leaders and policy developments have, at most levels, taken the concept of diversity seriously. One way teachers and students experience diversity is when schools accommodate and include different identities, beliefs, and values into the classroom and allow it to guide pedagogy, curriculum, knowledge formation, and assessment strategies. Sometimes educators refer to this as a practice of "excellence" and "equity," and it is often expressed through ongoing curriculum advances.[11]

Some educators are committed to leading people by equipping them to lead themselves, to self-govern and self-determine. Also, the teachings and values treasured by family and faith communites become important to educators. In some sense, educators who believe and are committed to a constructivist paradigm of learning in the classroom become unnecessary educators, because rather than try and control what people should believe and value, they understand the meaning of unity in diversity and are content with knowing that there is more going on than they can see or get their hearts and minds around. They become learners and pilgrims offering open hands of gratitude and hope to others in the community. Wholesome inclusion and human connections become possible when "people know who they are and who they are not, what they bring to the relationship and what they do not, what they seek from it and what they might want to avoid."[12]

At the same time, although educators believe in inclusion at a theoretical level they often find it difficult to implement. Sometimes educators are unclear of their role. At other times, they find inclusive practices hard to sustain so they eventually stop trying.[13] Whatever the reason, a deficiency of inclusive policy and practice often relates to "deeply embedded attitudes to, and beliefs about, human differences."[14] Professor Emeritus

---

11. One example is the new BC Education Plan. The Ministry of Education in British Columbia conducted interviews with all post-secondary institutions of education to assist with creating a new inclusive educational vision for British Columbians that would take seriously the diverse social and cultural needs of the communities it serves. For more information on these curriculum changes related to inclusion and diversity, please visit http://www2.gov.bc.ca/gov/content/education-training/k-12/support/bcs-education-plan.

12. Westerhoff, *Good Fences*, 56.

13. Rouse, "Developing Inclusive Practice."

14. Ibid., 3.

at the University of Florida and member of the Faculty Ministry Advisory Council John Sommerville[15] argues that one of the main problems with modern education, particularly at the post-secondary level, is the trouble it has defining the human, and yet education outside of the context of the human makes no sense. Moreover, to be a great leader, one has to also understand what disadvantage is, most certainly, but to do that we also have to recognize what advantage is and how you and I benefit from the privileges we already have and expect.

It is quite possible that future educators, policy makers, institutions of education, and significant stakeholders with vested interest in the teaching and learning of all people will one day look back to the inclusion effort and wonder why it took so long.[16] We have been separating people because of their beliefs and identity for a very long time. Some of the following examples highlight this reality.

In the 1870s the Government of Canada proposed that the separation of Aboriginal children from their parents would be the best way to achieve their assimilation into European culture. This continued into the twentieth century where many Aboriginal children were taken from their homes and often forcibly removed and separated from their families to attend residential schools. They were often prohibited from speaking their language or seeing their families, and were ultimately forbidden to live the identity of an Aboriginal person. Their identity and ways of knowing were denied.

Another example of exclusion occurred in January 1939, when a professor at the University of Berlin was summoned by the minister of education and given notice that he could no longer teach as a professor at the university. The reason he was given—"when the state itself has a worldview, there can be no room for a chair of Catholic *Weltanschauung* at the university."[17] This echoes an example of epistemic exclusion.

A significant event occurred in 1976 when school children in Soweto, South Africa, rioted against exclusive practices as the government planned to introduce Afrikaans as the official language of instruction. Forty years later, in 2016, students once again protested at a South African university over the use of Afrikaans as an official teaching language—a demonstration that echoed students' demands for identity inclusion decades ago.

These are examples of exclusion and the separation and devaluing of identity and epistemic differences from those in privileged positions of power. Epistemological inclusion requires the presence of various

---

15. Sommerville, *Decline of the Secular University*.
16. Henley, *Creating Successful Inclusion Programs*.
17. Krieg, "Romano Guardini's Theology," 457–74.

epistemologies and worldviews in teaching and learning, while identity inclusion comprises the integration of personal identification in the teaching and learning process.

Consequently, this book is about what teachers should know about two types of inclusion—identity and epistemic inclusion. The chapters collected offer important perspectives from experts in the field who care deeply about people and hope to inform, stimulate thought, and encourage reflection for all types of diversity workers.

Why a Book on Inclusion in Education

In 2017 debates for and against diversity are at an all-time high. An increasing flow of people to Western societies, together with values, beliefs, information, and goods, brings a diversity of people to interact and collaborate. Institutes of education have been under scrutiny over the successes and failures to reflect this reality and be inclusive places where all people can flourish. Schools in the Western context have often been described as factories, prisons, businesses, legacies of colonial conquests, and so on. Critics argue that schools do not embrace diversity in practice, encourage creativity and difference, or prepare students adequately for the outside world that is more diverse than it is similar. Some educational stakeholders have responded by suggesting that schools are neutral places that should enforce a common curriculum, and while diversity and difference are important, this should not be a priority. Sheldon Chumir supported such a view when he said that "public schools were designed to mix children of different ethnic and religious groups and eliminate those differences."[18]

However, inclusive schools along with enlightened curriculum initiatives have embraced, at least in theory, a long-term commitment to "open its arms" wider and encourage a greater diversity of identities, perspectives, and approaches, and over time changes to educational policy have occurred. The educational language of teaching and learning is gradually advancing from "individualized learning," which is inward looking and solitary, associated more with Western values, to what is now referred to as "personalized learning,"[19] which is outward-looking, community-based, and human-centered. Personalized learning with the *person* at the center of their learning and in community is a recognition of "personhood."[20] In this context,

---

18. Bateman, "Exploring the Limits of Pluralism," 27–39.
19. See Ministry of Education, "BC Education Plan."
20. Sokolowski, *Phenomenology of the Human Person.*

personhood is understood in holistic terms of mind, body, and spirit, with people as bearers of rights and status, responsibilities and moral standing.[21]

Inclusive schools, teachers, and educational institutions are becoming more sensitive to their students as people with complex, rich, and diverse backgrounds, with prior life experiences that do influence how they learn and how the perceive their learning. Although this awareness and admission by some has been slow, it is happening and when it does it is encouraging for all diversity workers, because when human beings experience positive and affirmative inclusion of their identity and epistemological ideals, beliefs, and hopes, it is axiomatic that they will learn, grow, and cooperate together.

Epistemology and Identity Inclusion

Inclusion is practiced in education and experienced by learners in two different ways. The first involves a commitment to affirm and accommodate identity, that is, who a person is. The second is the recognition, accommodation, and affirmation of different beliefs, worldviews, and values regarding what a person believes about the world.[22] The practice of inclusion that is currently adopted within the English education system is typically attentive to identity inclusion rather than epistemic or epistemological inclusion.[23] As discussed below, I suggest that the reason for this might be because epistemology, or as it is sometimes described as *ideological inclusion*, is not well understood by teachers compared to identity inclusion, which in some cases is more visually obvious and therefore more pragmatically obtainable for educators to implement.

The author recounts an example of epistemic exclusion, which is related to the topic of critical thinking at the post-secondary level. This experience transpired while attending an education conference held annually in Canada. In this particular gathering teacher educators and participants had the opportunity to hear—in one double session—different practices of critical thinking within a variety of teacher education programs.[24]

The main pair of presenters, both experienced education professors, described in detail an approach they employed for integrating critical thinking strategies in the classroom for their student teachers. The professors explained in detail the strategies they used for provoking critical thinking,

21. Taylor, "Moral Topography," 298–320.
22. Ipgrave, "Religious Diversity," 94–109.
23. Ibid., 95.
24. See my chapter in this volume: Etherington, "Uncritical Critical Thinking in Teacher Education."

which was grounded in a conviction that critical thinking required scientific approaches. The description they gave was "smashing down old ways of thinking,"[25] and it was in relation to what they would do to students who didn't think in scientific ways but instead drew on traditional epistemologies of the past which they considered "nonscientific."[26]

In the question-and-answer time, the two professors clarified their practice as "utilizing new and innovative ideas and not previous [old] knowledge or values from a bygone era."[27] While their original explanation of "smashing down old ways of thinking" remained, in the question-and-answer period they spoke about an ultimate objective to advance critical thinking by steering their education students away from their traditional beliefs and replace them exclusively with scientific points of view. No one present in the room showed any surprise that education professors might not appreciate the possibility that in diverse pluralistic communities in which their university was housed, "smashing down old ways of thinking" may in fact exclude numerous students who value their traditions, and who have no intention of replacing their beliefs with another.

This lack of surprise and the experience itself is worth thinking about because educators are supposed to promote and actualize inclusive learning environments, otherwise they serve to breed unsafe and unwelcome settings where diversity is frowned upon and students are restricted from joining together in the riches of learning different ways. Moreover, surely the vision of higher education has not "progressed" to the point where the young, once provided with leadership and initiated into the wisdom of the past, has now turned into places where less diversity exists, traditions of inquiry in dialogue are absent,[28] and the old abandon the young to their resources because the old are irrelevant and have nothing of value to say anymore.[29] This sounds like the complete opposite of diversity and inclusion.

Deep learning requires the humility to admit that you do not know everything there is to know and that the past, present, and future all have value. Learners can look back to the past and look forward to the future, it doesn't have to be one or the other. Thus, deep learning takes both the time and patience to acquire insight from others who think differently. Learning from others is a necessary component of caring about people, even learning

---

25. Personal communication, CSSE Conference, Brock University, Ontario, Canada, May 2014.

26. Ibid.

27. Ibid.

28. Sommerville, *Decline of the Secular University*.

29. Ibid.

from those who we experience or think of as strangers.[30] In the words of Baruch Spinoza, "I have striven not to laugh at human actions, not to weep at them, nor to hate them, but to understand them."[31] Realizing that we are all cultural creatures, and often blind to our own cultural filters, requires us to be acutely aware of the feelings, values, and attitudes of others and understand that learning is a process of discovering, acknowledging, considering, and valuing different ideas, theories, people, policy, practices, and structures.[32]

Historically, K–12 schools and institutes of higher education have responded to identity and epistemological inclusion in two ways. Either they have believed in it, and have offered opportunities for learning communities to experience diverse identities, perspectives, talents, and links across a whole range of disciplines, or they have resisted by throwing a blanket over people and competing ideas and in doing so smothered diversity.[33]

Schools, teachers, and curriculum initiatives need to recapture the purpose of education. The great teacher Aristotle observed that where anything has a function the virtues of that thing is when it performs its function well. For example, a knife has a function to cut, and it performs its function well when it cuts well. This has application if we consider the function of education. A positive example of function is taken from Sandridge Independent Secular School in Australia.[34] This particular school adopts a vision of education that includes a philosophy of connectedness and prosperity. They state that the purpose of education is a commitment to nourish people's lives by encouraging teachers and students to thrive first as human beings. When the goal of education is to help all learners flourish as human beings, they will experience an education that functions to encourage one another to pursue what is good and worthy, and at the same time develop a heightened respect for difference within an increasingly diverse population.[35] Some might argue that this would mean that disagreements over truth or reality can never be resolved. If the goal is merely agreement, then indeed a resolution may never transpire, but what if the function of education is understanding rather than agreement? We might then learn to respect those who disagree radically.[36]

30. Smith, *Learning from the Stranger*, 9.
31. Spinoza, *Tractatus Politicus*, ch. 1, sect. 4.
32. Smith, *Learning from the Stranger*, 45.
33. Miller and Katz, *Inclusion Breakthrough*.
34. Visit Sandridge Independent Secular School at http://www.sandridge.vic.edu.au/wp-content/uploads/Sandridge-School_Organisational-Objectives.pdf.
35. de Ruyter, "Pottering in the Garden?," 377–89.
36. Sommerville, *Decline of the Secular University*, 71.

Once our epistemic boundaries and differences are welcomed, then questions of hospitality arise. This welcome must include a "willingness to struggle with people's ideas, and happenings that are strange or intimidating to us."[37]

The Purpose of Inclusion

Aristotle, Plato, John Amos Comenius, John Locke, Rousseau, Mo Tzu, Confucius, and John Dewey—all educators who thought extensively about the function and role of education and schooling in their respective societies.[38] Anyone who has completed a social foundations course in education can attest to the fact that there are a multitude of responses to the question, *What is the purpose of education?* However, because this book is about inclusion, I want all educators to consider the possibility that one of the main goals of education is to increase human worth. Unfortunately, the experience of many school students suggest that education can work against inclusive practices that permit diverse identities and epistemologies to unfold.[39]

Schools should not operate monochromatically, compartmentalizing knowledge and identities in isolation. In fact, if we want our young people to feel good about learning and in particular learning historically unpopular subjects like mathematics, which most students often express scorn over, and if we want them to experience the importance of transferring what they learn at school to their lives, then schools must stop compartmentalizing and privileging certain types of knowledge. We don't live our lives like that as human beings. There is plenty of room for education and schooling to expand the capacity for acquiring knowledge in all its forms.[40] As John Dewey famously said, "Education should not be a preparation for life but life itself."[41] In pluralistic classrooms, institutions of teaching and learning can come together and take hold of the opportunities that exist for inclusive practices that can highlight to all learners, the classroom, and the school community, the importance of understanding the diversity of humanity.

If the inclusion of all people is an important function of education, then teachers and schools must work toward building a culture of learning that reflects such a commitment. Everyone must be invited to the table of conversation and decision making and contribute toward a combined wisdom of interaction and dialog, so a culture of authentic inclusion in schools

37. Westerhoff, *Good Fences*, 32.
38. Noddings, *Philosophy of Education*; Reed and Johnson, *Philosophical Documents*.
39. Kanu, "Introduction," 17.
40. Miller and Katz, *Inclusion Breakthrough*, xiii.
41. See Dewey, "My Pedagogic Creed."

can be unleashed. A commitment is made to unite with local community, parents, Indigenous leaders, churches, synagogues, mosques, temples, and other organizations. Curriculum would be informed by many voices and not just a dominant privileged few. In diverse classrooms all people work together, complementing, supporting, and including one other.[42]

As our world becomes more technological, it becomes harder to slow down and listen to other voices. But who is going to do it if not our students, our current and future teachers and educators? No one else has the opportunity and calling we have as teachers. Eugene Peterson writes that "if you look at it from a strictly professional point of view, we as teachers are possibly the only identifiable groups (besides clergy) commissioned to teach, reflect and listen. If we don't who will?"[43]

Inclusion—In and About

Martin Buber speaks of the interchange and symmetrical space of the I-Thou relation. Similarly, Nel Noddings imagines a caring and inclusive relationship in schools dependent on reciprocity. Alternatively, Emmanuel Levinas intersects with education and inclusion as he envisions a responsibility and respect to the Other even when no reciprocity or respect is experienced.

What can we gain from these important thinkers in relation to inclusion? First, educators must ask themselves if their classrooms serve to embrace all in the learning process. Do educators really believe that inclusion and diversity matters, and if so, how should they live out such an ideal as they walk alongside their students. An educator can be knowledgeable about inclusion, what it is and how it can be practiced in a classroom setting, but still not fully embrace the inclusion experience. An example might be the case of a teacher knowing *about* her student Sebastian. For a specific time, she knows important objective data about him, that is, she knows his academic background, his organizational skills, and through her regular classroom observations even knows his social strengths and challenges within a variety of contexts. These are important data that teachers need to know about their students, but although the teacher has such information, she may not in fact believe *in* him or know what he values about the world. When a teacher believes *in* her students, she places her confidence, hope, and trust in them as human beings and is cognizant and inclusive of their distinctive identities and future hopes. Ask a graduate of any learning institution to name the teachers who believed in them, and they will immediately remember

42. Ibid., 48.

43. Chan et al., *Road We Must Travel*, 80.

the names of teachers who they recognized as having understood them as people first and foremost.

We all know the difference between believing *in* someone and simply knowing superficially *about* someone, because chances are we have experienced both realities. The distinction is important to topics of inclusion because authentic inclusion requires not only a cognitive awareness and knowledge about the learner but a heart knowledge and commitment to the learner. To have a heart knowledge and commitment to a person requires a yearning to experience them as a whole, with many different parts to their identity together with a commitment to walk alongside them with open hands of understanding and trust. As I heard a student once say in class, "I just want to be heard, valued, and respected." There are many pieces to the person-puzzle, and the hope of any teacher should be to help bring all the pieces together to form the whole person.

Consequently, authentic inclusion presupposes and values diversity. Schools and educational institutions of all creeds and none are supposed to reflect the communities they serve and communities are made up of diverse people. As students learn to live alongside their peers, they also learn how to play together, agree and disagree together. And in the process they likewise learn that their neighbor holds to beliefs and values that are similar and also different to their beliefs. Schools then act as hosts to receive, support, and welcome all and reject none, including the diverse epistemologies that people use to make sense of the world. Inclusive education puts the values of pluralism, tolerance, and equity into action. Diversity practitioners sometimes use the metaphor of the institution as an organic singular body or entity, made up of multiple interrelated parts all of which contribute and communicate within and to the whole system and give health and vibrancy to the institution.[44]

Therefore, if inclusion as a theory recognizes the whole person—that is, their identity and epistemology—then the practice of inclusion always honors diversity. Yet there are examples where this still does not occur. For example, in British Columbia, Canada, which is noted by the Ministry of Education as "the most ethnically diverse province in Canada,"[45] the

---

44. Ahmed, *On Being Included*, 29.

45. The Ministry of British Columbia website notes that "multiculturalism is a way of life in BC. By law, you have to respect other people's lifestyles, beliefs, religion, and culture, and they have to respect yours. When you move to BC, you can continue practising your religious beliefs and cultural traditions. As a member of our ethnically diverse communities, you will also be able to experience the cultural heritage of other people from around the world." For more, please visit https://www.welcomebc.ca/Choose-B-C/Explore-British-Columbia/Multicultural-B-C.

Public Schools Act under Section 76 concerning conduct in public schools states that all public schools should be conducted "on strictly secular and nonsectarian principles".[46] In the 2001 Statistics Canada Census,[47] out of a total population in British Columbia of 3,868,875, only 1,388,300 people identified as nonreligious. This is compared to 2,480,575 people who identified as religious, which is a clear majority. In a more recent survey conducted in 2011, the National Household Survey Profile, for the census metropolitan area of Vancouver, British Columbia,[48] revealed figures at 950,170 people representing themselves as religious, while the nonreligious were registered at 945,405. Consequently, one could reasonably claim that the *Public School Act*, which is still active in 2017 does not appear to reflect the diversity of people living in British Columbia.

Attempts to ignore or control ideas and beliefs is on occasion resisted while others stay silent or even find themselves terminated from their place of work. One example of resistance is the Valley Park Middle School in Toronto, involving Hindu families and students protesting against the marginalization of Friday prayer sessions for Muslim students.[49] An example of epistemic exclusion is situated in the debates over science and the value of religion in schools and classrooms, which continues to divide students, teachers, and parents. For example, in 2008, a professor from the Royal Society attempted the inclusion of religion and science in class debates stating that the teacher should discuss and include all current and controversial issues that relate to the topic and held by rational people of all professions and none. An outcry ensued and the professor resigned.[50] Another example of those in privileged positions of decision making deciding what is acceptable or not occurs when Aboriginal students are included in mainstream education, but with the constitution still ignoring the cycle of poverty and systemic disadvantage in many Aboriginal communites; consequently, the education gap between Native Canadians and the rest of the country shrinks but with comparative slowness.[51] And in a recent report from the UK, the identity of a special needs student will ensure her removal from the mainstream classroom.[52]

46. For more information, see School Act.
47. For more information, see "Population by Religion, by Province and Territory."
48. For more information, see "NHS Profile, Vancouver, CMA, British Columbia, 2011."
49. "Hindus Protest Muslim Prayers.
50. Ipgrave, "Religious Diversity."
51. Sniderman, "Aboriginal Students."
52. Garner, "Pupils with Special Educational Needs."

The inclusion of different cultural identities in schools also receives only superficial recognition. For example, most K–12 schools celebrate diversity by hosting an annual multicultural day. This includes singing traditional songs, eating exotic foods, and observing a parade where students and parents display their traditional clothing to the school community. Universities will sometimes include a week in the academic calendar celebrating diversity. For example, in May of each year, the University of Queensland celebrates Diversity Week.[53] The university gives out prizes and arranges a variety of events held on the campus, all related to diversity. This recognition is important and valuable; however, diversity is more than food, clothes, and dancing. Diversity embodies everything; our basic beliefs and values, our sense of who we are, what we should do, what we should hope for, and how we should relate to other people.[54] And yet after the multicultural day is over any deeper understanding of people's beliefs and worldviews, and any application of those beliefs into pedagogy, curriculum content, assessment or learning outcomes, often does not transpire.

Educators who believe in authentic inclusion understand that students are three dimensional people. Classrooms and institutes of learning will be vehicles that open opportunity for deep learning from a diversity of thought.[55] Therefore, authentic inclusion will consist of the integration of diverse identities and epistemologies into the curriculum. This should inform and change learning outcomes, instructional methods and strategies, curriculum content and learning resources, and assessment strategies. An inclusive practice must value and nourish the human spirit and edify the whole person—physically, socially, emotionally, spiritually, and cognitively. It is now time for teachers, schools, and all educators to consider how they will alter the way they do things.[56] When diversity of identity and epistemology is not evident in the life of the school, "classrooms become echo chambers rather than sounding boards—and we all lose."[57]

This book is about teachers, educators, diversity, and topics related to epistemology and identity inclusion. Like all human beings, teachers and educators have a lot to know about inclusion and diversity, hence the need for this book. What should educators know about the inclusion of students with special needs, religion and spirituality, Aboriginality, the

53. See "UQ Diversity Week," http://www.uq.edu.au/about/uq-diversity-week.
54. Smith, *Learning from the Stranger*.
55. Woods, "Thinking about Diversity of Thought."
56. Ibid.
57. Kristof, "Confession of Liberal Intolerance."

role of storytelling, the environment, tolerance, families, and school choice? Although teachers have knowledge of their subject matter, this knowledge alone is not sufficient. They must know and understand how people think about the world. They must also care deeply about who they teach.

In regards to inclusion, no teacher preparation will be sufficient by itself because there will always be discussions that were never had, people that were never known or invited to share, and knowledge that was never investigated. With limited time and resources, there is only so much a formal education can do to prepare teachers and students for inclusion in diverse learning environments. Therefore, this book provides an additional resource to help satisfy a cavity in K-12 and higher education that teachers and students are either not aware of or not able to achieve. A cavity of inclusive learning and perspectives is the catalyst for this book so that teachers can begin the journey of inclusive practices. What are the parameters of an inclusive pedagogy? Who defines its principles? How should these principles be taught and by whom? And by what authority shall they be grounded?[58] These types of thorny questions occupy the thoughts of most educators and the authors of this book.

The authors are attentive to what it means to educate for human flourishing. Chapters comprise topics related to the inclusion of lived experiences, storytelling, the historical underpinnings of education, Indigenous ways of knowing, special education, family pedagogy, worldview, the environment, tolerance, and spirituality, just to name a few. These topics are intended to expose the reader to perspectives that highlight the need to consider carefully how they might respond to issues related to diversity of identity and ways of knowing. Each chapter offers varied ideas all centered on the theme of inclusion, which any educator, leader, or classroom teacher can find valuable for their educational setting. In the end, this book has an ultimate goal and that is to help educators make teaching and learning simply more human.

Bibliography

Ahmed, Sara. *On Being Included: Racism and Diversity in Institutional Life*. Durham: Duke University Press, 2012.
Bateman, T. "Exploring the Limits of Pluralism." *Catalyst* 12 (1988) 27–39.
Bennett, Christine. *Comprehensive Multicultural Education*. New York: Pearson, 2011.
Chan, Francis, et al. *The Road We Must Travel*. Brentwood, TN: Worthy, 2014.
de Ruyter, Doret. "Pottering in the Garden? On Human Flourishing and Education." *British Journal of Educational Studies* 52 (2004) 377–89.

---

58. Hunter, *Death of Character*, 78.

Dewey, John. "My Pedagogic Creed: Article II–What the School Is." Infed, n.d. http://infed.org/mobi/john-dewey-my-pedagogical-creed.

"Education For All 2000–2015: Achievements and Challenges." Education for All Global Monitoring Report. Paris: UNESCO, 2015. http://unesdoc.unesco.org/images/0023/002322/232205e.pdf.

"Fixing the Broken Promise of Education for All: Findings from the Global Initiative on Out-of-School Children." Montreal: UNESCO Institute for Statistics, 2015. http://www.uis.unesco.org/Education/Documents/oosci-global-report-en.pdf.

Fant, Gene. *The Liberal Arts: A Student's Guide*. Wheaton, IL: Crossway, 2012.

Garner, Richard. "Pupils with Special Educational Needs Are Being Failed by Mainstream Schools, says Mencap." *Independent*, December 13, 2014. http://www.independent.co.uk/news/education/education-news/pupils-with-special-needs-are-being-failed-by-mainstream-schools-says-mencap-9923366.html.

Henley, Martin. *Creating Successful Inclusion Programs*. Bloomington, IN: Solutions Tree, 2004.

"Hindus Protest Muslim Prayers at Public School." *Toronto Sun*, July 4, 2011. http://www.torontosun.com/2011/07/04/hindus-protest-muslim-prayers-at-public-school.

Hunter, James. *The Death of Character: Moral Education in an Age without Good or Evil*. New York: Perseus, 2000.

Ipgrave, Julia. "Religious Diversity: Models of Inclusion for Schools in England." *Canadian and International Education* 40 (2011) 94–109.

Kanu, Yatta. "Introduction: Why Does It Matter Now?" In *Integrating Aboriginal Perspectives into the School Curriculum*, edited by Yatta Kanu, 3–33, Toronto: University of Toronto Press, 2011.

Krieg, Robert. "Romano Guardini's Theology of the Human Person." *Theological Studies* 59 (1988) 457–74.

Kristof, Nicholas. "A Confession of Liberal Intolerance." *New York Times*, May 7, 2016. http://www.nytimes.com/2016/05/08/opinion/sunday/a-confession-of-liberal-intolerance.html?emc=eta1&_r=1.

McDonald, Heather. *Blood, Bones, and Spirit: Aboriginal Christianity in an East Kimberley Town*. Victoria: Melbourne University Press, 2001.

McIsaac, Elizabeth, and Carrie Moody. *Diversity and Inclusion: Valuing the Opportunity*. Toronto: Mowat Centre for Policy Innovation, University of Toronto, 2014.

Miller, Frederick A., and Judy Katz. *The Inclusion Breakthrough: Unleashing the Real Power of Diversity*. San Francisco: Berrett-Koehler, 2002.

Ministry of Education. "BC Education Plan." Updated January 2015. http://www2.gov.bc.ca/gov/content/education-training/k-12/support/bcs-education-plan.

"NHS Profile, Vancouver, CMA, British Columbia, 2011." Statistics Canada, September 11, 2013. http://www12.statcan.gc.ca/nhs-enm/2011/dp-pd/prof/details/page.cfm?Lang=E&Geo1=CMA&Code1=933&Data=Count&SearchText=vancouver&SearchType=Begins&SearchPR=01&A1=All&B1=All&Custom=&TABID=1.

Noddings, Nel. *Philosophy of Education*. Boulder, CO: Westview, 1995.

"Population by Religion, by Province and Territory: 2001 Census." Statistics Canada, January 25, 2005. http://www.statcan.gc.ca/tables-tableaux/sum-som/l01/cst01/demo30c-eng.htm.

Reed, Ronald F., and Tony W. Johnson, eds. *Philosophical Documents in Education*. White Plains, NY: Longman, 1996.

Rouse, Martyn. "Developing Inclusive Practice: A Role for Teachers and Teacher Education." *Education in the North* 16 (2008) 6–13. https://www.abdn.ac.uk/eitn/documents/issue16/EITN-1-Rouse.pdf.

Ruitenberg, Claudia W., and D. C. Phillips, eds. *Education, Culture and Epistemological Diversity: Mapping a Disputed Terrain*. New York: Springer, 2012.

School Act. RSBC, ch. 412 (1996). British Columbia Ministry of Education. http://www.bclaws.ca/civix/document/LOC/complete/statreg/--%20S%20--/05_School%20Act%20[RSBC%201996]%20c.%20412/00_Act/96412_06.xml.

Smith, David. *Learning from the Stranger*. Grand Rapids: Eerdmans, 2009.

Sniderman, Andrew. "Aboriginal Students: An Education Underclass." *Maclean's*, August 8, 2012. http://www.macleans.ca/news/canada/an-education-underclass/.

Sokolowski, Robert. *Phenomenology of the Human Person*. New York: Cambridge University Press, 2008.

Sommerville, John. *The Decline of the Secular University*. New York: Oxford University Press, 2006.

Spinoza, Benedictus de. *Tractatus Politicus*. In vol. 1 of *The Chief Works of Benedict de Spinoza*, translated by R. H. M. Elwes, 279–385. Whitefish, MT: Kessinger, 2010.

Taylor, Charles. "The Moral Topography of the Self." In *Hermeneutics and Psychological Theory*, edited by Stanley Messer et al., 298–320. New Brunswick: Rutgers University Press, 1988.

Westerhoff, Caroline. *Good Fences: The Boundaries of Hospitality*. London: Morehouse, 2004.

Woods, Susan. "Thinking about Diversity of Thought." Working Paper, School of Industrial and Labor Relations, Cornell University, 2008. http://www.workforcediversitynetwork.com/docs/articles/article_thinkingaboutdiversityofthought_woods.pdf.

Part One

Ethics

1

Family Pedagogy: (Re)claiming a Topic of Inclusion for Teacher Education

Sherick Hughes

Introduction

TWO OF THE MOST important, interdependent skills that novice teachers can learn in teacher education is (a) how to begin building upon the knowledge that diverse children bring into the classroom and (b) how to understand the role that family histories play in shaping that knowledge.[1] One entry into these diverse family histories is through the examination of family pedagogy. While the actual origins of the construct, *family pedagogy*, in the literature are difficult to defend, the constructs of *nuanced Black Family Pedagogy* (n-BFP) and *Oppressed Family Pedagogy* (OFP) were coined by the author of this chapter.[2] At the time these constructs were introduced, there was virtually nothing on the topic of family pedagogy in the discipline of education. There was, however, a plethora of research on family/parent involvement, led by pioneering scholar-activists like Dr. Joyce Epstein of Johns Hopkins University. Six types of family/parent involvement toward school improvement emerged from Epstein's work: (1) establishing home environments that support learning, (2) facilitating effective communication between school and home, (3) helping the school and supporting students, (4) learning at home, (5) participating in school decision-making processes, and (6) working with other stakeholders (i.e., students, school staff, and community).[3] Those six types of parent involvement were later

---

1. Hughes, "How Can We Prepare Teachers?"

2. Hughes, "Pedagogy of Educational Struggle"; Hughes, *Black Hands*, 49, 163; Hughes, "Theorizing Oppressed Family Pedagogy."

3. Epstein, "School/Family/Community," 81–96.

grouped by other scholars into two categories: (1) home-based parent involvement (H-BPI) and (2) school-based parent involvement (S-BPI).[4]

Although, this work has been invaluable to the field of education, the work is limited in that it tends to (a) ignore the explicit critical exploration of any perceived racism among the parent(s) on socioeconomic status or race, (b) center the "parent(s)" in ways that exclude other family members involved in the children's lives as primary caregivers, and (c) diminish a deeper, critical discussion of the pedagogical nature of school-related messages from oppressed family elders shared with children at home across generations and grade levels to improve their school experiences.[5] Since its inception, family pedagogy signaled the importance of educators learning from the teaching and learning that occurs between children and their families, yet it is routinely absent from teacher education curriculum. This chapter seeks to reclaim family pedagogy as a topic of inclusion for teacher education. It is guided by one central question: why is it important to reclaim family pedagogy as a topic of inclusion for teacher education and what evidence supports this reclamation? The remaining text provides a brief review of relevant literature on family pedagogy, before describing the *worked example* method. A worked example of OFP is applied here (which is broad enough to encompass n-BFP and other family pedagogies) to illuminate the implications of family pedagogy. Moreover, the chapter ends with concluding thoughts on the importance of (re)claiming family pedagogy as a topic of inclusion in teacher education.

Brief Review of Relevant Literature on Family Pedagogy

There is paucity in scholarship on family pedagogy. Using the *Articles+* search engine with key words "family pedagogy," there were hundreds of hits; however, upon further inspection only ten specifically discussed family pedagogy as a construct. This scholarship included four dissertations (including the author's dissertation), three peer-reviewed journal articles (including the author's article), and three chapters.[6] A Google search for family pedagogy revealed approximately seven pages of relevant websites; however, the vast majority of them presented overlapping information. Some new information emerged from the Google search including a relatively new journal (2011) titled *Family Pedagogy* (*Pedagogika Rodziny*), a

---

4. Murray et al., "Barriers and Opportunities," 2.

5. Ibid., 8.

6. Cross, "Homeplace"; Baker, "Black Families' Pedagogies"; Hughes, "Theorizing Oppressed Family Pedagogy," 45–72; Meng, "Chinese Culture Themes."

quarterly journal of the Academy of Management. Another Google page revealed family pedagogy as an area of concentration for graduate students studying during the 2011–12 and 2012–13 academic years at Krakow: the Jesuit University of Philosophy and Education Ignatianum. The university's faculty of pedagogy[7] justify their inclusion of family pedagogy as a "specialization." Graduates of the program are expected to reflect at least one of the following profiles:

- The graduate has acquired basic knowledge of education, history, philosophy, sociology, and psychology necessary for understanding the sociocultural context of the upbringing process and direct one's professional development. The graduate is competent at interpersonal communication and can analyze and diagnose educational reality. The graduate speaks foreign language at B2 level according to the European Framework of Reference for Language developed by the Council of Europe. The graduate has the ability to reflect on his/her own professional role and is open to the need of professional, personal, and social advancement.

- The graduate has obtained professional qualifications for work as a primary school teacher of "Family Life Education." The graduate is theoretically and practically prepared to work as a career educator in educational, community, therapeutic, and sociotherapy centers, in domestic violence shelters, adoption centers, educational care centers, emergency facilities, family centers, and family courts. The graduate can also work as a counsellor and consultant in institutions catering for the needs of children and families. The graduate is prepared to undertake second cycle and postgraduate studies.

Despite paucity in family pedagogy research on this specific construct, it has been described as an "upcoming discipline."[8] There is some evidence to support this claim with an international audience, including *the SAGE Handbook of Educational Action Research*,[9] and a book published in Russia titled *Special family pedagogy: Family education children developmental disabilities*.[10] This text interprets pedagogy as an integral approach to scholarship because it can engage actions like studying a child's upbringing from different "specialisms" of pedagogy including "social pedagogy and family pedagogy." Family pedagogy as a research direction and social pedagogic

7. Faculty of Pedagogy, *Pedagogy for Students*.
8. Kornbeck and Jensen, *Social Pedagogy*, 113.
9. Noffke and Somekh, *SAGE Handbook*, 328.
10. Seliverstov, Denisova, and Kobrina, *Special Family Pedagogy*, 238.

action answers parents' need to be helped in better educating their children. The qualities of a "good parent" require effort and specialty training, continuous improvement and self-improvement, and are based on science, on competence and skill, and may even suppose a certain vocation.[11] In another study (using approximately seventy hours of video observations collected over nine months), researchers found that the primary caregiver participates in shared book reading in ways that illustrate promising family pedagogical practices for heritage language development, and offers insights into building pedagogical practices for education in the early years.[12] While not speaking of family pedagogy directly, a recent study of preservice teachers[13] underscores the potential for preservice teachers to be educated, via teacher education coursework, about how to begin engaging local family pedagogy, particularly in desegregated, multiethnic/multiracial schools. One preservice teacher from their study elaborates on this point: "It was the first time I've ever been in a room where English was not the dominant language, so communicating in my native language was challenging. It brought me out of my comfort zone. . . . I see the need to include these families in my classroom."[14]

Pre-service teachers in the study agreed unanimously "that doing the family night was a positive experience that they would repeat as classroom teachers, because they felt that working with parents and children together would give them a better sense of the context in which their children live, and would help them get to know the parents."[15] Pre-service teachers also began to internalize the point that "this would be important in working with the parents to support their children's education, and that although they hadn't considered this before, it was important to be comfortable working with the adults that are from minority groups, as much as the children."[16] Moreover, preservice teachers in the study "were living in an entirely different field, interacting and working with diverse Others: situations such as family literacy nights and multicultural events were readily arranged to further challenge PTs' conventional epistemology."[17] This teacher education experience demonstrates that preservice teachers are capable to studying family pedagogy in a manner that instills within preservice teachers "the

---

11. Neacsu and Dumitru, "Family Pedagogy," 212.
12. Li and Fleer, "Family Pedagogy," 1944–60.
13. Han, Madhuri, and Scull, "Two Sides of the Same Coin," 626–56.
14. Ibid., 646.
15. Ibid., 646–47.
16. Ibid.
17. Ibid.

need for advocacy for Others' educational equity and deepened critical consciousness and praxis to include Others and Other epistemology in their pedagogic practices and relationships."[18]

Methodology:
The Worked Example from a Larger Ethnography

Data presented here were drawn from a long-term ethnographic study in the southeastern region of the United States. This larger ethnographic study occurred 2001–03 with additional follow-up questions of participants 2004–06.[19] The ethnographic methods included the study of three generations of six African-American families from that region via oral history interviews, intergenerational focus group dialogues, archival document analysis, and focused observations. Interviews were transcribed by a paid transcriptionist and data were analyzed using critical narrative analysis in search of larger themes that emerged from a compilation and comparison of family pedagogical narratives and the observations and archival data. One of the families centered in the ethnography will be highlighted in the worked example, the Foresight family (a pseudonym). The ethnographic methodology was most conducive to exploring and identifying family pedagogy because of its designed ability (a) to search for ways the sociocultural, historical, and geographical context shapes family pedagogy, (b) to be concerned for issues of intersubjectivity, and (c) to include a social constructionist interpretation.

One of the most important pieces of historical data that emerged from the study was the information regarding the *freedom of choice*. The freedom of choice was a discursive innovation that grew out of *separate but equal* and gained momentum from the discourse of the excellence vs. equity debate. Indeed, it was espoused as a good, democratic ideal alternative for balancing excellence and equity. However, it would not lead to an ideal "free and intellectual search," but seems to have led to both anticipated and unanticipated negative conditions and consequences. Following the rise of the deceiving political discursive innovation of freedom of choice, it was not unusual for a black family to find themselves yet again at the intersections of tradition and transition, resistance and accommodation, law and oppression.

The worked example involves a way to present a shortened version of a synthesis while demonstrating the process.[20] A signature mark of family pedagogy is its dialogic approach, and accordingly, the iteration of the worked

18. Ibid.
19. Hughes, *Black Hands*, 12.
20. Britten et al., "Using Meta Ethnography."

exampled applied in this chapter relies on heavy quotations, so as not to hide the actual text from which our emergent metaphors and analogies originate and to remind the reader that the words reflect interpretations not objective data. Given space limitations, this chapter follows their protocol. The worked example demonstrates the potential of family pedagogy as a defensible milieu to consider in teacher education because of its potential to generate unasked questions, improve interpretations and deepen understandings of the children. The process of engaging the worked example to illustrate an exemplar of family pedagogy is intended to provide more continuity and clarity for the reader, and the author, as well. In the following worked example, the Foresight family pedagogy provides evidence of de facto desegregation and Oppressed Family Pedagogy as a form of family pedagogy to consider.

Oppression has been described as extant interlocking systems that comprise a matrix of domination in which "race, class, and gender" are particularly dominant and oppressive.[21] Oppression is perpetuated, exposed, and resisted "on three levels: personal biography, group or community level of the cultural context created by race, class, and gender; and the systemic level of social institutions."[22] The author of this chapter introduced the construct, Oppressed Family Pedagogy (OFP) in 2005. As applied in this article, OFP *involves the intergenerational art of critical and reciprocal teaching and learning that is engaged at home by families battling oppression.* Oppressed families live at the crossroads of domination, accommodation, and resistance. They tend to represent numerical or political minorities who are often perceived to be a threat by a dominant group who sees them as potentially encroaching upon their values, beliefs, and/or resources perceived as precious and/or limited.

Within the Foresight family's response to the discursive innovation of freedom of choice, educators can find spaces for both languages, so to speak, in a joint effort to disarm its potentially harmful innovative bearings. In short, the Foresight family presents counter-discursive family pedagogy of struggle and hope. Both struggle and hope pedagogies seem to induce conditions that help the family endure the arduous counter-discursive homework of problem posing, problem finding, and problem solving to prepare for the inequities of desegregated schooling. The worked example highlights two specific lessons from Foresight family pedagogy through the voices of the elderly father, Warren Foresight, and his two middle-aged daughters who experienced the initial years of school desegregation. Information from their family pedagogy can be incorporated into teacher education,

---

21. Hill Collins, *Black Feminist Thought*, 226–27.
22. Ibid.

particularly for schools and colleges of education and other programs preparing teachers to lead diverse, equitable, and socially just desegregated schools and classrooms that don't oppress black families in the southeastern region of the United States.

Oppressed Family Pedagogy: A Worked Example of Family Pedagogy

Lesson Number 1:
Freedom of Choice is Not Free, So Work Twice as Hard

Foresight children did not receive meals at home, unless they went to school and did well at it. Fortunately, none of the Foresight children would go hungry by this rule. It was all part of Warren "Daddy" Foresight's pedagogy and his fight to prevent and to counter any possible thoughts his children might have about receiving handouts from anyone during the turmoil of the freedom of choice period. It may initially seem cruel or indicative of pre-abuse and neglect at first read, but his children seemed to understand the message as he intended it.

My interpretation of his message was that it was intended to counter discursive innovations including freedom of choice, because he knew his children would never be afforded such a freedom. Following her father's teaching me the no-school-no-food lesson, Joanne Foresight alluded to the rule as one family counter-discursive tool to push the children to seize every learning opportunity in school.

Joanne (Daughter 1): "No we sure didn't [miss any meals]. We sure didn't. Not any. Like he said, we wanted to go to school. We loved school. And that [was] a big difference."

Warren and Janice provided additional evidence that the family shared narratives of struggle and of hope that were educative and intergenerational.

Warren (Father): "They had to do what white children didn't do. . . . Um hum, yeah. A black child had to be prepared to do something in order to make a living, and other children didn't. I think [that's] why I was so hard on my children. . . . And our children had to work twice as hard to get what he was getting in order to compete with the white, and he wasn't doing as much, because they just do enough to get by with a lot of other things that our children couldn't. And it's still like that now. A colored person has to learn how to give their children something of substance [at home while they're] in school."

Janice (Daughter 2): "But every grading period [during freedom of choice] they kept me off the honor roll. That's how they did. And that's how they do now. That's why I tell my niece and nephew, they have a plan to keep us down. But we've got to do double and triple and quadruple what they do. We can't just get by and 'do good' and do better. But we've got to do the best. And that's the only way we're going to make it. . . . And I try to let them know [things are different for most whites here]. My nieces and nephews may say, 'Well, they [whites] do . . .'. So what? You know. 'They didn't go to college.' 'But their mamas or their daddies own Wachovia Bank,' I remind them. . . . And it's Serby and Sons. They are looking out for their children. But [even after freedom of choice], we don't own anything, so we can't pass anything along to our children and grandchildren. We don't have anything. So one thing I would encourage any black is that they try to get into a profession where you can go in business and be your own boss. That's what I wish more blacks would do."

Warren Foresight taught his children (implicitly and explicitly) and they taught their children, nieces and nephews (and other black children in their community) that no matter what was publicly espoused, their lived in a condition that exposed underlying motives of oppression. Their family pedagogy was set to counter the messages of political discursive innovation in order to navigate a sometimes shady desegregated educational system. For local teachers (largely white teachers) in the newly desegregated school setting, knowing that some black children were taught at home that (a) the freedom of choice was not free (at least not for them), and (b) that they would need to work twice as hard as whites to be treated equitably in schools was invaluable information. Evidence of this point was found in the narratives of white teachers from the area, one of which was mentored by black teachers and families, Barbara Needham (pseudonym).

Barbara Needham (White Teacher): "During integration all white commissioners made the funding decisions [not to build a new school out in plain view like the other two formerly all white schools] . . . it's like they said, 'Let's hide them, so people can't see the inequality.'"

Barbara also spoke highly of the black female teachers and families with whom she later worked as an assistant and learned as a mentee. The backlash she notes from other whites helps to support the Foresight stories of oppressive white teachers.

Barbara Needham (White Teacher): "Most people probably would say 'oh my, I work for a black woman.'"

During the early transition into school desegregation, one teacher in the system asked Barbara, pejoratively "how can you take orders from a black?"

Barbara Needham (White Teacher): (Sighs) "She thinks she's above and beyond anyone. I enjoyed her the least. And she was white."

While Barbara Needham did not have family pedagogy in her teacher education program, she learned nuanced black family pedagogy by necessity. Barbara had been a student during the freedom of choice period and she befriended black students and continued relationships with their families. So, when she returned to the area as a middle school teacher assistant and then later was awarded Teacher of the Year at the desegregated school, those relationships and lessons learned from black families were invaluable. Unfortunately, most white teachers in desegregated schools have no such relationship with the local communities. With the advent of Teach For America, and other alternative teacher programs, as well as funding cuts for fellowships to grow-your-own local teachers programs (Like the North Carolina Teaching Fellows program), few white teachers entering desegregated schools have the knowledge, skills, and dispositions to engage local family pedagogy to improve student learning.

Therefore, it is imperative that family pedagogy become a legitimate topic of inclusion in teacher education. With the evidence of continued gaps in the opportunity to learn in those schools that separate students disproportionately along racial lines, the region should not rely on trial and error strategies to engage local families. It is past time to consider family pedagogy in the teacher education programs that filter teachers into regional schools. Janice Foresight speaks to this point in a final note on Lesson Number 1:

Janice (Daughter 2): "It was an all-white school. . . . It was like a trial-and-error thing. I think they were trying to see. First of all I don't think they thought the blacks were going to go. That's number one. And we shocked them when we went. And when we stayed the whole year. Because they probably didn't think we were going. So they really didn't make any plans for us."

Lesson Number 2:
Faith in God, Faith in Family, and Faith in Learning from Others

The Foresight family like many other nuanced Black families countered the esoteric, Machiavellian characteristics of freedom of choice with two faiths: faith in family and faith in God. These two faiths also can be interpreted as a limited faith in school to provide a sound basic education that is also equitable and socially just for oppressed families.

Janice (Daughter 2): "I think family is number one—having that good support from the family, and my oldest sisters and brothers. Family support. I mean, knowing that they were always there. Because see, my mother did not work outside the home, per se. She was here when I was here. When they were growing up, she might have worked in the fields or something, but

Mama was home. So I knew what it was like to have a good home, nutritious meals, warmth and love and encouragement. And my Daddy just instilled in us that he only went as far as the tenth grade, because I think that's as far as they went back then. And he knew. He used to tell us stories about what he had to go through at the shipyards. And he was determined that his children would be three or four times better than he was. And the only way to do that was education. He stressed, 'You've got to get it.' It was only because of him that I went back and got my master's. Because I had no intention, but the more you get, he would always let us know, you've got to have it. You've got to. And that's what I try to tell young black kids now. A high school degree now is nothing for blacks. It's like fifth grade graduation. And even four years [of college] now is almost like a high school, for us. I mean, it's so sad that . . . we are still behind."

Janice (Daughter 2): "My daddy's thing was, 'You need to go [to the newly desegregated school]. And it'll help you.' I said, 'Why?' And he said, 'First of all, it will prove to you, to let you know you're just as smart as the white kids. And it will give you some experience in knowing how to deal with people other than your own people.' And so they checked it and I went. And I was in the eighth grade. It was in the 1966–67 school year. And I can tell you it was an experience I will never forget. And I think that's why I push my nieces and nephews so hard. . . . And I was telling a group of black kids, one Sunday—I was speaking at a church in Windsor—and I told them what I did was I found out who the smartest whites were. And I sat with them. Because I knew they were going somewhere in life. And that's what I wanted to do. And if some of the blacks would say, 'You think you're better than me?' 'Call me what you want. I'm going somewhere.' And I found out who the smartest whites were, and the Puerto Rican guy there . . . were the smartest, about six whites. I mean smart. And in class I'd get me a chair and my desk, and I'd be right in the midst of them listening. Seeing how they take notes. When I graduated, I graduated right along with them. They were number six and I was number seven. The only black. Um hum. With the gold ring around the neck."

Warren (Father): "They would say the Lord's Prayer every morning. I don't know whether they allow it now or not. That's the first thing you done when you got in your classroom was say the Lord's Prayer. I suspect a lot get grown now and don't even know it. . . . They're kind of busy now, they ain't got time.

Joanne (Daughter 1): "I think prayer really helped because I can't remember in school, but we did a lot of praying. . . . You know that prayer was the foundation of things."

Janice (Daughter 2): "We were raised in the church. My parents were praying parents, and they had to be back then. I think most black parents back then had to know something about God, because we wouldn't have been where we are. You know, in the fields, they sung hymns to keep them going. And like I say, we were raised in the church. We had to go to church, and it did not hurt me. You know, as I got older it has strengthened me and helped me to know that because of God I have gotten some things in life that I would not have, probably, if I did not have education and God.... And I was still preaching [the Foresight family pedagogy and religious faith] back then. I babysat them for summers at a time, preaching.... I would always let them know that they could be anything they wanted to, even the president of the United States, if they wanted to. And I really believe, Terrence [nephew], the one that is with the city, he's going to go places. I don't know how far."

With family and religion as such an integral part of Foresight family pedagogy, it is imperative for teacher education programs in their local universities to prepare novice educators with this lesson in mind. The family pedagogical lesson of faith in learning from others was clear in the intergenerational narratives from Janice and her father Warren. This family pedagogy could be quite useful in teacher education as we educate teachers about how to engage peer collaboration. Janice learned from her father to have faith in learning from others, including white peers, who may know more about the given concept, until she reaches her highest potential[23] with that concept. Janice proceeded to share that family pedagogy with her nephews and church members from the next generation of black learners in her school community. Knowledge of this family pedagogy would be useful a priori for any teacher entering a classroom with concerns about flexible and appropriate peer collaboration and peer support in lieu of traditional, static ability grouping.

Interpreting the family lesson of faith in God and faith in family might begin logically by revisiting the separation of church and state, which exists in the region. Education policy for public schools in the region does prohibit school faculty and staff members from leading prayers; however, individuals can pray over their own meals and even small student groups can and do pray at the public school together without legal ramifications. This element of Foresight family pedagogy is of particular concern in the region, commonly considered as part of the "bible belt" of the US. Thus, this intergenerational family lesson can be important for teaching novice educators about how to respond to local family pedagogy by being knowledgeable about their places of worship. As we learn from Foresight family pedagogy, gospel music from their church choir was central to worship, so teaching

---

23. Walker, *Their Highest Potential*, 206.

educators to genuinely support the participation of such choirs in school musical assemblies could go a long way in connecting educators with an integral lesson of family pedagogy.

Implications: Family Pedagogy as a Topic of Inclusion for Teacher Education

As demonstrated in the narratives from the Foresight family, intergenerational family narratives are educative and, indeed, pedagogical in ways that expose and resist, as well as value and support, education at home. Moreover, the worked example provides evidence of at least three implications of family pedagogy to be considered as educational leaders contemplate its inclusion in teacher education. These implications are articulated below through an adaptation of Clark's work on the implications of local oral history:[24]

1. Family pedagogy can restore the importance of local history by documenting the history of communities that have been excluded from historical accounts and encouraging individuals to see themselves as historical actors. It is possible to encourage people to remember, as a way of entering and transforming history and our understanding of the past, for future reference.

2. Family pedagogy can spark a dialogical encounter based on rapport between the teacher education researcher and the researched local families. It can support healing, reconciliation, and developmental teaching and learning, affording educators the currency to validate and to exchange important K–12 experiences with local families.

3. Family pedagogy can work as an artistic practice that can transform relationships and build new cultural perspectives, thereby opening new dialogues to engage positive K–12 home-school-community-university relationships.

Family pedagogy offers suggestions for ways (a) to collaborate and (b) to expose any barriers of oppression that limit the type of praxis that optimizes the potential to liberate our K–12 school communities. Albeit based in family narratives, family pedagogy has the potential to convey some convincing evidence to teacher education research, rendering it a useful scholarly tool for highlighting and critiquing the counter discursive possibilities of critical pedagogy.

24. Clark, "Oral History," 91, 94–95.

(Possibility 1) FP is conceptualized broadly for teacher education to consider pedagogy from families privileged and penalized* by racism, social classism, sexism, heterosexism, ableism, ageism, and religion-based discrimination.

(Possibility 2) FP has intergenerational lessons for teacher education to prepare new educators to entire school communities with the tools for engaging more meaningful, critical and reflexive actions, which is crucial but often neglected in desegregated school settings.

(Possibility 3) FP acknowledges pedagogy at home as a form of curriculum with planned lessons and units that can be transferable and translated by generations of family members, and has lessons that can be particularly important for teacher education programs preparing teachers for that locale.

(Possibility 4) FP centers the family as a primary source, and as a link to secondary sources, of evidence from historical documents that also can validate their narratives. With FP as a primary source, teacher education can help fulfill a promise to local families to develop "nothing about us without us."**

(Possibility 5) FP can be instructive in teacher education for additional evidence to be used against the banking model of learning, because it offers an example of the potential learning that can surface from what families teach and learn at home, and it can respond to daily trials and triumphs associated with local schools.

(Possibility 6) FP attends to oppressed family needs for legitimate authority and regards oppressed family members as legitimate school decision-makers. Teacher education can prepare educators for co-equal planning and performing teams to create necessary in-service lessons and units for their peers regarding pertinent pedagogical issues at home and school.

(Possibility 7) FP suggests a need to find spaces for oppressed families in teacher education, where school/college of education faculty could involve local, historically oppressed or privileged families as co-equal instructors. As incentivized partners, local families could inform electives and core courses in the curriculum.

(Possibility 8) FP can be applied in teacher education to create anti-oppressive lesson plans and unit plans that also move children toward proficiency in literacy, the arts, and STEM. School/college of education alumni from oppressed families represent a promising population for this type of university engagement with local families and schools.

* Hill, *Black Feminist Thought*.
** "Nothing about us without us" is a phrase borrowed from critical disabilities scholars in the United States to ensure that no activity was planned on behalf of children and adults labeled with disabilities without their consultation and representation on decision-making groups, teams, or committees.

Reclaiming 8 Possibilities of Family Pedagogy (FP) for Teacher Education

Concluding Thoughts: (Re)claiming Family Pedagogy as a Topic of Inclusion

In summary, the aim of reclaiming family pedagogy as a topic of inclusion in teacher education is to enable educators to consider children holistically toward helping them reach their highest potential.[25] This (re)claiming of family pedagogy in teacher education necessitates a concerted effort to develop curriculum toward an understanding of family as arguably the most powerful non-school force in the milieu of children's lives,[26] whereby:

- Children are reconceptualized as human agents in schools, and their actions are greatly influenced by family pedagogy;
- Children are reconceptualized as learners in schools, and their abilities, work ethic, and willingness for learning a given concept at a given time is greatly influenced by family pedagogy;
- Children are reconceptualized as young scholars with funds of knowledge they bring to school that is greatly influenced by family pedagogy.

Reflection Questions

1. What is family pedagogy, and how is it linked to nuanced black family pedagogy (n-BFP) and oppressed family pedagogy (OFP)?
2. Imagine what and how you may need to learn differently in order to approach educating diverse students with family pedagogy in mind.
3. From your own schooling experience as a student, think of one salient narrative where educators' preparation for engaging family pedagogy would have improved how they addressed any school-based adversity that you faced.
4. Take time to record some notes on your understanding of the relationship between the family and the school. Do they reflect the arguments given by the author for the importance of reclaiming family pedagogy as an area of inclusion in teacher education?
5. Think of some of the possibilities that engaging family pedagogy has for how you educate children more or less different from yourself.

---

25. Walker, *Their Highest Potential*, 206.
26. He, Schultz, and Schubert, *SAGE Guide*, xxv.

Bibliography

Baker, Aaliyah. "Black Families' Pedagogies: Pedagogical Philosophies and Practices Surrounding Black Parents' Decisions to Homeschool." PhD diss., University of Wisconsin–Madison, 2013.

Britten, Nicky, et al. "Using Meta Ethnography to Synthesize Qualitative Research: A Worked Example." *Journal of Health Services Research and Policy* 7 (2002) 209–15.

Clark, Mary Marshall. "Oral History: Art and Praxis." In *Community, Culture, and Globalization*, edited by Don Adams and Arlene Goldbard, 86–105. New York: Rockefeller Foundation, 2002.

Cross, Paulette Theresa. "Homeplace: Unearthing and Tracing the Oral Traditions and Subjugated Knowledge of a Multigenerational Woman-Centered African American Family." PhD diss., University of Utah, 2014.

Epstein, Joyce L. "School/Family/Community Partnerships: Caring for the Children We Share." *Phi Delta Kappan* 92 (2010) 81–96.

Faculty of Pedagogy. *Pedagogy for Students Beginning in the Academic Year 2012/2013 and 2012/2011.* Krakow: The Jesuit University of Philosophy and Education Ignatianum, 2016. http://www.ignatianum.edu.pl/institute-of-educational-sciences/about-the-institute/graduates-profile---pedagogy.

Family Pedagogy (Pedagogika Rodziny) Quarterly 1 (2011). http://pedagogika-rodziny.spoleczna.pl/attachments/article/PR_1_1.pdf.

Han, Keonghee Tao, Marga Madhuri, and W. Reed Scull. "Two Sides of the Same Coin: Preservice Teachers' Dispositions towards Critical Pedagogy and Social Justice Concerns in Rural and Urban Teacher Education Contexts." *Urban Review* 47 (2015) 626–56.

He, Ming Fang, Brian D. Schultz, and William H. Schubert, eds. *The SAGE Guide to Curriculum in Education.* Washington, DC: SAGE, 2015.

Hill Collins, Patricia. *Black Feminist Thought: Knowledge, Consciousness, and the Politics of Empowerment.* London: HarperCollins, 1990.

Hughes, Sherick. *Black Hands in the Biscuits, Not in the Classrooms: Unveiling Hope in a Struggle for Brown's Promise.* New York: Peter Lang, 2006.

———. "How Can We Prepare Teachers to Work with Culturally Diverse Students and Their Families?" Harvard Family Research Project, the Family Involvement Network of Educators, n.d. http://www.hfrp.org/family-involvement/fine-family-involvement-network-of-educators/member-insights/how-can-we-prepare-teachers-to-work-with-culturally-diverse-students-and-their-families-what-skills-should-educators-develop-to-do-this-successfully.

———. "Pedagogy of Educational Struggle and Hope: Black Families Responding to Desegregated Schooling." PhD diss., University of North Carolina at Chapel Hill, 2003.

———. "Theorizing Oppressed Family Pedagogy: Critical Lessons from a Rural Black Family in the Post-*Brown* South." *Educational Foundations* 19 (2005) 45–72.

Kornbeck, Jacob, and Niels Rosendal Jensen, eds. *Social Pedagogy for the Entire Lifespan.* Vol. 2. Bremen: Europäischer Hochschulverlag, 2012.

Li, Liang, and Marilyn Fleer. "Family Pedagogy: Parent-Child Interaction in Shared Book Reading." *Early Child Development and Care* 185 (2015) 1944–60.

Meng, Nan. "Chinese Culture Themes and Cultural Development: From a Family Pedagogy to a Performance-Based Pedagogy of a Foreign Language and Culture." PhD diss., Ohio State University, 2012.

Murray, Kantahyanee, et al. "Barriers and Opportunities to School-Based Parent Involvement: Implications for Adolescent Violence Prevention." *SAGE Open* (2014) 1–12.

Neacsu, Mihaela Gabriela, and Georgiana Dumitru. "Family Pedagogy: Research Direction and Social and Pedagogic Action." *Journal Plus Education/Educatia Plus* 8 (2012) 212–17.

Noffke, Susan E., and Bridget Somekh, eds. *The SAGE Handbook of Educational Action Research*. Washington, DC: SAGE, 2009.

Seliverstov, V. I., O. A. Denisova, and L. M. Kobrina. *Special Family Pedagogy Family Education Children Developmental Disabilities*. Russia: Vlados, 2009.

Walker, Vanessa. *Their Highest Potential: An African-American School Community in the Segregated South*. Chapel Hill: University of North Carolina Press, 1996.

2

A Role for Teachers and Teacher Education in Developing Inclusive Practice[1]

Martyn Rouse

Introduction

ALTHOUGH THERE IS WIDESPREAD support for inclusion at a philosophical level, there are some concerns that the policy of inclusion is difficult to implement because teachers are not sufficiently well prepared and supported to work in inclusive ways. Inclusion requires teachers to accept the responsibility for creating schools in which all children can learn and feel they belong. In this task, teachers are crucial because of the central role they play in promoting participation and achievement, particularly with children who might be perceived as having difficulties in learning. This chapter reviews some of the barriers to the development of successful inclusive schools and suggests that one way to overcome these difficulties is to reconsider the roles, responsibilities, and identities of teachers. It also provides some suggestions about the role of teacher education in the development of teachers' skills, knowledge, attitudes, and beliefs. In this context, the Inclusive Practice Project (IPP) at the University of Aberdeen has been working with colleagues on the reform of the Professional Graduate Diploma of Education (PGDE)[2] to look at different ways in which teachers and schools can become more inclusive of children who might have found learning and participation difficult in the past. Some details of the project are provided.

1. An earlier version of this chapter appeared as: Martyn Rouse, "Developing Inclusive Practice: A Role for Teachers and Teacher Education?" *Education in the North* 16 (2008) 6–13. Reproduced with permission.

2. The PGDE is a full-time, one-year, postgraduate program leading to qualified teacher status for candidates with (at least) a bachelor's degree.

This chapter addresses a series of key questions:

- What is the current international policy context for inclusion?
- Why are inclusive practices difficult to develop?
- How do teachers perceive their roles in supporting inclusion and reducing underachievement?
- How might teacher education contribute to the development of inclusive practices?

This chapter also locates recent developments in inclusive education in a broader discussion about the role of teachers in educating *all* children more effectively than may have been done in the past. It considers broad issues of achievement, underachievement, and participation, and the roles, responsibilities, and identities of teachers, as well as the development of their skills and knowledge. In particular, it argues for the central role of teachers in promoting inclusion and achievement, particularly when dealing with children who are perceived as having difficulties in learning.

Inclusion: The Current International Context

Extending access to education is part of a worldwide agenda. The Education for All (EFA) initiative from the United Nations was an essential element of the Millennium Development Goals, in part because education continues to be seen as crucial to human development, and also because so many children do not have access to education.[3] Across the world, there are many reasons why children do not attend school, including high levels of mobility, social conflict, child labour and exploitation, poverty, gender, and disability. Many children are at risk of not attending school or of receiving a substandard education. In some parts of the world, schooling is not available because of a shortage of school places, a lack of quality teachers, or because schools are too far from where children live. Sometimes families choose not to send their children to school because of fears about safety and security, the poor quality of schooling (which may be seen as irrelevant), or because of the economic costs. Such costs might include school fees, having to buy uniforms, books, and materials, and so-called "opportunity costs" that arise when young people are not economically active because they are in school.

Differences in access to, and outcomes from, education depend not only on children's individual circumstances, but also crucially on the country in which they live, and in many cases, where they live within that

3. "Children Out of School."

country. In well-schooled, internationally successful countries, such as Scotland, with its long history of compulsory school attendance, such concerns may seem irrelevant. But even here, not all children are in school. And even when they are in school, some children do not have positive experiences of education, nor do they have much to show for their time in school. The so-called "achievement gap" between those who achieve most and those who achieve least is a major concern in many countries, including Scotland, as outlined in two reports by the Organization for Economic Cooperation and Development (OECD).[4] In many countries, the concern is not only about access to schooling, but it is also about ensuring meaningful participation in a system in which achievement and success is available to all.[5] But why is there such a long tail of underachievement in many countries? Why do educational systems have institutional barriers to participation and achievement? And why do so many teachers think that the problems that some students have in learning should not be their responsibility? Is it because they have not been trained to deal with these matters?

Throughout the world, there is an increased awareness of differences in access and outcomes of education. This has to be understood in the power of education to reduce poverty, to improve the lives of individuals and groups, and to transform societies.[6] Developing "schools for all" is important because schooling is linked to human, economic, and social development goals. But at the same time, it is apparent that many school systems perpetuate existing inequalities and intergenerational underachievement. The reasons for this are complex, but it often relates to deeply embedded attitudes to, and beliefs about, human differences. Nevertheless, dealing with exclusion, marginalization, and underachievement is not only the right thing to do; it makes sound economic and social sense. Failure to develop schools capable of educating all children not only leads to an educational underclass, but also a social and economic underclass which has serious consequences for society now and in the future. Therefore, the development of successful inclusive schools, "schools for all," in which the learning and participation of all children is valued is an essential task for all countries. It is hardly surprising therefore that tackling underachievement and increasing inclusion are part of a worldwide agenda. As a result of this interest, a series of national and international initiatives intended to broaden participation for vulnerable groups of children have been enacted over a period of more than twenty years. These include the United Nations Education for All

4. OECD, *Review of the Quality*; OECD, *Improving Schools*.
5. Florian, Black-Hawkins, and Rouse, *Achievement and Inclusion*.
6. Grubb and Lazerson, *Education Gospel*.

initiative (EFA), which was launched in Jomtien, Thailand, in 1990, and the Dakar Declaration.[7]

As previously mentioned, many countries have educational systems that work better for some children than for others. These concerns have become more apparent because of concerns about global competitiveness and the rise of the so-called knowledge economy. In response, many systems have introduced "standards-based" reforms.[8] The process of mainstream education reform began in many countries in the mid-1980s when concerns about economic competitiveness and the efficiency of school systems led to the introduction of marketplace principles in education.[9] Such reforms were underpinned by the idea that competition and choice raise standards and accountability. However, it could be argued that competitive environments result in winners and losers, and that in such a climate, some children may be seen as more attractive to schools than others. Children who are considered difficult to teach and those who find learning difficult are at increased risk for exclusion when schools operate in a competitive educational marketplace.[10]

At the same time, but mostly independent of the "mainstream" reform legislation, many countries have enacted educational policies designed to develop their special education systems or to encourage greater inclusion of children considered to have disabilities or difficulties for whatever reason. Examples can be seen in a series of initiatives and reports from the European Agency for the Development of Special Needs Education[11] and OECD.[12] At the national level, there is the Education (Additional Support for Learning) (Scotland) Act of 2004, which points out that a child may require additional support for a variety of reasons. It is clear that such legislation will not only have an impact on the roles of teachers and schools but also significant implications for professionals working in health, social work, and other agencies.

In spite of a positive policy framework in many countries, achieving inclusion and reducing underachievement is a daunting task. The European Agency on the Development of Special Needs Education[13] reports that dealing with differences and diversity continues to be one of the biggest problems

7. "Education for All."
8. McLaughlin and Rouse, *Special Education*.
9. Ball, *Education Policy*.
10. Gillborn and Youdell, *Rationing Education*.
11. "Inclusive Education and Classroom Practice."
12. OECD, *Students with Disabilities*; Field, Kuczera, and Pont, *No More Failures*.
13. "Inclusive Education and Classroom Practice."

faced by schools across Europe. It is suggested that difficulties in creating schools for all are often associated with low expectations and aspirations, migration, intergenerational poverty and underachievement, and a belief by some that education is a privilege and not a right that should be available to all. In addition, barriers to participation arise from inflexible or irrelevant curricula, didactic teaching methods, inappropriate systems of assessment and examinations, and inadequate preparation of and support for teachers. In some countries, schools are operating in a hostile policy environment that results in insufficient "capacity" because of restrictive school structures, a competitive ethos, negative cultures, and a lack of human and material resources. In turn, these views lead to negative attitudes about learners who struggle, low expectations, and a belief that some children are "worthy" of help but others are "unworthy" because their difficulties are their own (or their parents') fault.

It is important to reiterate that this broader policy context can affect the development of inclusion. Mainstream educational reform initiatives designed to raise standards can be both a facilitator and a barrier to the education of children with learning needs. In many cases, these two strands of policy development, inclusion on the one hand and higher standards on the other, do not necessarily make comfortable partners. On the one hand, it can be argued that higher standards are good for all children because schools are held accountable for the progress of all learners. On the other hand, it has been argued that the difficulties children experience in learning are a consequence of unresponsive education systems. As a result, children are often seen as having "additional support needs" when there is a discrepancy between what a system of schooling ordinarily provides and what the child needs to support their learning. Thus, the professional focus tends to be on what is "additional to or different from" the provision that is generally available, rather than on what can be done to make schooling more accessible for all.[14]

In addition, there are persistent beliefs that when children find learning difficult, it is because there is something wrong with them. The "classic" special education view assumes that it is not possible to include children with learning difficulties in mainstream settings because they have deficits and their needs are different. The assumption that underpins this view is that it is desirable to group children according to the nature of their abilities, disabilities, or difficulties. There are those who claim that because children are different, there will be a diversity of instructional needs. In turn, this requires teaching groups to be formed according to these perceived individual characteristics. Successful teaching of children who are different requires

---

14. Florian, "Reimagining Special Education," 9–22.

that they be grouped homogeneously so that special pedagogical approaches can be deployed by teachers who have been trained to use them.[15] It could be argued that when special education is conceptualized in this manner, it is a barrier to the development of inclusion because it absolves the rest of the education system from taking responsibility for all children's learning.

The research literature suggests that the implementation of inclusion policies has been uneven.[16] While there are many success stories to be told about inclusion over time,[17] there have also been failures and difficulties. Such difficulties have been blamed on a variety of factors including competing policies that focus on competition and ever-higher standards, a lack of funding and resources, and existing (separate) special education practices. It has also been suggested that one of the greatest barriers to the development of inclusion is because most teachers do not have the necessary knowledge, skills, and attitudes to carry out this work.[18]

Therefore, although inclusion is seen as important in most countries, experience tells us that it is difficult to achieve for children with additional support needs for a number of reasons, including

- uncertainty about professional roles and the status of teachers, especially those who have responsibilities for additional support needs;

- a lack of agreement about the nature and usefulness of specialist knowledge;

- territorial disputes between professionals associated with certain "special" practices; and

- inadequate preparation of teachers and a lack of ongoing professional development opportunities.

Teachers' Views of the Inclusion Task

The current context in which teachers are working is one of rapid change. All areas of education have changed during the past decades, with major changes to the role of teachers together with the introduction of new approaches to the curriculum and assessment. In addition, the legislation has seen changes in how difficulties in learning are conceptualized, from deficit-based approaches

---

15. Kauffman et al., "Diverse Knowledge," 2–6.

16. Evans and Lunt, "Inclusive Education," 1–14.

17. Ainscow, "Towards Inclusive Schooling," 3–6; Florian, "Reimagining Special Education."

18. Forlin, "Inclusion," 235–45.

to broader "ecological" concepts of special educational needs to additional support for learning, which recognizes that children may have difficulties for all kinds of reasons. These changes have involved the development of new understandings about the interactive nature of children's needs and a shift in focus from "what is wrong with the child?" to "what does the child need to support their learning?" Such developments have substantially affected the professional identity as well as the roles and responsibilities of many teachers. It also has implications for how teachers are trained and supported in their professional development to enable them to become inclusive practitioners in the increasingly diverse schools of today.

In Scotland, as in many other countries, there is currently very little time allocated within initial teacher education programs to cover issues of inclusion and additional support needs. Further, with the exception of teachers of the blind and the deaf, there are no nationally mandated qualifications for teachers of pupils with additional support needs. The General Teaching Council for Scotland and the Scottish Teacher Education Committee (STEC) have been reviewing the best way to develop teachers' values, skills, and knowledge to deal with diversity as part of the National Framework for Inclusion.[19] Although specialist courses for experienced teachers are available in a number of universities, funding is scarce and many teachers do not have the opportunity to pursue courses leading to higher-level qualifications in the area of diversity, learning support, and inclusion.

In addition, the rapidly changing policy context together with uncertainty about how best to organize provision leads to a range of understanding about the purpose and nature of the support needs task. Provision varies from school to school and from local authority to local authority. Therefore, any exploration of the role, status, and identity of teachers who teach children who have support needs has to take into account the complexity of the task. Such complexity arises from uncertainty about who these children are, the "type" of needs they have, the range of settings in which they are educated, the professional qualifications of the teachers themselves, how teachers construct their own professional identity, and how they should work with other adults as well as children.

It is clear that teachers are crucial in building more inclusive schools. But how do they feel about this task? And how do they perceive their roles, status, and identity. In the past I was involved in one aspect of a large-scale study of the status of teachers in England for the Department of Education and Skills.[20] This strand of the research was based on a series of focus group

19. "National Framework for Inclusion."
20. Hargreaves et al., *Status of Teachers*.

discussions with teachers designed to explore their perceptions of working with children designated as having special educational needs (SEN). Although the research was conducted in England, where the policy context is somewhat different, there are many resonances with the current situation in Scotland and in many other countries. The findings of this research inform the sections that follow.

Teachers' Roles and Identities

First, it is important to point out that there have been no separate routes to becoming a "special education" teacher in initial teacher education in any of the countries of the UK since 1988. All preservice teachers train to work in general education and they may chose to specialize later, normally after a minimum of three years of teaching. The range of teachers who have responsibilities for learning support is wide, as are their professional identities. Primary teachers are more likely to see their identity as a class teacher first, then as a learning support teacher second, whereas secondary learning support teachers probably will have made a specific career choice and are more likely to have undertaken additional professional development leading to qualifications. Thus, secondary teachers more commonly describe themselves as "a learning support teacher" than do primary teachers. Similarly, teachers in special and local authority support services are more likely to have a clear professional identity as "support teachers." There is considerable variation in status among learning support teachers between different schools and local authorities. In some schools, provision for learning support is marginalized. In other schools, the principal teacher (PT) learning support will have significant influence and a high level of management responsibilities, often as a member of the senior management team. Although status is linked to pay and position in the management structure, it is also associated with personal and professional credibility, knowledge, skills, and responsibilities.

Differences in professional identity are associated with whether the teachers have specialist qualifications and have made deliberate career choices to work in this field. Many teachers who have responsibility for learning support in primary schools see it as a stage in their career, something they will undertake to get extra experience or because "it's my turn." Several teachers reported that they became interested in the work by accident or because it was available on a part-time basis and it fitted well with other commitments when they returned to teaching.

The picture then is complex. Learning support teachers come from a range of different professional backgrounds, their identity and status is influenced by a variety of factors including by where and who they teach, their experiences, and their qualifications. Nevertheless, a common theme emerged throughout the focus group discussions with teachers. Most believe that they can make a difference to children's lives. Many said they were motivated by a desire to help vulnerable children, but they were frustrated that not all colleagues shared their commitment to this task.

The Nature of the Work

The support for the learning task is complex. In part, this is because of the contested nature of the concept of learning support outlined above and a lack of agreement about what constitutes best practice. Given the rapidly changing policy context and a lack of shared understanding about what constitutes good practice, it is inevitable that roles and responsibilities will vary between schools. However, when mainstream teachers were asked about the nature of their roles and the tasks they undertake, a long list was produced. It includes teaching, assessing, counselling, administrating, organizing, liaising with external agencies, consulting with colleagues, providing staff development, and managing other adults. Many reported tensions between the teaching functions and the management and consultancy functions of the role.

Such wide-ranging tasks require knowledge, skills, and attributes that not all feel they possess. One commented:

> When I came into the work, it was to teach children. Now most of my time is spent working with other adults, such as colleagues and assistants, external agencies and families. I have never received any support in making this move, so whilst in some ways it has raised my status, it has undermined my credibility.[21]

Recent initiatives in integrated children's services and multi-agency working, such as *Getting it Right for Every Child*,[22] are likely to mean that teachers will be undertaking more multi-professional work with social services, school psychology services, and health authorities. Most respondents saw such initiatives as a positive development for vulnerable children, but also wondered whether it would be properly funded and supported. Many respondents spoke of the difficulty in managing the demands from colleagues, children, and parents. One of the biggest challenges is convincing

---

21. Ibid., 301.
22. *Getting it Right*.

their colleagues that there should be a shared responsibility for children who face difficulties.

> My colleagues always want me to deal with their problem pupils and I find it difficult to say no because I don't want to see the kids struggling. I know that the more I agree to do this for them the less likely they are to see it as their responsibility.... It leads to a kind of learned helplessness I suppose.[23]

The overall picture is one of a rapidly changing field in which there is a lack of consistency in the role and responsibility of many teachers of children with additional support needs. The nature of tasks and responsibilities varies from school to school. In part, this variation arises from differences between school policies and the perceived skills and attributes of teachers. Many, however, speak of a role that is overloaded and confused.

Teachers of children with support needs cover a wide spectrum of professional roles and responsibilities. Thus, the views of other teachers are complex and vary from context to context. Crucially, it seems to be the skills and attributes of the teachers themselves that seem to be the determining factor when it comes to whether they have status in the eyes of their colleagues. However, there was widespread consensus that teachers who do this work are held in high esteem by parents and the community, and most of them feel that they do make a positive contribution to children's lives and learning. Overwhelmingly, they expressed the view that more sustained professional development opportunities would help raise the status of the work and enable them to work more effectively with, and through, colleagues in a consultative capacity.

Central to this task was widespread agreement of the need to reform initial education so that all beginning teachers enter the profession better prepared to deal with diversity in their classrooms and also more aware that they will be working with adults as well as pupils.

Teachers' Roles in Developing Inclusion

Teachers are crucial in determining what happens in classrooms, and there are those who would argue that the development of more inclusive classrooms requires teachers to cater to different student learning needs through the modification or differentiation of the curriculum.[24] For some, this approach has been interpreted as requiring individualization. At its most

---

23. Hargreaves et al., *Status of Teachers*, 301.
24. Forlin, "Promoting Inclusivity," 183–200.

extreme, this view can be seen in the call for one-to-one teaching of students with learning difficulties. Questions about the sustainability of such provision are rarely adequately answered. Further, there are those who argue that there are specialist teaching approaches for children with different kinds of disabilities and that specialist training is required.[25] An unintended consequence of these views is that most mainstream teachers do not believe that they have the skills and knowledge to do this kind of work and that there is an army of "experts" out there to deal with these students on a one-to-one basis or in small, more manageable groups. Teachers express concerns about their lack of preparation for inclusion and for teaching all learners.[26] But in settings where teachers are encouraged to try out a range of teaching strategies, they report that they knew more than they thought they knew and, for the most part, children learn in similar ways. Although some children might need extra support, teachers do not distinguish between "types" of special need when planning this support.[27] Many teachers reported that they did not think they could teach such children, but their confidence and repertoire of teaching strategies developed over time. This would suggest that by "just doing it," teachers are capable of developing knowledge and positive attitudes to inclusion.

I have suggested elsewhere[28] that developing effective inclusive practice is not only about extending teachers' knowledge, but it is also about encouraging them to do things differently and getting them to reconsider their attitudes and beliefs. In other words, it should be about "knowing, doing, and believing." But what might this look like in practice?

For many years, teacher development courses focused on extending knowledge and skills. Courses would often concentrate on the characteristics of different kinds of learners, how they should be identified, and the current policy context. In addition, they would cover the specialist teaching strategies that should be used. In other words, these courses focused on knowing about:

- Teaching strategies
- Disability and special needs
- How children learn
- What children need to learn
- Classroom organization and management

25. Kaufman et al., "Diverse Knowledge," 2–6.
26. Forlin, "Promoting Inclusivity," 183–200.
27. Florian and Rouse, "Inclusive Practice in English Secondary Schools," 399–412.
28. Rouse, "Enhancing Effective Inclusive Practice," 8–13.

- Where to get help when necessary
- Identifying and assessing difficulties
- Assessing and monitoring children's learning
- The legislative and policy context

It is important to point out that such content knowledge is important, but the evidence suggests that it is insufficient to improve practice in schools because many teachers did not act upon this knowledge when they returned to the classroom. It was clear that there was a big gap between what teachers knew as a result of being on a course and what they did in their classrooms. In an attempt to bridge this gap, initiatives have been designed to link individual and institutional development. In other words, "doing" has become an essential element of professional learning and institutional development. In many cases this involves action-research type initiatives built around school or classroom-based development projects and new ways of **doing**:

- Turning knowledge into action
- Moving beyond reflective practice
- Using evidence to improve practice
- Learning how to work with colleagues as well as children
- Becoming an "activist" professional
- Becoming an inclusive practitioner

Although many action research initiatives to develop inclusion have had positive outcomes and have resulted in changes to practice, it became apparent that some were "content-free" and only focused on process. Others ran into barriers associated with negative and deterministic attitudes about children's abilities and "worth." Sadly, there are those who believe that some children will never be able to learn those things that are important to their teachers. Further, there are teachers who do not believe they have the skills to make a difference, perhaps because they have not been on the course and they lack confidence. Therefore, it is also important to consider how it might be possible for teachers to develop new ways of **believing**:

- That all children are worth educating
- That all children can learn
- That they have the capacity to make a difference to children's lives
- That they can create greater opportunities for learning
- That such work is their responsibility and not only a task for specialists

Changing attitudes is difficult, particularly for those teachers whose professional identities are fixed. If a teacher sees her/himself as a teacher of, let's say chemistry or French, it is likely that the subject they teach will play an important part in the construction of their professional identity. Further, if their subject is seen as intellectually demanding, then why would they be expected to have to teach it to all learners? But it is not only subject specialist teachers in secondary schools who have difficulty redefining their professional identities. Some special needs teachers see themselves as experts in dealing with children's difficulties in learning. It is an identity built upon certain beliefs about specialist knowledge and skills for the work. In this view, other teachers not only do not know how to do it, but they wouldn't want to do it if they did know how. Inclusion threatens assumptions that some teachers have about many aspects of schools and schooling. In particular, it can threaten teachers' identity. If responsibilities are to be shared and teachers are to take on new roles, then there have to be changes to the way inclusion is conceptualized and a realization that it can only be achieved if all teachers are supported in the development of all aspects of this process: knowing, doing, and believing.

But how might this be brought about? As pointed out earlier, the traditional way of attempting to bring about developments in inclusion was to focus on improving teachers' knowledge and skills, but this did not always work. Providing new knowledge has been seen as a necessary but not sufficient condition. Equally, it was not sufficient to establish "content free" action-research development projects as they often drift aimlessly. As previously mentioned,[29] if two of the three aspects of development (knowing, doing, and believing) are in place, then it is likely that other aspects will follow. In other words, if teachers acquire new knowledge and they are supported in implementing new practice, using a "just do it" approach, then attitudes and beliefs will change over time. Equally, if teachers already have positive beliefs and they are supported in implementing new practices, then they are also likely to acquire new knowledge and skills. Therefore, if two of the three elements of developing inclusive practice are in place, the third is likely to follow.

Conclusion

A crucial element in the development of inclusive practice is better preparation of and support for teachers that incorporates the elements outlined above. One way of conceptualizing this task might be to take the lead from Lee Shulman, who talks about the need to ensure that training and

---

29. Ibid.

induction in all the professions has three essential elements.[30] He refers to these elements as the "three apprenticeships." The first is the "apprenticeship of the head." By this he means the cognitive knowledge and theoretical basis of the profession. The second is the "apprenticeship of the hand," which would include the technical and practical skills that are required to carry out the essential tasks of the role. And finally the "apprenticeship of the heart," which are the ethical and moral dimensions, the attitudes and beliefs, that are crucial to the particular profession and its ways of working.

So how does this relate to developments in the University of Aberdeen? The Inclusive Practice Project worked with colleagues on the reform of the one-year Professional Graduate Diploma of Education (PGDE). The project reflects an ongoing interest in the School of Education to reform initial teacher education, and it ensures that it is more responsive to the demands facing schools today. At the heart is the involvement of the staff in the school in developing new approaches to training teachers to ensure that new teachers

1. have a greater awareness and understanding of the educational and social problems/issues that can affect children's learning; and
2. have developed strategies they can use to support and deal with such difficulties.

Florian has identified three areas that deserve particular attention in the reform of teacher education based on the argument that future progress in inclusion requires new ways of thinking about provision and practice.[31] These are: clearer thinking about the right to education, the need to challenge deterministic views about ability, and a shift in focus from differences between learners, to learning for all.

Major changes have been made to the structure and content of the PGDE programs for primary and secondary teachers to ensure that social and educational inclusion is addressed at the heart of the professional studies element of the program rather than being an elective selected by only a few student teachers. Florian's "three areas" (educational rights, anti-determinism, and learning for all) have been embedded in the course. It is also informed by the principles of learning, participation, collaboration, and activism as drivers of teacher professionalism in changing contexts of education that include the multiple overlapping layers of teaching and learning, the community of a school, and the school in the broader social

---

30. Shulman, *Wisdom of Practice*.
31. Florian, "Reimagining Special Education," 9–22.

and political context.[32] The overriding aim is to help new teachers accept the responsibility for the learning of all pupils in their classrooms and to know where to turn for help when required. If this task is to be successful, it will entail addressing all three of Shulman's apprenticeships.[33] A research program has explored the impact of these changes on the content of the course, the practice of colleagues, and the knowledge, skills, and attitudes of students in order to inform future developments in the course.[34]

The development of inclusive schools is not an easy task and not all people are committed to the development of inclusion because they have strong beliefs about where and how different "kinds" of children should receive their schooling. In particular, there are still unanswered questions about the purpose and nature of specialist knowledge in the area of additional support needs. In spite of these difficulties, there are sufficient examples of good practice across the world and particularly here in Scotland for us to be optimistic that, if we so wish, we can create successful inclusive schools for all. If the Inclusive Practice Project can support new teachers in "believing, knowing, and doing," it will be an important step in this vital task.

Reflection Questions

1. Why is it important that all teachers are prepared to deal with diversity in their classrooms?
2. What do teachers need to believe, to know, and be able to do if they are to be inclusive practitioners?
3. To what extent is the reform of preservice teacher education sufficient to create a teaching workforce that builds capacity for inclusion in schools? What else needs to be done?
4. What challenges are faced in reforming teacher education for inclusion?
5. What might be the future role for specialist knowledge about diversity and disability?

---

32. Sachs, *Activist Teaching Profession*, 1–154.
33. Shulman, *Wisdom of Practice*.
34. Beacham and Rouse, "Student Teachers' Attitudes," 3–11; Florian and Rouse, "Inclusive Practice Project in Scotland," 594–601; Florian and Spratt, "Enacting Inclusion," 119–35; Florian, Young, and Rouse "Preparing Teachers," 709–22; Rouse and Florian, "Inclusive Practice Project," 1–52.

Bibliography

Ainscow, Mel. "Towards Inclusive Schooling." *British Journal of Special Education* 24 (1997) 3–6.

Ball, Stephen J. *Education Policy and Social Class: The Selected Works of Stephen J. Ball.* London: Routledge, 2006.

Beacham, Nigel, and Martyn Rouse. "Student Teachers' Attitudes and Beliefs About Inclusion and Inclusive Practice." *Journal of Research in Special Educational Needs* 12 (2011) 3–11.

"Children Out of School: Measuring Exclusion from Primary Education." Montreal: UNESCO Institute for Statistics, 2005. http://www.uis.unesco.org/Library/Documents/ooscO5-en.pdf.

Deppeler, Joanne, et al., eds. *Inclusive Pedagogy Across the Curriculum.* International Perspectives on Inclusive Education 7. Melbourne: Emerald, 2015.

"Education for All: Meeting Our Collective Commitments." Paris: UNESCO-Dakar, 2000. http://www.unesco.at/bildung/basisdokumente/dakar_aktionsplan.pdf.

Evans, Jennifer, and Ingrid Lunt. "Inclusive Education: Are There Limits?" *European Journal of Special Needs Education* 17 (2002) 1–14.

Field, Simon, Malgorzata Kuczera, and Beatriz Pont. *No More Failures: Ten Steps to Equity in Education.* Paris: Organisation for Economic Development and Cooperation (OECD), 2007.

Florian, Lani, ed. "Reimagining Special Education: Why New Approaches Are Needed." In *The SAGE Handbook of Special Education: Two Volume Set*, 9–23. London: SAGE, 2014.

Florian, Lani, and Kristine Black-Hawkins. "Exploring Inclusive Pedagogy." *British Educational Research Journal* 37 (2011) 813–28.

Florian, Lani, Kristine Black-Hawkins, and Martyn Rouse. *Achievement and Inclusion in Schools.* 2nd ed. London: Routledge, 2016.

Florian, Lani, and Martyn Rouse. "Inclusive Practice in English Secondary Schools: Lessons Learned." *Cambridge Journal of Education* 31 (2001) 399–412.

———. "The Inclusive Practice Project in Scotland: Teacher Education for Inclusion." *Teaching and Teacher Education* 25 (2009) 594–601.

Florian, Lani, and Jenny Spratt. "Enacting Inclusion: A Framework for Interrogating Inclusive Practice." *European Journal of Special Needs Education* 28 (2013) 119–35.

Florian, Lani, Kathryn Young, and Martyn Rouse. "Preparing Teachers for Inclusive and Diverse Educational Environments: Studying Curricular Reform in an Initial Teacher Education Course." *International Journal of Inclusive Education* 14 (2010) 709–22.

Focusing on Inclusion and the Education (Additional Support for Learning) (Scotland) Act 2004: A Paper for Professional Reflection. Glasgow: Learning and Teaching Scotland, 2006. http://www.educationscotland.gov.uk/images/FocusingOnInclusion_tcm4-342924.pdf.

Forlin, Chris, ed. *Future Directions for Inclusive Teacher Education: An International Perspective.* London: Routledge, 2012.

———. "Inclusion: Identifying Potential Stressors for Regular Class Teachers." *Educational Research* 43 (2001) 235–45.

———. "Promoting Inclusivity in Western Australian Schools." *International Journal of Inclusive Education* 8 (2004) 183–200.

Getting It Right for Every Child: Implementation Plan. Edinburgh: Scottish Executive Education Department, 2006. http://www.gov.scot/Resource/Doc/131460/0031397.pdf.

Gillborn, David, and Deborah Youdell. *Rationing Education: Policy, Practice, Reform and Equity.* Buckingham: Open University Press, 2000.

Grubb, W. Norton, and Marvin Lazerson. *The Education Gospel: The Economic Power of Schooling.* Cambridge: Harvard University Press, 2004.

Hargreaves, Linda, et al. *The Status of Teachers and the Teaching Profession: Views from Inside and Outside the Profession.* London: Department for Education and Skills, 2007.

"Inclusive Education and Classroom Practice." European Agency for the Development of Special Needs Education, n.d. https://www.european-agency.org/agency-projects/inclusive-education-and-classroom-practice.

Kauffman, James, et al. "Diverse Knowledge and Skills Require a Diversity of Instructional Groups: A Position Statement." *Remedial and Special Education* 26 (2005) 2–6.

McLaughlin, Margaret, and Martyn Rouse, eds. *Special Education and School Reform in the United States and Britain.* London: Routledge, 2000.

"The National Framework for Inclusion." Revised ed. Edinburgh: Scottish Teacher Education Committee. http://www.frameworkforinclusion.org.

OECD (Organisation for Economic Development and Cooperation). *Improving Schools in Scotland: An OECD Perspective.* 2015. https://www.oecd.org/education/school/Improving-Schools-in-Scotland-An-OECD-Perspective.pdf.

OECD (Organisation for Economic Development and Cooperation). *Review of the Quality and Equity of Education Outcomes in Scotland.* December, 2007. http://www.oecd.org/education/school/39744132.pdf.

OECD (Organisation for Economic Development and Cooperation). *Students with Disabilities, Learning Difficulties and Disadvantages—Statistics and Indicators.* 2005. http://www.includ-ed.eu/sites/default/files/documents/sen_students_-_statistics_and_indicators_-_oecd.pdf.

Rouse, Martyn. "Enhancing Effective Inclusive Practice: Knowing, Doing and Believing." *Kairaronga* 7 (2006) 8–13.

Rouse, Martyn, and Lani Florian. "Inclusive Education in the Marketplace." *International Journal of Inclusive Education* 1 (1997) 323–36.

———. "Inclusive Practice Project: Final Report." Aberdeen: University of Aberdeen, 2012. http://www.academia.edu/4432038/The_Inclusive_Practice_Project_Final_Report.

Sachs, Judyth. *The Activist Teaching Profession.* Maidenhead, UK: Open University Press, 2003.

Shulman, Lee S. *The Wisdom of Practice: Essays on Teaching, Learning, and Learning to Teach.* Edited by Suzanne M. Wilson. San Francisco: Jossey-Bass, 2004.

3

Achieving Culturally Sensitive Education with Faith-Informed Discourse

Jonathan Anuik

Introduction

IN 2014, A COLLEAGUE of mine at a Canadian faith-based university and I discussed how we as teacher educators indigenize our practices. He sent me his course outline for his School of Education's mandatory Issues in Indigenous Education class, and I read an objective rarely considered when indigenizing practice and discussing culturally sensitive education. He expects his students to "[e]xplore faith informed, ethical responses to current issues affecting Indigenous education."[1] My colleague's course outline enables us to consider what faith-informed teachers' practices with children were supposed to accomplish and the Christian educational context desired for children. Teachers need to know what faith-informed responses shaped public schools' foundations and practices.

This purpose justifies my discussion about concepts of who a Christian Indigenous child was in Canadian schools; student teachers need to understand the origins of faith-informed responses that shape our contemporary public schools' foundations. Faith informed what Christians saw as ethical responses to the absence of formal educational opportunities for children in western Canada at the turn of the twentieth century. Education was a faith-informed public good for consumption by children, a benign liberator of the mind linked to social and economic advancement in North America.[2]

---

1. Matthew Etherington, EDUC 496: Issues in Indigenous Education. Langley, BC: Trinity Western University, School of Education, 2013.
2. Battiste, "M'ikmaq Literacy," 23; Battiste, "Post-Colonial Remedies," 224.

For me, the time period 1880–1950 is an ideal era for preservice teachers to examine how faith shaped foundations of education and influenced the evolving western Canadian public school system. I start in 1880 and inform students of the Christian sources and domains of knowledge that are the education system's roots. The knowledge is in the Christian newspapers and clergy's contributions to secular newspapers. The goal is to help students comprehend the effect of Christianity on Indigenous children's education. Although conceived in public schools, implicit in the concepts of childhood conveyed in the system of public schooling was the superiority of Protestantism as the faith of Canadians and the stabilizer of Canadian society. Teachers were expected to speak of the blessings of church and Christian life to their students.

Grant locates missionaries in Canada as newcomers who worked to replace Indigenous knowledge, spiritual beliefs and practices, epistemologies, and worldviews with Christian sources and domains of knowledge.[3] Missionaries' adventurous nature enabled them to spread the gospel to those whom they believed needed it.[4] They perceived Indigenous peoples' beliefs as inferior to their own. Battiste considers missionaries' beliefs in their benevolence and their actions as misguided.[5] Christian educators turned their knowledge into commodities and over time made these items necessary for human development. These items were schools and curricula. For Battiste, the actions of clergy and their lay supporters were acts of cognitive assimilation and cognitive imperialism.[6] Missionaries replaced Indigenous peoples' knowledge with their knowledge systems and implied they were superior to "lower" Aboriginal "cultures." Monture-Angus agreed, saying a missionary ideology of education took hold in Canada.[7] It resulted in an import of truth to the field, and clergy assumed everyone wanted to hear this truth. It was a gift assumed to be wanted by all children.

Starting in the 1830s, schools in central Canada reached out to the masses to serve and stabilize the public good. Historians of education have documented the formation of ministries of education, school boards, and schools—known collectively as the educational state—and the academic consensus of childhood in English Canada at the turn of the twentieth century.[8] The implication from the literature is that schools were able to

---

3. Grant, *Moon of Wintertime*, 75, 90–91; Grant, *Church in the Canadian Era*, ix–x.
4. Huel, *Proclaiming the Gospel*, 104; Grant, *Moon of Wintertime*, 49.
5. Battiste, "M'ikmaq Literacy," 23.
6. Battiste, "Maintaining Aboriginal Identity," 192–93, 200–204.
7. Monture-Angus, *Thunder in my Soul*, 94, 114–15, 117.
8. Curtis, *Building the Educational State*, 72, 169–70, 184–85, 187, 201, 299, 311;

neutralize Christian and all so-called religious values in favour of educational practices that imparted to children lessons in English literacy, numeracy, citizenship, and a grand narrative of Canadian history.[9]

In late-nineteenth-century western Canada, Christian churches preceded public education promoters and stepped in to fill a perceived void in educational opportunities for First Nations, Métis, and newcomer or immigrant children. The clergy and their lay staff drew on Christian understandings of childhood and youth to lay the foundations for instruction in their new schools. The then Northwest Territories government recognized the contributions of Catholic and Protestant clergy to schooling and sought their advice on school system formation. In 1884, the Northwest Territories established a publicly funded Board of Education, although the board would be run until 1892 by appointees from Protestant and Catholic churches. These religious educationists brought with them foundational knowledge that influenced instruction of children in the west.[10]

The first Christian teachers came to western Canada from Ontario, and the first one arrived in 1866.[11] To these progenitors of modern teachers, who were selected based on their dedication to their respective churches, becoming educated meant becoming civilized, and the way to a civilized life involved a three-part process. Children had to first convert to Christianity, if they did not already identify as Christian; second, accept academic and practical instruction in English or French, instruction often delivered by clergy, nuns, and lay teachers dedicated to their churches; and third, abandon mobile occupations such as fur trading, trapping, and hunting. The reason for the latter choice was that clergy did not want children to grow up and live transient lives among the same gender, known also as homosocial groupings, individuals whom missionaries thought would become involved in homosexual relationships.[12] The above occupations were usually done by their parents. The shortage of certificated teachers and an absence for the most part of any formal teacher training system in the west at the end of the nineteenth century necessitated involvement of Protestant and Catholic

---

Houston and Prentice, *Schooling and Scholars*; Sutherland, *Children in English-Canadian Society*; Wallner, *Learning to School*.

9. Stanley, "Whose Public?" 34.

10. Anuik, "Métis Families and Schools," chapter 2; Anuik, "From Protestant and Roman Catholic Missions."

11. To learn about the educational administration and leadership history behind the formation of the Northwest Territories Board of Education and Council of Public Instruction, see Anuik, "From Protestant and Roman Catholic Missions."

12. Missionaries located in British Columbia in the nineteenth century observed these "problems" with men. Perry, *On the Edge of Empire*.

clergy. These clergy and their lay flock who ventured west were often the only ones with formal schooling past elementary school.[13] Back then and now, teachers assumed students and their families wanted the instruction offered.[14]

Christian missionaries set up schools in the service of First Nations, Métis, and newcomer families and communities. They sincerely believed their work improved Indigenous peoples' and their newcomer counterparts' quality of life. The missionary model of "doing good" through Christian service and salvation justified erection of schoolhouses and churches. These fortifications were spaces where everyone could learn the truths they would need to know to live in the new Dominion of Canada. Lessons would counter the desire to be mobile, a deficit the missionaries reported when they observed that "[t]o be a cowboy seems to be the goal of ambition of most of the boys," a typical quotation appearing in newspapers discussing children in western Canada in the 1890s.[15]

The missionary plan Anuik articulates illuminates Monture-Angus' missionary idea of education.[16] However, it has three flaws. First, she did not identify the missionary educational ideology. Second, she implied it was a singular perspective that all proponents shared. From reading Monture-Angus, one is led to think that Christian educators and their colleagues in the mission field never discussed nor critiqued the Christian educational agenda that would sustain churches and schools. Third, by concluding that assumptions guided missionary work, she suggested it lacked a scientific base from which to operate. Similarly, she suggested belief in Christianity implied one operated in a stasis and mindlessly repeated the same rituals in all contexts without any attention to circumstance.

The assumption that Christian knowledge does not change and evolve in new circumstances affects how educators approach Indigenous knowledge in their practices. The most important objective of education grounded in First Nations and Métis sources and domains of knowledge is to nourish the learning spirit. There is recognition of every human being's inherent capacity to learn, and the purpose of learning is to find one's interests and capabilities.[17] However, the principles of nourishing the learning

13. Anuik, "Forming Civilization"; Anuik, "Métis Families and Schools"; Anuik, "From Protestant and Roman Catholic Missions."

14. Monture-Angus, *Thunder in my Soul*, 94, 114–15, 117.

15. Maclean, *Regina Leader*.

16. Anuik, "Forming Civilization"; Monture-Angus, *Thunder in my Soul*, 94, 114–15, 117.

17. Anuik, Battiste, and George, "Learning from Promising Programs," 65–67, 75, 78.

spirit lead teachers to the understanding that Indigenous knowledge is religious knowledge.[18] If they work from this position, they believe Indigenous content is religious content. In public schools, teachers gain the option not to nourish students' learning spirits and journeys because they assume Indigenous content is solely religious content. The use of religious knowledge as a point of reference for knowing is then considered inappropriate in the classroom. The consequence is that whatever First Nations and Métis curriculum teachers can share becomes packaged into a unit. The teacher distances the content from discussion of principles and values. The content becomes historical because teachers think it lacks a contemporary, modern, and secular grounding in philosophy. It is judged old knowledge.[19]

Battiste exposes teachers who work from the position that religious content must be taught in a dispassionate and nondevotional manner as unable to indigenize their practices.[20] Such educators confine Indigenous knowledge to a religious sphere and expel it from school. They argue that schools are public spaces and supposed to be free of religious influence and persuasion. The spiritual sources and domains of knowledge that sustain Indigenous learning make teachers uncomfortable with such content. Teachers who avoid Indigenous content through identification of it with religious knowledge deanimate ideas and look away from Indigenous children because they think religion and spirituality don't belong in public schools. For them, public schools don't promote a faith position, and this perspective gives teachers a flawed justification for exclusion of Indigenous perspectives on learning.

When content becomes old knowledge, and old knowledge is associated with a religious position, teachers think the material interferes with the progress of modern society. They see it as incompatible with the advanced work of educational thinkers, according to a conversation I had with Matthew Etherington on August 22, 2014. Students who reason through problems from Indigenous and Christian frames experience the classroom as an adversarial space. So what is left for students to do in a class with a teacher who discredits the knowledge of their parents, faith communities, elders, and other nurturing guides? Students may feel the teacher is not worth listening to and consequently, the class experience can become adversarial in its execution. Students emotionally drop out before physically dropping out of class and school.[21]

---

18. Battiste, *Decolonizing Education*, 169.
19. Etherington mentioned this to me in an e-mail message on August 22, 2014.
20. Battiste, *Decolonizing Education*, 169.
21. Ningwakwe George, as cited in Anuik and Gillies, "Indigenous Knowledge."

The conflation of Indigenous knowledge with religious knowledge and their tethering to a stasis pole begs unpicking in teacher education and among teachers. Pre-service teachers need to recognize how their beliefs about teaching and the content students need to learn originated in musings of clergy and their lay supporters at the turn of the twentieth century. They spread truths that were initially devotional and later academic in curriculum.[22]

Faith-informed responses to children are part of educational discourse but exist outside of the legislative record that comprises secular educational history. This omission creates the impression in neophytes that the path to a secular school system was achieved without much involvement from authorities in the sacred sphere. Such a conclusion is incorrect. One only has to read the Christian periodicals published at the turn of the twentieth century to see contributors and readers interested in public schools. Teachers need to see these discussions; the discourse can debunk the myth of an inevitable transition from sacred schools to secular practice.

I want preservice teachers to explore First Nations and Métis children and their educational experiences from their own faith locations. I want preservice teachers to know that they draw from a faith base when they practice. Teachers need to know this lesson; Christianity inspired the formation of public schools and continues to have an effect on schools' pedagogical objectives. Faith influenced secular and modern society's objectives for what children needed to know at school. I educate students that children would be expected at school to rely on faith-informed concepts when they were taught literacy, numeracy, and citizenship lessons. They were supposed to then promote these understandings and the skills they acquired to their families and to their own children so they would understand teachers at school.

Teachers need to consider how nascent boards of education addressed the shift from Christian to state-controlled schools and school boards in their objectives and practices, which were to train children to be loyal to the Canadian state.[23] I then ask students to consider how teachers adjusted to Christian practices becoming state practices in their work with children. Who was a Christian child at public school, and what were teachers expected to do to make a child Christian and reinforce Christianity?

The requirement that students consider Christian faith in Indigenous education courses makes space for neophytes to discuss Christianity and First Nations and Métis children and youth in education. There can be discussion of spirituality as it affects learning and opens a door to consideration

---

22. Monture-Angus, *Thunder in my Soul*, 94, 114–15, 117.
23. Anderson, *Education of the New Canadian*, 93, 147.

of how to nourish the learning spirit in Christian and Indigenous schools.[24] The classroom can become a space where teachers can learn what faith-informed Christian concepts grounded teachers' practices in the first schools for children in western Canada and how these ideals continue to shape schools' rhythms. Pre-service teachers can consider what faith-informed practices teachers needed to know and what teachers needed to accomplish when they worked with children and the Christian educational contexts their contemporaries who wrote on childhood wanted.

Investigation of concepts of Christian childhood can come when students read about the concepts of childhood communicated in Christian books, pamphlets, and newspapers published in Canada at the turn of the twentieth century. The contributors pursued educational research in a Christian context. The nuances gleaned from these sources remain unknown to most preservice educators. Consideration of faith-informed perspectives from the Christian press in educational scholarly and practical work is necessary because the missionaries' moorings informed what the first teachers saw as their "ethical responses" to the problems they thought First Nations, Métis, and newcomer children faced. Contributors shared practices they thought were necessary for these first teachers to know.

Missionaries sought practical guidance from Christian education scholars in Ontario, some of whom trained missionaries and clergy and published in both the Christian periodicals and local newspapers. These missionaries would read this work as they set up the first schools. While these de facto teachers practiced, the Protestant press discussed modern childhood in a nation becoming economically and socially complex.

Christian educators' work was not guided by assumptions. Faith informed what Christian education scholars saw as ethical responses to the absence of schools for children in turn-of-the-twentieth-century western Canada. Their evidence came from their periodicals, newspapers, magazines, and textbooks. The observation of boys aspiring to be cowboys became a deficit attributed to the absence of a mission field and a gap in educational opportunity. Consequently, educators who came west were not only teachers of English literacy, numeracy, and citizenship lessons, they were also responsible for producing the impression among students that Christianity was of as much importance as the vowel and the fraction.

However, the Protestant press had to discuss secularization of schools at the turn of the twentieth century. The press at times contained scathing critiques of the movement toward public education, and schooling not

---

24. In conference presentations and informal communications, Marie Battiste suggests that outside of faith-based education, discussion of spirituality and nourishing the learning spirit are, for the most part, nonexistent.

directly controlled by church authorities and their lay supporters. There was also a network of writers who believed that religion was a necessary part of one's life but not necessarily the responsibility of new public school boards that formed on the prairies.

Protestant Christians, whether they represented the Anglican, United, Methodist, or Presbyterian Churches[25] invested in "giving children a working knowledge of western civilization and above all a personal knowledge of Christ" amid a period of mass immigration of continental Europeans to Canada.[26] Schools were thought to be necessary for a Christian society in the west. Presbyterian John Maclean identified this need for universal education in an 1891 column in the *Regina Leader*. Children now

> belong[ed] to the state, and it is the duty of the state to supply the best means possible for training the young.... Higher education does not mean a special education for any section of the country, or any class. The education which includes languages, drawing, and music applies to the training of the individual in the broad principles and is not a class education.... [T]o teach the young the principles [of] hygiene, chemistry, and physiology is to give a harmonious education which will fit the individual to perform his [sic] duties as a member of the state.[27]

Maclean assumed children's families and communities did not provide any sources and domains of knowledge relevant to Canadian society. The school represented the state and was responsible for giving children knowledge they needed for life in modern Canada, and children were expected to be grateful for this offering.

Christian educators wanted to develop a school system supported and directed by faith-informed and ethical responses given by churches. In 1910, Reverend William Hincks wrote that teaching "national strength" in the public schools "can only come from a religious foundation.... Civilization depends on religion" and faith. Donald Ross told Professor Maclean on September 6, 1880 that Christian influence assured students and hopefully their families would be drawn in by "Christ and the power of His gospel above, [it] can bring them together" through schooling and "through him, they are being brought together." By the middle of the twentieth century, missionaries took credit for establishing schools run in rural and remote

---

25. The United Church of Canada formed in 1925 from the merger of Congregationalist, Methodist, and the majority of Presbyterian churches.

26. Paul, Trail of the Cross, 5.

27. Maclean, *Regina Leader*. Hygiene and physiology would be the predecessor subjects of health and biology in contemporary schools.

areas of Canada. In 1957, E. L. Homewood suggested his predecessor clergy and lay supporters of the United Church of Canada—the Methodists and Presbyterians—"pioneered much of the work for which the State now assumes responsibility. Day schools were established by the church, and every mission house had a dispensary."[28] The idea of schools for all children where everyone gained a common set of skills originated according to this missionary with the ideas, visions, and dreams of late-nineteenth-century Christian missionaries. Homewood also identified that the United Church of Canada set up the structures of the modern school system. He did not mention that the role of missionaries as teachers and curriculum developers in schools would begin to decline almost as soon as schools were established.

Commentators bristled at the prospect of schools under exclusive control of ministries of education and school boards without any religious oversight. For them, "the school-house and the church are the only sure fortifications" of what Reverend Abel Stevens called a Christian nation.[29] "Education and religion must keep up" with the population growth, "or they will break down the strongholds of our public safety, and submerge the national morals and order." For Stevens, public schools slayed church from the state. Methodist Reverend Alexander Sutherland agreed:

> [A]n education which excludes the religious elements tends toward infidelity and atheism. . . . We must remember that education is carried on by a two-fold process—the knowledge communicated and the impressions produced. The one largely determines what the student shall know; the other determines what he [sic] shall become. Now what are the impressions that will inevitably be left upon the mind of a youth by an education that is purely secular? As a rule, the impressions will be that religion is a very secondary matter; that it is out of place in the spheres of philosophy and science, and is antagonistic to the advanced thought of [the] age.[30]

For Sutherland, public schools would excise Christianity and faith as foundations of learning. Opponents suggested pedagogy and curriculum would over time weaken the effect of Christianity as a fortification of modern society. For writers like Sutherland, students in a public school system would face two problems in their lives. First, they would grow up to see churches as mere structures they could choose to enter or decide to ignore. Second, if they chose to ignore lessons in faith contained in churches, they would

---

28. Day schools are today known as K–12 schools. Homewood, "Okemow," 10.
29. Stevens, "Priesthood of the People."
30. Sutherland, "Religious Element," 31.

grow up adrift from ethical and moral roots and sources and domains of knowledge that they needed as adults.

For others, the prospect of a publicly funded school system could cement the church's interdependent relationship with the state in publicly funded schools. Educated folks received instruction at both of the state's fortifications, the church and the school, as Donald Solandt said, "Education means the 'stimulation and enrichment of the soul,' a training of the mind 'to see greatness and beauty of the world.' An educated man [sic] is a world citizen. To be such he [sic] should know the general history of the world, know the history of human ideas, know one science, and know one language . . . [and] live . . . a great religious life."[31] For Solandt, learners who did not participate in church life were lopsided individuals ignorant of one of the pillars that held up their nation. Their citizenship education was incomplete because they did not connect Christianity to patriotism and loyalty to Canada. Nelson Chappell of the United Church of Canada approved of Saskatchewan public school teachers who provided "physical, intellectual, social, and spiritual" activities for children.[32] The integrated model of church and schoolhouse as fortifications of modern Canada came into sharp relief when teachers spoke of "the blessings and privileges of home life, school life, community life, and church life."

In between the fortifications of the church and schoolhouse would be farmland. In the twentieth century, the Saskatchewan government's educational policies supported the churches' desire for an agrarian society between these two poles. By mid-century, Protestant clergy and church members looked to public schools to fulfill and complement their goals for the teaching and learning of children in what they saw as Christian Canada. Public schools taught agriculture, academics, and citizenship and inspired patriotism and loyalty to Canada at one fort, and students learned ethics at churches at the fort on the other end. Together, the two parties taught children to claim the land in between the two sides as their own. Schools and churches coexisted but were always separate entities responsible for educating children in distinct and different areas of their lives.

By the turn of the twentieth century, church control over education gave way to a public school system where school and church were the fortification of modern Canada. Christian educators debated but ultimately conceded academic instruction to schools. However, they fortified their churches alongside schools. Concerns of Christian educators that children would lose their spiritual identities as a result of academic instruction in

---

31. United Church of Canada Archives, "A Synopsis."
32. Chappell, "A New Curriculum," 15.

schools were assuaged as clergy erected their churches beside schools. In their newspapers and magazines, Christians discussed how teachings at church and school could make a good Christian child.

As Canadian society secularized, schools accepted their Christian foundations as part of the public good. Even though students would not be subject to direct proselytizing, they would continue to be marinated in the state's mainline Protestant objectives for achievement. The modern child, whether First Nations, Métis, or newcomer, was to be formed as a Christian child in the public school system. Parents took their children to the nearby churches on Sundays where students learned lessons in ethics and morality.[33]

Teachers need to know where Christian concepts of childhood in western Canada began, how they took root in communities, and why missionaries and their intellectual contemporaries considered them necessary for children to know. Teachers need to be able to think of Christian discourse as Canadian educational thought and map the reach of the ideas into their predecessors' minds and hearts. They need to discuss the legacy of Christianity for modern schools and their practices. They must understand how Christian childhood informed and influenced what became accepted educational practices to meet students' so-called needs. It is necessary for neophytes to examine Christians' hopes for and anxieties about nineteenth- and twentieth-century Canadian children. The reason is that contemporary Canadians promote the view that their publicly funded schools are a logical result of governments' and educational researchers' interventions to provide children with a common set of skills and improve their health and wellness.

When clergy and their lay supporters saw an absence of schools in western Canada, they invested their intellectual energies in discussions of what children needed and the foundations teachers were to create in schools. One of the plans by Christian educators was to replace children's aspirations toward now unacceptable pursuits like being a cowboy, fur trader, or miner with lessons that taught children to settle, to farm, and to marry. Teachers' lessons were to impart to children the importance of a civilized life. Schools in the mission field worked alongside churches that sought to convert children to Christianity. The two parties instructed them in academic (i.e., English literature, math, science, and social studies) and practical (i.e., agricultural) subjects, and in those first schools started in the late 1860s, they used the Bible to teach children to speak and write academic English. For Christian education scholars, curriculum communicated to students that they were to use the education being offered to improve their character

---

33. Owram, *Born at the Right Time*.

and behavior through sacrifice and service. They would learn respect for and deference and service to the authority of the Canadian government and its laws and justice system. Teachers were to gain authority over youngsters, and although teachers in public schools did not remove them physically, students would be cognitively removed from their families' authority.

Teachers need to know Christian scholars conceived of public schools as interdependent with churches; the two were fortifications of modern Canada. Churches' erection beside schools assured the ideas of missionaries, clergy, and lay supporters would be part of western Canada's public school system. Sunday school lessons were to reinforce lessons from school. Teachers there would provide the ethical and moral base to engage problems at school.[34] For Christian educational scholars, schools and churches needed to be interdependent, although at the end of the nineteenth century, as Stevens and Sutherland suggest in their writing, not all commentators were ready to cede total authority for academic instruction to public schools.

There was a position that the educational administrative and leadership structure of public schools directed by a provincial or territorial ministry of education and elected school boards was an unnecessary intrusion into churches' control over educational opportunities in western Canada. Supporters thought teachers would detach academic knowledge from a value base and pull, even if unintentionally, the spiritual moorings from lessons. A consensus formed that the school could never be a marionette pulled by a distant set of Ministry of Education policies. In this consensus, teachers needed to know they would provide academic instruction at school on one side of the fortification while lessons about faith would be shared at church on the other side. Consequently, critique of public schools—thought to be secular in intent—gave way to recognition that Christianity was important for a student's learning journey. It was a source and domain of knowledge clergy believed all children should have. Teaching and learning provided in Sunday schools could craft each student's ethical compass. The compass would guide students as they learned scholarly knowledge.

With the privilege placed on Christianity as a coconspirator in the formation of modern Canada's fortifications, Indigenous learning moved to the background when students came to school. Teachers—first missionary and then lay—pushed Indigenous students to turn their gaze toward a new system of education. Most often, this action was taken to satisfy the consensus reached in the Protestant press that later became accepted education rhetoric. Teachers could not understand the knowledge systems students brought and instead sought to replace them. Thus, to build an education

---

34. Blackman, Stewart, and Sparling, *Primary Teacher's Guide*, 60.

that is culturally sensitive requires teachers to understand the Christian origins of the modern system of education and its consequences for students.

If teachers understand this, then they are likely to be less resistant to classification of Indigenous knowledge as religious belief and more apt to seek out new understandings that could shape modern childhood. If they see Christian education discussions as dynamic and contested and in a process toward consensus at the turn of the twentieth century, then it is likely they will be more open to comprehending how Indigenous knowledge changes and grows as schools became part of students' lives. The modern child was made a Christian child, and teachers need to know what faith-informed discourse looks like in children and how First Nations and Métis children's sources and domains of knowledge can become an authentic part of this discourse. Then, teachers can start to build a culturally sensitive education with a faith-informed foundation.

Reflection Questions

1. Why would provinces and territories form departments and boards of education and agree that academic instruction of children was their responsibility?

2. Why would Christian churches take on responsibility for education of children and youth in religion and ethics, especially in Sunday school lessons on ethical conduct and moral discipline?

3. Is it possible to truly separate church from state? Is it necessary?

4. If you had a class of grade one students in 1900, what is one thing you would teach them about the 1800s in order for them to persevere in twentieth-century Canada?

5. Why do teachers need to know how faith affects public schools?

Bibliography

Anderson, James T. M. *The Education of the New Canadian: A Treatise on Canada's Greatest Educational Problem.* Toronto: J. M. Dent, 1918.

Anuik, Jonathan. "Forming Civilization at Red River: 19th-Century Missionary Education of Métis and First Nations Children." In *The Early Northwest*, edited by Gregory P. Marchildon, 249–69. History of the Prairie West Series 1. Regina: University of Regina, Canadian Plains Research Center, 2008.

———. "From Protestant and Roman Catholic Missions to Public Schools: Educating Métis and Settler Children in the West to Be Citizens of Modern Canada, 1866–1939." *Saskatchewan History* 62 (2010) 22–35.

———. "Métis Families and Schools: The Decline and Reclamation of Métis Identities in Saskatchewan, 1885–1980." PhD diss., University of Saskatchewan, 2009.

Anuik, Jonathan, Marie Battiste, and Priscilla N. George. "Learning from Promising Programs and Applications in Nourishing the Learning Spirit." *Canadian Journal of Native Education* 33 (2010) 63–82.

Anuik, Jonathan, and Carmen Gillies. "Indigenous Knowledge in Post-Secondary Educators' Practices: Nourishing the Learning Spirit." *Canadian Journal of Higher Education* 42 (2012) 63–79.

Battiste, Marie. *Decolonizing Education: Nourishing the Learning Spirit*. Saskatoon: Purich, 2013.

———. "Maintaining Aboriginal Identity, Language and Culture in Modern Society." In *Reclaiming Indigenous Voice and Vision*, edited by Marie Battiste, 192–208. Vancouver: University of British Columbia Press, 2000.

———. "Mi'kmaq Literacy and Cognitive Assimilation." In *Indian Education in Canada*, edited by Jean Barman, Yvonne M. Hébert, and Don N. McCaskill, 23–44. The Legacy 1. Vancouver: University of British Columbia Press, 1986.

———. "Post-Colonial Remedies for Protecting Indigenous Knowledge and Heritage." In *Teaching as Activism: Equity Meets Environmentalism*, edited by Peggy Tripp and Linda Muzzin, 224–32. Kingston: McGill-Queen's University Press, 2005.

Blackman, Edwin Cyril, Charlotte Stewart, and Olive D. Sparling. *The Primary Teacher's Guide: A Guide for Teachers of Six-, and Seven-, and Eight-Year-old Children in the New Curriculum of the United Church of Canada for Year 2 Emphasis: Jesus Christ and the Christian Life*. Toronto: United Church Publishing, 1965.

Board of Home Mission Fonds, General Files. 83.050C, 509/15/105. United Church of Canada Archives/Victoria University Archives.

Chappell, Nelson. "A New Curriculum: Saskatchewan Proposes Changes in Rural Education." *The United Church Observer* 1 (1939) 15.

Curtis, Bruce. *Building the Educational State: Canada West, 1836–1871*. London, ON: Althouse, 1988.

Grant, John Webster. *The Church in the Canadian Era*. Vancouver: Regent, 1998.

———. *Moon of Wintertime: Missionaries and Indians in Encounter Since 1534*. Toronto: University of Toronto Press, 1984.

Homewood, E. L. "Okemow and His Crees." *The United Church Observer* 19 (1957) 10.

Houston, Susan E., and Alison Prentice. *Schooling and Scholars in Nineteenth-Century Ontario*. Toronto: University of Toronto Press, 1988.

Huel, Raymond J. A. *Proclaiming the Gospel to the Indians and Métis*. Edmonton: University of Alberta Press, 1996.

Maclean, John. *The Regina Leader*, 1891. Fonds, 3270/42/471. United Church of Canada Archives/Victoria University Archives.

Monture-Angus, Patricia. *Thunder in My Soul: A Mohawk Woman Speaks*. Halifax: Fernwood, 1995.

Owram, Doug. *Born at the Right Time: A History of the Baby Boom Generation*. Toronto: University of Toronto Press, 1996.

Paul, W. E. J. The Trail of the Cross, Indian Missions & Indian Work—Reports, 1928–1955, Vol. 3/3 I2, Ca. 1950. Anglican Diocese of Saskatchewan.

Perry, Adele. *On the Edge of Empire: Gender, Race, and the Making of British Columbia, 1849–1871.* Toronto: University of Toronto Press, 2001.

Records Pertaining to Missionaries to the Aboriginal People in Western Canada. Fonds. Presbyterian Church in Canada. Home Mission Committee, Correspondence, Manitoba. 79.199C 122-series 14/1/1. United Church of Canada Archives/Victoria University Archives.

Stanley, Timothy J. "Whose Public? Whose Memory? Racisms, Grand Narratives and Canadian History." In *To the Past: History Education, Public Memory, and Citizenship in Canada*, edited by Ruth W. Sandwell, 32–49. Toronto: University of Toronto Press, 2006.

St. Denis, Verna. "Silencing Aboriginal Curricular Content and Perspectives: 'There Are Other Children Here.'" *Review of Education, Pedagogy, and Cultural Studies* 33 (2011) 306–17.

Stevens, Abel. "The Priesthood of the People." *The Christian Journal* XIII 33 (1875).

Sutherland, Alexander. "The Religious Element in Education." *Methodist Magazine and Review* XLIV (1896) 31.

Sutherland, Neil. *Children in English-Canadian Society: Framing the Twentieth-Century Consensus.* Waterloo, ON: Wilfrid Laurier University Press, 2000.

United Church of Canada Archives/Victoria University Archives, Board of Home Mission Fonds, General Files, "A Synopsis of the Marks of an Educated Man (Dr. A. E. Wiggam's book)," Donald M. Solandt, M.A., Associate Book Steward, United Church of Canada (1931), 83.050C, 509/15/105.

United Church of Canada Archives/Victoria University Archives, Rev. Wm. H. Hincks, LL.B., "Present Day Lessons for Practical People," *The Adult Class* II.1 (1910) 31.

Wagamese, Richard. *Indian Horse: A Novel.* Vancouver: Douglas & McIntyre, 2012.

Wallner, Jennifer. *Learning to School: Federalism and Public Schooling in Canada.* Toronto: University of Toronto Press, 2014.

Financial support for my archival research came from a Native-Newcomer doctoral scholarship with supplements from the Messer Scholarship for Research in Canadian History. The research for this paper originated in my PhD dissertation "Métis Families and Schools: The Decline and Reclamation of Métis Identities in Saskatchewan, 1885–1980," defended successfully in 2009 at the University of Saskatchewan in Saskatoon, Saskatchewan, Canada. I thank my PhD supervisor Dr. J. R. Miller and my dissertation committee for their comments on earlier drafts of this work. I thank Dr. Matthew Etherington for our discussions about Indigenous education in a Christian context. My greatest gratitude goes to the students who have taken Concepts of Childhood in History over the last four years, where I have delivered this lesson. I am grateful for their comments and feedback.

4

Toward an Ecologically Informed Paradigm in Thinking about Educational Reforms

Chet Bowers

Introduction

THE USE OF WORDS and phrases such as "individualism," "empowerment," "transformative learning," "critical pedagogy," and so forth, are intended to signal to readers that they are about to encounter the latest thinking of a liberal educational reformer. Unfortunately, this vocabulary, along with its underlying deep cultural assumptions that exclude other vocabularies better suited to clarifying the life-threatening challenges we now face, is still in the grip of centuries-old ways of thinking.

The invitation to write on the influence of liberalism on educational policies, practices, and discourse acknowledges that there are two traditions of liberalism: the liberalism focused on social justice issues and the neo- or what I prefer to refer to as the market liberalism that is focused on economic globalization and maximizing profits for the few at the expense of the environment and the many. Both traditions of liberalism share many of the same deep cultural assumptions. The assumptions they share in common: that rational/critical thinking leads to a linear form of progress, that this is a human-centered world, that the individual is the basic social unit and source of intelligence, that traditions must be overturned in order to free the forces of innovation and individual emancipation, that technologies are both culturally neutral and the expression of progress, and that these assumptions should be the basis for promoting on a global scale the West's approach to social justice and economic development. The tradition of social justice liberalism is often in conflict with that of market liberalism, and this conflict is ignored in the same way that the western thinkers who laid the conceptual basis for these assumptions were also ethnocentric thinkers.

The Marginalization of Knowledge

John Locke's epistemology marginalized the importance of traditional knowledge and established the conceptual basis for the ownership of private property (including as much as the individual could acquire). His ethnocentric and abstract thinking was matched by the ethnocentrism and abstract thinking of Adam Smith (who wrote the important yet neglected *A Preface to Moral Sentiments*), as well as the thinking of John Stuart Mill, and more recently John Dewey and Paulo Freire. They also shared other core assumptions that are still in vogue among both social justice and market liberals—assumptions that demonstrate how different genres of liberalism are still in the grip of a past that was unaware of environmental limits. Then and now, references to the need for critical thinking to focus on what needs to be conserved as well as changed are still missing. What has become part of the litany of liberal educators is promoting the students' ability to engage in critical thinking in order to change the world—as if scientists, technocrats, and market liberal politicians are not changing the world fast enough. Critical thinking and transformative learning are now the mantras of the liberal educators guiding UNESCO's project of promoting sustainability thinking in teacher education programs around the world—which is yet another example of ethnocentric thinking. To fully understand this criticism, one needs to recognize the diverse cultural traditions that strengthen community, have a smaller ecological footprint, and have enabled people to live largely non-monetized lives.

Liberalism

One of the problems is that the word "liberalism" is a context-free metaphor. That is, it is the outcome of abstract thinking that has become disengaged from the historical experiences that shaped its earliest social justice priorities. Thus, it is Ayn Rand's theory that promotes the idea that individuals should pursue a life of self-interest and that capitalism represents the economic system, which best allow the virtue of selfishness to be fully realized. Her brand of liberalism holds that altruism and government regulations undermine both the basic rights of the individual and social progress. She also promoted critical thinking as essential to recognizing how governmental efforts to provide a safety need for the disadvantaged is a violation of the individual's basic right to fail. Today's Tea Party activists are relying upon another liberal idea that has been widely promoted by educational reformers: namely, that individuals should construct their own knowledge and values. Scientific facts, knowledge that has been revised over generations of experience and varies from culture to culture, are to be ignored in favor of the individual's subjective decisions. Underlying the thinking of social justice liberals, market liberals, libertarians, Tea Party activists, and followers of Dewey and Freire, is that their various approaches to educational reforms are assumed to lead to social progress (which is another context-free metaphor).

Scientists are now claiming that their studies of the rate and scale of environmental changes mean that we may have only a few decades before we become overwhelmed by rising levels in the world's oceans, droughts, the increasing scarcity of potable water, dooming hundreds of millions to a level of poverty where life itself cannot be sustained, and the disappearance of species that rivals earlier mass extinctions. The majority of liberal educators seem not to recognize the connections between the deep cultural assumptions that underlie their interpretation of progress and how these assumptions guide policies and actions that are exacerbating the crisis—especially as these assumptions are being embraced by other cultures that want to identify themselves as becoming modern and technologically developed.

The language of liberalism is like a Tower of Babel discourse, with widely diverse groups using seemingly the same vocabulary of liberalism to achieve radically different social, economic, and colonizing agendas. What the followers of classical liberalism (Locke, Smith, Mill), of today's social justice liberals (Ayers, Dewey, Freire, Gadotti), and of the libertarian liberals (Rand, Norquist, the Republican alliance of Tea Party activists, corporate heads, and the military establishment) all ignore is that the ecological crisis has moved from being the focus of scientific research and publications to massively impacting people's daily lives. Fisheries are disappearing, droughts are spreading and jeopardizing the food security of entire nations, and glaciers are melting at a rate that is threatening the prospects of billions of people. In the face of these immediate threats, it is necessary to ask whether there is an alternative paradigm that avoids the following: the ethnocentrism inherent in all genres of liberal thinking, the deep cultural assumptions derived from liberal thinking that underlie the industrial/consumer culture that is a major contributor to accelerating the rate of environmental change, and the Social Darwinian thinking that prevents many liberals from recognizing what can be learned from other cultures, including the traditions within our own dominant culture, that are more community- rather than consumer- and individualistic-centered.

Ecological Intelligence

There are many Indigenous cultures that have developed what can be referred to as ecological intelligence. That is, they learned by carefully observing the cycles of life-renewing processes within their bioregion, and this knowledge was encoded in their languages. They also learned how to adapt their technologies and rituals in ways that did not destroy these ecological cycles of renewal. Of course, there are many Indigenous cultures, as Jared Diamond points out in his book, *Collapse: How Societies Choose to Fail or Succeed* (2005) that failed to recognize how ecological uninformed practices and values were leading to their demise.

The important point here is that there is a small group of scientists and others who are beginning to understand the characteristics of ecologies in ways that take into account cultural practices and how even modern individuals exercise a limited form of ecological intelligence. The leading thinkers who are rescuing the concept of ecology from scientists who have traditionally understood it as the study of natural systems, which reflected a radically limited way of thinking, are now associated with the biosemiotic movement and with the followers of the ideas of Gregory Bateson. For educators willing to move beyond the double-bind thinking of classical and contemporary interpretations of liberalism and to explore the educational reform implications of Bateson's ecological interpretative framework, his insights on the role of language are especially important. Chapter 2 of my recent book, *Perspectives on the Ideas of Gregory Bateson, Ecological Intelligence, and Educational Reforms* (2011), pulls together his ideas on language that are interspersed in various places in his *Steps to an Ecology of Mind* (1972), which many find difficult to understand because of their own taken-for-granted liberal/Enlightenment assumptions. Why Bateson, rather than the writings of the biosemiotic thinkers, should be the starting place for educational reformers is that Bateson's ideas help to clarify how cultural practices, including the role of language, need to be understood as ecologies. The emerging field of biosemiotics provides a way of understanding all natural systems, including cultural practices, as semiotic systems dependent upon the constant exchange at different levels and of kinds of information—chemical, temperature changes, genetic, silences, metaphorical, patterns of metacommunication between people, and so forth. But as biosemiotics is now dominated by scientists, the cultural/langauging processes are given less attention. I will reverse their orientation by presenting the characteristics of an ecological paradigm of understanding that avoids the ethnocentrism, Social Darwinian bias, and deep cultural assumptions that represent the individual as an autonomous, rational/critical thinker, and the rest of the world, in Cartesian fashion, as unintelligent and as a nonparticipant in the dynamic nature of all living systems.

Autonomy and Language

The cultural assumptions shared by different interpretations of the liberal agenda that were mentioned at the outset have no place in an ecological paradigm. But this paradigm provides a way of understanding how these assumptions continue to be perpetuated in the language of the classroom and in the media generally. Indeed, this explanatory framework brings into question the central value of liberalism: the freedom of the individual. Bateson's famous saying that the "map is not the territory" is a key to understanding that there is no such entity as an autonomous individual and that students and even the most creative thinkers do not construct their own ideas. Language, as Bateson and others have pointed out, is metaphorical, and the analogs that frame the meaning of such words as "individual," "data," "intelligence," "woman," "progress," "technology," and so forth, were settled upon in earlier times, and in cultural contexts, that lead to these words now carrying forward the earlier ways of thinking—including misconceptions, silences, and prejudices. When the infant begins to think and communicate in the metaphorical language of her/his linguistic community, the earlier patterns of thinking become taken for granted. Over time, some of these earlier meanings are recognized as too restrictive and as sources of injustice, which then leads to adopting new analogs. This process of revising the meaning of words seldom involves the deep root metaphors such as progress, individualism, mechanism, anthropocentrism, economism, and so forth. The best example of how current interpretations of liberalism continue to perpetuate these deep root metaphors is that the word (metaphor) "tradition" still carries forward the failure of Enlightenment thinkers to recognize the traditions that sustained the skilled craftspeople and others who sustained the cultural commons of their day.

Ecologies, even ecologies of bad ideas or what Bateson refers to as ecologies of weeds, are sustained through various forms of communication. But unlike the liberal assumptions that represent individuals as rational actors in a nonintelligent world, Bateson claims that what circulates through all ecologies are differences which make a difference. He further argues that these differences are the basic units of information the lead to responses by the Other. The differences which make a difference, such as how toxic chemicals interact with the genetic codes regulating the development of the immune system and how the teacher observes students texting messages (to cite just two examples), lead to communication that is interactive. The Other responds, which then becomes a difference that leads to further exchanges. For example, at the micro level of the ecologies within the human body, the receptors in cells respond to what is being communicated at the level of chemical/electrical processes. It is an interactive form of communication of information, and not a matter of thinking and acting on an inert world. Perhaps it is easier to recognize what Bateson means by a difference which makes a difference being the basic unit of information, and how it leads to interactive responses, by considering how a soccer player responds to the differences in the other players' behavior, which leads, in turn, to a dance in the interactions of the two or more players. New ideas may also be the difference which makes a difference in thinking and behavior—or the awareness that the use of genetically modified seeds that resist Roundup has an adverse impact on the environment, which in turn is communicated through the growth of pesticide resistant super-size weeds. Everything in both natural and cultural ecologies communicates in responses to differences which make a difference, and there are consequences that follow. But the misconceptions and silences encoded in the language of the culture may lead to consequences that are life threatening if they go unnoticed. That is, many of the differences which make a difference in the viability of natural systems to support life are going unnoticed—which brings us to the question of how language inherited from the past continues to influence awareness.

Relationship with the Other

The ecological paradigm of thinking leads to recognizing that what liberals represent as individual freedom should be more accurately understood as individuals *always* being in a relationship with the Other—another person or group, changes in the natural environment, the history of their own cultural ecology—including the ecology of its guiding languages, unjust and exploitive acts by others, behaviors that are mutually supportive, and so forth. Bateson's saying about maps (metaphorical language systems constituted in the past) not accurately representing the territory (today's problems and possibilities—including social injustices and ecologically unsustainable policies), also clarifies why the liberal view of individualism, including how individuals think about and use language, is also a product of abstract theory that has been repeated over the centuries. In order to maintain the myth that rational/critical thinking is free of cultural influences and thus of ethnocentrism, it is necessary, as Michael Reddy pointed out, to think of language as a conduit in a sender/receiver process of communication. This is the view of language reinforced at all levels of formal education, in the use of digital technologies, in the media, and in everyday conversations.

When Bateson's observation about the map/territory disconnect is related to what we now understand about the nature of metaphorical thinking, it becomes clearer that when supposedly autonomous thinkers engage in critical and transformative learning, they are reproducing with only minor variations the conceptual maps of an earlier era when there was no understanding of environmental limits—and no understanding that not all cultures equate our hyper-rate of change with progress. An ecological perspective brings out that words, whether spoken or written, have a history, and that they are metaphors whose meaning were framed by the earlier selection of analogs that reflected the power relationships, misconceptions, and silences of earlier times. When a person is born into a language community, she/he learns to think in the metaphorical language inherited from the past. As we are witnessing, some of these earlier analogs are being revised—such as thinking of a woman as an artist and mathematician (excluded possibilities in terms of earlier analogs), or the wilderness as a sign of a healthy ecosystem (rather than wild and needing to be brought under technological control). What is being suggested here is that we can recognize important reforms that must be undertaken in the area of curriculum when we recognize that most of the language of liberalism (how traditions, individuals, intelligence, language, technology, and so forth are understood) is metaphorical and still carries forward the misconceptions and silences of earlier thinkers who did not recognize how relying upon print promotes abstract thinking that is ethnocentric and that undermines the exercise of ecological intelligence. Only then can we recognize important reforms that must be undertaken in the area of curriculum. The cultural assumptions identified earlier as being shared by different interpretations of liberalism—such as an anthropocentric world, individualism, progress, mechanism, economism, and so forth—are also root metaphors that influence thought and behavior across a wide range of cultural activity, and over hundreds of years. Some root metaphors are being challenged, such as patriarchy, while new ones are beginning to provide different ways of understanding, such as evolution (which can be interpreted as supporting the assumptions of market liberals) and ecology (which helps us understand how mechanistic science can lead to misconceptions that threaten life itself). As evidence of the latter we have only to consider the role of Social Darwinian thinking in the shaping the internal and foreign policies of Nazi Germany. Two more observations need to be made about the role of root metaphors: as powerful interpretative frameworks they control which vocabularies are conceptually coherent while at the same time marginalizing other vocabularies. They also operate below the level of conscious awareness, which is further aided by thinking of language as a conduit in a sender/receiver process of communication.

The metaphorical nature of words illuminate and hide. Root metaphors do the same thing but operate on a scale that has global consequences—which we can now witness in the globalization of the market liberal agenda. Hidden by the language-controlling root metaphors are the changes occurring in the natural system.

Educational Reforms that Address Social and Eco-Justice within an Ecological Paradigm

What are the pedagogical and curricular reforms that will help the younger generations avoid the conceptual grip of classical and current social justice and market liberal ideologues? The initial reaction to the following proposals may be to claim that the teachers' professional courses did not prepare them to introduce students to an in-depth examination of the cultural patterns in their own cultural ecologies. And they may also protest that there are no written texts on how to proceed. What needs to be understood is that a curriculum that focuses on the lived cultural ecologies of the students should not be derived from printed accounts, either in textbooks or on a computer screen. Rather, it can be described by students if the teacher asks them the right questions that will bring to their attention to patterns of communication and behavior that were previously taken for granted. The teachers' task is to name the patterns and then engage with students in the process of examining how the patterns affect other patterns, relationships, and long-term consequences.

What students will be learning is the key characteristics of ecological thinking: that is, learning to give explicit attention to what is being communicated in their relationship, both natural and cultural, are that it is part of their embodied experiences. They will also be learning that the ecological conceptual framework is not ethnocentric, nor does it lead to a human-centered way of thinking and acting in the world. As students become aware of the metaphorical language of their own culture (including its history) and the differences which make a difference when foreign metaphors are introduced, they will then be able to recognize how the language processes that are taken for granted hide and illuminate changes occurring in the ecological systems they depend upon. As suggested earlier, naming the patterns that are part of the students' everyday experiences should be the starting place for in-depth discussions. From time to time the teacher may need to explain how the patterns connect and interact on each other.

Introducing Students to the Ecology of Languaging Processes

1. Recognize that words have a history and how their meanings change over time.
2. Discuss how most words can be understood as metaphors and how the change in meanings can result from different groups in the past succeeding in replacing old analogs (what something is like) with analogs that reflect their economic, political, and religious interests.
3. Identify examples of how analogs settled upon in the past by specific cultural groups become the basis of cultural colonization when introduced within different cultures. Examples could include "modernization," "individualism," "wealth," "success," and so forth.
4. Examine how supposedly original thinking and objective knowledge often are influenced by a vocabulary that carries forward the insights, misconceptions, and silences of earlier eras.
5. Discuss how the taken-for-granted use of language serves to hide that words have a cultural history.
6. Using examples of the vocabulary of the ethnically diverse classroom, discuss the different analogs that frame the meaning of words commonly taken for granted in curriculum materials, in the media, and in dominant discourses.
7. Discuss how certain metaphors marginalize taking seriously the meaning of other metaphors that lead to behaviors and values that have a smaller ecological footprint and that strengthen the patterns of self-sufficiency within communities. Select examples that marginalize awareness of what needs to be conserved, such as civil liberties, the cultural and natural commons, linguistic/cultural diversity, and so forth.
8. Using the root metaphor of patriarchy as an example, have students identify the vocabulary used in a variety of activities that reflect the influence of other root metaphors such as progress, individualism, mechanism, and evolution.
9. Identify the root metaphors or mythopoeic narratives of cultures that have developed an ecological understanding of human/nature relationships.

Introducing Students to Ecological Sustaining Patterns of Living: The Cultural and Environmental Commons within Their Communities

1. Have students identify the largely non-monetized skills and knowledge that are intergenerationally passed along and are part of their family and community.

2. Have students create a map of where their mentors live, and invite mentors in the various cultural commons activities to share their experiences that led to the discovery of a personal interest in cultural commons activities, how they were mentored, and their community networks of support.

3. Engage students in a discussion of the differences in their experiences as they engage in cultural commons and consumer-based experiences. Which experiences lead to a sense of community and which lead to the discovery of personal talents and skills?

4. Identify different cultural commons activities that can be used as the basis for comparing the ecological footprint of food shared within the family and industrially prepared food, of practicing a craft and purchasing something ready-made, and so forth.

5. Discuss with people who are carrying on different cultural commons activities about how they understand the nature of wealth, and if they feel pressures to earn a high income. Ask them to comment on why the cultural commons is often referred to as a gift economy.

6. It is important to have students discuss the cultural commons within their ethnic group and the role that mentors play in their community. Do these cultural commons activities represent an alternative economy— especially for the unemployed and those working for a minimum wage?

7. Introduce students to how the cultural commons are being enclosed; that is, being integrated into the market economy, which leads to greater dependency upon a money economy, while at the same time computer-driven technologies are reducing the need for workers. This would be a good place to introduce Bateson's concept of double-bind thinking.

8. Discuss how the educational process, with its silences as well as ideologies that represent traditions and the spoken word as sources of oppression, leaves many students unaware of the ecological importance of the cultural and environmental commons.

9. Encourage students to study how wealth and property are understood in cultures that have not taken the industrial/consumer pathway to development.
10. Have students do a survey of the environmental commons that have not been enclosed by private ownership and the market system.

Introducing Students to the Cultural/Ecological Differences Between the Spoken and Printed Word

Students experience both the spoken and printed word, with students from some ethnic cultures learning to rely more upon oral communication where the senses and an ability to give close attention to context play a larger role as sources of information. As Walter Ong, Eric Havelock, and Jack Goody point out while acknowledging cultural variations, a greater reliance upon the spoken word for cultural storage and communication leads to a different form of consciousness than found in cultures that rely more upon the printed word for cultural storage and thinking. This difference is becoming increasingly important as the abstract thinking reinforced by print-based thinking and communication are becoming a global phenomenon—with the spread of computers and other digital technologies, and with the modernizing appeal of various interpretations of Western liberalism. In introducing students to the following questions, it is important that students acquire a balanced understanding of the benefits of print-based cultural storage and thinking as well as how oral cultures often have a record of perpetuating misconceptions and prejudices from the past. Yet the differences between what separates oral- from literacy-based cultures are critical to whether students will learn to think and act in ways that are ecologically informed.

Introducing Students to How They Exercise a Limited Form of Ecological Intelligence

One of the major challenges facing educators is to assist students in recognizing the differences between when they are exercising ecological and individual intelligence (the latter coming into play when their thinking is based primarily on what their abstract language dictates as worthy of attention). As suggested earlier, print fosters abstract thinking rather than awareness of tacit understanding and local contexts. It also reinforces reliance upon sight and thus the perspective of the individual. As print is also static, it allows for making comparisons that are essential to critical analysis. The core ideology shared by different interpretations of liberalism permeates every aspect of daily life—from the incessant promises that connect consumerism with personal happiness to the claims that critical reflection empowers people to control their own future—which should be free of past influences. As suggested earlier, the original Greek word that was translated as ecology was quickly narrowed in meaning to encompass the scientific study of natural systems. Building primarily on the writings of Gregory Bateson, as well as the more recent writings of biosemiotic thinkers, all aspects of culture, including different cultures, need to be understood as ecological systems. Thus, educational reforms should provide students with the language that more accurately represents the interactive nature of their experiences, and they should recognize the impact their ideas and values have on the life sustaining process within the larger ecology. The following represents a way of bringing about this transition in thinking and acting.

1. Ask students to identify an experience, aside from being asleep or unconscious, when they are not in a relationship with the natural environment (the soil under foot, water, mircoorganisms, air, light, silences, and so forth).

2. Discuss how the language in the curriculum and the media, including its abstract representations, marginalize awareness of their relationships with the natural world.

3. Helping them to recognize the influences of language on their relationships with both natural and cultural ecologies provides a good opportunity to examine how the language systems of other cultures, including those represented by students in the classroom, foster the exercise of ecological intelligence, where the differences in the behavior of the Other lead to different responses.

4. Bateson's statement that differences which make a difference are the basic units of information that circulate through all levels and kinds of ecosystems will be difficult to understand, as it will at first appear as yet another abstract statement that can disregarded. It is important, therefore, that students be asked to give careful observation to how the behavior and thinking in playing a game illustrates the accuracy of Bateson's insight. Have students observe a musical performance, a soccer, basketball, or chess game, the act of cooking a meal, a conversation, planting a garden, and so forth. Ask them to give close attention to how differences communicated in the behavior of the Other leads to changes in one's own responses and how this is an ongoing cycle of information

exchanges. Most important is to name these interactive relationships as ecologies, and understand that taking into account what is being communicated by the myriad participants in the relationships (which might include the wet surface of the playing field, the instrument not properly tuned, etc.) is exercising ecological intelligence.

5. Introduce the characteristics of individually centered ecological intelligence, where the individual gives attention to the differences in the Other that enable her/him to achieve a personal objective while ignoring the adverse impact on natural and cultural ecologies. Also discuss how the liberal emphasis on freedom, shared by market and social justice liberalism, can lead to promoting this level of ecological intelligence.

6. Promote a discussion of the characteristics of a social justice oriented exercise of ecological intelligence. What are the differences which make a difference that would be the focus of attention by someone exercising this level of ecological intelligence? What are the silences and misconceptions?

7. Having discussed the two previous examples of ecological intelligence, engage students in a discussion of the characteristics of ecological intelligence that are oriented toward long-term sustainability of one's own culture, other cultures, and the life-sustaining characteristics of natural systems. Expand the discussion to how people often move between the exercise of these three levels of ecological intelligence, and how some individuals never move beyond the first level. The influence of religious and ideological beliefs should be taken into account.

8. Have students examine the mythopoeic narrative of cultures that live more consistently at level three ecological intelligence, such as the Hopi in the American Southwest and the Quechua of the Peruvian Andes. Many other Indigenous cultures could be used as examples that contrast sharply with the mythopoeic narratives inherited from early western cultures.

Conclusion

If the above analysis were to be boiled down to the most essential points, it would be that liberalism, for all the gains made in moving us beyond the constraints of feudalism and early capitalism, carries forward too many of the assumptions that have contributed to the industrial culture that is now accelerating the degradation of the natural environment. The conceptual roots of liberalism are in print-based abstract thinking that failed in the past and continues to fail today in recognizing the cultural roots of the ecological crisis and in the different cultures that have taken other routes to development while having a smaller adverse environmental impact. Bateson and other thinkers have laid the groundwork for recognizing that all ecological systems, both natural and cultural, possess the observable characteristics that suggest the nature of educational reforms that must be undertaken. Engaging students in deep ethnographies of their own cultural patterns will enable them to make explicit the ecologically destructive patterns that they will otherwise continue to take for granted unless patterns and relationships are made explicit and examined in terms of their environmentally destructive consequences and their other life-enhancing possibilities.

Reflection Questions

1. What are the cultural assumptions that make it difficult for people to respond to questions about how language carries forward the misconceptions and silences of earlier eras when there was no awareness of environmental limits?

2. What are the characteristics of print and data (in spite of all their many positive uses) that undermine the exercise of ecological intelligence? Is ecological intelligence an abstraction or do we exercise it in limited ways even while thinking we are autonomous and inner-directed thinkers. What are the characteristics of the cultural ecologies within which we live, and what could Christian students learn from becoming aware that they live in an emergent, relational, and interdependent world.

3. Does the dominant Christian understanding of eco-justice address the deep linguistic and cultural roots of the ecological crisis?

4. What are the critical questions that Christians should be asking about the conscious shaping influence of computer-mediated learning? In what ways does the digital revolution threaten Christianity as well as other world religions? What should teachers bring to the attention of students about this threat?

5. What is distinctive about the epistemology of Jesus, and how does it differ from the epistemology reinforced by the digital revolution? What are the moral values that can be derived from reducing human experience to that of data? What are the issues that teachers should raise with students? Is the digital revolution a secularizing force?

6. Is print, even when used by a careful observer, able to account for the full range of the experiences—differences in the students' emotions, interaction to behaviors, memories that provide the analogs for understanding unfamiliar aspects of the experience?

7. Is print able to represent the taken-for-granted patterns of thinking that students bring to the experience? Does the taken-for-granted assumptions of the writer, as well as her/his vocabulary, influence what aspects of experience will be written about? Is there such a thing as objective knowledge?

Bibliography

Bateson, Gregory. *Steps to an Ecology of Mind.* New York: Ballantine, 1972.
Bowers, Chet. *An Ecological and Cultural Critique of the Common Core Curriculum.* New York: Peter Lang, 2015.
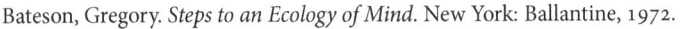. *The False Promises of the Digital Revolution: How Computers Transform Education, Work, and International Development in Ways That Are Ecologically Unsustainable.* New York: Peter Lang, 2014.
———. *How the Digital Revolution Undermines Democracy and the World's Cultural Commons.* Denver: Paradigm, 2015.
———. *In the Grip of the Past: Educational Reforms that Address What Should Be Changed and What Should Be Conserved.* Eugene, OR: Eco-Justice, 2013.
———. *Perspectives on the Ideas of Gregory Bateson, Ecological Intelligence, and Educational Reforms.* Eugene, OR: Eco-Justice, 2011.
———. *University Reform in an Era of Global Warming.* Eugene, OR: Eco-Justice, 2011.
———. *The Way Forward: Educational Reforms That Focus on the Cultural Commons and the Linguistic Roots of the Ecological/Cultural Crises.* Eugene, OR: Eco-Justice, 2012.
Diamond, Jared. *Collapse: How Societies Choose to Fail or Succeed.* New York: Viking, 2005.
Kolbert, Elizabeth. *The Sixth Extinction: An Unnatural History.* New York: Henry Holt, 2014.
Reddy, Michael. "The Conduit Metaphor—a Case of Frame Conflict in Our Language about Language." In *Metaphor and Thought*, edited by Andrew Ortony, 164–201. 2nd ed. Cambridge: Cambridge University Press, 1993.
Smith, Adam. *Theory of Moral Sentiments.* New York: Economic Classics, 2013.
Weikart, Richard. *From Darwin to Hitler: Evolutionary Ethics, Eugenics, and Racism in Germany.* New York: Palgrave Macmillan, 2006.

5

Self-Worth and Meaning-Oriented Education

Eva Maria Waibel[1]

Introduction

ARE WE NOT PROMISING too much when we speak of a meaning- and existence-oriented education? Indeed, perhaps we are: there is no education that guarantees children will grow up to become adults who possess a strong sense of self-worth and lead a meaningful and, therefore, existential life. But in trying to find possible paths through the thicket of education, existential education is on a good course.

Existential education demonstrates a theoretically founded praxis knowledge that aims to be precisely this: a self-worth and meaning-oriented education. In a time of depersonalization and massification through various media worlds and in a time of value diversity and devaluation, an acceleration of lifeworlds, globalization, and social change, it is especially challenging to assert oneself as an independent person.

Existential Philosophy and Existential Analysis

The theoretical substantiation of my observations is based on existential analysis and logotherapy, the so-called third Viennese school of psychotherapy. What do we mean by existential analysis? Existential analysis is one of the most important schools of psychotherapeutic thought of the twentieth century. It is based on existential philosophy and phenomenology. Viktor Frankl initially

---

1. Quotations from German sources for which there is no English translation have been translated by the author in notes found throughout this chapter.

developed it between 1926 and 1933 as a complement to psychoanalysis and individual psychology. Later it became its antithesis. His theory, existential analysis, and logotherapy are not geared toward an analysis of existence but an analysis *for* existence. Existential analysis aims to show to the individual human being personal freedom and responsibility. It wants to enable the person to live free and responsible in accordance with personal values. Logotherapy has become a therapy that is focused on meaning.

Viktor Frankl (1905–97) was a Viennese psychiatrist and psychotherapist. At first, he intensively dealt with Sigmund Freud and Alfred Adler. After a committed exploration, it became apparent to him that Freud and Adler neglected one important question: namely, what moves a person in his or her innermost; one may also say: the question of the meaning of life. Frankl criticized this reductionism of psychotherapy during that time. Initially, he only wanted to add these topics to the existing schools of psychotherapeutic thought. Yet, from these reflections, the third Viennese school of psychotherapy eventually grew. Frankl was also a philosopher and was, therefore, involved with one of the most important schools of philosophical thought of the twentieth century, namely existential philosophy. The philosophers Max Scheler, Karl Jaspers, Martin Heidegger, Søren Kierkegaard, as well as Edmund Husserl influenced him. The central question for him was: what helps a person to come to a meaningful existence?

But first of all the following question must be answered: what does existence mean? Existence means to create something valuable out of the present conditions and to mould oneself as a person within these conditions. "Existence, in the framework of existential analysis, means a meaningful life, formed freely and responsibly; a life that the person experiences as his own and in which he understands himself to be a cooperator."[2] To attain this, we need a twofold dealing-with: an inner dealing with oneself and an outer dealing with the world.

To put it simply: the person who more and more reaches him- or herself and is in a meaningful exchange with the world leads an existential life. This, indeed, is the aim of existential education: to become more and more like yourself within and through the world. This is valid for children but also for educators. Existential education is oriented toward the child developing an appraisal and a feeling for him- or herself as well as for others. Therefore, the main concern is not to prescribe a path of life for children but to help them find their path and accompany them on this path.

---

2. Längle, *Lehrbuch der Existenzanalyse*, 99.

Frankl's existential analysis focuses on the spirituality of the human being. Frankl has taken over this term from Max Scheler.[3] With his theory he, above all, wants to counterbalance the "spiritual" deficit in psychotherapeutic treatment.[4] He wants to go beyond a perspective of humanity that is purely based on natural sciences since such a perspective can—according to his viewpoint—never do justice to the whole person. Thus, Frankl understands existential analysis as a process in which the person becomes aware of his or her spirituality and in particular of his or her freedom and responsibility. The aim is to live as free and responsible as possible.

The Implications for Education

Existential education focuses on the spirituality of the child; it neither sees the person as a result of psychological or inner-psychological processes nor as a result of an environmental influence, but as a being that can take charge of oneself and mould oneself. Existential education wants to enable children to "freely become themselves."[5]

Existential analysis also focuses on the persons that are involved in the educational process, namely the child and the educators. This pedagogy lays claim to existentialism because it also aims to contribute to a successful and fulfilled, i.e., an existential life. Another aim is implied, namely the aim to strengthen children in their self-worth. This implies that the educators also deal with their own existential questions. Yet, the main concern is dealing with one's own questions of value. Through this process, educators become clearer about their educational attitudes and actions and, therefore, about their authenticity.

Existential education is a pedagogy that takes young people seriously; it promotes dialogue, relationships, and encounters, and develops the person in the sense of unfolding him or her. This education primarily attends to the potential of the children and not to functionality. The person is to live as him/herself—just as he/she deeply is—but even more than this: as he/she ought to live and is able to live. Fundamentally, existential analysis extricates itself from theory in a twofold manner as it demands personal responses from the two parties involved in the educational process: the person to be educated and the educators.[6]

---

3. Henckmann, "Geistige Person," 150.
4. Viktor Frankl, quoted in Längle, *Lehrbuch der Existenzanalyse*, 5.
5. Jaspers, *Origin and Goal*, 88–96.
6. Waibel, *Erziehung zum Sinn*, 161.

The Spirituality of the Persons Involved in Relation to Each Other

At least two people are involved in education, the educator and the child. Every pedagogical action has effects and side effects on the other person. This implies that not only the educator influences the child in a very specific way but also that every child has an effect on the educators. Thus, education takes place in a multilayered reciprocity between educators and the individuals to be educated. It develops through the persons involved and reacts back toward them. A further consequence of spirituality is this: nobody is able to control another person's way of thinking or acting.[7]

The Self-Formation of a Person

Therefore, any change a person may undergo is not possible without his or her cooperation. Besides a possible stimulation from the outside, a person's self-formation most certainly requires an inner cooperation. Whether education sparks the forces of self-formation in children cannot be clearly determined. We can try to work toward this. The more the forces of self-formation are mobilized in children, the greater effect education will have. To this end, it is necessary to include the child's will to decide for him- or herself. Yet, one way or another, the person cooperates in moulding himself. Even when a person drifts along and does not participate inwardly with ongoing events, this is nonetheless a form of self-formation, albeit a passive form. The more actively someone forms his or her own life, the more this person is able to unfold his or her real person. Existential education, which aims to attain a fulfilled life, has always required the consistent integration of the child and the strengthening of the child's will.[8]

The Lack of Predictability and Feasibility of Education

Life, our entire Dasein, is—when viewed existentially—not feasible and not plannable, and therefore, it is not predictable. The same is also true for education. Education is only an offer. How children and adolescents receive this offer is beyond our capabilities. In the end, it is always uncertain how children and adolescents will respond, whether the answers will be active or passive, conscious or unconscious. At first glance, we wish, for the most

---

7. Ibid., 160f.
8. Ibid., 162f.

part, that a person would implement the things we deem important for him or her. Yet, what would the consequences be? Thus, at a second glance, we see that the entire responsibility for the life of this person would have been transferred over to us. Power as great as this could corrupt us. And what would happen if we, aware of it or not, used this power? Fortunately, the spirituality of humankind is the decisive counterweight for such possible encroachments. Education is not feasible or plannable since we cannot control the spirituality of another human being.[9]

Parents enable the Dasein of the child. Yet, they cannot compel the child to be as he/she is. The child must accomplish this being as he/she is. Yet, how a person deals with an impulse or stimulation is unpredictable. The addressed children or adolescents determine what they accept, seize, or discard. And it is good that this should be the case. Plannability and predictability in education would otherwise mean that young people function like robots upon being given a command and react without having a will of their own. They would be at the mercy of the educators and unable to develop themselves. They would be rubbed out by the conflicting demands from the outside. There would be no instance that allowed them to see themselves. Thus, they could not develop into independent persons. An educator who takes the spirituality of a child seriously cannot combine education with making, manipulating, and creating a person according to one's own images and ideas but must pledge allegiance to the idea of "paring the person" from obscuring and possibly hindering their unfolding. Thus, the dilemma of education often lies in the discrepancy between intention and effect. Education—from this viewpoint—does not always go according to plan. It is an open, unplannable, and complex phenomenon. It not only produces effects but also side effects. On account of all these reasons, education always includes a risk and requires courage and patient endurance.

Education Is More than Knowledge Acquisition

When we seriously consider the singularity and uniqueness[10] of the child ,and when we realize that no child or educational situation is like another, it becomes apparent that formulas will not help us here. First and foremost, we would not be doing justice to the person of the child and also not to ourselves. Our actions would be apersonal instead of personal. Yet, these questions also reveal that although there are some guidelines in existential education the main concern is to align oneself according to the concrete child person and

9. Ibid., 164ff.
10. Frankl, *Der Mensch auf der Suche*, 99.

its situation. From this viewpoint, education and in particular existential education is always a renewed creative and existential action. It includes a clear admission and agreement to subjectivity. Education can never be objective. The more "objective" it is, the less it aligns itself according to the respective person. Education—just like life itself—again and again proves to be like a sphinx.[11] Both are not truly palpable; they constantly change and, thereby, divest themselves of being accessed by humans. No educational methods are always valid, and no means and aims are valid for all children and in all situations. On account of this, it also becomes clear that existential education is not a dogmatic or enclosed system. It is open to new insights and has a fundamental attitude that is continuously developing.[12]

Educators are not Perfect

As educators, we do not have to be perfect. People who tend toward perfectionism often suffer on account of excessive and unrealistic demands toward themselves. The problem is: others suffer with them. Perfectionists not only put themselves under great pressure but also transfer this pressure onto others. They are frequently impatient with those who refuse to function like clockwork and question them. They are impatient and unforgiving with those who make mistakes or fail at something. For people who desire to act perfectly, a smooth process and superb workmanship are always the top priority. The other human being as a person is only secondary. Thus, perfectionism creates personal expectations and demands on the environment and is harmful within education. We could state the following: The more we want to be perfect, the more we distance ourselves from other persons and from ourselves. We do not have to be the best parents or educators. It is sufficient if we engage the child's person and potential. Educators must not and should not be perfect, but they must be truly present. Above all, educators are allowed to be and should be human.[13]

Education Is an Unfolding Development (German: Ent-wicklung)

There is a close reciprocity between development and education. Education should be a pacemaker for the development of the person. It is the aim of

---

11. Bollnow, *Existenzphilosophie*, 12.
12. Waibel, *Erziehung zum Sinn*, 167ff.
13. Ibid., 171ff.

existential education for the increasingly emerging person to grasp himself more and more and, thereby, to cooperate in moulding his or her life. At times, educators must accompany, encourage, or confront. Sometimes they are needed to provide an incentive for overcoming fear, to give feedback, to clarify a choice, to challenge a choice, to provide an impulse by challenging someone to attempt individual activities.[14]

Thus, in summary, it is necessary on the basis of the spirituality of the child to mobilize the forces of self-formation within the child and to support it in leading a life with consent, agreement, and respect for himself, i.e. an existential life. Therefore, education always means—as Romano Guardini expresses it—"to encourage this person to be himself. So that his task may be shown to him, his path revealed, not mine."[15] Karl Jaspers sees it as the following: "Nurturing as an aid to becoming fully human and education as the fruit of nurturing are carried out by taking the whole person seriously."[16]

The Human Image in Existential Education

The term "person" first appears with Seneca.[17] Yet, only Christianity shifts the importance of the individual toward the center of reflection since, according to this point of view, every person "was not only wanted and created by God for his own sake but also freed and redeemed through Christ for his own sake."[18] In pedagogics, the school of thought that orients itself along the lines of the person is initially found with Friedrich Schleiermacher in the nineteenth century and then more prominently in the pedagogical personalism of the twentieth century.

The person, the spirituality within human beings, also forms the hub for existential education. It is the active and visible expression of the spirit. Personhood can be described as what constitutes the person in his or her innermost. It is the human being's existential core and what makes up the person in his or her singularity and uniqueness. This essence of the human being is invisible and expresses itself indirectly through the body, the psyche, and the spirit. For the most part, it divests itself of any access through rationality. Personhood can also be seen as what is unconditional in a human being, what does not stem from outward conditions. Therefore, it transcends every role. It

---

14. Ibid., 173.
15. Quoted in Krieg, "Romano Guardini's Theology," 457–74.
16. Jaspers, *Origin and Goal*, 88–96.
17. Böhm, *Geschichte der Pädagogik*, 31.
18. Ibid., 33.

is difficult to fathom, and, when possible, it is understood via encounter and comprehension. Yet, a residual mystery always remains.

Thus, the methods of natural science only provide a limited access to personhood. From the viewpoint of existential analysis, personhood cannot be grasped but can nevertheless be understood. In existential analysis we define personhood as that which can choose, confront, distance, and deal with something. Personhood can therefore also be understood as that which is "free in a human being."[19] As the source of freedom on a deep and final level, personhood is responsible to itself. It deals with the world, with hereditary factors and with its own fate. It establishes a relationship with that group of parameters. What does it do with it? What does it make of it? How does it do it? It not only cooperates in being moulded by education but also moulds the environment. The changing of a person originates from it and leads back to it. Therefore, personhood also incorporates the alterable in and through the human being. Each person can be seen as his or her own possibility. In these possibilities also lies his or her potential. That potential describes what the person is capable of, a potential for both good and bad. It lies idle within as something the person is spiritually unaware of, until it is brought to life.

Personhood, therefore, is that which is able to deal with the world and with itself and that which brings it into relationship and enables encounters. Alfried Längle widens Frankl's understanding of personhood by his work on dialogical ability.[20] In existential education it is necessary to feel and understand the other person, to be in a relationship and in an exchange with him or her. What does the child need? What is necessary for his/her development? But also, which chords does the child strike in me? Which wounds of my own educational biography are affected? When do I react out of a sense of injury or prior deficiency?

In Summary

- Personhood is that which is free in a human being.
- Within the person, there is an inner counterpart.
- Personhood cannot be grasped but may always change.
- Personhood can behave in one way or another.
- The person is given over to himself through his/her capacity for choice.

---

19. Frankl, *Der leidende Mensch*, 173f.
20. Längle, *Lehrbuch der Existenzanalyse*, 31.

The Fundamental Motivations from a Pedagogical Perspective[21]

In the fundamental motivations developed by Alfried Längle,[22] all essential themes of humankind and, thereby, of existential education are illustrated. These are:

- The world—its conditions and possibilities.
- One's own life—one's own nature with its "experienced vitality."
- Being one's own person—being oneself, realness, and distinctiveness.
- The future and its prompting for active participation.

The four fundamental motivations—to put it simply—deal with one's own being, one's own values, one's own person, and one's own meaning. As stated earlier, they therefore revolve around life's central and vital questions. They illustrate the essential focal points along which people move. They can also be understood as existential queries to humankind, namely as life questions we encounter repeatedly if we have the mind to pay attention to them. They can also be interpreted as developmental steps for human beings. They are, furthermore, the structure of the person. They can likewise be seen as a foundation for human existence, and "based on these observations, personal maturity and psychological health appear to be contingent on how well the fundamental motivations can be lived out in relation to oneself and in reciprocal relation to the world."[23] If the fundamental motivations are fulfilled, the human being will experience meaning in his or her life. If these conditions are not fulfilled, emptiness, loss of orientation, existential vacuum, despair, and addiction may ensue. In the following section, the pedagogical aspects of the four fundamental motivations will be described.

The First Fundamental Motivation

The first fundamental motivation deals with Dasein, with one's own being in the world. It deals with the question of how a person copes with his or her own life. Existential education is geared toward offering *support*, *space*, and *protection* to children.[24]

---

21. Längle and Holzhey-Kunz, *Existenzanalyse und Daseinsanalyse*, 29.

22. Längle, "Was bewegt den Menschen? Die existenzielle Motivation des Menschen"; Längle, "Was bewegt den Menschen? Die existenzielle Motivation der Person"; Längle, "Die Grundmotivationen."

23. Längle and Holzhey-Kunz, *Existenzanalyse und Daseinsanalyse*, 29ff.

24. Ibid., 37.

A person experiences *protection* when he or she feels accepted. This is true for every phase of life, from youth to old age. For children it is especially important to feel accepted by their most prominent attachment figures. Up to a certain degree, one can make up for a deficiency in unconditional acceptance later in life. In this regard, the aspect of self-acceptance, which identifies a mature person, becomes increasingly important.

Children need sufficient *space* on a multitude of levels. Space is needed for one to be allowed to move physically, psychologically, and mentally. To be allowed to think and act freely is just as much a part of it as having sufficient space for one's own development; space is needed for one's own ideas and thoughts but also for the world as a living environment. Space also means not to be constantly "occupied" by educators. But for educators to take space means to stand up for their own values and convictions. Children should also have the possibility to appropriate as much of the real "world" as possible in order to "grasp" it.

Where it is necessary, children experience *support* through the assistance of others. For the most part, this happens through a regular daily schedule, clear rules and values, a dependable attitude of the educators, educators who are at rest with themselves, educators who know what is important to them and who are not needy themselves, and quite frequently also through siblings. Opposition may also be supportive. It leads to an experience of firmness and stability. Support may also be found in oneself—and this is already true for children: one may experience support through one's own body; e.g., by depending on the ability to control the body, having sufficient strength and endurance for a venture but also having acquired a specific knowledge (athletic, musical, life-practical, intellectual, craft-related). Yet, ultimately, it depends on being reconciled to all of one's strengths and weaknesses, to one's biography and possibilities. In doing so, the person accepts the conditions to which he or she is exposed.

If the conditions for the first fundamental motivation are fulfilled, experiences of *trust* take place. Out of these experiences *basic trust* or *fundamental trust* develop—as we say in existential analysis. It is based upon a deep feeling of being held in the world. In this state, the adult or the child feels safe. Fundamental trust is not given once and for all but is constantly reformed through later experiences.[25]

---

25. Längle, "Die Grundmotivationen," 5f.

In summary, the first fundamental motivation focuses on:

- *Protection* through being accepted.
- *Space* through places where we can dwell, where we have room for actual development, where we have distance and maneuvering room.
- *Support* through everything that has solidity, rests in itself and provides resistance.

The Second Fundamental Motivation

The second fundamental motivation revolves around the question of whether there is sufficient value in one's life and whether life is, therefore, viewed as valuable. In order to develop such an attitude children require *relationship, time,* and *closeness*.[26]

In the same way a bridge connects two shorelines, *relationship* forms a bridge and creates connectedness from one person to another. People draw strength for their lives from relationships. What measures can be taken in education to catch up on deficiencies in these experiences? Educators, who turn toward it deliberately, listen to it, are interested in its life, and try to understand it, fulfill this fundamental motivation. This means:

- Attending occurs within the framework of relationship.
- Relationship means to feel something that connects, something communal.
- Relationship enables access to other humans and objects.

Without the gift of *time*, a relationship is hardly conceivable. Only when we take time and give our time to another person is there room for feelings and their reverberations. "Time is the space for relationships."[27] This is especially true for the time in which educators fully turn toward the children, in which they are fully present to them.

- Having time means "turning toward someone."
- Turning toward someone means abiding.

Turning toward someone can be deepened by *closeness*. Through closeness we experience the other person, but also ourselves, more intensively. Thus, we become effortlessly aware of personal values (i.e., of what is important

---

26. Ibid.
27. Ibid., 6.

in our life). In all experiences of this kind there is an accompanying reverberation of the value of life. We feel finally and deeply touched by life and experience the so-called fundamental value.

Turning toward someone and being in relationships makes us come alive. Through such experiences, children view life as valuable. "The experience of life includes information about the value of life . . . and represents the background for what the person feels to be valuable."[28] Therefore, this experience forms the foundation for one's own feeling of value, for the ability of a person to be aware of value in the world. We orient ourselves according to this fundamental value; it includes an assessment of the value of life as well as previous value experiences and culminates in the following questions: Is it a good thing that I exist? Is life essentially good?

The Third Fundamental Motivation

Every person wants to unfold and develop, wants to become fully him- or herself. In the third fundamental motivation the child asks the question whether he/she is allowed to be as he/she is. There are three preconditions for this: *justification, recognition*, and *appreciation*.[29]

Justification—doing justice to oneself—includes an inner agreement of the person, allowing him/herself to be as he/she is. Only the person can decide whether something is good or right for him or for her, thus, the person becomes the final instance for his or her actions. It is very important to convey to children that they are allowed to be as they are, that they do not have to align themselves according to the wishes and ideas of the educators and may implement what is personally important to them. When educators discover abilities within the child of which the child has yet to become aware, it is especially challenging. A "just" treatment of the child, therefore, means that the child's own must be seen and conceded to the child. The human being who is aware that he/she means something to others by being as he/she is and with his/her values comes "alive." He or she develops a feeling for him/herself and for his/her essence. This is the foundation for authenticity.[30]

Through *recognition*, a person and his or her values can be observed. When the child is recognized in his/her distinctiveness and uniqueness, he/she is noticed for his/her otherness. To be noticed in such a way helps "in finding one's own and delineating it from the other."[31] Therefore, it can never be about

28. Ibid.
29. Ibid.
30. Ibid., 7.
31. Ibid.

a conformity-oriented education. To like children only when they "behave," when they comply with the norms of society or the norms of the parents, indicates that we do not accept the child as a person. Through such conditional love, the child learns conformity instead of courage for independence.[32] Also, when we only attend to the child lovingly after it performs well in school, in music, in sports, it means that our acceptance is conditional. The same applies to parents who would much rather have had a boy instead of a girl or vice versa. Getting to know oneself, therefore, requires respectful recognition (German: *Be-Achtung*) from others; one's own recognition may attach itself to this recognition from others. This being-seen-by-others connects with self-experience to form the image of the self or the self-image.

Through recognition, the person receives *appreciation*. This takes place when we perceive the child as something special for its own sake. To have such an attitude toward the child especially promotes the ability to find him/herself. If these preconditions are fulfilled, the child feels that he/she is allowed to be him/herself. The third fundamental motivation forms the basis for self-worth. At the same time, personal encounters are enabled since encounters presuppose that we leave the other person as he or she is. What makes it now possible for a child to be as he/she is, to say what he/she thinks, to follow his/her own values? How can appreciation be expressed to the child? What does appreciation consist of? What does the child receive appreciation for? What can the child value him/herself for? In summary, self-worth can be defined as follows:

- Self-worth forms on the basis of justification, recognition, and appreciation.
- Self-worth is a personal position toward one's own person, which includes recognition of oneself; it integrates ability and feeling.
- Self-worth is the sense of "being someone" and "letting oneself be seen."

The Fourth Fundamental Motivation

Humans want to view their sasein within a larger context; in other words, they want meaning in their lives and are searching for their own connection to other people and to the world. Here also, three preconditions must be fulfilled, namely *structural context, field of activity*, and *future*.

Structural contexts such as family, school, circle of friends, clubs, nature, etc., link people to each other and illustrate the value an individual has for

---

32. Längle, "Was bewegt den Menschen? Die existenzielle Motivation der Person," 28.

others. In existential education it is therefore important to let children experience a variety of structural contexts, communities, and nature. In doing so, they learn from each other and view themselves as part of something larger.

A *field of activity*, in which children complete a task and carry responsibility, also forms the foundation for an existential life. For children it can be decidedly helpful to be confronted with tasks and carry responsibilities (e.g., for a pet, for class duties, for tasks within the family).

Duties that are particularly exciting to children are ones that do not involve helper tasks they dislike but esteemed tasks or even tasks that only they can perform in their unique way, like being in charge of the family's computers, providing a meal once a week, performing supervision tasks for younger siblings or grandparents, and so on.

In this way, children learn for their *future*. Yet, it is crucial that children can orient themselves according to what is important and valuable for them and according to activities in which they want to invest their own time. In this way, even children can already live with inner consent when they are permitted to carry out activities that seem worthwhile to them. In the fourth fundamental motivation, we realize our personal meaning. From the existential analytical viewpoint, meaning is the most valuable possibility in a given situation.

Existential meaning is something that is possible here and now (not tomorrow or under better circumstances) on the basis of the present facts, something that is possible for *oneself* (not for others or a theoretical possibility), and something that is needed right now or what is the most urgent, valuable, interesting object at the moment.[33]

The Characteristics of Existential Education

Education is subjective and situational. It is good that this is the case, otherwise it would not orient itself according to the child. The wishes, ideas, and needs of the educators take a subordinate role in a child-oriented education. Education, therefore, is not "pulling" someone along but accompanying someone in a sensitive manner. Informed guides accompany someone on the path of life. Paul Moor expressed it as follows: "Education consists in taking our children along on our path to maturity."[34]

Here it is apparent, once again, that education is not a one-sided event. Education always means questioning oneself, reflecting on one's own actions as well as being open and ready for one's own continued development.

33. Längle, "Was bewegt den Menschen? Die existenzielle Motivation des Menschen."
34. Rotatori et al., *Special Education International*, 257.

In concrete terms, it is about training and expanding one's own perception of the child, of oneself, and of existential living situations. Educators are to let go of their own wishes and ideas and fully involve themselves with the child. They are not to orient themselves according to a superficial purpose but according to their own values and the values of the children.

Conclusion: The Aims of Existential Education

In summary, is the aim of an existential education to enable children to lead a fulfilled life. This means in particular:

- Children and adolescents are strengthened in their person, in their self-worth, and in their access to meaning.
- They are strengthened to lead a self-determined and fulfilled life, to give themselves over to themselves.
- They learn living by experiencing what is important in life.

Reflection Questions

1. What are some of the real roadblocks to existential education that come to mind?
2. Imagine some of the likely consequences if you approach your teaching with an existential philosophy of education.
3. From your own experience as a student, think of one notable situation in which you were not able to lead a self-determined life.
4. Take time to record some notes on your understanding of the human condition. Do they reflect the arguments given by the author for the importance of existential education?
5. Think of some of the consequences that your philosophy has for how you educate children?

Bibliography

Böhm, Winfried. *Geschichte der Pädagogik von Platon bis zur Gegenwart*. München: Beck, 2004.
Bollnow, Otto Friedrich. *Existenzphilosophie*. Stuttgart: Kohlhammer, 1984.

Clandinin, D. Jean, and F. Michael Connelly. *Narrative Inquiry: Experience and Story in Qualitative Research*. San Francisco: Jossey-Bass, 2000.

Craig, Cheryl J. "Narrative Inquiry in Teaching and Teacher Education." In *Narrative Inquiries into Curriculum-Making in Teacher Education*, edited by Julian Kitchen, Darlene Ciuffetelli Parker, and Debbie Pushor, 19–42. Advances in Research on Teaching 13. Bingley, UK: Emerald, 2011.

Dewey, John. *Experience and Education*. New York: Collier, 1938.

Frankl, Viktor. *Der leidende Mensch: Anthropologische Grundlagen der Psychotherapie*. München: Piper Verlag, 1990.

———. *Der Mensch auf der Suche nach einem letzten Sinn*. Wien: Gesellschaft für Logotherapie und Existenzanalyse, 1988.

Henckmann, Wolfhart. "'Geistige Person' bei Viktor E. Frankl und Max Scheler." In *Viktor Frankl und die Philosophie*, edited by Batthyany Dominik and Otto Zsok, 149–62. New York: Springer, 2005.

Howe, Edward R., and Masahiro Arimoto. "Narrative Teacher Education Pedagogies from Across the Pacific." In *International Teacher Education: Promising Pedagogies*, edited by Cheryl Craig and Lily Orland-Barak, 212–32. Advances in Research on Teaching 22(A). New York: Emerald, 2014.

Howe, Edward R., and Shijing Xu. "Transcultural Teacher Development Within the Dialectic of the Global and Local: Bridging Gaps Between East and West." *Teaching and Teacher Education* 36 (2013) 33–43.

Jaspers, Karl. *The Origin and Goal of History*. Translated by Michael Bullock. New Haven: Yale University Press, 1968.

Krieg, Robert. "Romano Guardini's Theology of the Human Person." *Theological Studies* 59 (1988) 457–74.

Längle, Alfried. "Die Grundmotivationen menschlicher Existenz als Wirkstruktur existenzanalytischer Psychotherapie." *Fundamenta Psychiatrica* 16 (2002) 1–8.

———. *Lehrbuch der Existenzanalyse (Logotherapie), 1. Teil: Grundlagen*. Wien: Eigenverlag, 2001.

———. "Was bewegt den Menschen? Die existenzielle Motivation des Menschen." Lecture, Unterägeri, Switzerland, March 4, 1992.

———. "Was bewegt den Menschen? Die existenzielle Motivation der Person." *Existenzanalyse* 3 (1999) 18–29.

Längle, Alfried, and Alice Holzhey-Kunz. *Existenzanalyse und Daseinsanalyse*. Wien: Facultas, 2008.

Rotatori, Anthony F., et al., eds. *Special Education International Perspectives: Practices Across the Globe*. Bingley, UK: Emerald, 2014.

Waibel, Eva Maria. *Erziehung zum Sinn—Sinn der Erziehung: Grundlagen einer existenziellen Pädagogik*. Augsburg: Brigg, 2011.

6

Uncritical Critical Thinking in Teaching and Learning: Smashing Down "Old" Ways of Thinking

Matthew Etherington

Introduction

THE APPLICATION OF CRITICAL thinking in K–12 and higher education enjoys universal approval at most levels of learning and unites educators. However, there is one view of critical thinking that perceives traditions (i.e., non-scientific ways of knowing) as an impediment to learning.[1] The educator's role is to encourage an abandonment of such "old ways of thinking" and adopt a pragmatic interpretation of critical thinking. The author recounts an example of this and then argues for an inclusive perspective of critical thinking that accommodates all teaching and learning practices.

Enter "Old Ways of Thinking"

At a recent conference of educators, participants had the opportunity to hear—in one double session—different understandings of critical thinking integration in teacher education. The first pair of presenters, both education professors, described in detail an approach by which student teachers were taught to integrate critical thinking based on the following definition:

---

1. Traditions include beliefs, values, and knowledge that are passed down from families or elders or are held individually and influence how someone understands the way the world (reality) is and the way it ought to be. This would include religious, Indigenous, and cultural traditions, beliefs, and values.

"Critical thinking," they said, "is the smashing down of old ways of thinking" and "the purpose [of critical thinking] is to always rock their boat."[2]

In the question-and-answer time, the professors clarified their definition as "utilizing new and innovative ideas and not previous [old] knowledge or values from a bygone era."[3] While their original definition of "smashing down of old ways of thinking" remained, in the question time they spoke about their ultimate objective to advance critical thinking skills by steering their education students toward reason, logic, and scientific evidence. No one present in the room (except the author of this paper) showed any surprise that education professors would choose to use the phrase "smashing down old ways of thinking" in relation to critical thinking.

This lack of surprise and the experience itself is worth laboring over. The professors' definition of critical thinking is problematic for a number of reasons. First, it discounts learners who value their so called old ways of thinking as an important part of their learning. Often, traditions and traditional ways of thinking have added significance because they were passed down from family, priests, rabbis, community, or elders. Second, the definition tacitly promotes the assumption that knowledge from the past is old, simplistic, out of date, and an impediment for thinking critically.

The danger that lurks here is that if such a definition were really acted upon, the diverse epistemologies and values that Indigenous, religious, and multicultural groups bring with them to the community and classroom would be underestimated at best and eliminated at worst. Moreover, such a definition, if realized, would encourage a homogenous student identity with only one methodology permissible for learning. Finally, a false dichotomy would be established between "old ways of thinking," represented as backward looking, lacking logic, reason, and evidence,[4] while "new ways of thinking" would be privileged as supposedly logical, reasonable, and evidence-based.[5]

Professors and teachers alike have been entrusted with the welfare and education of their students, and with this responsibility a learning environment that perceives critical thinking as the "smashing down of old ways of thinking" not only overlooks other diverse ways of knowing but fails to generate a safe and respectful place for all students to learn and grow. The "smashing down of old ways of thinking" is jarring because it neglects to uphold cultural inclusiveness and a respect for different epistemologies, groups, and identities within increasing multicultural and multiethnic

2. Personal communication, May 2014.
3. Ibid.
4. Widdowson, "Critical Thinking."
5. Egan, *Getting it Wrong*.

societies.⁶ It would be a daily reminder of not belonging, of being an outsider, marginalized, pushed to the fringe, and it would promote a prejudicial belief that there are some learners who will not fit in.⁷

Can learners retain their "old ways of thinking" and still be capable of thinking critically? Or should they allow faculty to determine what knowledge types to privilege? In the central sections of this chapter the author considers these questions and briefly examines the influence of pragmatic views of education, advocates of critical thinking, and the importance of making space in education for diverse ways of knowing and thinking in the classroom. Some suggestions are then raised to consider the possibility that "old ways of thinking" and other ways of thinking can and should peacefully coexist in any critical thinking model for teaching and learning practices.

Background and Influences

The phrase "smashing down of old ways of thinking" is a rational feature of education consistent with two unfortunate features of education today: a rampant and fierce pragmatism and the concomitant devaluation of nonscientific traditions.⁸ In the context of higher education, pragmatism is understood as "every situation learner's encounter is in some sense unique."⁹ Pragmatic critical thinking does not necessarily draw on knowledge from the past, but has a dialectical progressive, future-oriented approach to creating new knowledge. Traditional education, which includes time-honored ways of knowing, is then portrayed as old and irrelevant and judged to make students passive recipients of others' ideas.¹⁰

---

6. Samuels, "Faculty Preparedness."

7. Smith, *Learning from the Stranger*, 17.

8. By nonscientific traditions, the author includes the religious, cultural, and Indigenous traditions, ontology, and epistemology that have been handed down from one generation to the next for at least three generations and that inform people about what is real, what knowledge is important to have, and what is of value. The traditions act as a grid for which epistemological, axiological, and metaphysical claims are filtered. Although the traditions are not devoid of an empirical reality, I use the term "nonscientific" simply to make the distinction between scientific, empirical Western knowledge and other types of valid knowledge, such as intergenerational, personal, religious, and/ or cultural ways of knowing. Of course, it is entirely possible that some traditions neglect, abuse, or exploit by permitting inappropriate, damaging, unhealthy, or immoral behavior. But in this case we know that the "tradition" is perverted and we place the term "tradition" in quotation marks since the very meaning of tradition is at issue here.

9. Biesta and Burbules, *Pragmatism and Educational Research*, 13.

10. Egan, *Getting it Wrong*.

Enter John Dewey

Although progressivist standards have a long history in education, progressivism as an educational ideal is often associated with the Eurocentric views of John Dewey, who made progressivist principles and democracy in education increasingly popular.[11] In *The School and Society,* which began as a series of lectures given to parents, professionals, and others, Dewey mobilizes this approach as he imagines a pragmatic application of critical inquiry drawing from the ideas of an individual and never those of another person.[12] One of Dewey's central ways of achieving this was through the scientific method, which he considered the most reliable process for understanding reality and locating truth.[13] Dewey's pragmatic philosophy is important for this discussion because it echoes the narrow interpretations of critical thinking held by education instructors who publicly announce that critical thinking can only be achieved by the "smashing down [of] old ways of thinking."

Although Dewey's philosophy of education has much to offer teaching and learning today and admittedly his views of education did change over time, Dewey did not "recognize the world's culturally diverse knowledge systems, or understand how different knowledge systems are based on intergenerational knowledge and inform people's lives meaningfully."[14] One can make this claim knowing that it is professionally unwise to criticize the legacy that Dewey left. It seems that there are many defenders of his educational aspirations compared with those critical of his educational vision. That said, there is a case to be made that Dewey did not appreciate the possibility that nonscientific traditions and epistemologies are not necessarily an obstruction to scientific ways of thinking critically,[15] but give added meaning and attentiveness to the culture and worldview in which people are embedded, including his own cultural assumptions.[16]

A further misunderstanding is evident in *The School and Society* when Dewey (1899/1956) wrote that "many anthropologists have told us there are certain identities in the child's interests with those of primitive life . . . there is a sort of natural recurrence of the child mind to the typical activities of primitive peoples."[17] Dewey makes the association with old primitive ways of thinking and a child's simplistic thoughts.

11. Ibid.
12. Fallace, "Was John Dewey Ethnocentric?" 475.
13. Gribov, "John Dewey's Pragmatism," 375.
14. Bowers, *False Promises,* 17.
15. Bowers, *University Reform.*
16. Groome, *Educating for Life*; Valk, "Plural Public Schooling."
17. Dewey, *School and Society,* 48.

This is not surprising since Dewey understood the social world of learning as a series of developmental linear steps from simple to advanced, and it is the reason why Dewey disparaged traditional perspectives of learning and thinking in colleges and universities and advocated the superiority of a progressive "scientific definition of mission and identity."[18] Dewey assumed that by using traditional knowledge or perspectives to examine concepts, ideas, or topics other than the scientific method would make the pupil a mere passive recipient of others' ideas—a slave—an affair of telling and being told[19] supposedly leading to "old ways of thinking."

Over ten years ago, George Marsden[20] argued that there was a growing worldview perspective in education informed by advocates of John Dewey's pragmatic beliefs that should be recognized because of its antagonism toward traditions and traditional thinking. Marsden explains:

> This philosophy is found in the spiritual descendants of John Dewey, where the tendency has been to absolutize the pragmatic method in education. Absolutized liberal pragmatism has little tolerance for different perspectives and in particular groups that hold to traditional ways of thinking that might challenge the pragmatic absolutes.[21]

Unfortunately, the privileging of pragmatic education, a view that sees traditional or nonpragmatic ways of thinking as leading to passive understanding and the idea that to be a visionary and forward thinker requires a scientific approach offers a narrow and dualistic perspective of knowledge in general and critical thinking in particular. Knowledge comes in many different forms (i.e., mathematical, historical, aesthetics, etc.), and all knowledge is passed down within a particular cultural tradition. Secondly, because a learner always filters knowledge and truth claims through their traditional lens, no one is as objective and neutral as they would like to think they are. Since the 1960s, educational thought has recognized this, at least in theory, and the added value of including a multiplicity of epistemologies is significant for understanding reality in a deeper and more comprehensive way, and is especially relevant today for people living and learning within culturally diverse Western societies and classrooms.[22] Culture and learning is understood as both backward looking and forward looking.

---

18. Johnson, *Psychology and Christianity*, 23.
19. Egan, *Getting it Wrong*; Fallace, "Was John Dewy Ethnocentric," 474.
20. Marsden, *Outrageous Idea*, 26.
21. Ibid.
22. See "Focus on Learning," and Peters, *What is an Educational Process?*

It seems that although there are numerous definitions of so called twenty-first century learning, the overarching narrative has defined how critical thinking should be practiced. In the twenty-first century classroom, the critical thinking experience is predominantly pragmatic and scientific, with "schools producing the ultimate capitalist citizens combined with innovation, creativity, and entrepreneurship."[23]

What is missing in education are noncapitalist ideals such as traditional beliefs, values, justice, peace, empathy, varied worldviews about reality, and cultural understandings. Rather than teachers discussing these in the context of multicultural learning, they are seen as too controversial and even too hostile to a scientific privileging of critical thinking.[24] Regrettably, within institutes of education there is minimal opportunities for educators to engage in dialogue about other worldviews and ways of knowing besides the scientific discourse of so called twenty-first century education.[25]

Therefore, what it means to think critically is wedded to a rational orderly methodology drawn from "rigorous scientific evidence" and emphasized over "opinion-based" and subjective thought processes. The key point is that comparable with scientific pragmatism, "effective" pedagogy does not need to inform itself of traditional epistemologies because they are perceived as "unscientific." In fact, no one understood this better than John Dewey.[26]

Consequently, an increasing influence that encourages educators to believe that they must "smash down old ways of thinking" to produce critical thinkers is rooted in a pragmatic/scientific epistemology, and is compatible with the educational vision of Dewey. This forceful progressivist Eurocentric notion of learning promotes a shift from the locus of authority reflected in the local community and family to that of the "enlightened" modern pragmatic institution. This was confirmed at a recent conference in education[27] when representatives from a ministry of education stated that their focus is to "shift public thinking about what matters in education and to train the public to think about learning in a certain way." This is training people to think in prescribed ways rather than opening the conversation to other beliefs and values.

---

23. Ehrcke, "21st Century Learning," 67.
24. Kanu, *Integrating Aboriginal Perspectives*.
25. Nord, *Taking God Seriously*.
26. Spears and Loomis, *Education for Human Flourishing*.
27. Personal communication, University of Calgary, CSSE Conference, May/June 2016.

From the Is to the Ought

It is suggested that if critical thinking really entails the "smashing down [of] old ways of thinking," learners are left with a narrow and discriminatory epistemology devoid of other views and perspectives. The dichotomy of 'old' and 'new' fails to include the subjective and the intuitive voice of all learners, leaving students ignorant of other realities. It also presents a false contrast of choosing between traditional and scientific thinking. Setting up false dichotomies like this could require the teacher to identify her students with a committed attachment to social convention and a submission to traditions and authorities, and describe them as displaying a skills deficit.[28] Contemporary ideas and methods in education, Egan notes, "present learning as some kind of binary moral choice between the traditional, passive, forced, and vicious, and the progressive, active, reliable, and rational."[29]

The unnecessary concerns leveled against a commitment to traditional conventions are an abuse of critical thinking, which was precisely the criticism Socrates launched against the Sophists and their teachings. Certainly some traditional beliefs or values are unhelpful and could even be harmful for critical thinking, but the "smashing down of old ways of thinking" narrative is far removed from the classroom setting and as such lacks intellectual humility.[30] Critical thinking encourages the learner to display humility and a commitment to learn from others.[31] In the spirit of humility one would be better served to reflect upon a sensitive or controversial issue within its context where there are supporters and detractors on both sides, and then attempt to understand the arguments offered by another person. Critical thinkers could then examine and evaluate the propositions and logic involved—scientifically and nonscientifically. This would confirm to learners that there are other epistemologies besides only a scientific approach. There are three categories of legitimate knowledge in addition to scientific knowledge that could be included as critical thinking.[32] These comprise the mystical/spiritual, knowledge from Indigenous peoples and religion, and knowledge from fundamental traditions and beliefs.

The challenge for some educators is that they do not see the value of traditional knowledge in the same way as traditional groups do.[33]

28. Hurley and Hurley, "Enhancing Critical Thinking," 251; Widdowson, "Critical Thinking."
29. Egan, *Getting it Wrong*, 45.
30. Bowell and Kemp, *Critical Thinking*.
31. Portelli and Hare, *Philosophy of Education*.
32. Smoker and Groff, "Spirituality, Religion."
33. Tanaka, "Transforming Perspectives."

Knowledge is important only for what it can *do*. Knowledge is supposedly important only if it is useful, and what is perceived as "useful" is obvious only to those who share scientific values that render traditional knowledge as simple, and scientific knowledge as complex.[34] This view presupposes a narrow and timeworn perspective from a bygone era of the 1930s (i.e., logical positivism).[35] A positivistic epistemology cautions against any inherent reliance on the wisdom of practices embodied and transmitted by previous generations.

If we accept a privileging of scientific knowledge, we would have to abandon the traditions of art, literature, music, history, mathematics, and many other fields of human endeavor that are essential aspects of the modern world but are grounded in traditions that do not depend on the scientific method for validation.[36] Furthermore, no scientific endeavor could even begin without some set of received nonscientific beliefs, since science itself operates within traditional frameworks of assumption that cannot be empirically verified on scientific grounds.[37]

Critical thinking does not have to be understood in this way. The inclusive educator can offer a more comprehensive epistemology for consideration. Rather than ask the learner to adopt *the* critical view on an issue, which might assume that there is only one way to think, the teacher and learner take account of alternate stories and competing points of view while not jumping to judgment. The freeing of minds to think critically about issues would occur at the same time for developing awareness of the traditions in which all minds are embedded. A broader approach to epistemological diversity involves the understanding of what Homi Bhabha, a leading figure in contemporary cultural discourse called "the third space."[38] This includes the first space which is one's identity, the second space is one's culture and the third space is a place of difference where one can initiate and negotiate "new signs of identity, and innovative sites of collaboration and

---

34. Egan, *Getting it Wrong*.

35. According to the logical positivists of the 1920s to 1950s, there are only two sources of knowledge: logical reasoning and empirical experience. Nonscientific statements, those outside of science, are not empirically verifiable and are thus forbidden: they are meaningless. Today, theorists of knowledge understand that science is just one type of knowledge and that there are other credible types of knowledge that can enjoy warrant. This needs to be factored in when discussing how a person comes to know something.

36. Bailey, "What is 'Scientific Materialism.'"

37. Kuhn, *Structure of Scientific Revolutions*.

38. Bhabha, *Location of Culture*.

contestation."[39] A generous and inclusive model of critical thinking would negotiate all three spaces for thinking through idenity and learning.

Critical thinking should not require the learner to divorce herself from her traditional beliefs but rather make space available for the inclusion of all values in the process of education. Models of critical thinking must dialogue sensitively within the private and public domains of diversity, education, and schooling.

What a learner values and the knowledge they extract from their traditions should not comprise a "smashing down of old ways of thinking" but rather nurture a humility that seeks to understand why others adopt the knowledge and values they do. Respect of difference is important but so is understanding.

The Importance of Living Traditions

For thousands of years, traditions and intergenerational knowledge have been fundamental to how people have lived in societies and educated their young. Today, living traditions still provide a family flourishing and preserving of reality that is integral to identity formation. To be raised in a particular tradition "provides a necessary sense of identity and stable moral environment from which to explore the world."[40]

A living tradition adopts not only factual propositions but more importantly value claims,[41] and is often linked to a person's identity, that is, their core being. Critical thinkers should be encouraged to retain their traditional epistemologies because traditions provide knowledge, context, and value.[42] Moreover, there are different "traditions" of rationality, and being rational means being consistent within one of these traditions.[43] However, if traditional beliefs or practices prevent the forces of innovation and individual emancipation for thinking,[44] than educators would have a compelling reason to encourage the adoption of pragmatic scientific practices of critical thinking and discourage nonscientific epistemologies, although this would have to be discussed and discussed by all stakeholders. Nonscientific traditions are not in opposition to scientific ways of thinking critically but

---

39. Ibid.
40. Kroeker and Norris, "An Unwarranted Fear," 130.
41. Vaidya, "Epistemic Responsibility," 540.
42. Pelikan, *Idea of the University*.
43. Sommerville, *Decline of the Secular University*, 65.
44. Bowers, *University Reform*.

rather provide an awareness of the culture and worldview in which one is embedded and shared.[45]

Traditions are important for critical thinking because they are owned by people and are part of their story. Consequently, the educator's role should be as a "mediator between the young person and their tradition."[46] Having a traditional frame of reference makes a difference in how the data of human experience are seen and understood. Traditions are vital for critical thinking because they offer students some further questions to be answered, some additional theories to be examined, and some alternate projects to be undertaken, all of which should be of interest to a comprehensive education.[47]

Traditions are carried and embodied in people and communities and are located in the present.[48] If traditions are handed down from the past to the present and are a way for people to determine what is real and valuable, than educators ought to be gracious hosts and include multiple perspectives in the learning process, whether it be public or private institutions of learning. There must be public spaces made available in higher education for the conflicts that young people have with the knowledge, reality and values that higher education advances.

We can take an example of the importance of traditions and how they are understood within community from the traditional Māori people of New Zealand. In traditional Māori belief there is something beyond the cramped world of everyday empirical experience. They do not live in a closed system where what they see is all there is.[49] The traditional principle of interconnectedness and intergenerational knowledge is important and meaningful to the Māori people and other traditional groups too.[50] Their living tradition includes not only the physical world but also beyond the physical—the metaphysical or spiritual—with intergenerational knowledge passed down as truth from one generation to the next. For the Māori people to think and learn effectively entails the inclusion of their traditions.

---

45. Ibid; Groome, *Educating for Life*; Valk, "Plural Public Schooling."
46. Huebner, "Teaching as Vocation," 383.
47. Porath, "Response to 'The Outrageous,'" 238.
48. Huebner, "Teaching as Vocation."
49. Barlow, *Tikanga Whakaaro*.
50. It is important to note that in Canada there are numerous groups who practice their living traditions and epistemologies, some of which include First Nation epistemology and spiritual rituals; the religious practices of Chinese and Japanese immigrants; and the Sikhs, Christians, Muslims, and Hindus, each of which has a long history of varied traditions, worldviews, and presence in Canada.

Indigenous and feminist scholars have argued that there are multiple ways of knowing and some ways are privileged over others. Consequently, no one creates their own reality from scratch because we are all embedded in particular traditions. Traditions provide a normative force that holds a society together.[51] They provide remembered stories that "render a community or culture capable of ordering their new experience in a manner consistent with the story."[52] Traditions are reenacted and shared as knowledge between past generations and a younger one. They are a core feature of being human in community with like-minded people. Traditions are accumulated understanding and provide a pattern of thinking and learning that guides action. All societies, including Western societies, have been guided by both scientific and nonscientific traditions.

Education is also embedded in traditions and ceremonies of learning, so educators should be open to other views of reality and ways of knowing and learning in recognition of this fact and demonstrate a hospitality to all learners.[53] Educators act as good hosts, inviting young people into an open space of community and life together. Community life has a commitment to all traditions, and education acts hospitably to make room for the young person into the life of a diverse and rich community.

Teaching and Learning as a Hospitable Act

A comprehensive critical thinking model of learning should help students be inquisitive in nature, humble in approach, open-minded, flexible, fair-minded, have a desire to be well-informed, and most importantly be able to understand diverse viewpoints, traditions, and perspectives.[54] Critical thinking models should not make differences invisible but rather recognize differences and nurture commonalities. The "smashing down of old ways of thinking" simply lacks this comprehensiveness.

Society is diverse in thought, values, and beliefs and as such critical thinkers need to reflect and be engaged with such diversity as they learn. To do this well, teachers and learners must be incarnational and transformational and must exhibit the self-sacrifice to learn from others in order to welcome the Other with open hands in an act of respect. Education is relational, requiring meaningful inclusion, so teachers and educators must be open to the problems that a narrow perspective of critical thinking can have

---

51. Shils, *Tradition*.
52. Hauerwas, "Telling a Worldview Story," 86.
53. Wineberg, *Professional Care*.
54. Lai, "Critical Thinking," 11.

on learners with traditions outside of the scientific pragmatic model. This is because, like any pedagogical practice, critical thinking can be used as an instrument of emancipation or a tool of oppression. When John Dewey said that the task of the educator was to "emancipate the young from the need of dwelling in an outgrown past,"[55] he, similar to the educators who stated that old ways of thinking should be broken so "real thinking" can occur, did not understand that education itself is always embedded in and under the influence of a tradition.

Critical thinking should not require the student to choose either scientific ways or their traditional ways for investigation; rather, both can and should inform one another. As the educator Van Manen has said, "We need to be neither iconoclasts who only rebel and tear down traditions, nor iconolators who blindly submit to the monuments of traditions."[56] For learners and educators to gain a deep inside perspective of other types of knowledge, reality, and value so important in today's multicultural classrooms, an inclusive hospitable practice of critical thinking is needed. In the words of philosopher Emmanuel Levinas, education ought to be an unconditional responsibility *to* the Other. Levinas understood the Other to be "what I myself are not."[57]

If teaching and learning is a human flourishing and hospitable activity, than educators must practice the art of critical thinking in ways that abandon the expectation of homogeneity and move toward a genuine celebration of difference and heteronomy. To contribute to our diverse knowledge systems, a responsible approach to critical thinking should be to actively reach out to include learners with all traditions such as feminist, Indigenous, scientific, cultural, moral, or religious. This is necessary because all people are embedded in traditions and as such, pedagogues can learn from one another, and critical thinking itself is the result of cultural situatedness. Consequently, traditions themselves will and should play a significant and natural role in the development, and application of critical thinking.[58]

Although traditions can never serve as a substitute for truth, "the authority of a tradition should always be directed to the point which people see for themselves that something is true or not."[59] Embracing traditions through critical thinking does not mean "embracing conservatism or a

---

55. Gould, *Ontogeny and Phylogeny*, 73.
56. Van Manen, *Tact of Teaching*, 16.
57. Quoted in Egea-Kuehne, *Levinas and Education*, 30.
58. Pithers and Soden, "Critical Thinking in Education," 241.
59. Newbigin, *Gospel in a Pluralist Society*, 48.

retreat from progressive education;" rather, a hospitable education reflects conservative and progressive traditions—a synthesis of the two.[60]

Critical thinking could be practiced alongside learners and not *on* learners. It could entail an insider's perspective which requires relationship, community and hospitality.[61] The purpose would then be to develop knowledge and understanding, but also to advance an insider's perspective about the traditions that shape an individual's learning and values about life. Bernard of Clairvaux offers a view of critical thinking and learning that welcomes an insider's perspective by a focus on what Others help us see; a humility practiced "is a virtue by which a man [sic] recognizes his own unworthiness because he really knows himself."[62] This requires learning from and about the Other. Critical thinkers should reflect this openness to other ways of knowing rather than assuming that individuals who hold to nonscientific traditions have never examined their assumptions.[63] Under a more expansive conception of critical thinking, we embrace the idea of "learners forming a *critical identity* and having a *point of view* that derives from adopting a concern for specific values."[64]

A person can still be a critical thinker and accept nonscientific ways of pursing knowledge and truth. One can locate historians, Indigenous thinkers, logicians, and mathematicians throughout history who have thought critically and utilized methodology that was not contingent on the scientific method. An inclusive critical thinking model must honor the diversity of other knowledge systems, since the scientific-pragmatic model of critical thinking, while important, is not the only valid epistemological approach. Knowledge can be increased by quantitative and qualitative means. A broader practice of critical thinking can be advantageous for learners to understand the subjective and objective reasons people hold to their traditions and for making sense of motives and perceptions. Sensitivity to these ideas can facilitate a deeper and more profound practice of critical thinking for both teachers and learners.[65]

---

60. Wineberg, *Professional Care and Vocation*, 100.
61. Portelli, "Democracy in Education," 279.
62. Bernard of Clairvaux, *Selected Works*, 103.
63. Widdowson, "Critical Thinking."
64. Vaidya, "Epistemic Responsibility," 553.
65. Pithers and Soden, "Critical Thinking in Education."

Conclusion

If scientific knowledge is only one way of knowing, then critical thinkers should not be expected to draw merely on scientific knowledge.[66] The scientific bases, "while not superficial, do represent only a surface level of a complete understanding of the subject."[67] Moreover, when we judge a tradition, be it religious or cultural, we should not automatically go to some nonreligious or scientific basis to judge them but rather seek to understand them from *within* the tradition itself.[68]

Also as previously noted, to compartmentalize knowledge as scientific or not is to fail to recognize knowledge holistically, interwoven, culturally influenced, and interdependent. The obvious problem with compartmentalizing knowledge must be considered if critical thinking does not fall further into an epistemological prejudice of colonialism, where a Eurocentric education system has taught learners to distrust traditional-spiritual knowledge structures.[69]

Critical thinking should be a transformative experience for learners. It should promote participatory pedagogies with critical reflection engaging not just the intellect but also identity, worldview, beliefs, and values. A critical thinker is now transformed as someone with the freedom to "consider seriously other points of view than one's own."[70] Such a comprehensive education would encourage critical thinking and open-mindedness by drawing on the perspective of another practice.[71] This is not easy, but openness to others' ways of thinking is a virtue that any community should consider valuable. It will always be the case that "reasonable people differ on basic matters of the ultimate good; some of their starting points are religious, some philosophical."[72] Teachers and students must expose themselves to

---

66. Francis Widdowson claims that knowledge, such as faith, traditions, and spiritual claims of any type are actually an obstacle to the acquisition of knowledge, i.e., scientific knowledge ("Critical Thinking," 2). Widdowson assumes that other non-scientific claims to knowledge are static, old, and refuse to pursue questions to their conclusion. This is patently false. As Indigenous authors Battiste, Kanu, and others have argued, traditional knowledge is living knowledge because it pursues truth and reality, and always follows the evidence where it leads. Kanu suggests that criticisms like those of Widdowson are "inaccurate characterizations of the 'other' and their truth, knowledge, and histories (*Integrating Aboriginal Perspectives*, 47).

67. Bransford, Brown, and Cocking, *How People Learn*, 14.

68. Sommerville, *Decline of the Secular University*, 64–65.

69. Widdowson, "Critical Thinking."

70. Ennis, "Logic, Rational Thinking," 5–6.

71. Valk, "Plural Public Schooling," 280.

72. Nussbaum, "Moral Expertise?" 516–17.

topics and perspectives they might not have thought of, especially important in an era where many listen only to sources that reinforce their existing interests and prejudices.[73]

In the end, if educators desire their students to be well-informed, they must demonstrate a "respect for and willingness to entertain diverse viewpoints"[74] and not make differences invisible. They must, in the end, not "smash down old ways of thinking," but unite, include, and promote the importance of diverse ways of thinking so that teachers and students are informed and well educated for the broad range of ideas, values, and people that inhabit all classrooms and society at large.

Reflection Questions

1. How have you managed (or not) to keep your identity, worldview, and culture vibrant, healthy, and relevant to your education?

2. In what ways do you think critical thinking should be practiced in an open democratic society?

3. Respond to the following: "Models of critical thinking should recognize difference and nurture commonalities."

4. Do you believe that controversial topics should be unpacked, critically discussed, and questioned in schools?

5. What does "unity in diversity" mean to you, your family, and your community?

Bibliography

Ahmed, Sara. *On Being Included: Racism and Diversity in Institutional Life*. Durham: Duke University Press, 2012.

Bailey, David H. "What is 'Scientific Materialism' and How Does it Enter Into the Science-Religion Discussion?" Science Meets Religion, 2016. http://www.sciencemeetsreligion.org/theology/scientific-materialism.php.

Barlow, Cleve. *Tikanga Whakaaro: Key Concepts in Maori Culture*. Oxford: Oxford University Press, 1991.

Bernard, of Clairvaux, St. *Selected Works*. Translated by G. R. Evans. New York: Paulist, 1987.

Bhabha, Homi. *The Location of Culture*. London: Routledge, 1994.

---

73. Gill, "Jacques Ellul."
74. Lai, "Critical Thinking," 42.

Biesta, Gert J. J., and Nicholas C. Burbules. *Pragmatism and Educational Research.* New York: Rowman and Littlefield, 2003.
Bowell, Tracy, and Gary Kemp. *Critical Thinking: A Concise Guide.* London: Routledge, 2002
Bowers, Chet. *The False Promises of Constructivist Theories of Learning: A Global and Ecological Critique.* New York: Peter Lang, 2005.
———. *University Reform in an Era of Global Warming.* Eugene, OR: Eco-Justice, 2011.
Bransford, John D., Ann L. Brown, and Rodney R. Cocking, eds. *How People Learn: Brain, Mind, Experience, and School.* Washington, DC: National Academy, 1999.
Dewey, John. *The School and Society.* Chicago: University of Chicago Press, 1915.
Egan, Kieran. *Getting It Wrong from the Beginning: Our Progressivist Inheritance from Herbert Spencer, John Dewey, and Jean Piaget.* New Haven: Yale University Press, 2002.
Egea-Kuehne, Denise, ed. *Levinas and Education: At the Intersection of Faith and Reason.* New York: Routledge, 2008.
Ehrcke, Tara. "21st Century Learning Inc." *Our Schools Our Selves* 22 (Winter 2013). https://www.policyalternatives.ca/sites/default/files/uploads/publications/National%20Office/2013/02/osos110_21stCenturyLearning_0.pdf.
Ennis, Robert H. "Logic, Rational Thinking, and Education." In *Philosophy of Education 1979: Proceedings of the Thirty-Fifth Annual Meeting of the Philosophy of Education Society,* edited by Jerrold R. Coombs, 3–30. Normal, IL: Philosophy of Education Society, 1979.
Fallace, Thomas D. "Was John Dewey Ethnocentric? Reevaluating the Philosopher's Early Views on Culture and Race." *Educational Researcher* 39 (2010) 471–77.
"Focus on Learning." BC Education Plan, 2015. http://www.bcedplan.ca.
Gill, David. "Jacques Ellul and Technology's Trade-Off." *Comment,* March 1, 2012. https://www.cardus.ca/comment/article/4578/jacques-ellul-and-technologys-trade-off/?utm_medium=email&utm_source=newsletter&utm_campaign=Comment%20Weekly.
Gould, Stephen Jay. *Ontogeny and Phylogeny.* Cambridge: Harvard University Press, 1977.
Gribov, Shulamit. "John Dewey's Pragmatism and Moral Education." *Philosophy of Education* (2001) 373–80.
Groome, Thomas. *Educating for Life: A Spiritual Journey for Every Teacher and Parent.* New York: Crossroad, 2001.
Hauerwas, Stanley. "Telling a Worldview Story." In *The Crumbling Walls of Certainty: Towards a Christian Critique of Postmodernity and Education,* edited by Ian Lambert and Suzanne Mitchell, 75–98. Sydney: Center for the Study of Australian Christianity, 1997.
Huebner, Dwayne E. "Teaching as Vocation." In *The Lure of the Transcendent: Collected Essays,* edited by Vikki Hills, 379–97. Mahwah, NJ: Lawrence Eribaum, 1999.
Hurley, Martha H., and David Hurley. "Enhancing Critical Thinking Skills Among Authoritarian Students." *International Journal of Teaching and Learning in Higher Education* 25 (2013) 248–61.
Johnson, Eric. *Psychology and Christianity: Five Views.* Downers Grove, IL: InterVarsity, 2010.
Kanu, Yatta. *Integrating Aboriginal Perspectives into the School Curriculum: Purposes, Possibilities, and Challenges.* Toronto: University of Toronto Press, 2011.

Kroeker, Frances M., and Stephen P. Norris. "An Unwarranted Fear of Religious Schooling." In *Philosophy of Education: Introductory Readings*, edited by William Hare and John Portelli, 307–25. Toronto: Brush Education, 2013.

Kuhn, Deanna. "A Developmental Model of Critical Thinking." *Educational Researcher* 28 (1999) 16–26.

Kuhn, Thomas. *The Structure of Scientific Revolutions*. Chicago: University of Chicago Press, 1962.

Lai, Emily R. "Critical Thinking: A Literature Review." Pearson Research Report, June 2011. http://images.pearsonassessments.com/images/tmrs/CriticalThinkingReview FINAL.pdf.

Marsden, George. *The Outrageous Idea of Christian Scholarship*. Oxford: Oxford University Press, 1997.

Newbigin, Lesslie. *The Gospel in a Pluralist Society*. Grand Rapids: Eerdmans, 1989.

Nord, Warren. *Taking God Seriously in Our Schools and Universities*. Oxford: Oxford University Press, 2010.

Nussbaum, Martha. "Moral Expertise? Constitutional Narratives and Philosophical Argument." *Metaphilosophy* 33 (2002) 502–20.

Pelikan, Jaroslav. *The Idea of the University: A Reexamination*. New Haven: Yale University Press, 1992.

Peters, Richard Stanley. *What Is an Educational Process? The Concept of Education*. London: Routledge and Kegan Paul, 1967.

Pithers, R. T., and Rebecca Soden. "Critical Thinking in Education: A Review." *Educational Research* 42 (2000) 237–50.

Porath, Jerome R. "Response to 'The Outrageous Idea of Christian Scholarship,' by George Marsden." *Journal of Catholic Education* 1 (1997) 237–39.

Portelli, John. "Democracy in Education: Beyond the Conservative and Progressivist Stances." In *Philosophy of Education: Introductory Readings*, edited by William Hare and John Portelli, 275–78. Calgary: Detselig, 2001.

Portelli, John, and William Hare, eds. *Philosophy of Education: Introductory Readings*. Calgary: Temeron, 1996.

Samuels, Dena Renee. "Faculty Preparedness to Build Cultural Inclusiveness." PhD diss., University of Colorado at Colorado Springs, 2010.

Shils, Edward. *Tradition*. Chicago: University of Chicago Press, 1981.

Smith, David. *Learning from the Stranger*. Grand Rapids: Eerdmans, 2009.

Smoker, Paul, and Linda Groff. "Spirituality, Religion, Culture, and Peace: Exploring the Foundations for Inner-Outer Peace in the Twenty-First Century." *The International Journal of Peace Studies* 1 (1996) 57–113. http://www.gmu.edu/programs/icar/ijps/vol1_1/smoker.html.

Sommerville, John. *The Decline of the Secular University*. Oxford: Oxford University Press, 2006.

Spears, Paul D., and Steven R. Loomis. *Education for Human Flourishing*. Downers Grove, IL: InterVarsity, 2009.

Tanaka, Michele Therese Duke. "Transforming Perspectives: The Immersion of Student Teachers in Indigenous Ways of Knowing." PhD diss., University of Victoria, 2009.

Vaidya, Anand Jayprakash. "Epistemic Responsibility and Critical Thinking." *Metaphilosophy* 44 (2013) 533–56.

Valk, John. "Plural Public Schooling: Religion, Worldviews and Moral Education." *British Journal of Religious Education* 29 (2007) 273–85.

Van Manen, Max. *The Tact of Teaching: The Meaning of Pedagogical Thoughtfulness.* London, ON: Althouse, 1991.

Widdowson, Francis. "Critical Thinking, Secularism and Mount Royal University: Is 100 Years of Progress Under Threat?" *Mount Royal Centennial Reader*, August 19, 2010. http://blogs.mtroyal.ca/fwiddowson/files/2010/10/Secularism-Critical-Thinking-and-MRU-Frances-Widdowson.pdf.

Wineberg, Timothy W. *Professional Care and Vocation: Cultivating Ethical Sensibilities in Teaching.* Rotterdam: Sense Publishers, 2008.

7

Universities, Higher Education, and Ideological Diversity: Insights from Moral Foundations Theory

James Dalziel

Higher Education and Ideological Diversity[1]

WHILE UNIVERSITIES SHOULD FOSTER critical thinking about a wide range of ideas, there has been a recent rise in attempts to stifle the expression of certain types of ideas within universities—particularly ideas related to nonprogressive ideologies[2]. For example, "no platforming"[3] is a practice where prospective speakers at a university face resistance to speaking on campus (that is, their "platform" to speak is revoked). Potential solutions, such as offering an opportunity for a competing viewpoint to also be presented or encouragement of discussion and debate after a speaking event, are usually insufficient—the resistance seeks that the speaker is not permitted to speak at all.

"No platforming" has been used by some progressive student groups to put pressure on university administrations to stop a nonprogressive speaker

---

1. Alternative phrases to ideological diversity include political diversity, intellectual diversity, and viewpoint diversity.

2. This chapter will use "progressive" rather than "left" or "left-wing," but the same general meaning is intended. It will also use "conservative" and "libertarian" rather than "right" or "right-wing," and will generally distinguish between these two ideologies, based on the significant underlying differences in prioritization of moral foundations illustrated in Figure 1.

3. The phrase "no platforming" is more common in the UK than the US, but the practice is similar in both contexts regardless of the label. In the UK, "no platforming" is an official policy of the National Union of Students, but in this chapter, a broader version of this practice is considered.

from being invited. In some cases, invited guests (such as for graduation ceremonies) have been disinvited from speaking due to their nonprogressive views (even if these views are not the topic of the graduation speech). For example, Brandeis University disinvited Somalia-born Ayaan Hirsi Ali from speaking in 2014, and in response, Ali said, "Neither Brandeis nor my critics know or even inquired as to what I might say. They simply wanted me to be silenced."[4] In other cases, student protests lead a speaker to reluctantly decline an invitation, such as when Condoleezza Rice withdrew from speaking at Rutgers University.[5] Another variation is where a progressive speaker will refuse to participate in a panel discussion unless another panel member is disinvited, as recently experienced by Peter Tatchell.[6]

Sometimes the reasons given for "no platforming" are objections about the speaker's nonprogressive, or insufficiently progressive, views. Increasingly, these objections are combined with concerns for the well-being of certain students—that is, the speaker should not be allowed to speak because some students may feel harmed by discussion of certain ideas. For example, Christ Church College, Oxford, cancelled a debate about abortion culture following concerns raised by some students (this is one of a number of recent examples of "no platforming").[7] There was a significant attempt (ultimately unsuccessful) by academics and students to block Germaine Greer from speaking at Cardiff University in 2015 due to her past "transphobic" comments, even though her talk was not on this topic. And in a broader kind of "no platforming," in 2016 anthropology academics at the American Anthropological Association voted on a motion to boycott Israeli academic institutions. This motion was only narrowly defeated (50.4 percent against, 49.6 percent in favor),[8] and some pro-boycott actions were still enacted. These last two examples illustrate that problems with free speech are not limited to students, but also arise among academics.

"No platforming" is just one of a set of related free speech issues—others include the push for university courses to include "trigger warnings" about potentially troubling content, student complaints about certain types of offensive course content and words, and a variety of concerns related to the experiences of certain minority groups, including discrimination, "micro-aggressions," and cultural appropriation. An increasing number of

4. Leef, "Brandeis Caves."
5. Fitzsimmons, "Condoleezza Rice."
6. The cases involving Ayaan Hirsi Ali and Peter Tatchell illustrate how speakers who have argued for certain progressive views can nonetheless become targets for their other insufficiently progressive views. McVeigh, "Peter Tatchell: Snubbed by Students."
7. Richter, "'No-Platforming' on University Campuses."
8. Redden, "Anthropology Group Won't Boycott Israel."

academics, including some progressive academics, describe how the atmosphere on campuses has changed markedly in the last few years as students complain about harm they experience arising from these issues. As the title of one article put it, "I'm a liberal professor, and my liberal students terrify me."[9] Kimball is particularly critical of the way that concerns over student harm arising from exposure to nonprogressive views is used to stifle free speech.[10] Heller has recently provided a rich description of the current campus milieu in liberal arts colleges (such as Oberlin College), including the perspective of radical progressive students on the issues raised here.[11]

These problems are not unique to the United States, as the Christ Church College in Oxford and Peter Tatchell examples demonstrate. Similar recent issues in Australian universities include the decision by the vice-chancellor of the University of Western Australia to cancel its contract for the Australian Consensus Centre after a "passionate emotional reaction . . . that the university did not predict"—primarily from academics.[12] In another example at the University of Sydney, the student union threatened to deregister student religious groups (with a particular focus on the Evangelical Union—a Christian group) that included membership requirements that involved a creed or set of religious beliefs; this proposal was only abandoned after considerable pressure.[13]

More generally, the problem is not simply that certain speakers are being blocked from speaking, but rather that a particular cluster of ideas (usually nonprogressive ideas) is being marginalized or silenced in certain parts of the academy. If the purpose of a typical university[14] is to foster critical reflection and understanding, then exposure to a diversity of ideological views is essential to the formation of deep student understanding.

It is concerning that some modern universities are struggling to articulate, and put into practice, the importance of ideological diversity in their mission as a university. This is particularly concerning when support for diversity has been a significant positive focus for many universities, and yet ideological diversity—an essential kind of diversity for an institution that

---

9. Schlosser, "I'm a Liberal Professor." Although, as a follow-up piece argued, some progressive academics do not have similar concerns—see Taub, "I was a Liberal Adjunct Professor."

10. Kimball, "The Rise of the College Crybullies."

11. Heller, "The Big Uneasy."

12. "UWA Cancels Contract."

13. Holgate, "Sydney Uni Evangelical Union."

14. "Typical university" or "typical secular university" is not an ideal phrase, but it seeks to denote current mainstream universities in Western countries—which are also described here as "modern universities." There are some Christian and other religious universities (not just colleges), as well as some secular universities with explicit nonprogressive ideologies that do not fit the concerns raised in this chapter.

calls itself a university—is under threat. As Hayward has suggested, there are parts of some universities where the primary task of academics appears to be activism on behalf of certain groups, rather than fostering student understanding of competing ideas.[15] Some academics and students seem to be acting on the idea articulated by Herbert Marcuse in his essay "Repressive Tolerance."[16] "Liberating tolerance, then, would mean intolerance against movements from the Right and toleration of movements from the Left."[17]

In the particular case of Christian higher education, it could be assumed that there are greater challenges to achieving a diversity of ideological perspectives due to the religious beliefs of the institution and its academics.[18] And while this may be a challenge in practice in some institutions, it is noteworthy that Christian higher education has a long tradition of studying worldviews (including those that are not Christian) in order to better understand the assumptions of different ideologies.[19] It is the explicit recognition and discussion of ideological differences in the widespread worldview courses in Christian higher education that is noteworthy by comparison with the declining ideological diversity of traditional universities.[20]

Moral Foundations Theory

One way to understand these recent developments is through the lens of moral foundations theory (MFT) from the field of moral psychology. MFT describes six underlying moral foundations, with each foundation described as a continuum between opposites:[21]

15. Hayward, "Grievance School."
16. Marcuse, "Repressive Tolerance."
17. I am indebted to Chris Uhlmann's article on free speech for this quote—see http://www.theaustralian.com.au/news/inquirer/there-was-a-time-when-journalists-backed-free-speech/news-story/4704bea05341f9f674cb526470260601
18. While Christian higher education could refer to many different types of institutions, in the context of this chapter, it primarily refers to institutions that would be members of, or similar in beliefs to, the members of the Council of Christian Colleges and Universities. http://www.cccu.org/.
19. Wolterstorff, *Educating for Shalom*.
20. While the main focus of the examples provided is the lack of ideological diversity in traditional universities due to opposition to nonprogressive ideas, there may be different problems with ideological diversity within Christian higher education, as illustrated, for example, by recent debates at Wheaton College. Also, it should not be assumed that Christian higher education is ideologically conservative—there are various ideological views among Christian academics, including many Christians who would identify in some sense as progressive.
21. Haidt, *The Righteous Mind*, 127.

- Care/harm
- Liberty/oppression
- Fairness/cheating
- Loyalty/betrayal
- Authority/subversion
- Sanctity/degradation[22]

While a full discussion of MFT is beyond the current scope of this essay,[23] one of the key findings is that different people give different priorities to one moral foundation over another. For example, some people might feel that caring for others is the most important moral value, whereas others might weight care and liberty about equally and still others might feel that liberty is the most important moral value. As Haidt notes, different patterns of prioritizing moral foundations are observed across people with different political ideologies. Three of these patterns (progressive, conservative, and libertarian) are illustrated in Figure 1.

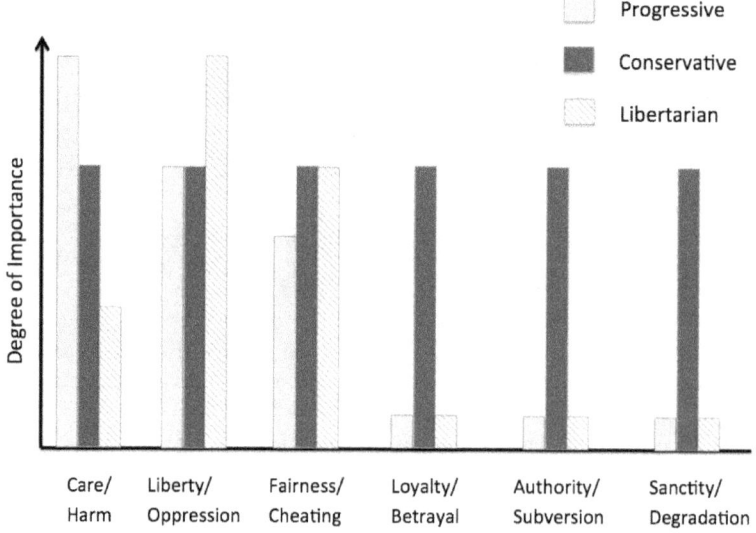

Figure 1:
Graphical illustration of the approximate generalized differences in prioritization of moral foundations across progressive, conservative, and libertarian voters.[24]

22. For a brief summary of each foundation, see http://moralfoundations.org.

23. For details, see Haidt, *The Righteous Mind*, and Dalziel, "Why Conservatives and Progressives Think Differently".

24. This diagram combines the ideas contained in Haidt, *The Righteous Mind*, 297,

While there has been growing discussion of how these different moral priorities apply to individuals, it is interesting to consider how the values of an institution could be represented in a similar way. For example, a university (or college) that places the highest priority on liberty (i.e., liberty in the form of free inquiry and free speech) could be thought of as having a similar moral prioritization pattern to that observed for libertarians. A university that places about equal value on care and liberty (as well as the other moral foundations) could have a pattern more similar to that observed for conservatives; and a university that places the highest value on care (rather than free speech and inquiry) could have a pattern more similar to that observed for progressives.

Using this approach, it could be argued that a typical Western university from the eighteenth and nineteenth centuries (which frequently incorporated a Judeo-Christian religious heritage) would be most similar in moral prioritization to a conservative pattern.[25] In the twentieth century, with the declining role of religion in universities coupled with the social changes of the 1960s and '70s (particularly the sexual revolution), yet combined with a continuing focus on free speech and inquiry, the university could be seen as most similar to the libertarian pattern. However, in the twenty-first century, the values of some universities (or more specifically, some parts of some universities) appear to be shifting, so that care is becoming the dominant value—even more so than free inquiry—with the resulting prioritization of moral foundations becoming more similar to the progressive pattern.

This analysis could explain the recent developments noted above—the rise of priority on the care foundation over the liberty foundation would explain why rigorous critical inquiry that encourages a wide range of ideological viewpoints is being challenged by a concern that free speech may be harmful to some students.

However, this might not fully explain why nonprogressive speakers have been the focus of "no platforming." Research shows that more academics now describe themselves as progressive than in the past, and that the percentage of conservative academics is small and falling.[26] While more

---

302, and 306, with the "audio equalizer" metaphor used by Haidt in an interview with Bill Moyes (see 17:30 and onwards) at https://vimeo.com/36128360. Note that Figure 1 is an approximate generalization for the actual data—for details, see Haidt, *The Righteous Mind*, and related research. For example, the average values for conservatives are not exactly equal across all six values, but their approximate equivalence compared to the other approaches is the point of Haidt's audio equalizer metaphor.

25. Given the importance of free speech and inquiry to a university's core purposes, it may be reasonable to argue for a slightly higher value to liberty than the other moral foundations.

26. Jaschik, "Moving Further to the Left."

research on this issue is needed, this and similar data, together with many anecdotal reports (see student examples referenced below), suggest a broad shift in the ideological character of the typical university from a progressive-leaning but still relatively diverse organization, toward an organization that is dominated by academics who hold progressive ideologies, with a diminishing number of those holding conservative and libertarian views.

Academic Locker Room Talk and Hidden Moral Curriculum

Haidt himself has focused on the problems of declining ideological diversity in universities, and has recently launched a website with colleagues to discuss these issues called "Heterodox Academy" (heterodoxacademy.org). In an early attempt to raise his concerns, Haidt explained these problems in a keynote address at a major psychology conference in 2011, and proposed solutions including the need for more conservative voices in psychology. Following a fierce backlash to this proposal, he documented the experience at the website "Post-Partisan Social Psychology,"[27] and subsequently with other colleagues.[28]

When discussing the lack of conservative views in universities, Haidt explored both self-selection[29] and discrimination explanations.[30] However, even just considering a self-selection argument, Haidt warns:

> My point was not that discrimination is the MAIN cause of underrepresentation. My point was that there is an underrepresentation of conservatives for many reasons, but once the percentage of conservatives drops below some threshold, we get the predictable problems of a large majority interacting with a small and disliked minority. Eventually liberals begin to assume that everyone around them shares their political views. At that point, "locker room talk" becomes much more public, the climate becomes more hostile toward non-liberals, and the few remaining non-liberals must either hide their views, leave the field, or endure criticism and social exclusion.[31]

---

27. Haidt, "Post-Partisan Social Psychology."
28. Duarte et al., "Political Diversity."
29. Gross, *Why are Professors Liberal*.
30. Inbar and Lammers, "Political Diversity."
31. For an Australian audience, the word "liberal" here should be read as "progressive" to avoid confusion (as the "Australian Liberal Party" is the main conservative party).

The idea of "academic locker room talk" is an important concept for understanding the realities of life in universities. While there are some disciplines where the curriculum illustrates progressive biases (e.g., sociology[32] and social psychology[33]), even when the formal curriculum does not demonstrate a bias against nonprogressive ideas, the lived practices of academics can convey powerful pro-progressive and anti-conservative messages. While these problems may be absent or minor in some parts of the academy (e.g., parts of the physical sciences), they appear to be more prominent in parts of the humanities and social sciences. (Yancey provides examples and a discussion of variation across disciplines in the humanities and social sciences.[34])

This is particularly relevant to students and junior staff with conservative ideologies who sometimes experience hostility in discussion with others when they present conservative ideological positions. (Haidt collated a list of unsolicited conservative student comments following his keynote.[35]) One of the ironies of this situation is that these students experience discrimination as a minority group within a university, which runs counter to common university goals promoting diversity and care for student well-being. Haidt's foregrounding of "academic locker room talk" draws attention to how universities can present a hostile social and intellectual environment for those with conservative or libertarian ideologies (especially those with socially conservative ideologies[36]).

Another way to think about this problem is using the concept of a "hidden curriculum," a topic discussed in higher education fields such as medicine.[37] The "hidden curriculum" captures the many beliefs and practices that are conveyed to students outside the formal curriculum. In medicine this often refers to the informal opinions and practices that students learn in clinical contexts from practicing doctors that are not part of traditional lectures. In K–12 education, the hidden curriculum is often conceptualized in progressive terms, such as the role of education in maintaining oppressive societal structures.[38] For this chapter, it is the hidden curriculum of progressive moral values in modern universities that is the current focus.

32. Smith, *The Sacred Project*.
33. Duarte et al., "Political Diversity."
34. Yancey, *Compromising Scholarship*.
35. Haidt, "Discrimination Hurts."
36. Yancey, *Compromising Scholarship*.
37. Hafferty, "Beyond Curriculum Reform."
38. Giroux, *Theory and Resistance*.

By combining the concept of a hidden curriculum with the insights of MFT and the experiences of conservative students noted by Haidt, it can be argued that some parts of some universities have a powerful "hidden moral curriculum" in which students are subliminally, and sometimes overtly, encouraged to adopt progressive beliefs and practices and to take a negative view of nonprogressive ideologies. Importantly, this hidden progressive moral curriculum goes beyond any particular ideological biases of specific discipline curriculum, and is part of a general milieu of pro-progressive and frequently anti-conservative and anti-libertarian "academic locker room talk."

In current typical Western universities, the hidden progressive moral curriculum is based on an increasing prioritization of the moral foundation of care over liberty. (Liberty in the form of free speech and inquiry.) It focuses on the negative experiences of certain minority groups (particularly related to race, gender, and sexuality issues). Regarding religion, it focuses on the negative experiences of some religious groups (e.g., Indigenous religious groups, Muslims), but not on other religious groups (such as Jews[39] or Christians[40]). Importantly, the hidden progressive moral curriculum of universities is not only a matter of ideas, but also of social practices, such as discrimination, shaming, and shunning of those who articulate conservative or libertarian views.[41]

The Hidden Moral Curriculum and Pedagogies of Desire in Universities

Many of the critiques of modern universities by Christian higher education have focused on worldview ideas.[42] While this is appropriate in one respect, it can be an overly cognitive view of the university experience that misses how a university's hidden moral curriculum can shape the deeper beliefs and practices of students. As has been said in other fields, such as IT security, "In theory, theory and practice are the same. In practice, they are not."[43]

This is where James K. A. Smith's concepts of cultural liturgies and pedagogies of desire are significant for understanding the problems

---

39. Freedland, "My Plea to the Left."

40. Yancey, *Compromising Scholarship*.

41. Haidt, "Discrimination Hurts," and Haidt, "Post-Partisan Social Psychology." It is important to note that discrimination, shaming, and shunning are also experienced by many other groups, such as the minority groups that are central to progressive concerns.

42. Samples, *A World of Difference: Putting Christian Truth-Claims to the Worldview Test*.

43. Schneier, "Cryptography is Harder."

identified above.[44] A "worldview" analysis directed only at bias in formal curriculum, based on a cognitive approach to the problem, misses the significant shaping of students' hearts and practices by the hidden progressive moral curriculum of typical universities. As Smith notes, it is the shaping of students' desires or loves that may be the most influential aspect of formation at universities—and if so, a hidden progressive moral curriculum can be a powerful shaping force on students.

Given that the shaping of pedagogies of desire goes well beyond the cognitive component of the university experience, any attempt to address the hidden progressive moral curriculum in typical universities will involve more than reform of curriculum or changes to academic hiring policies that encourage a diversity of ideological perspectives. It will need to address the wider socialization experience of student life at universities—such as how conservative and libertarian students are treated in tutorial discussions and assessments when they articulate nonprogressive views, as well as their treatment in social settings, such as student societies and representative bodies.

Ultimately, universities need to confront the question of whether they will prioritize free speech and ideological diversity over the position argued by Marcuse—that of intolerance of movements of the Right (i.e., conservatives and libertarians).

Interestingly, the demands of radical progressive students at institutions such as Oberlin College can be better understood using Smith's insights.[45] While some commentators have criticized these students,[46] some of their complaints arise from the perceived gap between the academic practices of the institution and its apparent support for progressive ideals. For example, students noted that in the 1970s, Oberlin modified its grading practices to accommodate student activism about the Vietnam War, but it was unwilling to do so for current students protesting against a fatal police shooting. In essence, students are calling attention to a mismatch between an increasingly corporate university culture (which wouldn't countenance changes to assessment methods) with a radical progressive ideology that students learn in many university lectures. In terms of the university's role in character formation, when these students tried to live out their progressive ideas in practice, they discovered that the university didn't share their integrated view of theory and practice.

---

44. Smith, *Desiring the Kingdom.*
45. Heller, "The Big Uneasy."
46. Trimpf, "Oberlin Students."

Discipline Examples:
Psychology, Sociology, Education, Law, and Theology

A lack of ideological diversity will affect specific disciplines in different ways, but the broad problem of insufficient critical thinking among students can occur across many disciplines. While it is beyond the scope of this chapter to analyze these problems in detail in specific disciplines, a few brief examples can be provided.

Haidt's keynote address to colleagues in social and personality psychology has sparked a significant ongoing debate within psychology. Empirical evidence has supported Haidt's concerns about a lack of political diversity in social and personality psychology,[47] including evidence for active discrimination against conservative psychologists by progressive psychologists. In a major recent article, accompanied by thirty-three commentaries on this article, Haidt and colleagues summarize the evidence for bias and discrimination by progressives in social psychology, and discuss ways in which it leads to poorer research within the discipline.[48]

An important aspect of their argument is that greater ideological diversity is needed to improve critical thinking within the discipline, and to foster a broader range of research topics. Their call for an increase in nonprogressive voices is not made for the sake of increased minority representation (it is not an argument for fairness)—rather, it is made for the sake of improving the overall quality of psychological science arising from a better contest between multiple ideological viewpoints.

In the field of sociology, there have been several important recent analyses of its lack of ideological diversity and its resultant problems. These include Christian Smith's *The Sacred Project of American Sociology*[49] and Yancey's *Compromising Scholarship*[50]—which covers other disciplines in addition to its in-depth study of sociology. A striking specific case is Mark Regnerus' study[51] showing that "adult children of parents who had same-sex romantic relationships, including same-sex couples as parents, have more emotional and social problems than do adult children of heterosexual parents with intact marriages."[52]

---

47. Inbar and Lammers, "Political Diversity," 499.
48. Duarte et al., "Political Diversity," 33.
49. Smith, *The Sacred Project*.
50. Yancey, *Compromising Scholarship*.
51. Regnerus, "How Different," 760.
52. Smith, "An Academic Auto-da-Fé."

This study led to a significant backlash against the author and the journal that published it—the author was investigated for potential academic misconduct (which was dismissed), and over two hundred academics wrote a letter to the journal criticizing the study,[53] while twenty-seven academics have written in support of the study.[54] While the study and its methodology remain highly contentious, Smith has observed that "without a doubt, had Regnerus published different findings with the same methodology, nobody would have batted a methodological eye."[55] From a statistical point of view, even when there is no actual population difference between two groups on some measure, if one hundred research studies are conducted on samples from this population, then using normal levels of statistical significance ($p<.05$), it is likely that a few studies will find a difference in favor of one group, and a few studies will find a difference in favor of the other group—simply due to artifacts of sampling.

Susan Robbins, editor of the *Journal of Social Work Education*, has raised concerns about the problem of requiring "trigger warnings" for certain content.[56] As Robbins notes, the difficulty with this approach is that students who wish to become social workers will need to deal with many upsetting situations in their professional life. Given this, students either need to find a way to work through any personal difficulties and build resilience during their time at university, or alternatively consider a different career. A similar argument about building resilience for upsetting work situations could be made for training in many of the caring professions. In another context, Haidt, together with Greg Lukianoff, makes a similar "building resilience" argument for all university students in "The Coddling of the American Mind,"[57] and concerns about coddling at universities were subsequently been echoed by then-President Obama:

> It's not just sometimes folks who are mad that colleges are too liberal that have a problem. Sometimes there are folks on college campuses who are liberal and maybe even agree with me on a bunch of issues who sometimes aren't listening to the other side. And that's a problem, too. I've heard of some college campuses where they don't want to have a guest speaker who is too conservative. Or they don't want to read a book if it has

---

53. Gates et al., "Letter to the Editors."

54. Johnson et al., "A Social Scientific Response." See also Redding, "Politicized Science."

55. Smith, "An Academic Auto-da-Fé."

56. Robbins, "From the Editor."

57. Lukianoff and Haidt, "The Coddling of the American Mind."

language that is offensive to African-Americans, or somehow sends a demeaning signal toward women. I've got to tell you, I don't agree with that either. I don't agree that you, when you become students at colleges, have to be coddled and protected from different points of views. Anybody who comes to speak to you and you disagree with, you should have an argument with them. But you shouldn't silence them by saying, you can't come because I'm too sensitive to hear what you have to say. That's not the way we learn, either. The way to do that is to create a space where a lot of ideas are presented and collide, and people are having arguments, and people are testing each other's theories, and over time, people learn from each other. The idea that you'd have somebody in government making a decision about what you should think ahead of time or what you should be taught, and if it's not the right thought or idea or perspective or philosophy, that that person would be—that they wouldn't get funding runs contrary to everything we believe about education. I mean, I guess that might work in the Soviet Union, but it doesn't work here. That's not who we are. That's not what we're about.[58]

In the context of K–12 education, particularly initial teacher education, there are many cases where the moral foundations of care and fairness will come into conflict—such as in classroom discipline scenarios,[59] and assessment of poor-quality student work. A recent case involved a letter accompanying school report cards that said:

> Since our goal is to share accurate information with the parents, and not to discourage or hurt a student, great discretion must be used before allowing your child to view his report card. . . . If after viewing the enclosed report card you would like us to develop a second version of this report card for your son with higher grades, please call.[60]

Teachers who have not considered how to manage the competing moral foundations of care and fairness may find it difficult to respond to challenging classroom or assessment situations that pit care for one student against fairness for other students.

The field of law has also seen recent discussion of the problem of ideological diversity, including a landmark study of the political ideologies of lawyers that illustrates the broad progressive leaning of the profession,

---

58. Byrnes, "Obama Hits."
59. Dalziel, "Implementing Developing Scenario Learning."
60. Locke, "School Offers to Change."

which is particularly strong among legal professors.[61] Phillips has recently investigated possible reasons for the low numbers of conservatives and libertarians among legal scholars in the United States (he also demonstrates the high productivity of these scholars).[62]

Theology is studied in many different kinds of institutions, such as university theology departments, liberal arts colleges, denominational seminaries, and bible colleges, and these institutions may exhibit overt or subliminal ideological biases—such as those described in the famous polemic *God and Man at Yale*.[63] However, despite a lack of intra-institutional ideological diversity in some cases (either progressive or conservative), the field as a whole provides significant inter-institutional ideological diversity. Theological education also has a long-standing focus on "formation," and hence issues similar to a "hidden moral curriculum" are more frequently discussed within this discipline than in others, though as James K. A. Smith notes, there is a need for ongoing reflection.[64]

Conclusion:
A New Argument for Christian Higher Education

Concerns about a lack of ideological diversity and anti-Christian bias in typical universities has been one factor behind the development of Christian higher education in recent decades, particularly in the United States.[65] In addition, concerns about the direction that modern universities shape students' hearts and practices—the "cultural liturgies" of universities—have also led to growth in Christian higher education.

However, for many Christians in the twenty-first century, a respect for the assumed ideological neutrality of universities (perhaps combined with a desire for universities known for their research excellence, which is less common among current Christian higher education providers) has seen only limited numbers of Christian students choosing to attend Christian higher education institutions over secular universities in many countries.

This chapter has illustrated the recent decline of ideological diversity in universities, and its negative impact on free speech and inquiry. It has also highlighted concerns about the hidden progressive moral curriculum of modern university intellectual and social life. For Christian students

61. Bonica, Chilton, and Sen, "The Political Ideologies."
62. Phillips, "Why Are There So Few Conservatives."
63. Buckley, *God and Man at Yale*.
64. Smith, *Desiring the Kingdom*.
65. Yancey, *Compromising Scholarship*.

choosing between typical universities and Christian higher education, the developments of the past few years in typical universities can be important factors to consider when choosing a higher education institution.[66]

Reflection Questions

1. In your experience, is learning best advanced by restricting or not restricting free speech?
2. Do schools and institutes of higher education provide students with a useful set of guidelines for identifying free speech rights?
3. Have new technologies such as social media complicated the way we think about and exercise free speech and ideological diversity in education?
4. Do you agree with the following statement: "The ideological imbalance that pervades academia fosters groupthink and undermines critical thinking." Have you experienced an unconscious bias in your education that expects everyone to think the same way?

Recommended Reading

Baklinski, Pete. "Quebec Can't Force Catholic School to Teach Ethics and Religion Course in 'Neutral' Way: Supreme Court." *LifeSite News*, March 19, 2015. https://www.lifesitenews.com/news/quebec-cant-force-catholic-school-to-teach-ethics-and-religion-course-in-ne.
"Trinity Western Law School Loses B.C. Law Society Vote." *CBC News, British Columbia*, June 11, 2014. http://www.cbc.ca/news/canada/british-columbia/trinity-western-law-school-loses-b-c-law-society-vote-1.2670688.
McCracken, Brett. "The Freedom to be a Christian College." *Biola Magazine*, Fall 2014. http://magazine.biola.edu/article/14-fall/the-freedom-to-be-a-christian-college/.

Bibliography

"UWA cancels contract for Consensus Centre involving controversial academic Bjorn Lomborg." *ABC News*, May 8, 2015. http://www.abc.net.au/news/2015-05-08/bjorn-lomborg-uwa-consensus-centre-contract-cancelled/6456708.
Bonica, Adam, Adam S. Chilton, and Maya Sen. "The Political Ideologies of American Lawyers." *Journal of Legal Analysis* 8 (Winter 2016): 227–335. http://ssrn.com/abstract=2652706.

---

66. By extension, it also provides a basis for reform of typical universities, but this goes beyond the scope of the current chapter.

Buckley, William F., Jr. *God and Man at Yale: The Superstitions of "Academic Freedom."* Washington, D.C.: Regnery, 1951.

Byrnes, Jesse. "Obama Hits 'Coddled' Liberal College Students." *The Hill*, September 15, 2015. http://thehill.com/blogs/blog-briefing-room/news/253641-obama-hits-coddled-liberal-college-students.

Dalziel, James. "Implementing Developing Scenario Learning with Branching for Moral Values in Teacher Training." In *Proceedings of The 9th International LAMS and Learning Design: Innovation in Learning Design*, 65–72. Edited by Leanne Cameron and James Dalziel. Sydney: Macquarie University, 2014. http://lams2014.lamsfoundation.org/docs/paper3.pdf.

Dalziel, James. (In press). "Why Conservatives and Progressives Think Differently: Insights from Moral Psychology." In *Proceedings of the 27th Conference of the Samuel Griffith Society*. Canberra, Australia: Samuel Griffith Society, 2015.

Duarte, José L., et al. "Political Diversity Will Improve Social Psychological Science." *Behavioral and Brain Sciences* 38 (2015): 1–13.

Fitzsimmons, Emma G. "Condoleezza Rice Backs Out of Rutgers Speech After Student Protests." *New York Times*, May 3, 2014. http://www.nytimes.com/2014/05/04/nyregion/rice-backs-out-of-rutgers-speech-after-student-protests.html.

Freedland, Jonathan. "My Plea to the Left: Treat Jews the Same Way You'd Treat Any Other Minority." *The Guardian*, April 29, 2016. https://www.theguardian.com/commentisfree/2016/apr/29/left-jews-labour-antisemitism-jewish-identity.

Gates, Gary J., et al. "Letter to the Editors and Advisory Editors of Social Science Research." *Social Science Research* 41 (2012): 1350–51.

Giroux, Henry A. *Theory and Resistance in Education: Towards a Pedagogy for the Opposition.* Westport, CT: Greenwood, 2001.

Gross, Neil. *Why are Professors Liberal and Why Do Conservatives Care?* Cambridge: Harvard University Press, 2013.

Hafferty, Fred W. "Beyond Curriculum Reform: Confronting Medicine's Hidden Curriculum." *Academic Medicine* 73 (1998): 403–7.

Haidt, John. *The Righteous Mind: Why Good People Are Divided by Religion and Politics.* New York: Pantheon, 2012.

Haidt, John. "Discrimination Hurts Real People." *Your Morals* (Blog), February 17, 2011. http://www.yourmorals.org/blog/2011/02/discrimination-hurts-real-people/.

Haidt, John. "Post-Partisan Social Psychology." John Haidt NYU faculty page, n.d. http://people.stern.nyu.edu/jhaidt/postpartisan.html.

Hayward, Steven F. "Grievance School." *National Review*, February 23, 2015. http://www.nationalreview.com/article/413675/grievance-school-steven-f-hayward.

Heller, Nathan. "The Big Uneasy." *New Yorker*, May 30, 2016. http://www.newyorker.com/magazine/2016/05/30/the-new-activism-of-liberal-arts-colleges.

Holgate, Tess. "Sydney Uni Evangelical Union Votes to Keep Faith-Based Declaration for Members." *Bible Society*, March 23, 2016. http://www.biblesociety.org.au/news/update-sydney-uni-evangelical-union-votes-keep-faith-based-declaration-members.

Inbar, Yoel, and Joris Lammers. "Political Diversity in Social and Personality Psychology." *Perspectives on Psychological Science* 7 (2012): 496–503.

Jaschik, Scott. "Moving Further to the Left." *Inside Higher Ed*, October 24, 2012. https://www.insidehighered.com/news/2012/10/24/survey-finds-professors-already-liberal-have-moved-further-left.

Johnson, Byron, et al. "A Social Scientific Response to the Regnerus Controversy." Institute for Studies of Religion, Baylor University, June 2, 2012. http://www.baylorisr.org/2012/06/20/a-social-scientific-response-to-the-regnerus-controversy/.

Kimball, Roger. "The Rise of the College Crybullies." *Wall Street Journal*, November 13, 2015. http://www.wsj.com/articles/the-rise-of-the-college-crybullies-1447458587.

Leef, George. "Brandeis Caves In to the 'No Platform for Our Opponents!' Crowd." *Forbes*, April 14, 2014. http://www.forbes.com/sites/georgeleef/2014/04/14/brandeis-caves-in-to-the-no-platform-for-our-opponents-crowd/#3559c4476811.

Locke, Judith. "School Offers to Change Children's Grades So Not to Hurt Students' Feelings." KidSpot, January 20, 2016. http://www.kidspot.com.au/school/secondary/real-life/school-offers-to-change-childrens-grades-so-not-to-hurt-students-feelings.

Lukianoff, Greg, and John Haidt. "The Coddling of the American Mind." *The Atlantic*, September 2015. http://www.theatlantic.com/magazine/archive/2015/09/the-coddling-of-the-american-mind/399356/.

Marcuse, Herbert. "Repressive Tolerance." In Robert Paul Wolff, Barrington Moore, Jr., and Herbert Marcuse. *A Critique of Pure Tolerance*, 95–137. Boston: Beacon, 1965. http://www.marcuse.org/herbert/pubs/60spubs/65repressivetolerance.htm.

McVeigh, Tracy. "Peter Tatchell: Snubbed by Students for Free Speech Stance." *The Guardian*, February 13, 2016. https://www.theguardian.com/uk-news/2016/feb/13/peter-tatchell-snubbed-students-free-speech-veteran-gay-rights-activist.

Phillips, James C. "Why Are There So Few Conservatives and Libertarians in Legal Academia: An Empirical Exploration of Three Hypotheses." *Harvard Journal of Law & Public Policy* 39 (Winter 2016): 153–207. http://www.harvard-jlpp.com/wp-content/uploads/2010/01/39_1_Phillips_F.pdf.

Redden, Elizabeth. "Anthropology Group Won't Boycott Israel." *Inside Higher Ed*, June 7, 2016. https://www.insidehighered.com/news/2016/06/07/anthropology-group-rejects-resolution-boycott-israeli-academic-institutions.

Redding, Richard E. "Politicized Science." *Society* 50 (2013): 439–46.

Regnerus, Mark. "How Different are the Adult Children of Parents Who Have Same-Sex Relationships? Findings from the New Family Structures Study." *Social Science Research* 41 (2012): 752–70.

Richter, Monica. "No-Platforming on University Campuses: Political Correctness and the Subversion of Free Speech." Free Speech Debate, March 3, 2016. http://freespeechdebate.com/en/discuss/no-platforming-on-university-campuses-political-correctness-and-the-subversion-of-free-speech/.

Robbins, Susan P. "From the Editor—Sticks and Stones: Trigger Warnings, Microaggressions, and Political Correctness." *Journal of Social Work Education* 52 (2016): 1–5.

Samples, Kenneth R. *A World of Difference: Putting Christian Truth-Claims to the Worldview Test*. Grand Rapids: Baker, 2007.

Schlosser, Edward. "I'm a Liberal Professor, and My Liberal Students Terrify Me." *Vox*, June 3, 2015. http://www.vox.com/2015/6/3/8706323/college-professor-afraid.

Schneier, Bruce. "Cryptography is Harder than it Looks." Schneier on Security, January/February 2016. https://www.schneier.com/essays/archives/2016/03/cryptography_is_hard.html.

Smith, James K. A. *Desiring the Kingdom: Worship, Worldview and Cultural Formation*. Grand Rapids: Baker, 2009.

Smith, Christian. "An Academic Auto-da-Fé." *Chronicle of Higher Education*, July 23, 2012. http://chronicle.com/article/An-Academic-Auto-da-F-/133107/.

Smith, Christian . *The Sacred Project of American Sociology*. Oxford: Oxford University Press, 2014.

Taub, Amanda. "I was a Liberal Adjunct Professor. My Liberal Students Didn't Scare Me at All." *Vox*, June 5, 2015. http://www.vox.com/2015/6/5/8736591/liberal-professor-identity.

Trimpf, Katherine. "Oberlin Students: Replace Midterms with Conversations and Erase Grades Below Cs." *National Review*, May 24, 2016. http://www.nationalreview.com/article/435810/oberlin-college-student-life-hard-without-grades-exams.

Wolterstorff, Nicholas. *Educating for Shalom: Essays on Christian Higher Education*. Edited by Clarence W. Joldersma and Gloria Goris Stronks. Grand Rapids: Eerdmans, 2004.

Yancey, George A. *Compromising Scholarship: Religious and Political Bias in American Higher Education*. Waco: Baylor University Press, 2011.

Acknowledgments

The author gratefully acknowledges the advice of Ben Myers on a draft of this chapter. An earlier version of this chapter was presented at the Christian Heritage College Research Symposium, "Learning and Loves: Re-imagining Christian Education," on July 18, 2016.

Part Two

Inclusion and Teacher Management

8

The Benefits of Choice in Education: A Canadian Perspective

Peter J. Froese

Introduction

TED WAS AN AIRLINE pilot based in Calgary, Alberta. When his son and daughter reached high school age, Ted moved the family to Abbotsford, British Columbia, to enable his children to attend an independent school of his choice with an academic emphasis, a superior music program, and faith values that supported his own—even though it meant he had to commute to Calgary for work until he was able to secure a transfer to Vancouver. It has been suggested that, in the absence of limiting factors such as availability, location, tuition cost, and restrictive government policies, up to 50 percent of Canadian families would choose a different school for their children than the one they currently attend.[1]

Educational choice is important to families in Canada, despite strong voices that argue against it. Numerous studies demonstrate that merely the act of choosing a school or program, whether in the public or in the private sector, can enhance both satisfaction and academic performance significantly.

A survey conducted by the National Center for Education Statistics in the United States in 2002–3 found that only 57 percent of parents with children attending traditional public schools were "very satisfied" with the education their children were receiving. By comparison, 68 percent of parents with children attending chosen public schools, 75 percent with children attending secular private schools, and 78 percent with children attending religious

---

1. Comment made by a senior BC government official during a meeting, May 2014.

private schools were "very satisfied."[2] These survey results suggest greater parental satisfaction with schools that parents have selected for their children.

According to the Fraser Institute, of the academic rankings of British Columbia schools based on provincial assessments at grades 4 and 7, only one of the sixteen elementary schools scoring a perfect 10 was a public French immersion school in West Vancouver (incidentally, also a school of choice within the public system); the other fifteen were all independent schools. In the top 100 of 978 elementary schools in the province, seventy-four were independent schools and twenty-six were public schools. Among high schools ranked according to provincial examination results in grades 10, 11, and 12, the highest ranking public school was in nineteenth place. Public schools and independent schools split the top 100 of 289 secondary school spots evenly with fifty schools in each category, while only four independent secondary schools had achievement levels in the lower 50 percent.[3] Though some university preparatory schools select their students for academic prowess, many high-ranking independent schools are faith-based and employ open admission policies. The purpose of highlighting these rankings is not to suggest that independent schools are superior to public schools, but to show these statistics suggest that higher academic achievement is strongly correlated to choice, as is higher satisfaction. Critics often question school rankings for not taking socioeconomic status, ethnicity, disabilities, and ESL status into consideration.

Despite these findings, there is no consensus that choice in education should be universally adopted. Proponents of unilateral public education believe that the state should exercise total responsibility for the education of all its children. Proponents of choice believe that all education should be locally developed and regulated in consultation with the families of school-age children, with the state providing only financial support, core curriculum, and guidelines for health and safety issues. Studies and publications can be found to support each perspective.

Current Status of Educational Choice in Canada (2015)

Surprising as it may seem, the educational structures of different provinces in Canada vary widely along this continuum. Following the repatriation of the British North America Act in 1867, the federal government assigned responsibility of education to the provinces, retaining direct involvement only

---

2. Walberg, *School Choice*, 96.
3. For more information, see "School Performance."

in the K–12 education of Aboriginal, military, and foreign service families.[4] Each province maintains its own Department of Education that determines curriculum standards, funding levels, capital costs, and policies to guide the provincial educational program.[5]

Basically, parents with school-aged children in Canada have three educational options: 1) public schools, 2) independent or private schools, and 3) home-schooling, though each of these options is funded and regulated differently in different provinces. In addition to physical brick-and-mortar schools, both public and independent systems now offer online curriculum to students at home, fully regulated by the provincial Departments of Education and supervised by certified teachers.

Canada's status as a bilingual nation provides one automatic element of choice, as all schools in English speaking Canada offer French as a second language, and some offer full French immersion programs. Each province also has a Francophone school board to serve children whose first language is French. In Quebec the situation is reversed, with Francophone schools offering English as a second language and English immersion, and Anglophone school boards as an option for children whose native language is English.[6]

Three provinces, Alberta, Saskatchewan, and Ontario, offer families fully funded Catholic education as an extension of the public school system, operated by a separate Catholic school board. Catholic schools in other provinces are independent or private schools, partially funded in some provinces but not in others. In British Columbia and Manitoba, Catholic schools are funded at 50 percent of operating costs, while they receive no funding in any of the maritime provinces.[7]

Alberta funds alternative educational programs the most liberally of any Canadian province. Thirteen of its public schools across the province are fully funded, autonomous, not-for-profit charter schools, which provide alternative educational programs with an emphasis on a specific discipline such as dance, drama, or music. Charter schools are highly popular in Alberta, with six charter schools in the city of Calgary having combined waiting lists of over eight thousand students.[8] Alberta also provides full funding for public Francophone, separate Catholic, separate Francophone, and separate Protestant schools.

4. Cunningham, *Justice Achieved*, 16.
5. Clemens et al., "Measuring Choice and Competition."
6. Ibid.
7. Ibid.
8. Ibid

Independent schools are outside of the public system and offer alternative approaches to teaching, and may include a religious orientation. All provinces in Canada have independent schools, with Alberta, British Columbia, Manitoba, Quebec, and Saskatchewan providing partial funding for operational costs. Operating grants for independent schools vary among provinces and range from 35 percent to 70 percent of the public sector average cost per pupil, with some exceptions.[9]

Independent schools are generally government regulated, which means that partial funding is conditional on meeting certain expectations set by the Ministries of Education. In British Columbia, for example, partially funded independent schools are expected to teach the provincially approved curriculum, employ only certified teachers, participate in provincial learning assessments, provide instruction in facilities that meet municipal building and safety codes, and operate their schools according to the standards set out in the Independent School Act, and its regulations and orders.[10] These schools are inspected regularly by external evaluation teams. The majority of British Columbia independent schools that meet the regulatory requirements are partially funded for operating costs only, placing British Columbia approximately midway among the many models of school funding that exist both nationally and globally.

Educational Choice

Educational choice is a topic of considerable interest for families in both public and independent school sectors. The "choice" aspect of the discussion is embraced in practice, if not in theory, by the growing number of options provided within the public system, from "mini-schools" within larger public schools that cater to special interests or abilities such as outdoor or fine arts programs, to whole schools with specific designations such as fundamental or French immersion schools. Interest in these special programs is significantly higher than the number of seats available. In one Vancouver public school, over two hundred students apply annually for a class with an enrollment cap of thirty. Despite the vehement views of proponents of universal public education systems, those very systems appear to be recognizing the power of choice to improve student satisfaction, motivation, and achievement.

Enrollment trends provide some illuminating insights into the appeal of choice. British Columbia independent schools show growth in each of the

9. Ibid.
10. Independent School Act, Schedule 2 and 3.

past forty years, including during the most recent decade when the overall K–12 enrollment declined in the province. In 2014–15, over five thousand additional students enrolled in independent schools in British Columbia, bringing the provincial total to over eighty thousand students or 13 percent of the overall K–12 enrollment. Waiting lists in many of the province's three hundred fifty independent schools ensure that these enrollment levels are unlikely to decrease.

Public and Independent Enrollment Comparison for British Columbia, 2005–15[11]

Year	Enrollment Public	Annual Growth %	Enrollment Independent	Annual Growth %	Enrollment Total	Independent Proportion of Total (%)
2004–05	588,007	-1.0	64,406	2.4	652,413	9.9
2005–06	582,100	-1.0	65,406	2.0	647,824	10.1
2006–07	572,161	-1.7	67,561	2.8	639,722	10.6
2007–08	568,090	-0.7	68,635	1.6	636,725	10.8
2008–09	561,471	-1.2	68,919	0.4	630,390	10.9
2009–10	558,000	-0.6	69,272	0.5	627,272	11.0
2010–11	553,828	-0.7	70,073	0.1	623,901	11.2
2011–12	546,219	-1.4	71,615	0.2	617,837	11.6
2012–13	540,490	-1.0	74,051	3.4	614,541	12.0
2013–14	537,765	-0.5	75,753	2.3	613,518	12.3
2014–15	535,309	-0.4	80,230	5.9	615,539	13.0

Funding Matters

Partial funding of British Columbia independent schools began in 1977 with the enactment of the Independent School Support Act, renamed the Independent School Act in 1989, at which time the province set independent school funding at 50 percent of the average operating costs of public schools in the same district, provided the independent schools' average operating costs are equal to or less than the surrounding district public school average student operating costs. Independent schools with operating costs

11. "Enrolment Comparing Public and Independent."

greater than the surrounding public school district receive 35 percent.[12] The balance of the schools' costs must be met through a tuition fee paid by the parents, donations from supporters, or support from affiliated religious organizations, such as the Catholic dioceses.

Independent schools confer a financial benefit on the province by educating their students for a fraction of the cost to the taxpayer incurred by public schools. In 2014–15, the province budgeted $320 million in operating costs for independent schools from a provincial education budget of $5.35 billion. Put another way, the province allocated 5.7 percent of its education budget to educate 13 percent of the K–12 enrollment.[13] In addition to a significant savings in operating costs, the assessed value of independent school land, buildings, and improvements in 2013 was $1.7 billion, none of which was provided by government.[14] Though financial concerns should not be the determining factor in decisions regarding educational matters, educational choice in British Columbia provides an appreciable benefit to the taxpayers.

International Declarations and Agreements Support Parental Choice

One of the principal arguments against choice in education is that the state possesses both the right and the need to develop its children into good citizens, and that this can be done only in a state regulated and administered system. This position arises from concern that minority groups that are allowed to develop their own educational institutions exist to serve only their own needs, and may inculcate students with values that are hostile to the country's interests.

Yet, strong arguments for a pluralistic approach to education can be found in historical events that led to several international treaties and declarations ratified by Canada. The right of parents to access schooling they felt was appropriate for their children was established in international law after World War II, due in part to a reaction against the use of schooling by fascist regimes to indoctrinate children.[15] Support for choice in education has its basis in law through the United Nations Universal Declaration of Human Rights, 1948, which exerts moral authority on nations that adhere to it, to provide the following rights:

12. Independent School Act, Section 4.
13. British Columbia Ministry of Finance, *Estimates*, 62.
14. Report provided to FISA BC by BC Ministry of Finance, Nov. 7, 2014.
15. Glenn, *Contrasting Models*, 154–55.

1. Equal rights and freedoms regardless of race, color, language, religion or other distinctions, and equal protection under the law to these rights (Art. 1, 2, 7, 8).

2. Freedom of thought, conscience, and religion, and the freedom to express these beliefs in teaching and practice (Art. 18, 19).

3. Right to free and compulsory education, "at least at the elementary and fundamental stages." This education should promote understanding and tolerance among people of all racial and religious groups (Art. 26:[1] and [2]).

4. The family is the fundamental unit in society and parents have a prior right to choose their children's education (Art. 16[3] and 26[3]).

5. No state has the right to destroy the rights and freedoms of others as set forth in this Declaration (Art. 30).[16]

The International Covenant on Economic, Social, and Cultural Rights, ratified by Canada in 1976, goes further than moral authority. It is a legal treaty containing clauses very similar to those in the Universal Declaration of Human Rights, but includes the provision that secondary education should be free for all (Art. 13[2-c]). It specifically provides for schools to be established and operated by parents or other groups without interference from the state, provided they meet the minimum standards laid down by the state (Art. 13[4])].[17]

A third international agreement endorsed by Canada, the UN Convention on the Rights of the Child, covers much of the same ground as the previous two documents, but adds the presumption that an education system should develop respect by children for their parents and for their own "cultural identity, language, and values," as well as the values of others (Art. 29[c]).[18] Wilkinson argues that, according to these international agreements, since groups have the right to establish schools that teach their values, the state has an obligation to fund those schools.[19]

The Principle of Subsidiarity

Another argument against a pluralistic education system is that centralization contributes to a more efficient distribution of financial and human

---

16. Wilkinson, *Educational Choice*, 46–47.
17. Ibid.
18. Ibid.
19. Ibid., 47.

resources. This principle has been enacted in the United States throughout the twentieth century. "In the 1937–38 school year, the total number of traditional public school districts was about 119,000. . . . [This] dwindled to fewer than 15,000 by 2001–02."[20] However, students in Montana, which has maintained a decentralized school system with a large number of tiny school districts, "have consistently ranked at or near the top of US state achievement rankings."[21]

Evidence of smaller school systems achieving better academic results abounds. Chubb and Moe (1990) identified autonomy as one of the most significant factors contributing to an effective school, which, in their view, is why private schools tend to be more successful than public schools. "A private school principal, for example, is less likely to face interference in school management by central authorities such as boards and superintendents. The resulting autonomy enables principals to adopt clear academic goals, strong educational leadership, professionalized teaching, ambitious academic programs, [and] team-like organizations."[22]

Valerie Lee's study of Catholic schools determined that one of the factors in their success was that they "are decentralized; funds are raised and decisions are made largely at the school level."[23] Peterson and Walberg found that Catholic schools in New York, particularly those in high poverty areas, did considerably better than public schools of a similar socioeconomic status, for less than half the cost.[24] These schools had "fewer centrally determined policies . . . strong site-level leadership, demanding academic curricula, frequent communication with parents, and high student retention based on parental and student satisfaction,"[25] as opposed to the public school staff who operated in an environment muddied by rules coming from central offices, community boards, and federal and state boards. "High staff turnover undermined curricula, instruction, and disciplinary policies. Central office administrators changed schools' attendance boundaries and even grade levels without consulting parents or school staff."[26]

The term by which local autonomy in the governing of a school—or any social system—is known is "subsidiarity."[27] Wilkinson defines it as

20. Walberg, *School Choice,* 84.
21. Ibid., 85
22. Ibid.,67
23. Ibid., 68
24. Ibid.
25. Ibid.
26. Ibid.
27. Glenn, *Contrasting Models,* intro, x.

"the tenet that decision making should be delegated to the smallest, most intimate groups of people possible, rather than being left with some strong centralized authority."[28] He explains that subsidiarity "is founded as well on the precept that individuals matter . . . and are capable of making sound decisions affecting themselves and their families' well-being."[29]

The Treaty of Maastricht (1992) outlines the policies governing the European Union, and contains a separate section entitled "Principle of Subsidiarity," which says,

> The Treaty on European Union has established the principle of subsidiarity as a general rule, which was initially applied to environmental policy in the Single European Act. This principle specifies that in areas that are not within its exclusive powers the Community shall only take action where objectives can best be attained by action at Community rather than at national level. Article A provides that the Union shall take decisions as close as possible to the citizen.[30]

Pope John Paul II comments as follows on this article of the treaty:

> The principle of subsidiarity must be respected: a community of a higher order should not interfere in the internal life of a community of a lower order, depriving the latter of its functions, but rather should support it in case of need and help to coordinate its activity with the activities of the rest of society, always with a view to the common good.[31]

Schools that "take decisions as close as possible to the citizens" are schools in which each participant experiences a strong sense of ownership as a result of a strong sense of efficacy. Montana's students do better than those of other American states, because "the school board members, administrators, and teachers often personally know students, their siblings, and their parents. . . . Their votes count heavily in school board elections. None of this tends to be true of large school districts."[32]

Subsidiarity enhances the quality of education and is particularly effective in societies that respect the diversity of minority groups and cultures. The state provides guidance regarding curriculum, student safety, and civic responsibility, while the school interprets the state-prescribed curriculum

---

28. Wilkinson, *Educational Choice*, 50.
29. Ibid.
30. "Treaty of Maastricht."
31. Glenn, *Contrasting Models*, intro, x.
32. Walberg, *School Choice*, 85.

in light of the cultural values of the local community. As a result, parents and students feel a strong sense of identity and ownership in their school, as demonstrated by improved academic performance by students and rapid response by the school when improvements are needed. Therefore, subsidiarity in education promotes the spirit and values that form part of the school culture, as well as the organizational requirements.

Egalitarianism and Elitism

A third allegation made by those who oppose choice in education is that independent schools promote elitism in two ways: only families of higher socioeconomic status can afford to pay the tuitions, and students are screened for academic ability. Therefore, public schools have had the "cream" taken off the top of their clientele, and to add insult to injury, the government is also diverting funds that should be going into the public system to support these rich, elite independent schools.[33]

Research by Statistics Canada (2015) indicates that academic performance is higher in independent schools, largely due to two factors: independent school students are more likely to have socioeconomic characteristics positively associated with academic success and to have school peers with university-educated parents.[34] Van Pelt, Allison, and Allison (2007) also suggest that parents of children who attend Ontario private schools tend to be more highly educated than parents of children who attend Ontario public schools.[35]

Ironically, socioeconomic status and higher education appear to exert a more dichotomous effect on public schools than on independent schools. Fraser Institute rankings indicate that the three highest performing public elementary schools are located in West Vancouver, the community with some of the highest property values in the province. The two highest ranking public secondary schools are in close proximity to the University of British Columbia (UBC). While most of the lowest ranking public schools are in rural areas of British Columbia, four of them are located in areas of East Vancouver with high indigent or immigrant populations. At the same time, five of the ten Catholic schools located in these same East Vancouver communities rank in the top 10 percent of schools in the province, and only one appears below the median.[36] The conclusion to be drawn from these

33. White and Kuehn, "Does Independent School Funding."
34. Frenette and Chan, "Academic Outcomes," 6.
35. Ibid., 10.
36. "School Performance."

facts must be that academic achievement is linked to factors other than, or in addition to, economic well-being and parental education levels.

While it is true that approximately 15 percent of BC independent schools do charge high tuitions and screen for academic or other abilities, over 65 percent are faith-based schools, many with open admission policies. Furthermore, any school that receives 50 percent funding from the province must have an equal to or lower per student operating cost than the surrounding public school district.[37] If partial government funding were withdrawn, many smaller independent schools might be forced to close, whereas withdrawal of government funds would have little effect on the high tuition schools. Rather than promoting egalitarianism, such a policy would simultaneously increase education costs for the government and widen the perceived gap between "privileged" independent school students and "disadvantaged" public school students.

Systemic academic skimming is also a fallacious claim. As indicated earlier, only 15 percent of British Columbia independent schools select their enrollment, whereas 85 percent tend to enroll families, including children with disabilities. Some independent schools choose to exclusively serve learning disabled students, reducing the burden on the public school sector. A recent study of special needs students in independent schools undertaken by the Federation of Independent School Associations in British Columbia (FISA BC, April 2011) reveals that the student body composition of public and independent schools is very similar. While funded special needs students comprise approximately 4.5 percent of the public school population, independent schools are close behind with about 4 percent funded special needs students.[38]

Values Education

One of the major challenges of a centralized public education system in a pluralistic society is the need to provide a values neutral position so as not to offend any particular group's values. The British Columbia School Act, section 76,[39] states:

1. All schools and Provincial schools must be conducted on strictly secular and nonsectarian principles.

2. The highest morality must be inculcated, but no religious dogma or creed is to be taught in a school or provincial school.

---

37. Independent School Act, Section 3(1)(a).
38. "Special Education Survey," 11.
39. School Act, Section 76.

Section 76 of the School Act indicates that there is likely general agreement that families and the state want to see schools provide a high quality of education, protect students while they are attending school, and teach values that support a free and democratic society. However, there is considerable disagreement on how best to achieve these goals, and considerable concern from many families that the values of the home are lost in a "strictly secular and nonsectarian" environment of public education.

Wilkinson argues[40] that parents are better served if their children are taught according to the values underlying their own culture, religion, and ethical beliefs. By attempting to avoid conflict with any specific cultural or faith community, the public system has created an environment in which many parents believe that the bureaucratic educational values bear little resemblance to their own strongly held cultural and faith values.

Thomas's position[41] is that when the state exercises too much control, the quality of education takes on a neutral perspective, which denies students valuable lessons that educational pluralism can offer them. Education needs to strike a balance between individual and group rights, with the state giving guidance regarding societal responsibilities and the local community providing individual perspectives. In a pluralistic democracy, differing communities should be free to express their values institutionally in their schools, churches, and cultural centers. Yet all schools need to be committed to teaching the universal civic values that are essential to living in a pluralistic society. "There needs to be a balance between an emphasis on particularistic education and an emphasis on universalist education."[42]

The fundamental requirements of equity, fairness, and justice are not met in the current universal public education system because school authorities make decisions on the education that students receive only during the time that the students are attending the school, and their influence and responsibility cease when the children leave the school grounds.[43] Schools are faced with the additional challenge that in many cases both parents are too busy to spend time with their children or the children have only one parent, so these children are coming to school less capable of learning than children in the past. "Schools are being asked to compensate for this decreased social capital by providing more living skills, conflict resolution, and other values that have been taught traditionally at home."[44]

40. Wilkinson, *Educational Choice*, 47.
41. Thomas, *Parental Choice*, 223.
42. Ibid.
43. Coons and Sugarman, *Education by Choice*, 54.
44. Wilkinson, *Educational Choice*, 11.

When parents have a choice in the educational experiences of their children, they take ownership for a process that includes them, and the result is a better coordination of effort between the school and the home. When families can place their children in an environment where the values of the home are mirrored in the values of the school, parents feel more comfortable in the school and contribute more willingly as volunteers, classroom assistants, and organizers of school events such as sports day concessions, set construction for drama productions, and parent advisory groups.

Government plays a legitimate role in ensuring that all schools exercise curricular, safety, and civic responsibility. Yet parents should have the assurance that, when they send their children off to school, the values expressed in the home will be reinforced, not undermined. When an appropriate balance between state responsibility and local autonomy is achieved, the result will be an environment in which the five aspects of community growth can flourish.

Choice alone is not sufficient. Merely the right or the opportunity to choose a school is insufficient to guarantee student satisfaction and success. Successful schools become communities, in which mutually beneficial interactions among administrators, teachers, students, and parents continually strengthen coproduction, trust, and social capital.[45] A common vision can both develop and reinforce these aspects of community, and result in a heightened sense of civic responsibility, within the school, toward the surrounding community, and both nationally and globally.

Coproduction

Children do not become educated only, or even chiefly, at school. Since only a small portion of their day is spent at school, the school's agenda is unlikely to succeed without the active involvement of parents. Equally importantly, parents are more likely to support what is being taught at school if they are in agreement with it. Though several researchers make this point, Ostrom expresses it most clearly: "If students are not actively engaged in their own education, encouraged and supported by their family and friends, what teachers do may make little difference in the skills students acquire."[46] This process of mutual support by multiple parties intensifying outcomes is termed coproduction.

Coproduction includes engagement of the school community with the greater community in supporting the common good. Successful schools

---

45. Schneider, Teske, and Marschall, *Choosing Schools*, 55–57.
46. Ibid., 55

involve themselves in events beyond their doors, such as Adopt a Street, recycling, salmon enhancement programs, fall fairs, music festivals, and athletic events. Coproduction develops a sense of community pride and participation in students, and it informs them about civic responsibilities, local government processes, and community dynamics. Parents tend to be more involved in their children's schooling, and power is shifted away from central administrators to classrooms, schools, homes, and communities.

Trust

One of the natural by-products of coproduction is trust. Many of the educational activities of the school take place outside of the direct view of parents.[47] Therefore, school staff is dependent upon parents trusting that they are doing the best thing for the children in their care. If parents are given a choice in the education of their children and become personally involved in school activities, they are more likely to trust in the competence and goodwill of their children's teachers. Trust is also strengthened when the values of the school are consistent with the values of the home.

Social Capital

Coproduction and trust are both components of social capital. When parents assist the teacher by volunteering as classroom aides, helping students who need additional support, or assisting in a joint school/community project, what emerges is a cooperative relationship that builds trust and support for the vision and purpose of the school. Social capital develops from "constructive intergenerational relationships at the person-to-person level."[48] Social capital in a [school] can reduce costs, mitigate conflict, and generate cooperation. The resulting advantage is that "a group within which there is extensive trustworthiness and extensive trust is able to accomplish much more than a comparable group without the trustworthiness and trust."[49]

It is more difficult to build social capital in the public sector than in independent schools, due to collective agreements between teachers, support staff, and the central Board of Education. However, Brown's research on three public choice schools in Langley and Abbotsford, British Columbia, which originated from parental demand, found a significant degree of

---

47. Ibid.
48. Lieberman, *Privatization*, 206.
49. Schneider, Teske, and Marschall, *Choosing Schools*, 224.

social capital in each school.[50] Parents, teachers, and administrators agreed on the goals of the schools and there was consensus on how to achieve them. There was a high degree of parental involvement in each school and levels of parental and student satisfaction were high. The academic achievement of students in the three schools, as measured by provincial and district assessments, was 7 percent higher than the district average in grades 4 and 7. Satisfaction indices were up to 17 percent higher for students and 10 percent higher for parents. The three schools achieved these results while operating under the governance policies and collective agreements of the two public school districts, leading researchers to make the following observation: "The evidence gathered suggests strongly that parental choice in public schools . . . is associated with a number of very positive attributes that serve our children, their families, and our entire society. They include high levels of academic learning, civility, and parental involvement."[51]

Common Vision

A common vision between home and school also creates a safe environment for students, who immediately feel at ease in the classroom. Student learning is enhanced when students feel safe to take risks and make mistakes in their learning, because they are more assured of being accepted when families and school staff hold common values. Thomas writes that accepting students for who they are, rather than for what they do, is integrally related to the idea of teaching the whole child.[52] The point isn't just to meet a student's emotional needs with one activity, her physical needs with another activity, her social needs with a third activity, and so on. Rather, it is an integrated self to whom we respond. It is the whole person whom we value.

He suggests that this may be one of the reasons students in Catholic schools tend to demonstrate better general progress than similar students enrolled in the public sector.

Civic Responsibility

Critics suggest that schools of choice are harmful to a free and democratic society in that the schools become enclaves that keep to themselves, do not participate in building a democratic community, and therefore do not serve

---

50. Brown, *Impact of Parental Choice*, 95–97.
51. Ibid., 98.
52. Thomas, *Parental Choice*, 161.

the public good. Campbell's survey of secondary students in 2006 regarding tolerance for anti-religious activities produced the surprising results that Catholic and nonsectarian private school students were more likely to express tolerant opinions of those who opposed their views than were public school students.[53] They were also more likely to participate in civic activities such as volunteering, public speaking, and writing editorial letters on public issues.

Greene's examination of eight studies comparing schools of choice to traditional public schools found that private schools are more likely to be integrated (having a racial composition that resembles the composition of the broader community) and less likely to be segregated (having a racial composition that is almost all white or almost all minority) than are public schools; and private schools are more likely to promote tolerance, voting, and social involvement than are public schools.[54]

The *Cardus Education Survey* of Canadian secondary school graduates aged 24–39 concluded that various nongovernment schooling sectors produce graduates who embody commonly desired characteristics in higher proportions than public schools.[55] Researchers found that independent school graduates participate more in community and neighborhood groups, as well as in arts and cultural initiatives. Independent school graduates vote more regularly, volunteer more frequently, and participate in a wide variety of community organizations. They are well represented in civic and political initiatives, despite having been educated in independent schools organized around common values.

Research conducted by *Illuminate Consulting Group* confirmed similar results in 2014 for independent school graduates in British Columbia.[56] The survey conducted on almost eight hundred graduates concluded that nearly three quarters indicated they actively participate in volunteer or community activities that contribute to society. Graduates frequently commented that their experience at an independent school instilled in them a sense of service to society and led them to give back to their communities.

Choice Empowers Individuals

Numerous studies indicate that the presence of private schools within a public school district has a positive impact on student learning in both sectors. Hoxby

---

53. Campbell, *Why We Vote* cited in Walberg, *School Choice*, 73.
54. Greene, "Survey of Results," 6.
55. Cardus Education Survey, *Rising Tide*, 5–8.
56. Guhr, Furtado, and Hovland, *Post-School Trajectories*, 7.

(1994) found higher public school performance in metropolitan areas with greater private school competition.[57] Similar effects on public school student performance were identified in research by Borland and Howsen (1992),[58] and Couch, Shughart, and Williams (1993).[59] Milliman and Maranto (1996) found that public school teachers' perception of public school performance was improved by competition from Catholic schools.[60]

Choosing a school can mean the difference between graduating and not graduating. The graduation rates of students in Washington, DC, who were offered a voucher to attend a school of choice, graduated at a 12 percent higher rate (82 percent) than control group students in an assigned catchment school (70 percent).[61] Parents also expressed more satisfaction with their child's school and viewed it as safer when they were provided with a voucher to choose the school.

The greatest benefit of choice is the freedom it gives to parents, students, teachers, and administrators. When parents have the opportunity to choose, a perception of ownership and attendant responsibility accompanies the choice. When parents have the opportunity to choose, they consider alternatives and decide on the option that best meets the family's requirements. If that choice includes an investment in tuition fees, the sense of ownership is increased and the reciprocal commitment by the school also increases. Teachers, administrators, and support staff know that choice can be removed as easily as it is given, so they give more attention to ensuring that student needs are met. Parent satisfaction surveys confirm that schools of choice are perceived to deal with issues more effectively and in a timelier manner than public sector schools.

Teachers in schools of choice frequently enjoy a greater degree of freedom to create a learning environment that meets the needs of individual students. The school may have specific goals that must be met, but these are generally developed in a collaborative fashion based on the needs of students attending the school, as opposed to district goals set by central office personnel.

The freedom experienced in a choice environment both empowers the individuals on the receiving end of the service, and elicits a greater sense of responsibility and commitment on the delivery end. The resulting social capital contributes to a strong sense of identity and efficacy in all members of the school community.

57. Hoxby, "Does Competition Among Public Schools," 26.
58. Schneider, Teske, and Marschall, *Choosing Schools*, 238.
59. Ibid.
60. Ibid.
61. Wolf et al., "Evaluation of the DC Opportunity," 41.

Conclusion

Evidence cited in this paper indicates that schools of choice satisfy many educational and societal goals. It does not appear to matter whether that choice is exercised inside or outside of the public system; the chief factor in parental satisfaction, student satisfaction, and student achievement is that the participants have exercised choice in selecting the school, and continue to exercise essential control over decision-making in the operation of the school. The more the principle of subsidiarity is enacted, the more effective the school.

Government funding of independent schools makes sense both financially and for the common good of the society. Independent schools contribute to egalitarianism by making excellent education available to economically disadvantaged families as well as advantaged families. They require less taxpayer support as public schools and produce graduates who are on average more involved in civic affairs, volunteerism, and leadership. Graduates of independent schools also tend to pursue higher education and choose "helping" careers more frequently than public school graduates.[62]

Providing choice in education demonstrates respect for the diversity that characterizes our pluralistic, democratic society. Canada's laws and policies enshrine the rights of citizens representing a wide variety of ethnic and religious values. A unilateral, one-size-fits-all educational system is not equipped to protect the heterogeneous racial-ethnic-cultural-religious character of Canadian diversity, making educational choice an important policy priority for all provinces.

Reflection Questions

1. The principle of subsidiarity recommends that decision-making be delegated to the smallest, most intimately involved group of people possible. How might this principle apply to the philosophy of personalized learning in today's classrooms?

2. The data regarding enrollment growth in British Columbia schools shows a continuing trend toward parents choosing independent schools for their children. What can the public sector learn from this trend? How can choice be integrated into public education?

3. Teachers often feel the volume of administrative tasks takes them away from engaging with the students. Discuss how a school system might

---

62. Cardus Education Survey, *Rising Tide*, 6.

more effectively free teachers and students to maximize the time spent in teaching and learning.

4. Most of us would agree that we value choice in our day-to-day lives. Why is there resistance to providing more choice to families, administrators, teachers, and students in education today?

Bibliography

British Columbia Ministry of Finance. *Estimates: Fiscal Year Ending March 31, 2016.* Victoria: Queen's Printer for British Columbia, 2015.

Brown, Daniel J. *The Impact of Parental Choice on Three Canadian Public Schools.* Kelowna, BC: Society for the Advancement of Excellence in Education, 1999.

Campbell, David. *Why We Vote: How Schools and Communities Shape Our Civic Life.* Princeton: Princeton University Press, 2006.

Cardus Education Survey. *A Rising Tide Lifts All Boats: Measuring Non-government School Effects in Service of the Canadian Public Good.* Hamilton, ON: Cardus, 2012.

Clemens, Jason, et al. "Measuring Choice and Competition in Canadian Education: An Update on School Choice in Canada." Fraser Institute, 2014. https://www.fraserinstitute.org/sites/default/files/measuring-choice-and-competition-in-canadian-education.pdf.

Coons, John E., and Stephen D. Sugarman. *Education by Choice: The Case for Family Control.* Berkeley: University of California Press, 1978.

Cunningham, Victoria. *Justice Achieved: The Political Struggle of Independent Schools in British Columbia.* Vancouver: Federation of Independent School Associations in British Columbia, 2002.

"Enrolment Comparing Public and Independent—Historical." Federation of Independent School Associations, British Columbia, 2015. http://fisabc.ca/stats-resources/statistics.

Frenette, Marc, and Ping Ching Winnie Chan. "Academic Outcomes of Public and Private High School Students: What Lies Behind the Differences?" Ottawa: Statistics Canada Analytical Studies Branch Research Paper Series, 2015.

Glenn, Charles L. *Contrasting Models of State and School.* New York: Continuum International, 2011.

Greene, Jay P. "A Survey of Results from Voucher Experiments: Where We Are and What We Know." In *Can the Market Save Our Schools?* edited by Claudia R. Hepburn, 121–49. Vancouver: Fraser Institute, 2000.

Guhr, Daniel, Nelson Furtado, and Andreas Hovland. *Post-School Trajectories and Social Contributions of BC Independent School Graduates.* San Carlos, CA: Illuminate Consulting Group, 2015.

Hoxby, Caroline Minter. "Does Competition Among Public Schools Benefit Students and Taxpayers?" Working Paper No. 4979, National Bureau of Economic Research. Cambridge, 1994. http://www.nber.org/papers/w4979.pdf.

Independent School Act. RSBC, ch. 216 (1996). British Columbia Ministry of Education.

Lieberman, Myron. *Privatization and Educational Choice.* New York: St. Martin's, 1989.

Schneider, Mark, Paul Teske, and Melissa Marschall. *Choosing Schools*. Princeton: Princeton University Press, 2002.

School Act. RSBC, ch. 412 (1996). British Columbia Ministry of Education.

"School Performance: Elementary and Secondary School Rankings." Fraser Institute, n.d. https://www.fraserinstitute.org/school-performance.

"Special Education Survey: Member Schools Within FISA BC." Federation of Independent School Associations, British Columbia, 2011. http://fisabc.ca/sites/default/files/Special%20Ed%20Survey%20Final%20Edited.pdf.

Thiessen, Elmer John. *In Defence of Religious Schools and Colleges*. Montreal: McGill-Queen's University Press, 2001.

Thomas, Paul Lee. *Parental Choice? A Critical Reconsideration of Choice and the Debate About Choice*. Charlotte: Information Age, 2010.

"Treaty of Maastricht on European Union,. EUR-Lex, 2015. http://eur-lex.europa.eu/legal-content/EN/TXT/?uri=uriserv:xy0026.

Walberg, Herbert J. *School Choice: The Findings*. Washington, DC: Cato Institute, 2007.

White, Margaret, and Larry Kuehn. "Does Independent School Funding Make a Mockery of the Public School Funding Formula?" Vancouver: BCTF Research Report, 2015. https://bctf.ca/uploadedFiles/Public/Publications/ResearchReports/RR2015-01(1).pdf.

Wilkinson, Bruce. *Educational Choice: Necessary but Not Sufficient*. Montreal: Institute for Research on Public Policy, 1994.

Wolf, Patrick, et al. "Evaluation of the DC Opportunity Scholarship Program: Final Report." National Center for Education Evaluation and Regional Assistance. Washington, DC: US Department of Education, 2010. http://ies.ed.gov/ncee/pubs/20104018/pdf/20104018.pdf.

9

Full Inclusion and Learners with Exceptional Needs: Educational Ideology vs. Practical Pedagogy

Ken Pudlas

Introduction

FULL INCLUSION—A TERM SURE to garner a visceral response either positive or negative from those involved in education. Variations in response derive from confusion over what inclusion is and is not, varied perspectives of stakeholders, and consequently the degree to which they are invested in the process and the outcome. The purpose of this chapter is to explore the genesis and goals of inclusion and, given that in the majority of Western cultures it is a dominating paradigm for delivering educational services for students with exceptional learning needs, to discuss the efficacy of this paradigm from the perspective of various stakeholders.

Terminology: Full Inclusion

Full inclusion, long the prevailing method of delivering special education services throughout Canada,[1] is becoming increasingly prevalent in developed and developing countries.[2] The term can be applied to both a philosophy and a pedagogy: therein lies part of the tension. Illustrative of themes

---

1. Edmunds, "Preparing Canadian Teachers"; Lupart and McKeough, "Editorial: Schools in Transition."
2. Canadian Council on Learning, "Does Placement Matter?"

common to definitions of inclusion,[3] the Ministry of Education in British Columbia, Canada, describes inclusion as follows:

> British Columbia promotes an inclusive education system in which students with special needs are fully participating members of a community of learners. Inclusion describes the principle that all students are entitled to equitable access to learning, achievement, and the pursuit of excellence in all aspects of their educational programs. The practice of inclusion is not necessarily synonymous with full integration in regular classrooms, and goes beyond placement to include meaningful participation and the promotion of interaction with others.[4]

One of the desired outcomes of full inclusion is that all students in the learning community are valued and accepted and are fully participating members of that community. It has been suggested that a school is inclusive if every student is able to identify and connect with the school's social environment, culture, and organizational life.[5] Thus, full inclusion speaks to goals that transcend objectively measurable academic learning outcomes and relates to the valuing of persons who may, in some instances or particular contexts, be deemed exceptional.

This chapter explores the genesis and goals of inclusion, challenges faced by educators, and briefly offers suggestions for meeting those challenges. Foundational is that in order to meet those challenges and to fulfill the goals of full inclusion it is necessary to bring into confluence the head (knowledge) and the hands (skills) and the heart (dispositions) of educators in order that they be intentionally inviting and inclusive in their praxis (Figure 1).

---

3. Pudlas, "Inclusive Praxis"; Dei et al., *Removing the Margins*, 13; Stainback et al., "Commentary on Inclusion."

4. British Columbia Ministry of Education, "Special Education Services," v.

5. Dei et al., *Removing the Margins*, 13.

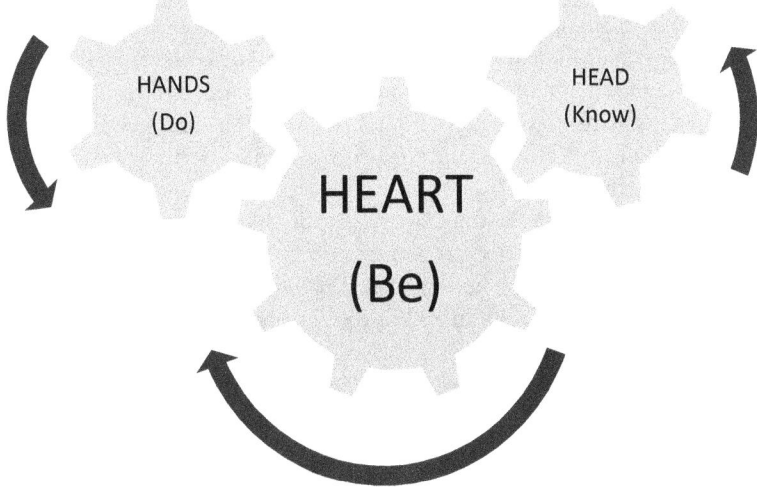

Figure 1. Confluence of head, heart, and hands toward development of inclusive professionals.

Exceptionality

A discussion of inclusion would be moot if all persons were inherently considered an integral part of a whole. For example, we do not speak of including an arm or a toe as part of a body; they simply are a part of the body. The following narrative is offered to set in context the discussion that follows; the story takes place in a church environment which should make the plot all the more surprising.

Cathy's Story

Picture the scene in your mind:

It is a sunny September Sunday morning. The meeting hall is full of children and parents, all dressed in their finest. The children, barely able to contain their excitement, sit in the front rows. Parents, silently hoping their sons and daughters will not somehow embarrass them in front of the entire congregation, sit toward the back.

It is "Promotion Sunday," and in a scene played out in countless churches, students are anxious to meet their new teachers.

One by one they are called to the front, and as the class list is complete they go off with their newfound mentor and spiritual guide. They may even discover some as-yet-unseen part of the church building as they find their new classroom together. First, the primary class goes, and then the older children. The excitement is electric, and the pride is evident on the faces of the parents.

One by one the rows empty. All the children are gone. All but one. She is a pretty girl, blonde and blue-eyed, wearing a new pink dress, sitting where moments before the primary grades had been. Slowly she turns her head, searches for the gaze of her parents, and with a plaintive expression on her face silently mouths the words: *But what about me?*

It is—without doubt—a pathetic scene.

Was this a deliberate slight on the part of the teachers or administrators? Doubtful. What happened? Who was this girl; perhaps a visitor that was overlooked? No, her family were founding members of the congregation, and she had been in the church for some time so she was not a newcomer to this community. I know, because I am a part of that family and Cathy was my younger sister.

Was Cathy included? Clearly not, and the ramifications of her pain and disappointment at being overlooked were felt by her parents and by her older brother. In fact, one of the reasons I am a special educator is because of that experience so many years ago. Cathy was profoundly deaf, and due to her sensory disability she was not one of the typical children in this congregation; rather, she was *exceptional* in that she had extraordinary learning needs.

From the earliest times, humans have been aware of and concerned with differences. As Margaret Winzer states, "Across the range of human behavior, there is some point at which different societies and cultures make a judgement as to whether an individual is normal or abnormal."[6] Those considered different or deviant have faced a different fate depending upon the era in which they were born. That is, the dominant discourse or prevailing worldview influences treatment of the other by those of the majority. One only need recall playground power-politics to see at a simple level how fickle those structures may be. Winzer suggests, "While all societies have faced the fact of individuals who differed physically, intellectually, or socially, how these differences have been addressed mirrors the vibrant and shifting gestalt of societal dynamics and forms one critical indicator of a society's humanity."[7]

6. Winzer, "Confronting Difference," 21.
7. Ibid.

It is a natural human trait to make interpersonal comparisons; societies and cultures determine what constitutes "normal" in a contextual but arbitrary manner. Western cultures have long taken a psychometric approach to intelligence and so approximately two-thirds of the population is considered to lie within one standard deviation of the mean and are thus considered "normal." Others have questioned whether IQ is a valid measure of normalcy, suggesting alternate ways of describing intelligence, that there are varieties of intelligence[8] or that the abilities to regulate one's own emotions and to relate well with others, that is, interpersonal and intrapersonal intelligence, were critical abilities.[9] Those who may have been considered abnormal have been defined differently over time and have been variously labelled as different, disabled, deviant, or exceptional. It is not surprising that "from the dominant discourse perspective, connotations of the opposite of normal tend to be derogative and include terms such as impaired, defective, faulty, damaged, deficient, incapacitated, or broken."[10] If exceptional learners are to be included, then dominant discourses need to be understood.

For the present purpose, and within an educational context, *exceptional learners* refers to those who need extraordinary intervention in order to reach their full learning potential. This functional definition covers a broad range of intellectual, behavioral, and social abilities, and various levels and types of intelligences; the formalized definitions of exceptional learners typically reference their need for *special education*.

Special Education

Generally speaking, special education is barrier removal: the interventions and various modifications and adaptations required by exceptional learners if they are to meet their full learning potential. Those barriers may take many forms and include physical, sensory, emotional, or social barriers and may be inherent in the learner or imposed by the ecology. The nature of the extraordinary interventions also may vary widely from simply providing more time to complete tasks to something as complex as integrating technologies such as communication boards or other devices for those whose barriers involve severe limitations in communication ability. How learners respond to those interventions and the consequent continuation, modification, or discontinuation of those interventions has come to be known as *response*

---

8. Gardner, *Frames of Mind*.
9. Goleman, *Emotional Intelligence*.
10. Fraser and Shields, "Leaders' Roles," 7.

to interventions (RTI).¹¹ Reschly further notes that RTI is evolving into the term *multitier system of supports* (MTSS). Regardless of the term used, the principle is that concerned educators attempt to empower less able learners and have done so throughout history. So while special education and RTI or MTSS are not new, what is new is that the implementation of the process in the current era is based on four principles, often entrenched in legislation, including: scientifically based academic and behavioral interventions, progress monitoring, data-based decision-making, and multitiered levels of intervention matched to student needs.¹²

The evolution of the terms and a focus on the importance of the process rather than merely the product or learning outcome alone are indicative of the educational zeitgeist. The ecology in which these interventions are undertaken is also indicative of the zeitgeist and the current paradigm for service delivery has become known as *inclusion*.

Historical Underpinnings

The treatment of persons deemed different has a long and varied history. A recounting of the nature of that treatment is available from many sources including, for example, the work of Margaret Winzer.¹³ History, however, is more than the recounting of events—that would be chronology. Rather, history examines the reasons surrounding those events. In effect, then, the history of special education, culminating in the most recent paradigm, full inclusion, is a reflection of the zeitgeist throughout various cultures and eras. It might be said that "the field [of special education] can catalogue a long series of reforms constructed in particular eras in response to political rhetoric, social perceptions, and fiscal conditions."¹⁴

Full inclusion (FI) in its current iteration, as a form of delivering services to learners who have exceptional needs, is derived from principles of *normalization* proposed by Wolf Wolfensberger, in which he espoused that all persons should live with dignity as close to normal as possible.¹⁵ While a full review of the history of the inclusion movement is beyond the scope of this chapter; nevertheless, two recent examples are instructive as to how and why education, in particular in North American cultures, espouses a

---

11. Reschly, "Response to Intervention."
12. Ibid., 40.
13. Winzer, "Confronting Difference."
14. Ibid., 22.
15. Wolfensberger, *Normalization*.

paradigm of inclusion and are discussed here prior to returning to a discussion of inclusive praxis.

The first example is taken from the early portion of the twentieth century and the second is taken from the latter half. During the rise of the Nazi regime, a time of extreme social and economic tension in Europe, the T4 Euthanasia Project in pre-war Nazi Germany used "science" to give legitimacy to a worldview that condoned the killing of persons with mental and physical disabilities.[16] Essentially, scientists proved that there were those in society who, due to some form of defect, consumed more energy than they contributed to society. Thus, as proven by science, which was considered at the time infallible, a class of humans became known as "Useless Eaters" and, again, based on science, these people were "euthanized" for the betterment of society as a whole. The atrocities committed as part of what has come to be known as the Holocaust used methods tried and perfected on those who did not fit into the norm of society.

The second example, that of normalization as espoused by Wolf Wolfensberger, came about during the zeitgeist after the Second World War in a time of economic and social renewal.[17] In the prior century in North America, the treatment of persons deemed exceptional is described as follows:

> Prompted by Enlightenment thought, early nineteenth century Americans found a common level of sympathy to improve the lives of people who were weak, dependent, or disabled. Founded on a humanitarian philosophy, evangelical commitment, and unbounded philanthropy, they established from 1817 onwards a complex of institutions designed to cater to the unique needs of exceptional individuals.[18]

However, what began with the best of intentions of protecting and providing for the vulnerable and weaker persons in society had a secondary consequence. The institutions that were built had the effect of limiting the opportunity and social interaction of those who were housed in them. Further, the role models in such institutions were also limited and thus, residents were often limited in their social growth and development.

Returning to the concise historical overview provided by Winzer, she describes the 1960s as a time of egalitarianism and humanism.[19] Along with race-related issues, questions arose concerning segregation of students with disabilities.

16. Mostert, "Useless Eaters."
17. Wolfensberger, *Normalization*.
18. Winzer, "Confronting Difference," 24.
19. Ibid.

So it was that into this environment, in what was at that time arguably the most affluent nation on earth (the United States of America), that Wolf Wolfensberger observed the plight of these exceptional and marginalized persons in large institutions.[20] His treatise, *The Normalization Principle*, helped give impetus to the movement to close institutions that historically had come to "warehouse" people, and it caused the critical examination of a worldview that during that same century had deemed it acceptable to exterminate persons deemed unfit for society. The zeitgeist during which Wolfensberger espoused normalization was also one where people of color in America were demanding equal rights. Also during this era young people, facing being drafted into military service in Vietnam, a war they considered not their own, began to question all forms of established authority. In this climate a movement toward integration grew.

More recently and as a result of over-familiarization and over-use of the term "normalization," Wolfensberger suggested the concept of *Social Role Valorization* (SRV).[21] Social Role Valorization refers to the application of empirical knowledge to the shaping of the current or potential social roles of a party (i.e., person, group, or class)—primarily by means of enhancement of the party's competencies and image—so that these are, as much as possible, positively valued in the eyes of the perceivers.[22] Note the SRV goal of seeing all persons as valued. This fits well with the previous discussion of the historical treatment of persons with disabilities.

A question that should continually be asked is whether all those in the community are fully participating and see themselves as valued and accepted. One empirical measure of community is a perception of acceptance by peers. Some early research suggested that those perceptions, based on measures of students' reported peer self-concept, are not necessarily positive.[23] In response to prompts such as "When kids go out to play they ask me to play with them," students with identified special needs responded significantly less positively than their peers who did not have identified special needs. More needs to be done by way of teaching prosocial skills in order to achieve more inclusive outcomes from the perspective of students.

As to teachers' perspectives, nearly two decades ago two-thirds supported the concept of mainstreaming/inclusion.[24] Fewer, however, were willing to put it into practice, and current results are similar. Teachers' con-

---

20. Wolfensberger, *Normalization*.
21. Wolfensberger and Thomas, *Introductory Social Role Valorization*.
22. Osborn, "Overview of Social Role," 4.
23. Pudlas, "Inclusive Educational Practice."
24. Scruggs and Mastropieri, "Teacher Perceptions."

cerns may derive from increasingly diverse educational communities. That diversity comes in many forms; while the focus here is on diverse learning needs in the traditional categories of special education, some of the principles apply more broadly. Other challenges derive from top-down legislation resulting in a kind of alphabet soup upon which we might choke: IDEA, which guarantees a FAPE in the LRE, and the President want NCLB, and the CAP has now focused primarily on FI. To clarify for those not conversant with "Ed-speak": Individuals with Disabilities Education Act (IDEA), Free Appropriate Public Education (FAPE), Least Restrictive Environment (LRE), No Child Left Behind (NCLB), Cascade of Alternative Placements (CAP), and Full Inclusion (FI). Perhaps the "R" in LRE comes (inadvertently) from the educational ecology. By that I mean any of a number of factors including both the skill set and the attitude of teachers (see Figure 2).

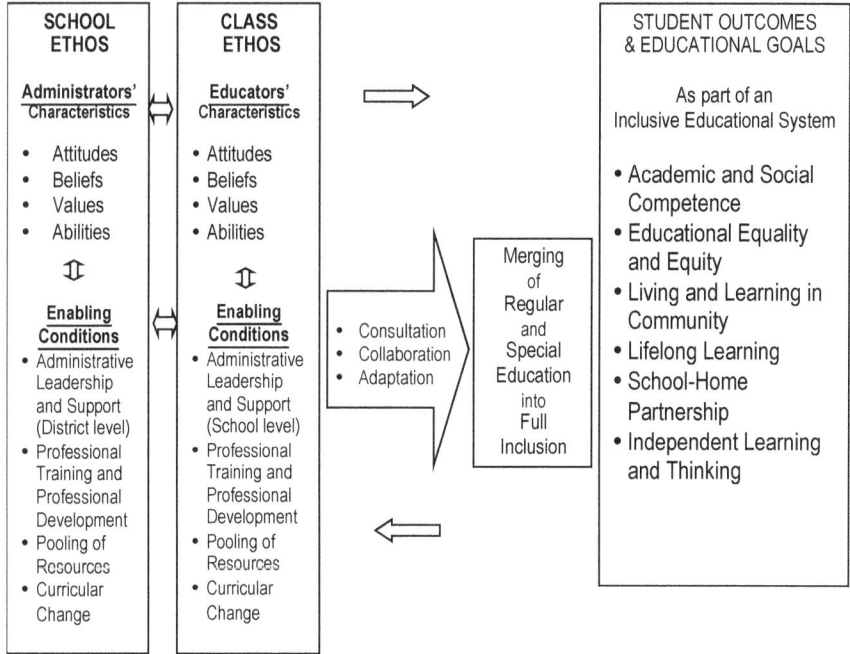

Figure 2.
Factors influencing positive outcomes of full inclusion. Kenneth A. Pudlas. (2010)

Vocation and Praxis

The act of teaching is represented by various metaphors, including as an art, a science, or gardening, and of course in religious settings, teaching is seen as ministry. Suggested here is a metaphor of teaching as a *vocation*. The metaphor with which we identify is critical. Fetterman and Robinson state, "In early 1999, Lakoff and Johnson suggested that conceptual metaphors guide thought, emotion, and behavior in a hitherto unappreciated manner."[25] Vocation, or literally calling, implies a purpose greater than merely a job or earning a living. The demands imposed by the confluence of increased diversity, an increasingly pluralistic worldview and a pervasive philosophy of full inclusion, plus the reality of reduced resources, pose challenges to teachers' efficacy in their calling. If educators' dispositions are such that they see teaching as a vocation and inclusion is a part of their praxis, the result will benefit both student and teacher. It is time we critically reexamine, in light of our current culture, the preparation of educators in regard to the knowledge and skills needed and the dispositions that motivate them both by way of preservice and in-service education.

Inclusive Praxis—The Heart of the Matter

The term *praxis* as used here refers to a habitual act or performance—something that is so ingrained in our nature that it does not require conscious thought; something that is done to a level of *automaticity*. For example, compare the actions of experienced drivers to those of a novice. The latter need to think about each action and may even plan their route in advance to avoid challenging intersections or having to stop and start on steep hills.

In contrast, experienced drivers may arrive at a destination without once having given thought to the driving actions required to get there; in fact, they may not even give thought to the route, they just leave with a goal in mind and arrive there safely. Or consider novice teachers who are so tied to their carefully composed lesson plan that they dare not deviate. This chapter suggests that including all learners in the learning community ought to be that automatic. Praxis, then, relates to and derives from how educators perceive their role and how they measure success in that role. In this context it refers to the very heart of who we are. The words of Parker Palmer are germane as he states, "Teaching, like any truly human activity, emerges from one's inwardness, for better or worse. As I teach, I project the condition of my soul onto my students, my subject, and our way of being

---

25. Fetterman and Robinson, "Do You Use Your Head," 316.

together."²⁶ As noted, any number of metaphors for teaching can be suggested; vocation is the focus here and some of the psychosocial literature on vocation is offered for consideration.

Vocation

This chapter adopts the metaphor of teaching as vocation. Answers to questions often begin with an attempt to simply make sense of the world, and humans depend heavily on language and narrative, and further metaphor serves the purpose well in that it enables us to conceptualize what we do not understand relative to that which we do.²⁷ Vocation or calling is not a new concept but has only recently been studied in the social science literature. Vocation connotes much more than merely a task or a job and even more than a career, and the term would connote an investment and a passion beyond merely doing a job. Concomitantly, there are numerous challenges such as cultural shifts, devolving family structures, and educational paradigm shifts that impact teachers' vocational satisfaction.

An interesting perspective on calling is presented by Lundmark in an article entitled, "Vocation in Theology-based Nursing Theories," in which he argues that "theology-based nursing theories are useful tools or frameworks for the discussion of intrinsic motivating factors, such as vocation."²⁸ In his discussion, Lundmark suggests that a correct understanding of the concepts of vocation is a personal identification with the social and moral meanings and values of [nursing] work.²⁹ In as much as nursing and teaching are related by being helping professions, this melding of scientific theory and theology is intriguing. In support of this notion, Wilson, as cited by Dukes et al., states, "Interdisciplinary thought is not new and many believe that even the most seemingly diverse fields can benefit from borrowing concepts and ideas from the other."³⁰ Given the metaphor of teaching as vocation and the prevailing educational paradigm of full inclusion, the discussion now turns to potential challenges to vocational satisfaction.

---

26. Palmer, *Courage to Teach*, 2.
27. Dukes et al., "Future Selection Pressures."
28. Lundmark, "Vocation," 767.
29. Ibid., 769.
30. Dukes et al., "Future Selection Pressures," 5.

Ego Integrity versus Despair

Erik Erikson's contributions to psychosocial development theory included his notion of eight dichotomous stages, beginning in infancy with trust versus mistrust and ending in later adulthood with wisdom and ego integrity versus despair.[31] At each stage a positive or a negative choice is available and the choice influences healthy development of the individual. It is the latter stage—wisdom and ego integrity versus despair—that is of import here. In this stage adults are said by Erikson to reflect on whether they have lived a life and reached a point in that life where they are true to themselves (ego) and to who they are relative to who they are meant to be; satisfied that they have done well in their vocation. When reflection leads to a sense that the true calling has been missed, or at least not fully achieved, the result is despair.

Challenges to Vocational Efficacy

In an issue of the journal, *Teacher Education and Special Education*, authors Rosenberg and Walther-Thomas opine that

> more than ever before, colleges and universities preparing teachers for work in complex learning environments (e.g. special education, low-income schools, urban and rural communities) must be able to demonstrate the value of the preparation their graduates receive.[32]

One source of complexity, inclusion, a term applicable to both service delivery for students with special needs and to multicultural classrooms, derives from a time of *optimism* and perhaps altruism. The zeitgeist saw racial integration and, in Canada, multiculturalism, during a time of *Trudeauian idealism*. Canada was officially proclaimed to be a multicultural country by then Prime Minister Pierre Elliott Trudeau on October 8, 1971, and in the early 1970s multiculturalism emerged as a new policy emphasis. Forty years after the birth of official multiculturalism in Canada the once-sacrosanct idea is met today with ambivalence by many Canadians. Recent humanitarian crises worldwide have brought a new influx of immigration to many nations. In Canada the multiculturalism policy may give rise to concern that nurturing a mosaic-like patchwork of cultures within a single country could undermine the creation of a coherent, unified national culture. Mosaics or quilts are only as strong as the glue or thread that hold the component parts together.

---

31. Erikson, *Life Cycle Completed*.
32. Rosenberg and Walther-Thomas, "Innovation, Policy, and Capacity," 79.

Demographics

Classroom ecologies are diverse—in cultures, abilities, and worldviews. In British Columbia's largest school district nearly, 42 percent of the sixty-five thousand students come from homes where English is not the primary language; in Vancouver, English is the language spoken in only 45 percent of the homes of the more than fifty-five thousand students.[33]

Individualism

From the early nineteenth century, Canadians held common ideals about the *value* of education, faced common *issues* concerning provision of schools and schooling, and historically met these issues with common *responses*. However, an increase in individualism and a subtle move toward secularizing society mean a changing paradigm. Understanding the relationship between education and society is the goal of sociology of education. Emile Durkheim, the acknowledged father of modern sociology, in light of the transition from traditional to modern societies, explored factors that provide for regularity in modern life.[34] In the face of increasing individualism, Durkheim questioned what was replacing the authoritative voice of religion, which had traditionally supplied the mores of a society.

Pluralism

As the purpose statement of the Ministry of Education in British Columbia suggests, it is the role of the school to develop knowledge, skills, and attitudes, and to do so in a democratic and pluralistic society.[35] This is to apply to all learners and is, therefore, inclusive. In a pluralistic society, however, no single worldview predominates, and if a society is increasingly bent on secularization by the removal of religion from the sphere of public influence, educators face a near impossible task: teaching values where all values are to be given equal weight. This may be yet another factor putting teachers' professional efficacy, not to mention the goals of full inclusion, at risk.

---

33. British Columbia Ministry of Education, "Overview of Class Size."
34. Wotherspoon, *Sociology of Education*.
35. British Columbia Ministry of Education, "2015/16–2017/18 Service Plan," 4.

Doing More with Less—
Simple Suggestions toward Inclusive Praxis

Ironically contrary to the spirit of LRE, as described in American legislation, public school educators perceive themselves as increasingly restricted and constrained and are thus less likely to provide the LRE experience for their students. A few simple ideas follow, all of which require a revisioning of what the vocation of teaching entails if educators are to be inclusive in their praxis.

Teachers' Professional Development

Professional development is as much the process of holistic development of the person who is the professional as it is a particular program or set of workshops or other learning opportunities.[36] Pre-service and in-service preparation of educators leads to more positive dispositions toward actual inclusion.[37] In this regard, the notion of "inviting school success" and principles of invitational education have implications for building more inclusive communities.[38] That is, educators may be more inviting if they adhere to five basic principles as discussed by Purkey and Novak and summarized here:

1. People are able, valuable, and responsible and should be treated accordingly.
2. Educating should be a collaborative, cooperative activity.
3. The process is the product in the making.
4. People possess untapped potential in all areas of worthwhile human endeavour.
5. This potential can best be realized by places, policies, programs, and processes specifically designed to invite development and by people who are intentionally inviting with themselves and others personally and professionally.[39]

The notion of inviting schools begins with attention to the conscious and subconscious perceptions of what makes an educator effective; that is, to be professionally inviting, educators need to be personally inviting. In

---

36. Pudlas, "Leading Teachers."
37. Ibid.
38. Purkey and Novak, *Inviting School Success*; Purkey, "Creating Safe Schools."
39. Purkey and Novak, *Inviting School Success*.

the context of this chapter personally inviting would derive from that sense of calling and of higher purpose that would necessarily result in a different assessment of effectiveness. As noted by Rosenberg and Walther-Thomas, unfortunately, today the overall "value" of a teacher's effectiveness is tied too closely to students' performance on standardized tests.[40]

Changing Dominant Discourses

The concept of *neurodiversity* is one example of a revisioning of how students who have atypical learning needs are perceived. It stands in contrast to some of the dominant discourses discussed earlier; perception matters, and it is important to rewrite dominant discourses. The current educational focus appears to be on what makes students different and on efforts to enable them to conform to the norm. Thomas Armstrong states, "The idea of neurodiversity is really a paradigm shift in how we think about kids in special education. Instead of regarding these students as suffering from deficit, disease, or dysfunction, neurodiversity suggests that we speak about their strengths."[41] In keeping with the earlier discussion in this paper concerning vocation and questions related to it—such as what are my strengths, what are my passions—this revisioning to thinking of neurodiversity rather than deficits applies to students as well. Armstrong refers to *positive niche construction* as an environment in which a student (with special needs) can flourish in school. This is not a dissimilar concept from the notion posited in this paper of vocational thriving. As it applies to students with diverse learning needs, Armstrong suggests seven factors:

1. A comprehensive assessment of student strengths
2. Use of assistive technologies and Universal Design for Learning methodologies
3. Provision of enhanced human resources
4. Implementation of strength-based learning strategies
5. Envisioning of positive role models
6. Activation of affirmative career aspirations
7. Engineering of appropriate environmental modifications to support the development of neurodiverse students[42]

40. Rosenberg and Walther-Thomas, "Innovation, Policy, and Capacity," 79.
41. Armstrong, *Neurodiversity in the Classroom*, 9.
42. Ibid., 4.

Knowledge and Skills for Inclusive Praxis

Five critical dimensions of successful inclusive classrooms have been identified as:

1. A sense of community and social acceptance
2. An appreciation of student diversity
3. Attention to curricular needs
4. Effective management and instruction
5. Personnel support and collaboration[43]

The first two of these have already been addressed as they relate to the heart of the teacher and the desire to create community. A full exploration of the other three dimensions is beyond the scope of the chapter; the extant challenges require much more training and education than have traditionally been available. Nevertheless, a few suggestions follow, including research-based strategies such as differentiating instruction, anchoring instruction, cooperative learning, peer tutoring, and strategic learning.

Differentiating instruction involves beginning where students are (rather than where curriculum says they should be). Teachers need to use time flexibly and employ a range of teaching strategies. It is important to create a community of learners where teachers and students are partners. Plan, for example, using preferred intelligences, which acknowledge how students are smart rather than how smart students are. In this regard, Howard Gardner's theory of multiple intellegences is instructive. Also plan and teach using cooperative activities based on authentic problems. It is imperative that students and teachers utilize inter- and intra-personal intelligences to understand themselves and to relate with one another.[44]

Anchoring instruction promotes higher-order thinking by using a conceptual anchor (e.g., video) so learners build a mental model. It allows for a common frame of reference. Students then construct their own knowledge through disciplined inquiry combined with problem-based or project-based learning. General guidelines include: choose appropriate anchor, set guidelines for group structure, practice general problem-solving skills (e.g., defining the problem), choose authentic problem, and have individual (as well as group) accountability.

Cooperative learning is another teacher-tool. Not all group work is cooperative learning. The human brain is a social brain and so cooperative

---

43. Smith et al., *Teaching Students*.
44. Goleman, *Emotional Intelligence*.

learning allows students to engage in instructional conversations that clarify, probe, and solidify learning. Teachers should group purposely (heterogeneously according to strengths/needs), model appropriate behavior in groups, and monitor learning (consistently interview students). It is important that teachers encourage groups to include diverse learners and that they clearly structure tasks with clear guidelines. The latter may mean task analysis and precision teaching application for those with diverse needs.

Peer tutoring has been proven successful for students with diverse learning needs. It can be cross-age or same age. Some guidelines for class-wide peer tutoring include: each member of a pair share roles, train each in giving feedback and error correction procedures, have each member practice—with teacher monitoring, and begin with less complex drill and practice (choose materials appropriate to skill level). Three important principles of instruction are individualization of the targeted skill, frequent opportunities to respond and rapid pace of instruction, and immediate corrective feedback.

Strategic learning may need to be taught. It is possible that some students simply have not learned how to learn; that is, they have no learning strategy. Students tend to intuit strategies and learn from observing others, but those with specific learning disabilities (SLDs) may not. Direct instruction of a specific strategy may pay dividends. One example is of a collaborative strategic reading process: *previewing* (reading title and headings) and *predicting* (what the passage is about); then get the *gist* (restating most important idea); finally *wrap up* (summarize what has been learned and ask questions that teacher might ask on a test). Strategic learning incorporates responsibility for mutual learning within a cooperative learning format. It uses think aloud techniques, modeling, and practice in using the strategies (i.e., verbal mediation is modeled).

Summary and Conclusions

A Reflective Retrospective

Imagine (recall) the initial optimism, boundless energy, and the outright idealism of beginning teachers; hopes, dreams, ambitions, and idealistic goals may succumb to fears, concerns, and unmet challenges. Educators may no longer be clear on individual and collective ultimate goals and a subsequent devolution to survival mode has come about because the vision of the original goal or a sense of hope and optimism are lost.

Full inclusion is not going away; nor should it, in a just and progressive society. Problems derive, however, when an ideological perspective becomes an educational imperative without the necessary preparation and supports. Teachers need to be willing to take advantage of every opportunity for professional development in order to become professionally inviting. Educators of teachers must also realize that their curricula should be viewed in a new taxonomy: head plus heart plus hands, or mind plus motive plus methods. The research on vocational satisfaction indicates that viewing work as a calling enhances outcomes. This chapter offered a brief exploration of how inclusive praxis might be fostered to achieve in reality what are certainly laudable goals.

Reflection Questions

1. Provide a rationale for the normalization movement.
2. From the perspective of all stakeholders, list and discuss the pros and cons for full inclusion.
3. Read several narratives of persons who may be deemed exceptional. Compare the lived experience of the protagonists. How do their lives differ depending on the era in which they were born and the nature of their disability.
4. Research the literature regarding the cost/benefit of providing special education. For example, what is the proportion of incarcerated persons who have a specific learning disability (e.g., dyslexia)?

Bibliography

Armstrong, Thomas. *Neurodiversity in the Classroom: Strength-Based Strategies to Help Students with Special Needs Succeed in School and in Life.* Alexandria, VA: ASCD, 2010.

British Columbia Ministry of Education. "2015/16–2017/18 Service Plan." Victoria, BC: Ministry of Education, 2015. http://www.bcbudget.gov.bc.ca/2015/sp/pdf/ministry/educ.pdf?page=#4.

———. "Overview of Class Size and Composition in British Columbia Public Schools 2015/16." Victoria, BC: Ministry of Education, 2015. https://www.bced.gov.bc.ca/reports/pdfs/class_size/2015/public.pdf.

———. "Special Education Services: A Manual of Policies, Procedures, and Guidelines." Victoria, BC: Ministry of Education, 2016. http://files.eric.ed.gov/fulltext/ED414703.pdf.

Canadian Council on Learning. "Does Placement Matter? Comparing the Academic Performance of Students with Special Needs in Inclusive and Separate Settings." March 18, 2009. http://files.eric.ed.gov/fulltext/ED519296.pdf.

Chapman, David, and Malcolm Lowther. "Teachers' Satisfaction with Teaching." *The Journal of Educational Research* 75 (1982) 241–47.

Dei, George, et al. *Removing the Margins: The Challenges and Possibilities of Inclusive Schooling.* Toronto: Canadian Scholars, 2000.

Dik, Bryan, et al. "Development and Validation of the Calling and Vocation Questionnaire (CVQ) and Brief Calling Scale (BCS)." *Journal of Career Assessment* 20 (2012) 242–63.

Dukes, Charles, et al. "Future Selection Pressures on Special Education Teacher Preparation: Issues Shaping Our Future." *Teacher Education and Special Education* 37 (2014) 9–20.

Edmunds, Alan L. "Preparing Canadian Teachers for Inclusion." *Exceptionality Education Canada* 13 (2003) 5–7.

Edmunds, Alan L., and Robert B. Macmillan, eds. *Leadership for Inclusion: A Practical Guide.* Rotterdam, Netherlands: Sense Publishers, 2010.

Erikson, Erik. *The Life Cycle Completed.* New York: Norton, 1998.

Fetterman, Adam, and Michael Robinson. "Do You Use Your Head or Follow Your Heart? Self-Location Predicts Personality, Emotion, Decision Making, and Performance." *Journal of Personality and Social Psychology* 105 (2013) 316–34.

Fraser, Deborah F. G., and Carolyn M. Shields. "Leaders' Roles in Disrupting Dominant Discourses." In *Leadership for Inclusion: A Practical Guide*, edited by Alan L. Edmunds and Robert B. Macmillan, 7–18. Rotterdam, Netherlands: Sense Publishers, 2010.

Gardner, Howard. *Frames of Mind: The Theory of Multiple Intelligences.* 3rd ed. New York: Basic Books, 2011.

Goleman, Daniel. *Emotional Intelligence.* Toronto: Bantam, 1995.

Lundmark, Mikael. "Vocation in Theology-Based Nursing Theories." *Nursing Ethics* 14 (2007) 767–80.

Lupart, Judy, and Ann McKeough, eds. "Editorial: Schools in Transition: International Perspectives." *Exceptionality Education Canada* 12 (2010) 3–6.

Mostert, Mark P. "Useless Eaters: Disability as Genocidal Marker in Nazi Germany." *The Journal of Special Education* 36 (2002) 155–68.

Noddings, Nell. "All Our Students Thinking." *Educational Leadership* 65 (2008) 8–13.

Osburn, Joe. "An Overview of Social Role Valorization Theory." *The SRV Journal* 1 (2006) 4–13.

Palmer, Parker. *Courage to Teach.* San Francisco: J. Wiley, 2007.

Pudlas, Kenneth A. "Inclusive Educational Practice: Perceptions of Students and Teachers." *Exceptionality Education Canada* 13 (2003) 49–64.

———. "Inclusive Praxis: Requisite Confluence of Head and Heart and Hands." Paper presented at Hawaii International Conference on Education, Oahu, Hawaii, January 2012.

———. "Inviting Inclusive Education: Affective Considerations." Paper presented at the Inclusive and Supportive Education Conference, University of Strathclyde, Glasgow, Scotland, August 2005.

———. "Leading Teachers in Professional Development for Inclusion." In *Leadership for Inclusion: A Practical Guide*, edited by Alan L. Edmunds and Robert B. Macmillan, 117–30. Rotterdam, Netherlands: Sense Publishers, 2010.

Purkey, William. "Creating Safe Schools through Invitational Education." *ERIC Digest* (1999) 1–6. http://files.eric.ed.gov/fulltext/ED435946.pdf.

Purkey, William, and John Novak. *Inviting School Success: A Self-Concept Approach to Teaching, Learning, and Democratic Process*. 3rd ed. Toronto: Wadsworth, 1996.

Reschly, Daniel J. "Response to Intervention and the Identification of Specific Learning Disabilities." *Topics in Language Disorders* 34 (2014) 39–58.

Rosenberg, Michael S., and Christine Walther-Thomas. "Innovation, Policy, and Capacity in Special Education Teacher Education: Competing Demands in Challenging Times." *Teacher Education and Special Education* 37 (2014) 77–82.

Scruggs, Thomas E., and Margo A. Mastropieri. "Teacher Perceptions of Mainstreaming/ Inclusion, 1958–1995: A Research Synthesis." *Exceptional Children* 63 (1996) 59–74.

Smith, Tom, et al. *Teaching Students with Special Needs in Inclusive Settings*. 5th Canadian ed. Toronto: Pearson, 2015.

Stainback, Susan, et al. "A Commentary on Inclusion and the Development of a Positive Self-Identity by People with Disabilities." *Exceptional Children* 60 (1994) 486–90.

Steger, Michael, et al. "Assessing Meaning and Satisfaction at Work." In *The Oxford Handbook of Positive Psychology Assessment*, edited by Shane J. Lopez. 2nd ed. Oxford: Oxford University Press, in press.

Usher, Ellen L., and Frank Pajares. "Sources of Self-Efficacy in School: Critical Review of Literature and Future Directions." *Review of Educational Research* 78 (2008) 751–96.

Winzer, Margaret. "Confronting Difference: An Excursion through the History of Special Education." In *The SAGE Handbook of Special Education*, edited by Lani Florian, 20–33. London: SAGE, 2006.

Wolfensberger, Wolf. *Normalization: The Principle of Normalization in Human Services*. Toronto: Leonard Crainford, 1972.

Wolfensberger, Wolf, and Susan Thomas. *Introductory Social Role Valorization Workshop Training Package*. Syracuse: Training Institute for Human Service Planning, Leadership, and Change Agentry, Syracuse University, 2005.

Wotherspoon, Terry. *Sociology of Education in Canada*. Toronto: Oxford University Press, 2009.

10

Building Resilience in Children in Relation to Bullying, Discipline, and Classroom Management

Lucinda Spaulding

Introduction

SCHOOLS AND TEACHERS HAVE had a long history of playing a significant role in fostering resilience in children and youth. Resilience is quite simply success in the face of adversity.[1] Resilience was first exclusively considered trait based, but as understanding of the construct developed, researchers began to compile lists of risk and protective factors, positing that students with a greater list of protective factors than risk factors would be resilient. However, recent research demonstrates that resilience is the result of a dynamic and multifaceted interaction between an individual and his or her environment.[2]

This chapter is grounded in a socioecological approach to resilience, which theorizes that an individual's environment and social interactions play a significant role in his or her ability to cope with adversity.[3] As one of the greatest adversities experienced by children in schools today is bullying,[4] the focus of this chapter is on preventative and responsive measures teachers can employ to foster students' resilience to bullying. This chapter begins with an overview of bullying and its effects on students and is followed by recommendations for educators to provide structure and support for stu-

1. Cefai, "Pupil Resilience."
2. Luthar et al., "Construct of Resilience."
3. Ibid.
4. Due and Holstein, "Bullying Victimization."

dents in the school environment in order to foster positive peer relationships and relational resilience. This chapter is based on the premise that educators are uniquely positioned within the context of schools to provide children the opportunity to learn skills and develop relationships that increase their potential to overcome, and even be made stronger by adversity.[5]

Bullying

Bullying is a systemic and persistent problem with school children today. On average, 31.2 percent of youth surveyed from sixty-six countries reported experiencing peer victimization in the two months prior to the survey; some countries reported rates up to 60 percent.[6] Considered the most prevalent form of youth violence, bullying can begin as early as preschool, progress through elementary school, peak in middle school, and persist in high school.[7]

Bullying is characterized by a power imbalance between the perpetrator and the victim as a result of repetitious behavior with intent to cause harm.[8] Bullying can be classified as *traditional* or *cyber*. Traditional bullying may be *physical* (e.g., hitting, kicking, spitting), *verbal* (e.g., oral, written, gestures that cause harm), or *relational* (e.g., ignoring, excluding, isolating). Cyber bullying is similar in nature and purpose, but the aggression is carried out via electronic media (e.g., hostile phone calls or texts, spreading rumors via social media, etc.). Cyberbullying differs from traditional bullying in that the bully may be anonymous and the network of relationships may be broader. While teachers have typically been most likely to intervene with traditional bullying involving physical aggression, teachers are beginning to realize their role in dealing with relational and cyberbullying given the effects such forms of bullying have on students in the classroom.[9]

Different types of bullying are associated with different ages and developmental phases. For example, physical bullying is more prevalent in the lower elementary years, while relational bullying tends to become more prevalent in older children and adolescents. Relational bullying, which has more typically been associated with girls, though can also surface among boys, tends to have more severe and longer term effects on victims than

---

5. Christiansen and Christiansen, "Using Protective Factors."

6. Due and Holstein, "Bullying Victimization"; Smokowski and Kopasz, "Bullying in School."

7. Chen and Astor, "Perpetration of School Violence."

8. Boulton et al., "Comparison of Preservice Teachers' Responses."

9. Ibid.

physical bullying.[10] Sadly, research suggests this form of bullying is often overlooked due to its covert nature or is viewed by teachers as normal behavior in school and just "part of the process of growing up."[11] While it is outside the scope of this chapter to discuss, it is important to note there are other types of bullying within the school context in addition to peer-to-peer victimization. Teachers can also be perpetrators and victimize students[12] and teachers can also be victims of bullying and cyberbullying by students.[13]

Characteristics of Victims and Bullies

Students fall into three general categories related to bullying: (a) bullies, (b) victims, (c) bully-victims.[14] According to Nansel et al., 13 percent of students are bullies, 10.6 percent are victims, and 6.3 percent are bully-victims.[15] While any child may become a victim, there are some children who are at higher risk of being bullied. Children with special needs and disabilities are more likely to be bullied than their general education peers.[16] Children with communicative disorders who may struggle to develop and maintain friendships are especially at risk.[17] Of a sample of thirty-four parents of children with autism spectrum disorder, 65 percent reported their children were bullied.[18] In a survey of 267 adults who stuttered, 83 percent reported experiencing bullying in school.[19] A study on students with learning disabilities (LD) revealed these students were bullied three times more than their general education peers.[20] In addition to having a disability, several other factors place students at higher risk of being bullied, including

---

10. Bauman and Del Rio, "Pre-service Teachers' Responses."
11. Ibid.; Feinburg, "Bullying Prevention."
12. Lyles, "School Psychologists' Experiences"; James et al., "Bullying Behavior"; Twemlow and Fonagy, "Prevalence of Teachers."
13. Davenport, "Educators' Perspectives"; Terry, "Teachers as Targets."
14. Berkowitz and Benbenishty, "Perceptions of Teachers' Support"; Nansel et al., "Bullying Behaviors."
15. Nansel et al., "Bullying Behaviors."
16. Blood et al., "Bullying in Children"; Cappadocia, Weiss, and Pepler, "Bullying Experiences"; Dev and Burdulis, "Bullying Among Female Elementary Students."
17. Cappadocia, Weiss, and Pepler, "Bullying Experiences."
18. Carter, "Bullying of Students."
19. Hugh-Jones and Smith, "Self-Reports."
20. Dev and Burdulis, "Bullying Among Female Elementary Students."

having poor parent-child relationships,[21] poor peer-relationships,[22] mental health problems,[23] or parents with mental health problems.[24] Additional risk factors include low self-confidence or lack of assertiveness.[25]

Just as any child may be a victim, any child may also be a perpetrator. In fact, many incidences of bullying fly completely under a teacher's radar as a child involved in more covert types of bullying (e.g., relational) or anonymous bullying (e.g., forms of cyberbullying) may not be easily identifiable. In fact, bullies and tormentors may even be "friends" of the victim.[26] However, bullies are typically characterized as having aggression, poor psychosocial functioning, physical strength, and "little anxiety or insecurity due to their strength and control over others."[27] Children who bully are also characterized by impulsivity, lack of empathy for others, a need for dominance, and aggression in conflict situations.[28]

Effects of Bullying

Bullying may have profound, significant, and long-term repercussions on victims *and* bullies. As a consequence of being bullied, victims may experience a range of short- and long-term social challenges, including loneliness, isolation, and poor social relationships with peers.[29] Victims tend to be unpopular and may struggle to identify even one friend.[30]

Victims may exhibit a host of emotional and psychological problems, including depression and anxiety,[31] hyperactivity, poor or low self-concept,[32] and low self-esteem, and self-efficacy.[33] Bullying can lead to self-injurious behavior and suicidal ideation.[34] In general, children who are bullied have

---

21. Spriggs et al., "Adolescent Bullying."
22. Delfabbro et al., "Peer and Teacher."
23. Fekkes et al., "Do Bullied Children Get Ill."
24. Cappodacia, Weiss, and Pepler, "Bullying Experiences."
25. Ibid.
26. Hammel, "Bouncing Back."
27. Berkowitz, "Student and Teacher Responses," 491.
28. Olweus, *Bullying at School*, 34–45.
29. Gini and Pozzoli, "Association Between Bullying."
30. Olweus, *Bullying at School*, 31–33.
31. Hawker and Boulton, "Twenty Years' Research."
32. Cappodacia, Weiss, and Pepler, "Bullying Experiences."
33. Kowalski et al., *Cyberbullying*, 30–31.
34. Herba et al., "Victimization and Suicide Ideation."

higher levels of mental health problems[35] and demonstrate more behavioral and emotional problems over time when compared to their peers who are not bullied.[36] Problems include maladjustment, disrupted concentration,[37] lack of interest in school, low appetite, and trouble sleeping.[38] Victims are also at risk for substance abuse and are more likely to carry weapons to school.[39] A history of being bullied has been attributed to school shootings.[40]

Bullying also impacts students academically, with victims experiencing attention and concentration difficulties, which naturally impede their ability to learn.[41] Sadly, victimization tends to exacerbate communication disabilities and further decrease a child's confidence and ability to take academic and relational risks in the classroom.[42] Further, victims may stop attending school to avoid being further victimized.[43] In fact, students who are bullied are more likely to drop out of school than peers who are not bullied.

The repercussions of bullying are not limited to victims. Perpetrators are also at risk for mental health disorders, conduct disorders, oppositional defiance disorder, and attention disorders.[44] Post-school outcomes for children who bully are also grim, with these students being at risk for poor career performance, engaging in criminal behavior, domestic violence, and substance abuse.[45] Clearly, bullying is a serious problem with profound repercussions for a significant number of children in schools around the world today. Further, "bullying doesn't occur in a vacuum. A host of factors contribute to its existence."[46] The section that follows discusses ways educators can proactively address factors associated with bullying.

---

35. Fekkes et al., "Do Bullied Children Get Ill."
36. Bowes et al., "Families Promote."
37. Boulton, Trueman, and Murray, "Associations Between."
38. Olweus, *Bullying at School*, 54–58.
39. Cappadocia, Weiss, and Pepler, "Bullying Experiences."
40. Nansel et al., "Bullying Behaviors."
41. Boulton, Trueman, and Murray, "Associations Between."
42. Cappodacia, Weiss, and Pepler, "Bullying Experiences."
43. Nansel et al., "Bullying Behaviors."
44. Kumpulainen, Rasanen, and Puura, "Psychiatric Disorders."
45. Carney and Merrell, "Bullying in Schools."
46. Allen, "Classroom Management," 11.

School Level Prevention and Response

Teachers and schools play a pivotal role in either preventing or maintaining issues related to bullying.[47] Students in positive school climates feel safe and cared for by their teachers and their peers and are "less likely to bully, more likely to report bullying if they observe it, and more likely to seek help if they are victims."[48] As public concern and understanding of the ramifications of bullying have risen, a myriad of school-based prevention and intervention programs have been developed in recent decades. A review of the primary components of effective programs demonstrates that schools equipped to deal with bullying have developed structures and supports at the school level, the classroom level, and the individual level. These interventions align with a resilience framework that targets prevention and intervention efforts on both the environment and the child. This multifaceted approach reduces children's risk by altering the environment to eliminate or minimize adversity and by equipping the child with the skills needed to cope with and overcome adversity.

School Policies

Levels of victimization in schools are very much influenced by school policies against bullying and violence.[49] Though rigid and punitive school policies (e.g., zero-tolerance) have not been effective in reducing violence and bullying, students and teachers benefit from school-wide initiatives like School-Wide Positive Behavior Support (SWPBS), where expectations are consistently reinforced across classrooms in the school. Irrespective of the program or initiative employed, school-wide policies and procedures should be clear and consistent, as teachers are better able to be proactive and responsive when there are established guidelines and school policies.[50] Consistency throughout the school is especially important in middle and high school settings where students move to different classes and teachers throughout the day. Schools best equipped to combat bullying have prevention and intervention programs that are multifaceted and comprehensive, and include a range of interventions. Further, school-wide prevention programs should begin early (i.e., kindergarten), be integrated into the curriculum, and be extended and reinforced across grade levels.[51]

47. Olweus, *Bullying at School*, 63–67.
48. Berkowitz and Benbenishty, "Perceptions of Teachers' Support," 497.
49. Eliot et al., "Supportive School Climate."
50. Berkowitz, "Student and Teacher Responses."
51. Ibid.; Cappadocia, Weiss, and Pepler, "Bullying Experiences."

Planning for Transitions

Many children struggle with the transition between grade levels and in transitions from elementary to middle to high school. Recognizing the challenges associated with transition, transition planning is mandated by law for special educators to ensure students with disabilities have the supports necessary to assist them in transitioning from an academic to post-school setting.[52] Similarly, it is important for administrators and teachers to plan for and help students who are vulnerable during grade level and school level transitions. For example, the transition from elementary to middle school can be difficult as children leave an environment where they are accustomed to spending most of their day with one teacher who knows them quite well, and then need to adjust to having multiple teachers who they may not develop personal relationships with.[53] To proactively provide support and enhance resilience at such crucial developmental stages, some schools are adopting *schools-within-schools* models that allow students to develop more personal and caring relationships with their teachers and peers. One example of this concept is the freshman academy in ninth grade, designed to ease the transition from middle to high school.

It Takes a Village

Bullying is part of a complex system of relationships, and developing not only within the context of the classroom, but the school, community, and the larger sociocultural environment. Consequently, strategies for prevention, intervention, and response to bullying need to be holistic, culturally sensitive, and multifaceted. In sum, effective prevention programs don't simply target the bully and the victim in the school environment, but rather, include a range of environmental and social supports, including the family.[54]

Families play a significant role in helping children cope with the effects of bullying. Research demonstrates that children who have a warm and positive relationship with their parents experience fewer repercussions from bullying than their peers without such stable relationships.[55] Sibling relationships are also significant to child resilience; strong and affectionate sibling relationships reduce the likelihood of emotional problems

---

52. Individuals with Disabilities Education Act, 2004.
53. Cassen, Feinstein, and Graham, "Educational Outcomes."
54. Ibid.
55. Patterson et al., "Maternal Warmth."

developing in children who have experienced stressful events.[56] Echoing the research on school environments, home environments that are calm, positive, and structured help ameliorate the effects of school stress on children.[57] In sum, a positive home environment and warm relationships with parents and siblings increases a child's resilience to the harmful behavioral and emotional effects of bullying.[58] These findings underscore the value of involving families in school based interventions and helping families understand their protective role in buffering the effects of bullying.

Teacher Training

Perhaps most important, school-level approaches should involve training teachers in prevention, identification, and intervention. Studies show that teachers tend to report low self-efficacy when it comes to their perceived ability to effectively identify and respond to bullying in their classrooms. As self-efficacy predicts behavior, and increased self-efficacy translates into increased action with regard to prevention and intervention,[59] administrators should survey their teachers and provide targeted training to increase teachers' skills and confidence in their ability to be proactive and responsive with bullying in their classrooms. Vignettes have been helpful to evaluate and train preservice and in-service teachers when and how to respond to bullying.[60] The section that follows provides recommendations for teachers to address bullying and foster emotional and relational resilience at the classroom level.

Classroom Level Prevention and Response

Teachers can prevent bullying and increase resilience in students by establishing a positive classroom culture and climate.[61] Teachers who have an *authoritative* style of management (e.g., rules are reasonable and designed to support change; students are treated with dignity and respect) create a classroom atmosphere that has reasonable boundaries for students to develop self-determination and independence. On the other hand, a bullying culture

56. Gass, Jenkins, and Dunn, "Are Sibling Relationships Protective?"
57. Bowes et al., "Families Promote."
58. Ibid.
59. Banas, "Impact of Authentic Learning."
60. Blood et al., "Bullying in Children."
61. Allen, "Bullying Intervention System."

can develop in classrooms governed by teachers with either *authoritarian* (e.g., rigid rules, power-asserted discipline) or *passive* approaches (e.g., lax, few limits or boundaries) to classroom management. From a comprehensive review of research on the relationship between classroom management practices and bullying, Allen concluded, "Just as parenting practices create a context and culture for development that either promotes bullying or does not, so too do teachers' classroom management practices contribute to a context or culture that either promotes or discourages bullying."[62]

Strong Behavior Management = Prevention

Teachers can head off bullying in their classes through strong classroom management skills. In fact, researchers have framed "bullying as a behavior management issue in the educational setting."[63] Research reveals a correlation between classroom management and bullying: bullying is less likely to take place where teachers create caring environments and develop social structures in their classrooms that promote positive peer relationships.[64] The goal is to foster a positive school climate in a structured environment. Research suggests that students perceive there to be more support in environments with more structure.[65]

One of the most effective forms of classroom management is providing good instruction that engages all learners. Children are less likely to engage in bullying when they are engaged in learning. Effective teachers differentiate instruction to meet the varied needs of their learners and carefully plan to ensure there is no "down time" giving students the opportunity to bully. Providing students the academic support they need is crucial, as when children are struggling in school and performing below their peers they are more likely to have low self-efficacy and low self-esteem. In the face of academic challenges, students may act out in frustration or seek to escape the situation through avoidance behaviors—both responses place them at risk for being bullied or choosing to bully.

---

62. Allen, "Classroom Management," 7.
63. Crothers and Kolbert, "Tackling a Problematic Behavior."
64. Ibid.
65. Gregory et al., "Authoritative School Discipline."

Social Skills Instruction

In addition to a strong emphasis on academics, teachers should directly teach and reinforce socially appropriate behavior and hold students responsible for inappropriate behavior. Teaching students socially appropriate behavior and fostering positive peer relationships is a very important prevention strategy, as negative peer relationships often predict bullying, while friendships protect against victimization.[66] In addition to decreasing the risk of being bullied, peers can also play a role in resolving issues related to bullying.[67] Social skills and conflict resolution strategies can be taught through role-playing, as well as through drama, puppetry, movies, personal stories, and books. The goal is to sensitize students to the issue of bullying and build individual assertiveness and empathy toward others. Discussion and role-playing can also equip students with the language they need to be assertive and advocate for themselves and others.[68]

Teachers can also use cooperative learning activities to develop familiarity and acceptance of others, being conscious of power differentials among students.[69] Groups should be created strategically to ensure that if potential bullies and potential victims are placed together, there is also a non-bully student with high social status who can and will intervene if needed. In sum, "Relationships are at the heart of growth, healthy resistance, and resilience."[70] Therefore, teachers should create caring classroom environments that foster positive peer relationships marked by empathy and concern for others. When relational problems arise, the focus should be on working collectively to solve the problem, rather than assigning blame.

Teaching Students to Seek Help

Teachers need to teach students to seek help from adults; teachers cannot intervene if they are not aware of the issue.[71] Unfortunately, many students feel that reporting an issue to a teacher will make things worse or that there will be no consequences for the bully.[72] Both perceptions decrease the likelihood that students will report future incidents. These findings underscore

66. Boulton, "Teachers' Views."
67. O'Connell, Pepler, and Craig, "Peer Involvement."
68. Crothers and Kolbert, "Tackling a Problematic Behavior."
69. Ibid.
70. Jordan, "Relational Resilience in Girls."
71. Berkowitz, "Student and Teacher Responses."
72. Jacobsen and Bauman, "Bullying in Schools."

how important it is for teachers to take matters seriously and actively intervene, affirming for the victim that teachers care while simultaneously sending the message that bullying, in any form, is not tolerated.

Prevention efforts also need to address the *bystander*. Graham urged, "Peers need to learn that as witnesses to bullying, their responses aren't neutral and they are either supporting or opposing bullying behaviors."[73] All students need to be taught how to respond when they observe bullying. As peers are often more aware of incidences of bullying than teachers,[74] teaching peers to defend and intervene is paramount. In fact, victimization is stopped 50 percent of the time when peers intervene.[75] To train students to intervene, teachers can create opportunities for students to role-play and practice advocating on behalf of a peer.

Altering the Physical and Social Environment

When seeing the potential for victimization, teachers can employ a range of strategies to alter the physical or social environment to minimize opportunities for bullying. Changes may be subtle, like increasing teacher presence near the bully, creating a new seating arrangement, or assigning new cooperative learning groups. Teachers may also give the bully a role or responsibility that capitalizes on his or her strengths while removing the student or shifting the student's attention away from the situation.[76] Situations may warrant avoiding opportunities for marginalization. For example, allowing students to choose their own teams in physical education (PE) class or form their own learning groups can result in exclusion and only serve to highlight students' high or low social status among peers. In such cases it may be helpful for teachers to assign students to teams, seats in the cafeteria, or seats on the bus.[77] An additional prevention strategy involves enlisting peer support or developing a buddy system, where a student who has the potential to be a strong advocate for a victim is paired with a student who is vulnerable.

---

73. Graham, "What Educators Need to Know," 15.
74. Holt and Keyes, "Teachers' Attitudes."
75. Fekkes et al., "Do Bullied Children Get Ill."
76. Allen, "Bullying Intervention System."
77. Cappodacia, Weiss, and Pepler, "Bullying Experiences."

Vigilance

Teachers need to be extremely vigilant, constantly observing their students in the classroom, on the playground, and during transitions. As bullying tends to take place when a teacher's attention is elsewhere,[78] teachers need to be relentlessly watchful, with a heightened awareness that bullying is often taking place without their knowledge and is most likely to occur in transitions or unstructured times of the day (e.g., transitioning to the cafeteria, bus, etc.). A teacher's failure to intervene can be interpreted by bullies, bystanders, and victims as tacit approval of behavior.[79] On the other hand, the support of one caring and concerned teacher can make all the difference in the world.[80]

Individual-Level Response and Intervention

It is crucial for teachers to take bullying seriously and to become knowledgeable of the prevalence and effects of bullying on their students; research consistently shows that students report higher levels of bullying than teachers, and students' awareness of bullying is significantly higher than teachers' awareness.[81] In fact, while teachers believe they would intercede in all cases of bullying, observational data suggests teachers intervene in only 15–18 percent of all bullying incidents in the class and on the playground.[82] These findings are devastating as students are more likely to continue to bully when there are no consequences for their actions. For this reason, this section begins with a discussion of interventions for bullies and concludes with a discussion of interventions for victims.

Interventions for Bullies

It is important for teachers to address bullying early, as addressing aggression in its early stages decreases the likelihood of later escalation.[83] In terms of how to effectively address bullying, Crothers and Kolbert recommend that before teachers approach a bully, they should gather as much

---

78. Dev and Burdulis, "Bullying Among Female Elementary Students."
79. Crothers and Kolbert, "Tackling a Problematic Behavior."
80. Downey, "Recommendations for Fostering."
81. Holt and Keyes, "Teachers' Attitudes."
82. Craig, Pepler, and Atlas, "Observations of Bullying."
83. Goldstein, *Low-Level Aggression*, 1–2.

information as possible about the incident first.[84] After they have met with the victim and witnesses, they should approach the bully in a straightforward manner, communicating that he or she is meeting with the student because of inappropriate behavior. This "straightforward delivery ensures that the student will not be trapped in a lie by asking for his or her version of events."[85] After addressing the issue in a serious tone, the teacher should transition into using a more caring and concerned tone, affirming the student's personal strengths and helping the student understand that victimizing peers is not necessary or helpful for maintaining or improving their social status. The goal of conferencing with the student is to foster self-reflection on actions and identify the motivation for actions (also referred to as *motivational interviewing*).[86] The teacher can also share with the student that research shows that while students who bully tend to be popular in the early school years, their popularity greatly wanes in later school years as their peers develop more empathy for each other and more assertiveness to stand up to bullies.[87] This conversation provides opportunity for the teacher to understand the function of the bullying behavior, gain the student's trust, and begin to build a teacher-student relationship where the teacher can, if needed, address the behavior directly and assertively in future incidences.

In considering how and when to involve parents of children who have bullied, it is important for teachers to be aware that children who bully often have parents whose parenting styles are authoritarian, characterized by discipline that is punitive, physical, and severe.[88] When discussing an issue with parents, Crothers and Kolbert advise teachers should simply present the evidence and outline the consequences for continued behavior.[89] They recommend concluding by discussing the student's strengths and inviting the parents to share their suggestions for helping the student develop in the identified areas. The goal is to create a partnership with the aim of supporting the student. The focus should be positive and supportive, non-punitive and non-disciplinary if possible, with the goal of helping the student identify an unhealthy relationship pattern and develop a holistic plan for supporting the student in changing or altering his or her behavior.[90]

---

84. Crothers and Kolbert, "Tackling a Problematic Behavior."
85. Ibid., 136.
86. Juhnke et al. "Using Motivational Interviewing."
87. Crothers and Kolbert, "Tackling a Problematic Behavior," 136.
88. Olweus, *Bullying at School*, 39–43.
89. Crothers and Kolbert, "Tackling a Problematic Behavior."
90. Allen, "Bullying Intervention System."

Interventions for Victims

When a student has been a victim of bullying, short- and long-term interventions are needed.[91] Short-term interventions should target the specific incident, while long-term interventions should be aimed at fostering resilience—increasing confidence and developing the skills needed to stand up to and report incidences. Teachers can increase a victim's confidence and trust by responding to the situation immediately and sharing with the student how the situation will be handled. It is also important for the teacher to frame the situation in such a way that the student does not attribute the bullying to his or her personal characteristics.

Victims cope with bullying by displaying a range of strategies, some more helpful than others. Helpful strategies include seeking advice and support, responding with humor or with assertiveness, and seeking to problem solve or resolve conflict.[92] Strategies that are generally ineffective, and may even perpetuate victimization, include retaliating or seeking revenge, reactive coping (e.g., crying, venting), and passive coping (e.g., ignoring, distancing, ruminating).[93] Unfortunately, the strategies found to be most effective are employed less frequently by victims than the practices found to be least effective. Therefore, it is important for teachers to teach effective coping strategies and encourage students to use them instead of employing ineffective strategies.

As students who are vulnerable or who are being bullied tend to be socially isolated, it is important to teach them social skills so they can develop friendships which can serve to buffer or ease the pain of victimization. Interventions need to target self-esteem and build on strengths so the student can develop the confidence needed to take the risk of being willing to seek out and try to connect socially with other students. Fostering *social intelligence* is also important, helping students to identify peers who may have a mutual desire or need for a friend, rather than seeking to befriend the most popular students or those who are prone to victimize others. Interventions aimed at increasing confidence and assertiveness can be done at the group or the individual level. It's important to note that social skills development is needed for victims *and* bullies.[94]

---

91. Crothers and Kolbert, "Tackling a Problematic Behavior."
92. Flanagan et al., "Coping with Bullying."
93. Ibid.
94. Dev and Burdulis, "Bullying Among Female Elementary Students."

Teachers may also employ *bibliotherapy*, the use of literature to foster emotional healing and growth.[95] Bibliotherapy can be used to assist victims in learning coping strategies through the experiences of characters in the story, though teachers should review the stories carefully to ensure they utilize effective rather than ineffective strategies.[96] An additional support for students who have been bullied involves inviting mature peers or older students to volunteer as friends and advocates for children who are vulnerable or who have been bullied. Such a relationship allows the student to begin to develop trust in others and provides a safe space to apply new social skills.

In terms of collaborating with parents of victims, it is important for teachers to help parents consider how they can foster resilience by nurturing their child's social development. Though well-meaning, parents of victims tend to overprotect and may try to meet the child's need for a best friend, failing to create opportunities for helping their child develop positive peer relationships. Rather than seeing their child as a victim, parents should see their child as capable of developing positive peer friendships and dealing with bullying situations, with assistance. Parents can support school prevention and intervention efforts by role-playing scenarios with their son/daughter, encouraging them to invite a friend home, and supporting their involvement in social activities. Crothers and Kolbert encourage parents of nonathletic victimized children to consider fostering their child's confidence and physical development through individual sports (e.g., swimming, karate, etc.) if they feel team sports may lead to further victimization.[97]

It would be remiss to conclude this section without stating that children who are bullied intensely or over a prolonged period of time may need professional mental health services.[98] Depending on school policies, teachers should begin with a referral to a school counselor or psychologist, who can assess and refer the family to the appropriate professional services if additional interventions and supports are needed.

Conclusion

The purpose of this chapter was to discuss structures and supports school communities can provide to foster students' resilience to bullying. This chapter was grounded in a socioecological approach to resilience, which

95. Heath et al., "Bibliotherapy."
96. Flanagan et al., "Coping with Bullying."
97. Crothers and Kolbert, "Tackling a Problematic Behavior."
98. Cappodacia, Weiss, and Pepler, "Bullying Experiences"; Cummings, Pepler, Mishna, and Craig, "Bullying and Victimization."

emphasizes that the ability to be resilient in the face of adversity is not simply dependent on individual traits and characteristics, but that resilience is a multidimensional construct, with a person's environment having a significant role to play in his or her positive adjustment to adversity. In the school context, teachers can prevent and respond to bullying through cultivating an environment that does not allow bullying to thrive and by equipping students to advocate for themselves and to intervene on behalf of others.

Reflection Questions

1. Can you define and identify bullying and cyberbullying?
2. What is the relationship between classroom management and bullying?
3. What are strategies for preventing bullying in schools?
4. What interventions are needed for victims of bullying? What interventions are needed for bullies?
5. How can teachers foster relational resilience in their students?

Bibliography

Allen, Kathleen P. "A Bullying Intervention System: Reducing Risk and Creating Support for Aggressive Students." *Preventing School Failure* 54 (2010) 199–209.

———. "Classroom Management, Bullying, and Teacher Practices." *The Professional Educator* 34 (2010) 1–11.

Amataya, Kishori, et al. "Concurrent and Longitudinal Links Between Friendship and Peer Victimization: Implications for Befriending Interventions." *Journal of Adolescence* 22 (1999) 461–66.

Astor, Ron A., Heather A. Meyer, and Ronald O. Pitner. "Elementary and Middle School Students' Perceptions of Violence-Prone School Sub-Contexts." *The Elementary School Journal* 101 (2001) 511–28.

Banas, Jennifer R. "Impact of Authentic Learning Exercises on Preservice Teachers' Self-Efficacy to Perform Bullying Prevention Tasks." *American Journal of Health Education* 45 (2014) 239–48.

Bandura, Albert. *Self-Efficacy: The Exercise of Control.* New York: Freeman, 1997.

Bauman, Sheri, and Adrienne Del Rio. "Pre-service Teachers' Responses to Bullying Scenarios: Comparing Physical, Verbal, and Relational Bullying." *Journal of Educational Psychology* 98 (2006) 219–31.

Berkowitz, Ruth. "Student and Teacher Responses to Violence in School: The Divergent Views of Bullies, Victims, and Bully-Victims." *School Psychology International* 35 (2013) 485–503. doi: 10.1177/0143034313511012.

Berkowitz, Ruth, and Rami Benbenishty. "Perceptions of Teachers' Support, Safety, and Absence from School Because of Fear Among Victims, Bullies, and Bully-Victims."

American Journal of Orthopsychiatry 82 (2012) 67–74. doi: 10.1111/j.1939-0025.2011.01132.x.

Blood, Gordon W., et al. "Bullying in Children Who Stutter: Speech-Language Pathologists' Perceptions and Intervention Strategies." *Journal of Fluency Disorders* 35 (2010) 92–109.

Boulton, Michael J. "Teachers' Views on Bullying: Definitions, Attitudes, and Ability to Cope." *British Journal of Educational Psychology* 67 (1997) 223–33.

Boulton, Michael J., Mark Trueman, and Lindsay Murray. "Associations Between Peer Victimization, Fear of Future Victimization and Disrupted Concentration on Class Work Among Junior School Pupils." *British Journal of Educational Psychology* 78 (2008) 473–89.

Boulton, Michael J., et al. "A Comparison of Preservice Teachers' Responses to Cyber versus Traditional Bullying Scenarios: Similarities and Differences and Implications for Practice." *Journal of Teacher Education* 65 (2014) 145–55.

Bowes, Lucy, et al. "Families Promote Emotional and Behavioral Resilience to Bullying: Evidence of an Environmental Effect." *Journal of Child Psychology and Psychiatry and Allied Disciplines* 51 (2010) 809–17. doi: 10.1111/j.1469-7610.2010.02216.x.

Cappadocia, M. Catherine, Jonathan A. Weiss, and Debra Pepler. "Bullying Experiences Among Children and Youth with Autism Spectrum Disorders." *Journal Of Autism & Developmental Disorders* 42 (2012) 266–77. doi: 10.1007/s10803-011-1241-x.

Carney, Amy G., and Kenneth W. Merrell. "Bullying in Schools: Perspectives on Understanding and Preventing an International Problem." *School Psychology International* 22 (2001) 364–82.

Carter, Susan. "Bullying of Students with Asperger Syndrome." *Issues in Comprehensive Pediatric Nursing* 32 (2009) 145–54.

Cassen, Robert, Leon Feinstein, and Philip Graham. "Educational Outcomes: Adversity and Resilience." *Social Policy and Society* 8 (2009) 73–85. doi: 10.1017/S1474746408004600.

Cefai, Carmel. "Pupil Resilience in the Classroom: A Teacher's Framework." *Emotional and Behavioral Difficulties* 9 (2004) 149–70.

Chen, Ji-Kang, and Ron Avi Astor. "The Perpetration of School Violence in Taiwan: An Analysis of Gender, Grade Level and School Type." *School Psychology International* 30 (2009) 568–84.

Christiansen, Jeanne, and James L. Christiansen. "Using Protective Factors to Enhance Resilience and School Success for At-Risk Students." *Intervention in School and Clinic* 33 (1997) 86–89.

Cohen, Jonathan. "Social, Emotional, Ethical, and Academic Education: Creating a Climate for Learning, Participation in Democracy, and Well-Being." *Harvard Educational Review* 76 (2006) 201–37.

Coloroso, Barbara. *The Bully, the Bullied and the Bystander: Breaking the Cycle of Violence*. New York: HarperCollins, 2004.

Craig, Wendy M., Debra Pepler, and Rona Atlas. "Observations of Bullying in the Playground and in the Classroom." *School Psychology International* 21 (2000) 22–36. doi: 10.1177/0143034300211002.

Crothers, Laura M., and Jered B. Kolbert. "Tackling a Problematic Behavior Management Issue: Teachers' Intervention in Childhood Bullying Problems." *Intervention in School and Clinic* 43 (2008) 132–39.

Cummings, Joanne G., Debra Pepler, Fay Mishna, and Wendy M. Craig. "Bullying and Victimization Among Students with Exceptionalities." *Exceptionality Education* 16 (2006) 193–222.

Davenport, Paula. "Educators' Perspectives on Having Been Cyber Harassed: A Phenomenological Study." PhD diss., Liberty University, 2014. http://digitalcommons.liberty.edu/doctoral/797/.

Delfabbro, Paul, et al. "Peer and Teacher Bullying/Victimization of South Australian Secondary School Students: Prevalence and Psychosocial Profiles." *British Journal of Educational Psychology* 76 (2006) 71–90.

Dev, Poonam, and Sarah Burdulis. "Bullying Among Female Elementary Students With and Without Learning Disabilities: An Exploration." *International Journal Of Learning* 14 (2008) 215–17.

Downey, Jayne A. "Recommendations for Fostering Educational Resilience in the Classroom." *Preventing School Failure* 53 (2008) 56–64.

Due, Pernille, and Bjorn Evald Holstein. "Bullying Victimization Among 13–15 Year Old School Children: Results from Two Comparative Studies in 66 Countries and Regions." *Journal of Adolescent Medicine and Health* 20 (2008) 209–22.

Eder, Donna. *School Talk: Gender and Adolescent Culture*. New Brunswick: Rutgers University Press, 1997.

Eliot, Megan, et al. "Supportive School Climate and Student Willingness to Seek Help for Bullying and Threats of Violence." *Journal of School Psychology* 48 (2010) 533–53. doi: 10.1016/j.jsp.2010.07.001.

Evertson, Carolyn M., and Alene H. Harris. "Support for Managing Learning-Centered Classrooms: The Classroom Organization and Management Program." In *Beyond Behaviorism: Changing the Classroom Management Paradigm*, edited by H. Jerome Freiberg, 59–74. Needham Heights, MA: Allyn and Bacon, 1999.

Feinberg, Ted. "Bullying Prevention and Intervention." *Principal Leadership* 4 (2003) 110–14.

Fekkes, Minne, et al. "Do Bullied Children Get Ill, or Do Ill Children Get Bullied? A Prospective Cohort Study on the Relationship Between Bullying and Health-Related Symptoms." *Pediatrics* 117 (2006) 1568–74.

Flanagan, Kelly S., et al. "Coping with Bullying: What Answers does Children's Literature Provide?" *School Psychology International* 34 (2013) 691–706. doi: 10.1177/0143034313479691.

Gass, Krista, Jennifer M. Jenkins, and Judy Dunn. "Are Sibling Relationships Protective? A Longitudinal Study." *Journal of Child Psychology and Psychiatry* 48 (2007) 167–75.

Gini, Gianluca, and Tiziana Pozzoli. "Association Between Bullying and Psychosomatic Problems: A Meta-Analysis." *Pediatrics* 123 (2009) 1059–65.

Goldstein, Arnold P. *Low-Level Aggression: First Steps on the Ladder to Violence*. Champaign, IL: Research Press, 1999.

Graham, Sandra. "What Educators Need to Know About Bullying." *Educational Horizons* 89 (2011) 12–15.

Gregory, Anne, et al. "Authoritative School Discipline: High School Practices Associated with Lower Bullying and Victimization." *Journal Of Educational Psychology* 102 (2010) 483–96. doi:10.1037/a0018562.

Hammel, Laura R. "Bouncing Back After Bullying: The Resiliency of Female Victims of Relational Aggression." *Mid-Western Educational Researcher* 21 (2008) 3–10.

Hawker, David, and Michael Boulton. "Twenty Years' Research on Peer Victimization and Psychosocial Maladjustment: A Meta-Analytic Review of Cross-Sectional Studies," *Journal of Child Psychology and Psychiatry and Allied Disciplines* 41 (2000) 441–55.

Heath, Melissa Allen, et al. "Bibliotherapy: A Resource to Facilitate Emotional Healing and Growth." *School Psychology International* 26 (2005) 563–80.

Herba, Catherine M., et al. "Victimization and Suicide Ideation in the TRAILS Study: Specific Vulnerabilities of Victims." *Journal of Child Psychology and Psychiatry* 49 (2008) 867–76.

Higgins, Gina O. *Resilient Adults: Overcoming a Cruel Past*. San Francisco: Jossey-Bass, 1994.

Holt, Melissa K. and Melissa A. Keyes. "Teachers' Attitudes Toward Bullying." In *Bullying in American Schools: A Social-Ecological Perspective on Prevention and Intervention*, edited by Dorothy Espelage and Susan M. Swearer, 121–40. Maywah, NJ: Erlbaum, 2004.

Hugh-Jones, Siobhan, and Peter Smith. "Self-Reports of Short- and Long-Term Effects of Bullying on Children who Stammer." *British Journal of Educational Psychology* 69 (1999) 141–58.

Individuals with Disabilities Education Improvement Act (IDEA). Pub. L. No. 108-446, 118 Stat. 2647 (2004). [Amending 20 U.S.C. § 1400 et seq.]

Jacobsen, Kristen E., and Sheri Bauman. "Bullying in Schools: School Counselors' Responses to Three Types of Bullying Incidents." *Professional School Counseling* 11 (2007) 1–8.

James, Deborah J., et al. "Bullying Behavior in Secondary Schools: What Roles do Teachers Play?" *Child Abuse Review* 16 (2008) 160–73.

Jordan, Judith V. "Relational Resilience in Girls." In *Handbook of Resilience in Children*, edited by Sam Goldstein and Robert Brooks, 79–90. New York: Springer, 2005.

Juhnke, Brenna A., et al. "Using Motivational Interviewing with School-Age Bullies: A New Use for a Proven, Evidence-Based Intervention." *Journal Of School Counseling* 11 (2013) 1–27.

Khanlou, Nazilla, and Ron Wray. "A Whole Community Approach Toward Child and Youth Resilience Promotion: A Review of Resilience Literature." *International Journal of Mental Health and Addiction* 12 (2014) 64–79.

Kowalski, Robin M., et al. *Cyberbullying: Bullying in the Digital Age*. 2nd ed. West Sussex, UK: Wiley-Blackwell, 2012.

Kumpulainen, Kristi, Eila Rasanen, and Kaija Puura. "Psychiatric Disorders and the Use of Mental Health Services Among Children Involved in Bullying." *Aggressive Behavior* 27 (2001) 102–10.

Luthar, Suniya S., et al. "The Construct of Resilience: A Critical Evaluation and Guidelines for Future Work." *Child Development* 71 (2000) 543–62.

Lyles, Sharon. "School Psychologists' Experiences with Teacher-to-Student Mistreatment." PhD diss., Liberty University, 2014. http://digitalcommons.liberty.edu/doctoral/855/.

Masten, Ann S., and Marie-Gabrielle J. Reed. "Resilience in Development." In *The Handbook of Positive Psychology*, edited by C. R. Snyder and Shane J. Lopez, 74–88. New York: Oxford University Press, 2002.

Molcho, Michal, et al. "Cross-National Time Trends in Bullying Behavior 1994–2006: Findings from Europe and North America." *International Journal of Public Health* 54 (2009) 225–34.

Nansel, Tonja R., et al. "Bullying Behaviors Among US Youth: Prevalence and Association with Psychosocial Adjustment." *Journal of the American Medical Association* 285 (2001) 2094–100.

O'Connell, Paul, Debra Pepler, and Wendy Craig. "Peer Involvement in Bullying: Insights and Challenges for Intervention." *Journal of Adolescence* 22 (1999) 437–52.

Olweus, Dan. *Bullying at School: What We Know and What We Can Do*. Cambridge: Blackwell, 1993.

———. "Bully/Victim Problems Among School Children: Some Basic Facts and Effects of a School-Based Intervention Program." In *The Development and Treatment of Childhood Aggression*, edited by Debra Pepler and Kenneth Rubin, 411–38. Hillsdale, NJ: Lawrence Erlbaum, 1991.

———. "Bully/Victim Problems in School: Facts and Intervention." *European Journal of Psychology of Education* 12 (1997) 495–510.

Patterson, Charlotte J., et al. "Maternal Warmth as a Protective Factor Against Risks Associated with Peer Rejection Among Children." *Development and Psychopathology* 1 (1989) 21–38.

Rigby, Ken. "What Children Tell Us About Bullying in Schools." *Children Australia* 22 (1997) 28–34.

Robert, Roland, and David Galloway. "Classroom Influences on Bullying." *Educational Research* 44 (2002) 299–312.

Sharp, Sonia, and Helen Cowie. "Empowering Pupils to Take Positive Action Against Bullying." In *School Bullying: Insights and Perspectives*, edited by Peter K. Smith and Sonia Sharp, 108–31. London: Routledge, 1994.

Smokowski, Paul R., and Kelly Holland Kopasz. "Bullying in School: An Overview of Types, Effects, Family Characteristics, and Intervention Strategies." *Children and Schools* 27 (2005) 101–10.

Spriggs, Aubrey L., et al. "Adolescent Bullying Involvement and Perceived Family, Peer, and School Relations: Commonalities and Differences Across Race/Ethnicity." *Journal of Adolescent Health* 41 (2007) 283–93.

Sullivan, Keith, Mark Cleary, and Ginny Sullivan. *Bullying in Secondary Schools: What it Looks Like and How to Manage It*. London: Paul Chapman, 2004.

Terry, Andrew A. "Teachers as Targets of Bullying by Their Pupils: A Study to Investigate Incidence." *British Journal of Educational Psychology* 68 (1998) 255–68.

Twemlow, Stuart W., and Peter Fonagy. "The Prevalence of Teachers who Bully Students in Schools with Differing Levels of Behavioral Problems." *The American Journal of Psychiatry* 162 (2005) 2387–89.

Wang, Jing, Ronald J. Iannotti, and Tonja R. Nansel. "School Bullying Among Adolescents in the United States: Physical, Verbal, Relational, and Cyber." *Journal of Adolescent Health* 45 (2009) 1–8.

Wang, Margaret C., Geneva D. Haertel, and Herbert J. Walberg. "Fostering Educational Resilience in Inner-City Schools." In *Children and Youth*, edited by Herbert J. Walberg, Olga Reyes, and Roger P. Weissberg, 2–23. Newbury Park, CA: SAGE, 1997.

Young, Sue. "The Support Group Approach to Bullying in Schools." *Educational Psychology in Practice* 14 (1998) 32–39.

11

Education and Mental Health: A Parent Perspective

Karen Copeland

Introduction

IT IS AN HONOR to be asked to write this chapter for this book. I will be honest; the thought is exciting, but also a bit nerve-racking. My hope is that what I have to say will be considered important enough to encourage others to make a shift in the way they think about child, youth, and family mental health. I have to believe that sharing our story will propel this shift in perspective forward.

An important disclaimer: while I have connected with a number of families over the years that have children and youth who experience mental health challenges, I do not presume to speak on behalf of all of them. While there will be themes of commonality that you will find in many family stories, every family has their own story to tell. The stories I will be sharing with you in this chapter are from our own family journey. I have written about many of them on my website Champions for Community Mental Wellness.[1]

As you will see in our story, sometimes there is a misunderstanding of what a mental health challenge is; other times, we may know a child is experiencing a mental health challenge but we have no idea what to do about it. Our family also faced views that children, especially young children, could not experience mental health challenges. This led to assumptions that our son's issues were a result of the way we were parenting him. Many parents

---

1. See Karen Copeland, "Champions for Community Mental Wellness," http://www.championsforcommunitywellness.com. A website where readers can learn more about mental health challenges and how these impact children, youth, and families in our communities.

are concerned they must be poor parents because of their child's behavior. At times, it can feel like professionals reinforce the idea of poor parenting.[2]

Educators need to know that there are opportunities available to develop more awareness and understanding about mental health, but they also need to be supported in this. Traditionally, educators have not received a great amount of formal training when it comes to recognizing, understanding, and supporting students who have mental health challenges in their classrooms. In fact, a national survey conducted by the Canadian Teachers' Federation in 2012, found that the majority of teachers had not received any professional development on how to support students who have mental illnesses.[3] Students who have mental health challenges are not going away, in fact, the numbers suggest that one in seven children will experience a mental health challenge.[4] More awareness and understanding is critical if we are going to have any kind of success with our vulnerable students.

My Journey

This was definitely not a journey I expected to go on when I became a parent. My thoughts of my children's future included sports, arts, academic achievement, and most importantly, a strong community with plenty of laughter and love; in short, similar to the way my own childhood and youth went. Sure, our family would face inevitable bumps along the way, but those challenges would happen perhaps later, in the adolescent years. Early in our family journey we took a detour away from what we had envisioned our lives would look like. I fought against this detour at the beginning. It simply couldn't be happening, and it must be related to something I was doing wrong in my parenting. I became firmer, stricter, and generally a very hard-hearted person. At some point I realized that I was repeatedly beating my head against the proverbial brick wall, and that if we were going to be able to manage this detour, it would be me that had to change the way I was thinking about what was happening with our son. This is our story.

My husband and I realized quite early on that our son was a little bit different from our daughter. Initially, we decided this must be a difference between boys and girls. As time went on and we met other families with boys, we began to understand it might be something more than that. Our son was very reactive, very sensitive. He had a hard time putting his emotions into

---

2. Inglis and Austin, "The Blame Game," 8–10.

3. Froese-Germain and Riel, "Understanding Teachers' Perspectives," 16.

4. Canadian Mental Health Association, "Mental Illnesses in Children and Youth," http://www.cmha.bc.ca/get-informed/mental-health-information/child-youth-md.

words. He also had a very difficult time with sharing any of his toys with other children; so much so that all his toys would have to be locked in his bedroom when other children came over to play. His fear of his toys getting broken was that strong. When family came to visit from out of town, our son would have tremendous difficulty with having someone new in our house, the change in routine, the change in the relationships in our home. It would take up to three days for him to finally accept and welcome the new person in our home. We would see our child retreat into his own world on a daily basis, a world we marvelled over—a world full of pacing and swinging arms and explosion noises. We didn't discourage this necessarily; however, we did guide him into doing this in private spaces versus in public, like at the mall.

I worked hard with my son, modeling and prompting appropriate emotional language and behavior. I created sticker charts and kindness journals, and played mediator when disagreements arose between my children. I registered him in preschool and dealt with ongoing resistance and refusal to attend. I coaxed and cajoled him into trying new things, often having to physically put him in the car to go on outings. I took him to the pediatrician when I had concerns about his sensitivity to high-pitched noises. I went to resource fairs and diligently completed screening tools and was always assured everything was well within range developmentally.

Kindergarten

Kindergarten started. The refusal and resistance we had seen with the preschool transferred into this new school environment. There was little reprieve. This does not mean his kindergarten teacher was not good. She was an amazing, loving teacher, who really took the time to problem solve and share ideas with us. Yet the challenges with school continued. He began having difficulties interacting with his peers. He did not like other children in his space and would react by pushing them away or screeching. He was easily frustrated. At the end of the school day, he would have a meltdown if he learned he could not go to the playground and would yell and stomp all the way home.

Toward the end of kindergarten, we experienced a significant family loss. My dad, whom our son had recently bonded with, passed away suddenly. This was a huge loss to try and process. Around this time, my husband left home for four months for work. Things really started to deteriorate. I was now on my own, trying desperately not only to get my daughter to school on time, but my son as well. I also started becoming very concerned about what was happening. Despite all my best efforts as a mom, things were getting worse instead of improving.

I reached out to my son's teacher and we had a good conversation about our mutual concerns. She arranged for us to meet with the school counselor. This was a brief meeting and it was recommended that I ask my child to tell me three positive things about his day every day after school. Easier said than done! I tried and tried, but could never get him to share much about his school day with me.

I reached out to my husband's Employee Family Assistance Program,[5] and my son and I met with a counselor. I went back to see the counselor a week later and she told me our son had high-functioning autism and recommended we find him a special school to attend. I was very upset. Not because I was blindsided by the word autism—I was upset because I knew there was more to diagnosing autism than a one hour visit.[6] My next step was to make an appointment with my doctor to get a referral to a pediatrician. This was also not a quick process. It took several months of waiting, we were nearing the end of grade one when we finally saw the pediatrician. The peer issues were continuing, my son was meeting regularly with the vice principal of the school and was refusing to do any work for one of his teachers. The pediatrician saw us for fifteen minutes and informed me my son had attention deficit hyperactivity disorder—ADHD—and that I should come back in September to get a prescription for medication for my son. To diagnose ADHD, checklists need to be completed by both family and school.[7] It is not a diagnosis that is made in a short visit to the doctor. I was furious. I returned to the school and informed my son's teacher of what I had been told. She was supportive; assuring me that this was not something she believed was going on for my son either. She believed it was something different.

I managed to connect to a peer-support person, who helped me understand that what my son was experiencing could be anxiety. She recommended I make a referral to our local Child and Youth Mental Health (CYMH) office,[8] as we might be able to join an anxiety group. I made the referral, only to learn that we would have to wait around six months before the next session started.

---

5. Homewood Health, "Employee and Family Assistance Programs," http://www.homewoodhealth.com/health/services/stay-at-work/efap. An employee and family assistance program provides employees with access to a registered counselor or psychologist for a finite number of sessions, paid for by the employer.

6. British Columbia Ministry of Children and Family Development, "A Parent's Handbook," 6.

7. Canadian Attention Deficit Hyperactivity Disorder Resource Alliance, "Canadian ADHD Practice Guidelines," vi.

8. Child and Youth Mental Health is a community-based service offered through the British Columbia Ministry of Child and Family Development that provides support to children and youth with mental health challenges.

Over the next several years, we attended groups and sessions with CYMH. We attempted to have our son attend one-on-one counseling sessions; however, he would refuse to go. We asked if we could see the community psychiatrist attached to CYMH and were told to go to our pediatrician instead. We presented at our local emergency department during one particular crisis, and the recommendation was to be seen by the community psychiatrist. We were again sent by CYMH back to the pediatrician, who told us our son needed to be referred to a psychiatrist. We ended up going out of community to access this. We pursued assessments for autism, for learning (psycho-educational), a sensory profile, and a full psychological profile. Our son was finally given an autism spectrum diagnosis after attending a five-week specialized assessment program at BC Children's Hospital. He was eleven years old.

All of these assessments provided us with information and recommendations on strategies to support our son. These recommendations were not always welcomed, though. In one instance, I had provided some information to one of my son's teachers and she dismissed it, telling me she preferred to learn the strengths and challenges of the child herself and not rely on outside information. I understand that teachers want to be objective and do not want to become biased by the information they read. I would like to provide an alternative perspective for educators to know.

When a child has mental health and other learning challenges, why would you not gather as much information as possible about what that means? I imagine this to be like looking at a picture in a magazine of an elaborate dinner menu item and deciding to make it without a recipe. Sure, you may get bits and pieces of it right, but without all the steps, how successful might you be?

Teachers need to know that parents may also appear to be resistant to labeling or diagnosing their child.[9] This is because we may not have a good understanding of why the behavior is occurring. When it was first suggested that our son was experiencing anxiety, I had a hard time understanding how this could be so. When I started reading more about anxiety and how it can manifest, things started to make sense. At other times we were told that the diagnosis didn't matter, that we knew our child best and therefore we knew what strategies would work best. This was somewhat true, in that we did have a pretty good idea of what would work, the challenge was getting our school team to listen. We were also told that a number of the things our child was experiencing were a part of normal development.

---

9. RBC Children's Mental Health Project, "Silent Families," 4.

Perhaps the worst of our entire journey, though, was all the questions and judgements about our child and our parenting. We would hear words like "willful" and "manipulative." We were even told our child was *passive aggressive* when he was in grade two. The problem with using words like these is they say more about adult judgement on why a behavior is occurring instead of looking deeper for the *why* and taking the time to understand and learn about the child. There were times when I felt completely isolated and alone. I questioned everything about who I was as a parent *and* as a person. And I wondered, if I feel this way, how must my child feel? This often happened with those who could have understood—family, friends, and professionals, they either chose not to or for whatever reason, could not.

Teachers need to know that learning to navigate systems proved to be very challenging. We did not have much guidance from school staff or even the pediatrician on how to get connected to resources or supports in our community. By the time our son completed elementary school, we had over thirty points of contact within the Ministries of Education, Health, Children, and Families, as well as connections with private service providers. This number does not include the number of phone calls or meetings we were involved in, nor does it reflect the time and energy spent on preparing for meetings or travel to and from appointments. It does not include the countless hours of research I completed, trying to figure out what systems existed to support our family, but also the language—jargon—of each, and what my rights were as a parent within these systems.

I have provided an illustration of the types of services a family may be involved in when their child or youth is experiencing mental health challenges. Some families will have fewer points of access, while other families may have many more. It is important to know parents are regularly expected to navigate all of these services on their own, without the assistance of a case manager. Many of these services do not communicate effectively with each other, so the parent is often left to provide this communication. This can be incredibly overwhelming and frustrating. Parents can also feel stuck trying to problem solve between other professionals and school teams.

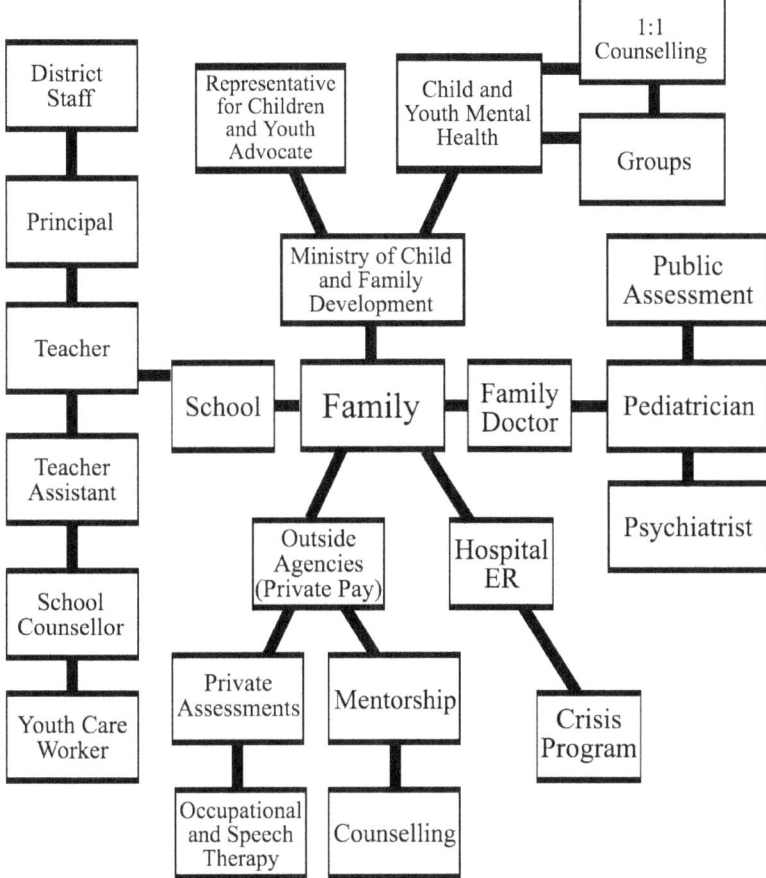

Figure 1: Sample map of services families may be involved with when their child or youth is experiencing mental health challenges.

What Teachers Need to Know

Reflecting on our journey, I wish everyone involved with my son had recognized my son was experiencing anxiety much earlier, instead of simply viewing his behavior—and our parenting—as a "problem." I believe this would have provided more understanding and empathy for my child.

I wish the school would have had information about Child and Youth Mental Health or other programs, and they would have informed us of these services and how to access them. I wish there would have been more curiosity from the school counselor in kindergarten, as well as the Employee

Family Assistance Program counselor and the pediatrician. I wish someone would have taught me how to navigate these systems so I did not have to learn how all on my own. I wish our concerns would have been heard the first time we spoke them, instead of having to go through many different systems for many years to get the diagnosis that fit our son the best. I wish there had been someone available to help me learn how to advocate effectively, as well as someone to assist with the school-based team meetings.

What You Need to Know About Mental Health Challenges

I have often said that when we are faced with a big problem, for some reason we think we need a big solution. I believe, though, that it is the smallest of changes that can make the biggest impact. That change starts by beginning to understand the various different mental health disorders, some of their common characteristics or symptoms, and how to respond to them.

The good news is there are a great number of resources available for educators to learn more about mental health challenges, not only through books but also online from a variety of reputable sites. I have listed some of my favorite mental health books and internet links in the additional resources section at the end of this chapter. When trying to understand mental health challenges and how they impact children, youth, and families, it is important to remember that everyone is unique in their experience. What this means is that even though our child experiences anxiety, how he experiences it can look quite different from how another child experiences it. This is where it is critical to connect with the parents to get a good understanding of what types of challenges exist for the child, as well as what strategies work best. As the child gets older, it is imperative they have access to a trusted adult within the school environment. Connecting with youth, listening to their experiences and insights into their challenges, and finding what works for them is important.

One of the best resources I have come across on our journey is the concept of Collaborative and Proactive Solutions by Dr. Ross Greene. He shifts our thinking from "kids do well if they want to" toward the more appropriate "kids do well if they can," meaning a child is lacking skills in specific areas that need to be taught versus being willful or purposefully misbehaved.[10] Greene also challenges adults to examine our own expectations when it comes to our children.[11] Are they reasonable? Can they be met? When I started looking at my son's own skill deficits—the areas he struggled—I began to realize that

10. Greene, *Lost at School*, 11.
11. Ibid., 12.

perhaps I needed to meet him where he was at, instead of expecting him to meet me. I highly recommend Greene's book *Lost at School*, as it provides a great illustration of how adults interpret behavior and how we can engage our kids to help them learn the skills they need to be more successful.

Know Your System

I can't emphasize enough the importance of knowing your education system, particularly the policies and guidelines that refer to students who have learning challenges. I would recommend directing parents to this information so they have an understanding of what they can expect for their child. Doing this can open the door for more communication and trust between home and school. Sharing information about processes is also important. For example, if you are asking a parent to attend an Individualized Education Plan (IEP) meeting, let the parent know who will be at the meeting, what is likely to be discussed, and how they can prepare for the meeting. Try to arrange the meeting for a time that works best for the parent's schedule. Providing information to a parent about what to expect helps lessen the stress they may have heading into the meeting.

I have heard the argument that teachers are not social workers. For example, Frank Furedi, an academic dealing with social policy has articulated this argument by stating that teachers should not be social workers. He asks why education and social policy appears to give parents the role of educators while teachers are encouraged to be carers, and he says that "professionalizing the management of children's relationships, parenting, and community attitudes weakens the ability of people to conduct their own affairs."[12] However, there is a growing movement toward recognizing that in order for children to learn and attend to academic lessons, they must first be able to regulate their emotions, both positive and negative.[13] Shanker states,

> While problems with self-regulation cannot be said to *cause* mental health problems, they can exacerbate them. By the same token, the ability to self-regulate contributes significantly to the development of the key attributes of mental health.[14]

In our own family situation, we found that when our son was calm and feeling safe, he was able to demonstrate his capacity for academic learning.

---

12. Furedi, "Teachers Are Not Social Workers"; Blamires, "Why Teachers Have to be Social Workers."
13. Shanker, *Calm, Alert and Learning*, 27.
14. Ibid., 138.

The challenge was getting him to this state of being. Positive adult connections within the school environment became a critical piece of the puzzle. Our son was more likely to be calm when he understood and trusted the adult who was making demands of him. Our son wanted to be connected. He wanted to feel safe, welcomed, and valued in his school environment, and his adult attachments were able to assist him with this.

> Secure human attachment promotes flexible self-regulation, pro-social behavior, empathy, a positive sense of emotional well-being, and self-esteem.[15]

When a student is recognized as experiencing or potentially experiencing mental health challenges, the teacher becomes an integral member of the team working with the child and family. It is important for teachers to be aware of the systems and services available in their community that support children and youth who have mental health challenges and their families, and how to direct families to these. There also needs to be an understanding of the limitations that exist within these services. Many of the programs often have wait lists, or the family does not qualify for service. It is important to avoid making the assumption that because a family has been referred to a service this means they will actually receive the service. Sometimes it may seem like a family is not doing anything to try and help their child. When this happens, it is important to start being curious and perhaps pulling in other professionals in your school community (for example, the school counselor) to assist the family in navigating any barriers to service they might be experiencing.

It is also important to connect families to other families who may be able to provide guidance and mentoring. We often feel very isolated when our children struggle, like we are the only parents going through this. Getting connected to other parents who had similar experiences was one of the best things that happened to me. It was important for me to realize that I wasn't the only parent experiencing challenges within service systems, and my knowledge, awareness, and curiosity blossomed because I had the support of my peers.

Connecting youth to other youth who are experiencing (or have experienced) mental health challenges can provide the same type of support and guidance. In British Columbia, youth can call and speak with a Youth in Residence at the Kelty Mental Health Resource Centre[16] for assistance with learning about and navigating services.

---

15. Ogilvie, *ConnectZone.org*, 62.
16. Kelty Mental Health Resource Centre. http://keltymentalhealth.ca/.

Our Champions

There is a TED Talk by Rita Pierson, titled "Every Kid Deserves a Champion." The description of the talk is this:

> Rita Pierson, a teacher for 40 years, once heard a colleague say, "They don't pay me to like the kids." Her response: "Kids don't learn from people they don't like." A rousing call to educators to believe in their students and actually connect with them on a real, human, personal level.[17]

Taking Pierson's statement a step further, I would suggest that every family deserves a champion as well. We had the fortune to have been connected with several different champions on our family journey. These are the people who have not only believed in our child—his gifts and strengths—but also believed in our family. Instead of meeting our concerns with resistance or defensiveness, they have welcomed us with respect and, most importantly, curiosity.

I recall our son's grade one teacher, who lived her truth of "firm but fair." Her communication was open and clear, with no judgement. She did not wait until there was a crisis to communicate, she would meet with me informally when necessary to let me know of concerns as they came up. She would regularly tell my son "tomorrow is another day, and I can't wait to see you!" regardless of how poorly the day had gone. When my son would go to her with a complaint about something, she would listen and respond instead of simply dismissing him. She would check in with me and provide me with guidance and suggestions, but would also welcome my input and ideas.

Our son's grade three teacher also welcomed our son into his classroom. He was a curious teacher, never hesitating to ask us questions about what we thought might be helpful to support our son in his classroom. He was also very reassuring. Our son's school refusal was quite significant during this grade year, and there were many mornings where I had a great amount of difficulty with him entering the school. His teacher had a great amount of empathy for the challenges we were all experiencing, and told us this. When our child would hide behind the bookcase during circle learning time, his teacher would check in with him after—asking him questions and discovering our son had been listening all along. When an occupational therapist provided strategies for the classroom, the teacher implemented many of them as best as he could. When peer issues would arise, he would not automatically jump to the conclusion that my son was solely responsible; rather, he would ask questions and allow time to pass before addressing the concerns. He asked if

---

17. Pierson, "Every Kid Deserves a Champion."

we would be comfortable allowing our son to chew gum in class, as he had noticed that our son was chewing on his fingernails constantly. While grade three was far from a successful year when it came to academics, we believe our son was valued and included by the teacher in his classroom.

Grade four did not start off well, but again, we were fortunate to be introduced to yet another champion. Our son continued to struggle academically and socially. Sometimes it is a subtle shift in how we, as adults, perceive things that make a difference. For instance, during one school meeting, our son's teacher stated that our son was "annoying" the other children in the class. My husband asked him what he meant. The teacher explained that while all the other students were working, our son would be trying to show them something he was reading in his book. Our support person at the meeting was able to present an alternative viewpoint—our son was actually trying to connect with his peers. To be clear, the way he was going about it was disruptive; however, his intent was not to annoy his classmates, he was trying to belong. This alternative perspective created such a shift in the teacher's perception of our child. He came to us with ideas of how to create positive connections between our son and his peers, in ways that would work for everyone. I recall a particular time when a large group of children, including our son, were involved in a game during recess and lunch hours. It was a game the group had created, and there were no hard and fast rules. This was particularly challenging for our son, who is quite rigid and rule-bound. After multiple incidents, the teacher mentioned to me they would probably have to discourage the kids from playing the game. I suggested that perhaps all the students involved could dedicate some time during one recess to create a written list of rules. This way, everyone would feel like they had a voice in the process, but would also walk away being clear on what acceptable play was and what was not. The teacher later told me how well the process had gone, and the challenges with the playground subsided. This particular teacher retired following our son's grade four year. He still e-mails our family every now and again to see how we are doing. It means a great deal to us.

Communicating with Parents

I recall one particular year that our son was struggling. He would regularly get notes home in his planner. These were not notes about positive behavior. These notes home had a tremendous impact not only on our son, but on me. They were written in his planner where anyone could see. I worried about what the impact would be on my son when he read them. I was fearful that another student or parent might see these notes and our son would be further marginalized by his peers. It is important for educators to share their concerns with a family about their child; this should be done in an objective and nonjudgmental way. I would suggest that it is better to address concerns face to face or verbally by telephone versus detailing incidents in daily planners.

It is also important to recognize and share the good things that are happening. Chris Wejr, an administrator in the Langley School District writes,

> Make the first contact with parents a positive one. It doesn't have to be about something the student has done but more about sharing that we value him/her and we know who they are.[18]

When educators build a foundation of trust and respect with a parent, the difficult conversations become easier to have. Consider the best ways to have these difficult conversations. Check with the parent to see what types of communication work best for them. Do they want notations in the planner? Or would they prefer an e-mail detailing the concerns? Are the parents able to attend school meetings or are their opportunities limited due to work commitments? At the same time, it is important for educators to also make sure parents know the best way to get in touch when they have a concern.

Two resources I found particularly helpful are available online. The Ontario Teachers' Federation has created an online parent engagement resource for educators. The website provides guidance on establishing relationships, communication, managing and resolving conflict, and more.[19] "Supporting Meaningful Consultation with Parents" is also a document that should be available in your school in British Columbia.[20] It details the requirement for parent consultation when decisions are being made about a child's school program.

We know that when parents are involved in their child's schooling, their child will generally do better, academically and emotionally. In fact, Wang and Sheikh-Khalil found that "parental involvement can promote positive adolescent development by motivating students to be behaviorally

---

18. Wejr, "10 Ways to Start." Chris Wejr believes that if we start looking at a child's strengths instead of only the challenges, we change our responses to become more supportive and can even change the story of that child from a negative one to a positive one.

19. For further information, see the Ontario Teachers' Federation, http://www.parentengagement.ca/. Find detailed information on how to create and sustain positive teacher and parent relationships.

20. "Supporting Meaningful Consultation with Parents" was created for British Columbia schools by the British Columbia Council of Administrators of Special Education (BC CASE) in 2008. The booklet details the different steps that must be taken when making decisions regarding a child's school program. School personnel are required to consult and provide information to parents throughout the decision making process.

and emotionally engaged in school."[21] While I have always strived to be involved in my child's schooling, I have not always been aware of the best ways to be involved. The successes came when there was clear communication between home and school about creative ways to be involved, because sometimes what works for everyone else doesn't necessarily fit when your child has a mental health challenge.

Wang and Sheikh-Khalil also found that schools could contribute to a student's academic success by providing parents with resources and information on how to support this development.[22] I would suggest that the same is true for emotional development. As my knowledge and understanding of anxiety increased, I was better able to support my son through conversations and modeling coping skills.

What Educators Want You to Know

One of the things I am very passionate about is being curious. As I was thinking about what to include in this chapter, I decided I should ask a few of my teacher connections for their thoughts on what preservice teachers should know about mental health. Here are their responses from an informal anonymous survey.

- Listen to the students. My instructor for the special education course from the University of British Columbia Bachelor of Education program invited students with designated Individualized Education Plans. With parents' consent, some students came with parents as well . . . as guest speakers. One of the most memorable lessons from my teacher training. It was mind blowing hearing students' perspective.
- Listen to the family, learn about their child, and work together with them and school based team to come up with a plan that includes all stakeholders in meeting the needs of the child.
- Know your community resources.
- Be patient. Be interested in your students. Know their strengths.
- Study up so you can better understand. Don't be scared to ask.
- I think we need to remember to be open-minded and nonjudgmental. We need to focus on the positives and strengths of our students—they all have them—regardless of any challenges they face.

---

21. Wang and Sheikh-Khalil, "Does Parental Involvement," 622.
22. Ibid., 623.

Where Are We Now?

We have had to make some difficult decisions over this past year in regard to our son's education. We have included him when making these decisions, because we believe that his voice is important. We have taken the time to listen to him, to discover what it is that he needs when it comes to his education. We had to evaluate the importance of academic work when compared to his overall mental health and feeling like he belonged.

We are fortunate to have access to an amazing special education teacher who has taken the time to understand who our son is and, most importantly, is not afraid to listen to what it is that he needs. We are accessing this teacher through a public distributed learning program. The goals in our son's Individualized Education Plan look much different now, but they finally truly reflect where he is at and where we hope to be.

While our journey is far from over, we celebrate the good things that have come our way and learn from the not-so-good experiences. We continue to encourage and support our son while surrounding ourselves with champions who believe in him and our family. We do not define or limit our son because of his diagnosis; instead, we honor his strengths and understand his challenges and let these guide us toward the strategies and supports that work best for him. Most importantly, we believe that he is and will continue to be successful.

I'd like to encourage anyone who lives with or works with children who have mental health and other learning challenges to embrace curiosity and understanding. It is important to take the time to learn about the different mental health disorders and explore which strategies may best support your student. Most critically, remember that relationships matter. A strong, positive relationship with a child and family leads to more opportunities for learning and understanding.

Reflection Questions

1. What are some of the challenges a teacher might face when they first identify a child in their class may be struggling?
2. Why is learning about mental health challenges and how they impact children, youth, and families important?
3. Why is it important to know about your local mental health resources?
4. What role does parent and school communication play in children's mental health?

5. How can you advocate for more mental health information and training in future curriculum? Is this important?
6. How can you be a champion for a future student and family? Why is it important to be a champion?

Bibliography

Blamires, Mike, "Why Teachers Have to be Social Workers: Adlerian Individual Psychology and Positive Approaches to Behaviour Management: A Lost Legacy in the UK." Geneva: European Conference on Educational Research, 2006. http://www.leeds.ac.uk/educol/documents/157654.htm.

British Columbia Ministry of Children and Family Development. "A Parent's Handbook: Your Guide to Autism Programs." August 2015. http://www.mcf.gov.bc.ca/autism/pdf/autism_handbook_web.pdf.

Canadian Attention Deficit Hyperactivity Disorder Resource Alliance. "Canadian ADHD Practice Guidelines." 3rd ed. 2010. http://www.caddra.ca/pdfs/caddraGuidelines2011.pdf.

Froese-Germain, Bernie, and Richard Riel. "Understanding Teachers' Perspectives on Student Mental Health: Findings From a National Survey." Canadian Teachers' Federation, 2012. http://www.ctf-fce.ca/Research-Library/StudentMentalHealthReport.pdf.

Furedi, Frank. "Teachers Are Not Social Workers." *The Telegraph*, November 8, 2003. http://www.telegraph.co.uk/education/educationnews/3320912/Teachers-are-not-social-workers.html.

Government of British Columbia. "Child and Teen Mental Health." http://www.mcf.gov.bc.ca/mental_health/.

Greene, Ross. *Lost at School: Why Our Kids with Behavioral Challenges are Falling Through the Cracks and How We Can Help Them*. New York: Scribner, 2008.

Inglis, Angela, and Jehannine Austin. "The Blame Game." *Visions: BC's Mental Health and Addictions Journal* 8 (2013) 10–11. http://www.heretohelp.bc.ca/visions/families-vol8/the-blame-game-is-it-my-fault-did-i-cause-it.

Ogilvie, Bev. *ConnectZone.org: Building Connectedness in Schools*. Vancouver, BC: Inside Out, 2014. http://www.connectzone.org.

Pierson, Rita. "Every Kid Deserves a Champion." TED, May 2013. https://www.ted.com/talks/rita_pierson_every_kid_needs_a_champion.

RBC Children's Mental Health Project. "Silent Families, Suffering Children, and Youth." 2012. http://www.rbc.com/community-sustainability/_assets-custom/pdf/Childrens-Mental-Health-Parents-Poll-White-Paper.pdf.

Shanker, Stuart. *Calm, Alert, and Learning: Classroom Strategies for Self-Regulation*. Toronto: Pearson Canada, 2013.

Wang, Ming-Te and Salam Sheikh-Khalil. "Does Parental Involvement Matter for Student Achievement and Mental Health in High School?" *Child Development* 85 (2014) 610–25.

Wejr, Chris. "10 Ways To Start With Strengths In Schools." The Wejr Board, November 30, 2014. http://chriswejr.com/2014/11/30/10-ways-to-start-with-strengths-in-schools.

12

Between Strangers and Friends: Toward a Theory of Hospitality, Reciprocity, and Respect for Difference in "Special Needs" Education[1]

Bruce Shelvey

Introduction

EVEN THOUGH INCLUSIVE AND democratic shifts in learning communities have made "special education" possible, exceptional students who do not establish an origin in the self in order to shape, categorize, and organize the present in planning for a certain future are either marginalized (excluded) or appropriated (integrated) within the educational system. However, a community of learning can be fostered when the self is understood in relation to each other and when associations of hospitality, reciprocity, and respect for historical difference are acknowledged and practiced.

Most exceptional learners[2] in today's educational settings find themselves in a minority position between strangers and friends. Based upon

1. Dedicated to all parents who have attempted to navigate the perplexing educational system into which their exceptional children have been born. And, to Ryerson, who "broke the mold."

2. For a list of possible definitions and categorizations relating to the term "exceptional learners," see the "Who are Exceptional Learners" page for the Council of Exceptional Children: The Voice and Vision of Special Education. https://www.cec.sped.org/special-ed-topics/who-are-exceptional-learners. While the CEC includes "gifted and talented" (high-achieving) learners and "twice exceptional" learners (high-achieving students with a co-occurring disability), I focus on the other "exceptional learners," identifying autism, deaf-blindness, deafness, emotional disturbance, intellectual disability, hearing impairment, multiple disabilities, orthopedic disabilities, specific learning disabilities, speech or language impairment, traumatic brain injury, visual impairments including blindness,

their exclusive nature or the unique symptoms of their condition, they are thought to lack a common "origin" that is shared by the majority of students, and their requirements for learning are processed in a manner that reflects the exception to the rule of pedagogical practice. While advocates for marginalized learners have made huge gains in the last twenty years, the idealism of the traditional educational paradigm and the pragmatism of various strains of progressive education remain centered on the development of a self-sufficient, independent person who makes their own future through the choices they enact. The learner that requires a "special education" is introduced into a no-person's land, a gulf between deviance and normalcy. They fit nowhere and everywhere at the same time; they reside in a "gap" that translates into policies of inclusion, toleration, and acceptance (of the condition) but also into isolation, loneliness, and alienation (for the person themselves).

Education, Personhood and History

In Western educational systems, the structure of schools, the language of progress, the objectives of learning outcomes, the measurements of assessment, and the coordination of classroom experiences, to name a few examples, place the subject-self-learner at the center of the educational model.[3] In more conventional settings, educators build up an individual self by encouraging students to construct their own sense of personhood in relation to supposedly self-apparent proven traditions or timeless values. In more liberal contexts, the student is encouraged to become self-aware by narrating a personhood around their social experience.[4] In both cases, the

---

and developmentally delayed. Note that "exceptionality," by definition, includes the two polarities (gifted and challenged) in relation to an educational "norm."

3. John Dewey's progressive educational model is premised upon the theory of nineteenth century German philosopher Georg Wilhelm Friedrich Hegel. Dewey's Hegelianism promoted the idea that personhood develops when the process-oriented individual critically reflects on their experience, organizes this experience into a series of relationships, and then synthesizes a particular, self-determined identity. Dewey, following Hegel, argued that the purpose and overriding aim of history (the self-conscious organization of the past) is the ongoing perfection of man. For Dewey's engagement with Hegelian philosophy, see his 1897 lecture at the University of Chicago as published in Dewey, "Hegel's Philosophy of Spirit." See also Hegel, *Reason in History*, and Hegel, *The Philosophy of History*.

4. Dewey, *Experience and Education*; See also, International Centre for Educators' Learning Styles, "John Dewey's Philosophy of Experience and Education" as found at https://eiclsresearch.wordpress.com/types-of-styles/teaching-styles/john-dewey/deweys-philosophy-on-experience-and-education/.

reliance on a self-determined history as a means to establishing a reasonable place within society—what progressive educator John Dewey called the "democratic fellowship of common humanity"—remains the cornerstone of educational philosophy.[5]

Scripting a particular past that relates to other pasts has become the crucial test of personhood because, as Dewey pointed out, "history began only when man came to know himself, when he became a conscious object of interest and of action to himself." The connection between cognition and meaning is explicit: "People who have left no historical records of their existence... cannot have had any true history.[6] In the positive sense, the created, self-aware individual, in their advancement toward maturity and through their ability to give meaning to their experience by consciously ordering the causes and effects of history, have the "power to develop."[7] A learner with physical or cognitive exceptionalities, on the other hand, may be excluded from a community where the relation of "reasonable" self-conscious beings determines membership.[8] As educational philosopher James Good explains about Dewey's philosophy, self-knowledge is "a means to the end of man's creating a home for himself by realizing his unity with nature, and the unity of his individual life and experience, within a larger, and perpetually evolving, whole."[9] Failure to script one's self-conscious awareness of difference translates into marginalization and isolation,[10] because diversity is tolerated only in as much as it provides the opportunity for the development of self-recognition.[11]

While educational systems today rarely exclude the exceptional learner, the preoccupation with self-actualization as the measure of successful teaching remains entrenched. After fifty years of experience and

---

5. Shook and Good, *John Dewey's Philosophy of Spirit*. Dewey's concept of personhood is taken from his interpretation of Hegel's philosophy of spirit. Hegel's reliance on history as a means to reason the "absolute" is similar to Dewey's conception of "nature."

6. Dewey, "Hegel's Philosophy of Spirit," 163.

7. Dewey, "Time and Individuality," as quoted in Good, "Rereading Dewey's 'Permanent Hegelian Deposit,'" 79.

8. Dewey, "Hegel's Philosophy of Spirit," 165.

9. Ibid., 89.

10. Dewey, for example, followed Hegel's idea of "identity in difference" (through his concept of negation) and agreed that this difference would be found in relation to "a process of development" (the absolute). Good, "Rereading Dewey's 'Permanent Hegelian Deposit,'" 56–92.

11. As Good so aptly points out, it is Dewey's application of Hegel's notion of property, as laid out in *Philosophy of Right*, that "gives man 'an external sphere of freedom' by enabling him to act in certain ways." Good, "Rereading Dewey's 'Permanent Hegelian Deposit,'" 85.

practice with marginalized learners, including the parental advocacy of the 1950s and 1960s that opened the doors for the inclusion of exceptionalities, the civil rights movement in the 1960s that prompted laws to protect the vulnerable in society, the changing political climate of the 1970s that de-institutionalized persons of difference, and the self-advocacy of marginalized peoples in the 1980s and 1990s that announced the voice of the other,[12] there still exists a tension between the spheres of "normal" and "special" education. No amount of innovation has bridged this great divide, even if practitioners share the unfortunate assumption that the person of difference lacks, either in kind or by degree, an identity. Educational environments that have become more nuanced and balanced have also retained the mandate to produce self-actualized individuals, and this has left few meaningful places for people of difference to exist in their own right when they do not create a self-affirming narrative.

In establishing models of exceptionality, "special education" itself reinforces the illusion that the diverse and dynamic community of learners in any classroom forms a coherent whole as opposed to the person of difference. In contrast to the assumed common origins of a typical learner, for example, the identity of each exceptional learner in *both* the medical and social models of analysis is premised upon the question: "What causes disability?" The answer, whether nature or nurture, predetermines how the educator interprets the challenged pupil and where they place her within the educational environment, precisely because of their search for a seminal cause for historical difference. And, both the determinist (hereditary/genetics) and constructionist (social/political) solution for learning deficiencies rely upon a common outcome of self-actualization even if they disagree on how to attain it. The criteria used to establish educational policy determines the kinds of research undertaken, the programs that are developed, and the interventions that are prescribed.

Once stigmatized with an objective, clinical label or identity, the learner with physical, cognitive, psychological, sensory, or behavioral abnormalities

---

12. For a sampling of the history of special education in the United States, see Martin, Martin, and Terman, "The Legislative and Litigation History," 25–39; US Department of Education, Office of Special Education and Rehabilitative Services, *Thirty-Five Years of Progress*; Osgood, *History of Inclusion*; Dudley, Burns, and Bridget, "Two Perspectives on Inclusion," 14–31. For a sampling of the history of special education in Canada, see Reaume, "Disability History In Canada"; Morgan, "A Brief History of Special Education," 10–14; Hutchinson, *Inclusion of Exceptional Learners*. The history of special education outside of North America is not easily accessible; however, interested researchers can consult the *International Journal of Special Education* (http://www.internationaljournalofspecialed.com) to review specific approaches taken by educators of exceptional learners in other parts of the world.

enters into a world of professional judgments, measures, and interventions designed to modify, treat, or improve their ability to participate in a self-affirming community.[13] Famed pioneer in special education studies, Dr. Samuel A. Kirk, who coined the term "learning disabilities" in 1963 and successfully lobbied Congress in 1964 for funding for specialized training for teachers, noted that this deterministic approach to learning anomalies promoted the understanding that the "abnormal within the child" was an inherent quality of their personhood. Even when environmental factors are considered and developmental psychological theories are applied, deterministic models make the exceptional learner's inability to narrate their personhood an inherent, generational, hereditary deficiency. Especially in the area of cognition, as researcher Scot Danforth suggests, both biological and psychological theories "do not differ in their orientation toward understanding intelligence as an individual attribute or intellectual disability as an individual condition of subnormal intelligence."[14]

In recent years, the advocacy of human rights activists, social theoreticians, and supportive educators has turned deterministic notions of deficiency and deviance into a social relationship between the exceptional learner and cultural and historical norms as represented by school systems, classically trained educators and traditional curriculum.[15] The diagnostic tools of these new experts and professionals probe the limits of the exceptional learner's ability to "fit" into the preexisting educational community, even as they recognize (and sometimes celebrate) the challenges of accommodating diversity. Specialized training, Independent Educational Plans (IEPs), classroom composition, and learning assistants have become a part of the language of integration. Not unlike the "ship of fools," however, the identity of the exceptional learner as a relation of power relative to normal learners serves as a proxy for societal relations.[16] The assumption that an exceptional learner is unable to form an identity independent from the self-actualization of others legitimizes the moral and ethical superiority of the "normal" individual, which makes practice of integration acceptable because it illustrates how exceptionality can be accommodated, even respected and valued, within a larger community.[17] It is instructive that moving the site of special education into the educational environment itself has not ended the

13. Educational theorist Ellen Brantlinger labeled this process "fixing other people's children." See Brantlinger, *Who Benefits from Special Education?*

14. Danforth, "John Dewey's Contributions," 56.

15. Castañeda, Hopkins, and Peters, "Introduction," 461–67.

16. Foucault, *Madness and Civilization*, Introduction and Chapter 1 ("Stultifera Navis").

17. Castañeda, Hopkins, and Peters, "Introduction," 461–67.

widely practiced personal, systemic, and institutional discrimination that excludes persons of difference and/or limits their opportunities.[18]

In the move from the institution to the classroom, the power relations between the physically or cognitively unique individual and the professional practitioner have remained intact. The school administrator and teacher now determine when and where exceptional learners will be "put on display," in order to validate the typical learner, or "kept out of sight/site," in order not to disrupt the typical learning environment.[19] Many of the typologies of "disability" employed in earlier periods have been translated into the perceptions of (and the homogenized identities of) an increasingly heterogeneous and diverse group of people of historical difference. At the level of popular culture, clinical terms that had defined persons with cognitive or mental "disorders," such as "idiot," "imbecile," "moron," "feebleminded," and "retarded," continue to function as demeaning epithets. At the professional level, the characterizations of "disability" operate with little scrutiny, making the exceptional learner's *function* within the classroom a naturally prescribed role as defined by their diagnosis. The social efficacy and scientific legitimacy of these and other forms of prejudice are reinforced each time they are combined to control and manage any specific educational anomaly.

Ideal Learners, Pedagogical Pets, and Problem Pupils

In light of all that we know about the impact of social and contextual influences, most educators today no longer hold to the perspective that nature endows certain humans with specific characteristics that act as a guiding force throughout the course of their development. Nevertheless, John Dewey's dictum that "a violet and an oak tree are equal when one has the same opportunity to develop to the full as a violet which the other has as an oak" remains a pedagogical truism.[20] Like Dewey, many educators assume that democratically inspired educational systems will act as a great equalizer and that the "inclusion" of all learners as part of a moral and ethical imperative

---

18. For example, educational philosopher Angela Carlson coined the termed "cognitive ableism," which she defines as, "a prejudice or attitude of bias in favour of the interests of individuals who possess certain cognitive abilities (or the *potential* for them) against those who are believed not to actually or potentially possess them." She goes on to further define these "others" as those persons who are perceived to lack "cognitive capacities which allow for rationality, autonomy, and relations with other human beings." Carlson, "Mindful Subjects," 142.

19. Foucault, "Subject and Power," 303–19; Foucault, *Archaeology of Knowledge*, 44–54.

20. See Dewey, "Ethics," in Boydston, *John Dewey: The Later Works*, 346.

will be the natural outcome of social justice.[21] These optimistic expectations extend to the individual learner, whose role is to dutifully contribute knowledge and obediently accept input from others within the community, while engaging in the collective social enterprise in their own unique way.[22] However, the "differences in kind" approach necessarily limits an individual's involvement based upon her ability to shape and form an experience that can be identified, defined, and categorized in relation to the experiences of others. So while the democratization of education has given thoughtful educators alternatives to the binaries of either the nature or nurture models when interpreting disability, the place of the exceptional learner continues to be defined by his ability to create and maintain a self-actualized proximity to the ideal of a typical learner. For most exceptional learners this process includes an assigned place along a spectrum as determined by educational professionals and medical practitioners.[23]

The myth of the ideal learner is most prominent in the educational setting when the exceptional learner is categorized according to standardized measurements, which have been naturalized by administrators and teachers.[24] A student's qualitative possibilities and assigned physical or cognitive

21. Scot Danforth points out that John Dewey did author a couple of articles in the *New Republic* that criticized the use of intelligence tests as both undemocratic and impractical, but it is not clear from Danforth's paper—which proposes a "Deweyan educational theory of intellectual disability"—how Dewey's commitment to "democratic faith in human equality" remained consistent with his idea that an individual participates in a community based upon the "development of whatever gift he has." For all of his writing on learning, education, and society, Dewey never once wrote specifically about the place of exceptional learners in the classroom. Danforth, "John Dewey's Contributions," 45–62.

22. Dewey understood biological function as movement and transformation in and of itself, a continuous and ongoing progression that combined the "natural" and the "social" spheres of human experience. He continuously worked against the nature/nurture dichotomy and proposed change itself as the only "natural" way to understand growth, learning, and development. Dewey, "Ethics," in Boydsten, *John Dewey: The Later Works*, 345.

23. For example, two predominant psychological theories on "mental retardation" are used to interpret quantitative data provided by standardized measurements: the Developmental Delay Theory (mentally handicapped are much the same as typical learners but have slower learning processes and may not have the capacity to realize full development) and the Deficit Theory (identifies the inherent shortcomings of personhood because of an (innate) inability to form an identity). Boddington and Podpadec, "Who are the Mentally Handicapped?" 177–90. The authors argue that reifying mental capacity is highly problematic given that psychologists are beginning to understand "handicaps" as "the outcome of a complex series of social negotiations," rather than an innate (or inherited) quality that existed within a person (182).

24. If Western liberal philosophical discourse on ethics and morality is any indication, the protection of peoples with cognitive variations may well be the last frontier of human

location are predetermined by an artificial quantitative standard, a norm that forms the basis of most educational policy. Defining the personhood of the exceptional learner in opposition to the individual identities within the learning community is especially evident in funding arrangements that depend upon the assessments of medical doctors, psychologists, and geneticists who use standardized measurements of diversity to identity the pathological condition that is worthy of a certain level of treatment. The educational deference given to these experts at the inception of a child's entry into the school system illustrates well the predisposition toward quantitative definitions and the subversion of qualitative difference. Medical quotients fortify an ongoing and internal bias that entrenches the notion that persons of difference are "deficit learners" by the very nature of their diagnosis. The emphasis on heritage, genetics, intellectual processes, and self-aware cognition in the form of an individual history *produces* a disabled learner who functions according to instinctual patterns. The Intelligence Quotient Test (IQT), for example, mechanizes a representation of a learner's mental proficiency and is utilized to determine everything from a legal right to be educated to appropriate funding levels.[25] Thus, the educational strategies employed to address the "problems," usually in the form of an Independent Educational Plan, are thought to be value-neutral even though for the sake of standardization and efficiency they are in the first instance, a *stereotype* of the medical/quantitative quotient that accompanied the diagnosis.

Placed at the mercy of the professional who conceived of them as blank slates that require a made-to-order identity if they are to survive in the classroom and in society, the exceptional learner has his agency (innocently) replaced by a matrix of social and environmental relationships that legitimize the typological histories acting as the measure of well-adapted human qualities.[26] Yet, the very presence of the physically or cognitively marginalized student disrupts or ruptures the utopian liberal notion of coherent self-actualization that is formed within the educational setting. Exceptional learners provide a constant reminder of the grand illusion of

---

rights. A representative sample can be seen in a quote from a book entitled *Ethics and Mental Retardation*: "Severely retarded persons normally have little chance of ever becoming autonomous.... Here we are dealing with a class of persons who will never be in a position where it could be reasonably claimed that their destinies ought to be determined by their own choices and decisions." Murphy, "Rights and Borderline Cases," 14.

25. Block and Dworkin, *IQ Controversy*. Scholars have made a direct link between the formalization of IQ testing and the early eugenics movement. See Carlson, "Mindful Subjects," 56–58. Recently, there have been discussions about whether special education has served as an organizational mechanism of racial resegregation in the United States. Ferri and Connor, *Reading Resistance*.

26. Scott, "Differences, Borders, Fusions," 16–24.

the independent, introspective, traditional/typical learner, especially when they compromise the purity of the educational ideal by refusing to cooperate with the appropriation of their unique identity. Because the typical range of responses available to innovative administrators, adaptive teachers, well-meaning parents, and understanding peers is limited to a pragmatic, logical positivism, the responses to these excesses of inclusion too often find their expression in cost-saving measures for an administration's classroom composition, or bargaining chips for teachers' workloads, or parental concerns over appropriate learning environments, all of which are manifestations of the notion that people of difference are integrated functions that rely upon the experiences of self-made others.[27]

Since a learner's agency is dependent upon the capacity and willingness to examine their own self-expressions in relation to that of others and to revise their expectations as a result of these assessments, the capacity for choice itself represents not only an intelligent approach to options but also the very freedom of the individual to act.[28] Schools, as social institutions and the medium for *creating* individuals,[29] are tasked with providing the freedom necessary for individuals to find their own path toward self-discovery.[30] Individualism is not taught as a fixed and preexisting state of nature, but as something that is in process and is achieved with the support of cultural and physical stimuli.[31] Therefore, when agency is exercised within a democratic classroom community, the ideal learner releases and fulfills their potential, regardless of differences, and realizes their preferred future.[32] On the other hand, a failure to *exercise* the choice over one's future amounts to a lack of liberty and thus a corresponding loss of one's indi-

---

27. The medical model predetermines a history based upon the narrow confines of a diagnosis and the body of literature that classifies the symptoms into a regime specifically designed to treat a pathological difference of kind. For an example of this kind of reasoning, see Spicker, "Mental Handicap and Citizenship," 139–51; Boddington and Podpadec, "Who Are the Mentally Handicapped?" 177–90. As Carlson points out, the issue is not the classification itself but rather "the assumption that it [the category of "mental retardation"] points to some real deficit, and that it is therefore unproblematic as a classification." Carlson, "Mindful Subjects," 131.

28. Dewey, "Individualism Old and New," in Boydsten, *John Dewey: The Later Works*, 121.

29. The role of the school in forming liberal citizens was developed in full by John Dewey. See Dewey, *School and Society*.

30. A very useful summary of Dewey's concept of freedom can be found at Festenstein, "Dewey's Political Philosophy." See also Dewey and Dewey, *Schools of Tomorrow*, especially chapter 6.

31. Dewey, "Future of Liberalism," in Boydsten, *John Dewey: The Later Works*, 291.

32. Dewey, "Public and Its Problems," in Boydsten, *John Dewey: The Later Works*, 329.

vidualism. As a result, the active and enterprising learner *discovers* their self experimentally within an intelligent and dynamic social environment, while the exceptional learner is expected to passively *accept* either intervention or exclusion as an essential part of their identity.

Rather than give up on their utopic vision of the ideal student, many educators have enveloped the exceptional learner into their existing paradigm by becoming more analytical and scientific in order to manage the diversity within the classroom.[33] Clinicians, administrators, teachers, and special education assistants diagnose, prescribe, surveil, and manage the exceptional learner's educational path for the purpose of humanizing their "underdeveloped" or "instinctual" habits.[34] Schools are understood, almost by default, as epistemological clinics where the deviant is programmed to learn through an experimental model of disability that interprets inclusion as a series of issues and problems.[35] IEPs, for example, adapt or modify the standard curriculum so as to mimic, as closely as possible, a set of prescribed learning outcomes even though its very application requires isolation or exclusion from learning community, and its implementation has little relevance to other learners. The exceptional learner, as a pedagogical pet, is a mirrored understanding that an ideal self can be impressed upon the life of an other, as if (in their innocence or their depravity) they constitute a blank screen upon which educators can project society's deepest fears and highest aspirations.

Navigating through the educational system as an exceptional learner also includes being stigmatized as an impediment to a learning community. Within the designation of special education, a distinct educational category of its own *kind* with specific and defined positions of power and experts vested with the authority to determine suitable treatment, exceptional

---

33. In the nineteenth century, attitudes toward persons of difference meant they were confined to the "private" sphere of the home and institution. See Kerlin, "Our Household Pets," 283–92. Kerlin held the position of superintendent of the Pennsylvania Training School from 1865 to 1893. See also White, *From a Philosophical Point of View*, 146, 149.

34. The recourse to scripting identity today may well be consistent with earlier educational practices when the historical construction of persons of difference as qualitatively and radically "other" meant the learner was not just in possession of lesser capacities and potential (quantitative) but is of their own kind and therefore in need of being possessed by an (assumed) individuality, one that is "given" to them or provided for them. One of the best summaries of this earlier period of education as it relates to cognitive variations can be found in Rosen, Clark, and Kivitz, *History of Mental Retardation*, introduction, xiii–xxiv.

35. The treatment of the human body in medical practice, where the organization of clinical knowledge enabled doctors "to *see* and to *say*," seems consistent with the structure of educational environments, which presume that anything that cannot be "seen" hides the system of thought that it supports. Foucault, *Birth of a Clinic*, xxi.

learners bear the weight of the politics of exclusion. The pressure to forgo educational opportunities because of the fear that they are a threat to a coherent student body is felt in so many gestures, snubs, and comments that express the responsibilities of prevention. As a form of discrimination bolstered by increasingly sophisticated and accessible prenatal testing and genetic identification mechanisms, the exceptional learner represents a "bad choice" or an opportunity missed.[36] The pressure to *screen* (make invisible) the exceptional learner appears to make their presence in the classroom an option.[37] Where prevention is not possible, the desire to discipline the diversity represented by the exceptional learner is most often treated with strategies of intervention. In utilizing comparative measurements in the form of quotients and standardized testing, social and cultural remediation is legitimized behind a veil of scientific neutrality that empowers clinicians, administrators, and teachers to intervene, surveil, and ameliorate the setting of abnormality.[38] Gratefully, associations that once guided interventionist

---

36. Perhaps the public debate on ethics of exclusion officially began in 1971 when the film *Who Should Survive?: One of the Choices on Our Conscience* aired at a conference for medical practitioners. The docudrama, financed by the Joseph P. Kennedy Jr. Foundation, followed a case at Baltimore's Johns Hopkins Hospital where, based upon the parents' wishes, an infant with treatable complications arising from being born with Down syndrome was intentionally neglected by the medical staff. The child died of starvation and dehydration. While the public reaction was generally critical of the parents' decision and the physicians' inaction, the film highlighted a general consensus that "prevention" would have been a more suitable option for the child than (non)treatment. Antommaria, "Who Should Survive," 205–24; Gustafson, "Johns Hopkins Case," 413–14.

37. Barbara Hillyer points out in her book *Feminism and Disability*, that the prenatal identification of genetic variations, for example, has put enormous pressure on mothers to make the preventative choice in order avoid the shame of "mother-blaming." Hillyer has been criticized, however, by self-advocates in disability studies who view her work as premised upon dependence and people-with-disabilities-as-children stereotypes. For a discussion of recent interlocutions between feminism and disability studies, see Silvers, "Feminist Perspectives on Disability"; Piepmeier, Cantrell, and Maggio, "Disability is a Feminist Issue." For an example of a self-advocacy position, see Morris, "Personal and Political."

38. As Amos Yong points out, in *The Bible, Disability and the Church: A New Vision of the People of God*, this prejudice against people of difference is not limited to scientific discourse but is also supported by a whole host of historical and religious assumptions. For example, Christian theological interpretations have tended to see "integration" in the context of a normalized eschatology that translates into the almost complete absence of persons of difference from religious communities. Further, the logic of a normalized heaven free from the evidence of all difference appears to give tacit support to a kind of societal utopia, which calls for interventionist strategies that marginalize exceptional individuals. The alternative for the Christian church, Yong argues, is to see a person with Down syndrome, for example, as "in the image of God." See Yong, *Theology and Down Syndrome*; Yong, "Disability Theology of the Resurrection," 10.

strategies are no longer practiced.[39] However, especially in areas of correctional action, the reaction to the distress of an exceptional learner is too often characterized by aggressive measures or with the removal of basic educational opportunities.[40] While not always abusive in nature, any treatment of the cognitively or physically diverse individual that justifies intervention as an appropriate substitution for their own agency should be understood as a diminishment (or loss) of their personhood.

Hospitality, Reciprocity, and Respect

Is there a way to turn learning environments into communities of learning given the progressive, pragmatic, and process-oriented educational system that we have inherited? Must we establish and enforce set categories of "disability" that are conceived as a deficit or defect? Is it possible to avoid putting exceptional learners into schools where they are either bound up in a process of socially constructed definitions of their diagnosis, or are the product of the identity they assume as a result of their treatment, or are the model of how their condition is interpreted, ordered, and categorized? The answer to these questions cannot come from a reduction of difference or the normalization of a condition, because arguments for biological similarities are not enough to overcome a long history of marginalization and appropriation. The preoccupation with biological origins can easily be shifted to exclude members of a *kind* based upon their character similarities to others where criteria such as self-awareness, future orientation, and relational acumen (all qualities held in high esteem by liberal democratic societies) are understood as a (more) suitable determination of individual being.[41] The

---

39. In institutionalized settings, for example, cognitively different children's supposed insensitivity to heat and cold justified the denial of basic warmth in their rooms, their assumed high tolerance to pain justified the use of electric shock as a means of punishment, and their apparent lack of social awareness justified isolation and exclusion. Wolfensberger, "Origins and Nature," 35–82.

40. Knowing the challenges presented by some exceptional learners, especially when faced with the possibility of violence toward others or of self-harm, one should not be judgmental but recognize that the reason why we see these treatments as options may be, at least in part, a hold-over from earlier associations of "disability" and the absence of full personhood.

41. For example, Peter Singer in *Animal Liberation* utilizes "permanently and profoundly retarded human beings" to argue for the rights of animals based upon their similar "level of awareness, self-consciousness, intelligence, and sentience of many non-human beings." While these "shells of humanity" may be *Homo sapiens*, they lack the human history that makes their lives morally relevant so as to provide a "legitimate bases for partiality." See Singer, *Animal Liberation*, 17–21. Philosophers have stretched

goal of creating self-sufficient and self-determined individuals has never guaranteed well-being for learners. Rather, it is the *indifference* to the historical uniqueness of others that blinds us to the interaction with difference that *makes* us human. In *difference* we (re)cognize our own self (know ourself again and again) by choosing to be in constant dynamic relation to each other. In affirming the classroom as an open location between strangers and friends, administrators, teachers, students, and parents transform curricular and pedagogical options once bound by the creation of a "productive citizen" into educational opportunities that promote the understanding of everyone's historical difference.[42]

Making the *end* of education a continuum of relational possibilities that realizes the diverse human representation and potentializes the agency of all students in our communities of learning is, in the first instance, premised upon hospitality. To invoke a spirit of hospitality for all persons participating in the community of learning is to recognize the desire to be known and to affirm the anticipation of knowing the other.[43] If, as philosopher and historian Paul Ricouer convincingly argues, "the shortest route to the self is through the other," then we need each and every other in order *to be* in a meaningful community of learning that encourages the presencing of unique gifts and contributions.[44] A hospitable approach to education makes any form of exclusion unthinkable.[45] Hosting each other makes new (and equally valid) ways of being in the classroom possible and opens up all areas of educational vitality, including assessment, collaboration, and correction, as opportunities for intellectual, physical, and spiritual well-being. Belongingness for all learners is possible when the beauty and mystery of a shared learning environment is the responsibility for the other's learning. It is a community-centric approach where a pedagogical space *in between* is nurtured so any person, indeed even ourselves, can be realized in relation to

---

the limits of this marginalization of persons of difference to the extreme in an attempt to prove their arguments, not (perhaps ironically) for the humanity of the person of difference, but rather for the relative similarities of animals and human communities in an effort to establish the moral and ethical standing of animals. For an especially unfortunate example see Murphy, "Do the Retarded Have a Right Not To Be Eaten?" 43–46.

42. Cole, *Teaching the Violent Past*. For an example of alternative models of education, see Sumara, Davis, and Laidlaw, "Canadian Identity," 150–51.

43. I am borrowing this phrase from Amos Yong. See Yong, *Theology and Down Syndrome*, 193–225.

44. See Kearney, *On Paul Ricoeur*, especially chapter 1, for what he calls the "eschatology of the sacred," 29.

45. Ricoeur, *Oneself as Another*, 1–23.

the other.[46] In the spirit of hospitality the desire to be known and to know the other is a hopeful reconciliation.

An educational model of possibility must also include an ongoing, open-ended, and dynamic pedagogy understood as reciprocity. Reciprocity is a commitment to the wager of (self) doubt so one can recognize the opportunities to "transform a stranger into a friend."[47] Unfortunately, the unknowns associated with exceptional learners have too often caused the rest of a learning community to avoid the risk of relationship because of the fear of being rejected by a person of difference. Tragically, we have replaced reciprocity with a "speaking for" in anticipation of a lack of agency (i.e., lacking a history independent from that of my own) and the relationship with the exceptional learner *becomes* an object lesson for our own purpose, an indignity of inclusion that only serves to validate a prescribed way of becoming. However, the community of learning transforms into a place of *being* that welcomes and receives the contributions, gifts, and talents of all learners across a diverse spectrum of abilities when we assume the risk of the stranger, a stranger that chooses to be our friend, and face our fear that we too are strangers to the other. The wager we accept is that the scapegoating of exceptional learners that is used to maintain a fixed, prescribed, and reasonable educational system[48] can be replaced with the possibility of a transfigured teaching and learning environment where all participants can thrive and have a meaningful part in the constant recreating of something new. In a community of learning where my self is the other, teachers have the opportunity in their role as translators to negotiate the worlds apart and facilitate mediums of understanding whereby the surprise between stranger and friend is reciprocated.[49] In assuming the wager of reciprocity, "betweenness" is transformed from a *location* in a classroom to a renewed *relation* in community.[50]

---

46. I am not aware of any work that applies Ricoeurian hermeneutics of the self to persons of difference; however, a good example of how it might be applied can be found in the interfaith dialogue as represented in the work of Richard Kearney and James Taylor. See Kearney and Taylor, *Hosting the Stranger*.

47. I am indebted to Richard Kearney for unfolding the concept of "the wager" in relation to an encounter with "the other." See Kearney, *Anatheism*, especially chapter 2. For quote, see Yong, *Theology and Down Syndrome*, 225.

48. The mythological origins of using "marked" individuals as scapegoats in order to create the illusion of a unified social order is best explained by Rene Girard. See Girard, *I See Satan Fall Like Lightening*.

49. Paul Ricoeur refers to this as "linguistic hospitality," which he defines as "where the pleasure of dwelling in the other's language is balanced by the pleasure of receiving the foreign word at home, in one's own welcoming house." Ricoeur, *On Translation*, 10.

50. An example of this can be found in the work and life of Jean Vanier who established these "in between" spaces in the L'Arche communities. See Vanier, *Becoming Human*.

Finally, the competition in our educational systems for either one or the other cannot be subverted by something else besides if we fail to respect the historical difference that makes each individual unique. When we understand that the specter of normalization poses a significant threat to interaction, we can then honestly examine the risk management positions that we adopt to limit the personal, emotional, and economic liability to which we feel exposed because of the presencing of the exceptional learner. Respect for historical difference counts on the wager of reciprocity and the spirit of hospitality to release the whole personhood of each individual as a gift to the other. In return, each participant in the community of learning has to choose whether to receive and honor the giving or to possess the gift as their own by making the other "fit" or adapt into a mythological world of reason or a fictitious, ready-made, pure social order.[51] To respect historical difference as a gift is to understand what theorist Homi Bhabha identifies as the most wonderful opportunity of an other's encounter with "us": "No name is yours until you speak it; somebody returns your call and suddenly, the circuit of signs, gestures, gesticulations is established and you enter the territory of the right to narrate. You are part of a dialogue that may not, at first, be heard or heralded—you may be ignored—but your personhood cannot be denied. In another's country that is also your own, your person divides, and in following the forked path you encounter yourself in a double movement . . . once as stranger, and then as friend."[52] The opening that provides the opportunity to give one's own story as a *gift* to an other is also "a collective, ethical, right to difference in equality."[53]

Postscript to teachers: As social theorist and historian Michel de Certeau points out (about France, but one could nevertheless apply it to all Western educational systems) the "school has been the weapon of a political centralization." As an "instrument that advertises democracy," the "implantation of schools" has "marked" cities and towns with "a unique and centralized Reason . . . as space infused by the state, that does not conform to the environment, it is a geometrical site, like a military barracks, with square rooms and rectilinear corridors, an architectural projection of the teaching

---

51. To paraphrase Vanier and his "moral philosophy for our time that is accessible to everyone," we should commit to three affirmations: First, that every human being, especially in light of the diversity of our limitations, cultures, or religions, is important and valuable and worthy of respect; second, that the worst evil is disdain of another person, which can lead to oppression, marginalization, and suppression of human life; and finally, that we can only experience the fullness of life inscribed on human beings when we realize our need of others. Vanier, *Made for Happiness*, 180.

52. Bhabha, *Location of Culture*, xxv.

53. Balibar, *Masses, Classes, Ideas*, 56.

formulated within it." But as the power relations have shifted away from the school toward other authoritative cultural sources (television, social media, advertising, and communications) the educational system, still representative of the imposition of state power, inherits the contested position of being both irreplaceable and yet irrelevant. In turn, educators find themselves saddled with all of the responsibility of proper socialization but lacking the authority to act. Perhaps the exception to this general rule is "special education," where learners are still socialized into a specific norm; the very designation encourages teachers to exercise a residual power that has long been lost in their relations with so-called typical learners. Interestingly, however, it is at this "critical crux where teachers and students develop their own practices from information that has come from different sources" that marginalized teachers (in a broader social context) and marginalized learners (in a specific educational context) can find a shared space of learning where a plurality of knowing can be practiced.[54] In schools where teachers are most likely to be confronted with heterogeneous references and multiple meanings, "special education" could be an opportunity to diversify our cultural understanding of "ability" and to expand our pedagogical parameters.

Reflection Questions

1. Do exceptional students face prejudice, discrimination, and marginalization in school contexts today?
2. In what ways does the necessity of self-actualization (i.e., narrating a coherent identity in relation to others) define a student and determine their place in the classroom?
3. How could the concepts of hospitality, reciprocity, and respect for historical difference be practiced in your educational settings today?
4. In what specific ways could "special education" provide opportunities to diversify our understanding of "ability" and expand the limits of our pedagogy?

Bibliography

Adams, Maurianne, et al., ed. *Readings for Diversity and Social Justice*. New York: Routledge, Taylor and Francis, 2013.

54. de Certeau, "Culture and the Schools," 64–65.

Antommaria, Armand Matheny. "Who Should Survive?: One of the Choices on Our Conscience: Mental Retardation and the History of Contemporary Bioethics." *Kennedy Institute of Ethics Journal* 16 (2006) 205–24.

Balibar, Etienne. *Masses, Classes, Ideas*. Translated by James Swenson. New York: Routledge, 1994.

Bhabha, Homi. *The Location of Culture*. New York: Routledge Classics, 2004.

Block, Ned, and Gerald Dworkin, eds. *The IQ Controversy: Critical Readings*. New York: Pantheon, 1976.

Boddington, Paula, and Tessa Podpadec. "Who are the Mentally Handicapped?" *Journal of Applied Philosophy* 8 (1991) 177–90.

Boydston, Jo Ann, ed. *John Dewey: The Later Works, 1925–1953*. 11 vols. Carbondale: Southern Illinois University Press, 1981.

Brantlinger, Ellen A. *Who Benefits from Special Education? Remediating (Fixing) Other People's Children*. Mahwah, NJ: Lawrence Erlbaum, 2006.

Carlson, Angela Licia. "Mindful Subjects: Classification and Cognitive Disability." Ph.D. diss., University of Toronto, 1998.

Castañeda, Carmelita (Rosie), Larissa E. Hopkins, and Madeline L. Peters. "Introduction to Section 8: Ableism." In *Readings for Diversity and Social Justice*, edited by Maurianne Adams et al., 461–67. 3rd ed. New York: Routledge, Taylor & Francis, 2013.

de Certeau, Michel. "Culture and the Schools: The Content of Teaching and the Pedagogical Relation." In *Culture in the Plural*, 53–68. Translated by Tom Conley. Minneapolis: University of Minnesota Press, 2001.

Chakrabarty, Dipesh. *Provincializing Europe: Post-Colonial Thought and Historical Difference*. Princeton: Princeton University Press, 2009.

Cole, Elizabeth A., ed. *Teaching the Violent Past: History Education and Reconciliation*. Lanham, MD: Carnegie Council for Ethics in International Affairs, Rowman & Littlefield, 2007.

Danforth, Scot. "John Dewey's Contributions to an Educational Philosophy of Intellectual Disability." *Educational Theory* 58 (2008) 45–62.

Dewey, John. *Experience and Education*. Toronto: Collier-MacMillan Canada, 1938.

———. "Hegel's Philosophy of Spirit." In *John Dewey's Philosophy of Spirit: With the 1897 Lecture on Hegel*, edited by John Shook and James A. Good, 93–176. New York: Fordham University Press, 2010.

———. *The School and Society: The Child and the Curriculum*. Reprint, Chicago: University of Chicago Press, 1990.

Dewey, John, and Evelyn Dewey. *Schools of Tomorrow*. Reprint, New York: E. P. Dutton, 1962.

Dudley, Marling, Curt Burns, and Mary Bridget. "Two Perspectives on Inclusion in the United States." *Global Education Review* 1 (2014) 14–31.

Ferri, Beth A., and David J. Connor. *Reading Resistance: Discourses of Exclusion in Desegregation and Inclusion Debates*. New York: Peter Lang, 2006.

Festenstein, Matthew. "Dewey's Political Philosophy." Stanford Encyclopedia of Philosophy Archive, 2014. http://plato.stanford.edu/archives/spr2014/entries/dewey-political/.

Field, Richard. "John Dewey." Internet Encyclopedia of Philosophy, n.d. http://www.iep.utm.edu/d/dewey.htm.

Foucault, Michel. *The Archaeology of Knowledge*. Translated by A. M. Sheridan Smith. Reprint, New York: Routledge Classics, 2002.

———. *The Birth of a Clinic: An Archaeology of Medical Perception*. Translated by A. M. Sheridan Smith. Reprint, New York: Routledge Classics, 2003.

———. *Madness and Civilization: A History of Insanity in an Age of Reason*. Translated by Richard Howard. Reprint, New York: Vintage, 1988.

———. "The Subject and Power." In *Critical Theory: The Essential Readings*, edited by David Ingram and Julia Simon-Ingram, 303–19. St. Paul, MN: Paragon, 1992.

Girard, Rene. *I See Satan Fall Like Lightening*. Translated by James G. Williams. Maryknoll, NY: Orbis, 2001.

Good, James A. "Rereading Dewey's 'Permanent Hegelian Deposit.'" In *John Dewey's Philosophy of Spirit: With the 1897 Lecture on Hegel*, edited by John Shook and James A. Good, 56–89, 181–190. New York: Fordham University Press, 2010.

Gustafson, James. "The Johns Hopkins Case." In *Contemporary Issues in Bioethics*, edited by Tom Beauchamp et al., 413–14. Belmont, CA: Wadsworth, 1994.

Hegel, Georg Wilhelm Friedrich. *The Philosophy of History*. Translated by John Sibree. Reprint, Mineola, NY: Dover, 1956.

———. *Reason in History: A General Introduction to the Philosophy of History*. Translated by Robert S. Hartman. Reprint, New York: Liberal Arts Press, 1953.

Hillyer, Barbara. *Feminism and Disability*. Norman: University of Oklahoma Press, 1993.

Hutchinson, Nancy L. *Inclusion of Exceptional Learners in Canadian Schools: A Practical Handbook for Teachers*. Toronto: Pearson Canada, 2010.

Kearney, Richard. *Anatheism: Returning to God After God*. New York: Columbia University Press, 2010.

———. *On Paul Ricoeur: The Owl of Minerva*. Aldershot, UK: Ashgate, 2004.

Kearney, Richard, and James Taylor, eds. *Hosting the Stranger: Between Religions*. New York: Continuum International, 2011.

Kerlin, Isaac N. "Our Household Pets." In vol. 1 of *The History of Mental Retardation: Collected Papers*, edited by Marvin Rosen, Gerald R. Clark, and Marvin S. Kivitz, 283–92. Baltimore: University Park Press, 1976.

Martin, Edwin, Reed Martin, and Donna Terman. "The Legislative and Litigation History of Special Education." *The Future of Children* 6 (1996) 25–39.

Morgan, Charlotte. "A Brief History of Special Education." *ETFO Voice* (Winter 2003) 10–14.

Morris, Jenny. "Personal and Political: A Feminist Perspective on Researching Physical Disability." *Disability, Handicap, and Society* 7 (1992) 157–66. http://www.um.es/discatif/PROYECTO_DISCATIF/Textos_discapacidad/00_Morris.pdf.

Murphy, Jeffrie. "Do the Retarded Have a Right Not To Be Eaten?" In *Ethics and Mental Retardation*, edited by Loretta Kopelman and John C. Moskop, 43–46. Dordrecht, Holland: D. Reidel, 1984.

———. "Rights and Borderline Cases." In *Ethics and Mental Retardation*, edited by Loretta Kopelman and John C. Moskop, 4–17. Dordrect, Holland: D. Reidel, 1984.

Osgood, Robert L. *The History of Inclusion in the United States*. Washington, DC: Gallaudet University Press, 2005.

Piepmeier, Alison, Amber Cantrell, and Ashley Maggio. "Disability is a Feminist Issue: Bringing Together Women's and Gender Studies and Disability Studies." *Disability Studies Quarterly* 34 (2014). http://dsq-sds.org/article/view/4252/3592.

Reaume, Geoffrey. "Disability History In Canada: Present Work in the Field and Future Prospects." *Canadian Journal of Disability Studies* 1 (2012) 35–81. http://cjds.uwaterloo.ca/index.php/cjds/article/viewFile/20/4.

Ricoeur, Paul. *Oneself as Another*. Translated by Kathleen Blamey. Chicago: University of Chicago Press, 1992.

———. *On Translation*. Translated by Eileen Brennan. New York: Routledge, Taylor and Francis, 2006.

Rosen, Marvin, Gerald R. Clark, and Marvin S. Kivitz. *The History of Mental Retardation, Collected Papers*. Vol. 1. Baltimore: University Park Press, 1976.

Scott, Charles E. "Differences, Borders, Fusions." *Journal Of Speculative Philosophy* 29 (2015) 16–24.

Shook, John R. and James A. Good. *John Dewey's Philosophy of Spirit: With the 1897 Lecture on Hegel*. New York: Fordham University Press, 2010.

Silvers, Anita. "Feminist Perspectives on Disability." Stanford Encyclopedia of Philosophy Archives, revised August 29, 2013. http://plato.stanford.edu/archives/spr2015/entries/feminism-disability/.

Singer, Peter. *Animal Liberation*. London: Pimlico, 1995.

Spicker, Paul. "Mental Handicap and Citizenship." *Journal of Applied Philosophy* 7 (1990) 139–51.

Sumara, Dennis, Brent Davis, and Linda Laidlaw. "Canadian Identity and Curriculum Theory: An Ecological, Postmodern Perspective." *Canadian Journal of Education* 26 (2001) 144–63.

US Department of Education, Office of Special Education and Rehabilitative Services. *Thirty-Five Years of Progress in Educating Children With Disabilities Through IDEA*. Washington, DC: US Department of Education, 2010.

Vanier, Jean. *Becoming Human*. Toronto: House of Anansi, 1998.

———. *Made for Happiness: Discovering the Meaning of Life with Aristotle*. Translated by Kathryn Spink. Toronto: House of Anansi, 2001.

White, Morton Gabriel. *From a Philosophical Point of View: Selected Studies*. Princeton: Princeton University Press, 2005.

Wolfensberger, Wolf. "The Origins and Nature of Our Institutional Models." In *Changing Patterns in Residential Services for the Mentally Retarded*, edited by Robert Kugel and Ann Shearer, 35–82. Washington, DC: President's Committee on Mental Retardation, 1976.

Yong, Amos. *The Bible, Disability and the Church: A New Vision of the People of God*. Grand Rapids: Eerdmans, 2011.

———. "Disability Theology of the Resurrection: Persisting Questions and Additional Considerations—A Response to Ryan Mullins." *Ars Disputandi* 12 (2012) 4–10.

———. *Theology and Down Syndrome: Reimagining Disability in Late Modernity*. Waco: Baylor University Press, 2007.

13

The Teacher's Authority
Ken Badley

Introduction

WHY SHOULD STUDENTS FOLLOW their teacher's lead? Why should they do what their teacher asks or tells them to do? These questions move us directly into the important and complex question of the teacher's classroom authority. The importance of understanding teachers' authority is obvious; classrooms without a leader usually sink into chaos. While almost everyone intuitively grasps the importance of teachers' authority, many miss its complexity. Even the two questions at the start of this paragraph reveal some of that complexity: *Why should students follow their teacher's lead? Why should they do what their teacher asks or tells them to do?* The two questions I began with look similar but the first more clearly asks about what most observers call *authority* while the second may connect more with what many call *power*. Even the differences between *asks* and *tells* in the second question denote different degrees of power. What do classroom teachers need: authority or power, or both?

Both beginning and veteran teachers can misunderstand classroom authority or misidentify its sources. Several such confusions come to mind. For example, some confuse or conflate the two concepts I distinguished in the above paragraph: authority and power. They think that the teacher's request or wish will become the students' command. Recognizably, to a degree, teachers can force most students to complete certain assignments and to behave in specified ways. That force connects to the ordinary sense of the word *power*, that someone or something can move objects that offer resistance, a concept to which I return in the "What Classroom Authority is Not" section of this chapter.

A second mistake, one that beginning teachers make more frequently than veteran teachers, is to try to become friends with students. Teachers who follow this path think that chumminess will lead students to like them and then willingly join them in the learning journey they have planned. In fact, this mistake has in it a seed of logic: the teacher's instructional program can only benefit if students *are on the teacher's side*, so to speak.[1] Still, I label this confusion because, as generations of teachers have learned, students want to learn in a classroom led by a professional, not by a "big friend or cheerleader."[2]

Some mistakenly believe that the teacher's authority relates only to classroom management and to the appropriate responses to specific misbehaviors and discrete discipline problems. On this account, classroom management becomes a stand-alone question, and, unfortunately, many teacher education programs treat it that way. This understanding is grounded in at least two errors. First, the goal of understanding our authority as teachers is not primarily to control aberrant behavior (even if we must do so periodically) but to create an ethos in which students succeed in learning. We are mistaken if we think that our authority relates only to controlling behaviors. Second, the teacher's authority has more to do with epistemology and the teaching-learning relationship than it does with classroom management. I use *epistemology* here to direct our attention to teachers' expert knowledge and to how we pursue with our students what Parker Palmer calls the big subject.[3]

Fourth, and finally, some mistake the three basic necessary conditions of expertise, teaching certificate, and employment contract for sufficient conditions to run a classroom program. Obviously, teachers do gain some authority from the basic three conditions; thousands of new teachers go to their first jobs every school year possessing only those three things. We also gain some room to move from traditional assumptions about classroom roles. But teachers—new teachers especially—can make the mistake of relying too heavily on traditional expectations and assumptions about the teacher's right to control the electronics in the room, or to determine seating plans, to stand or sit when and where she sees fit, and to carry out a hundred other ordinary classroom functions.

These confusions are not the only mistakes educators make related to authority, but they point to the truth that both experienced and beginning teachers need a more nuanced understanding of classroom authority. My

1. Spackman, *Teachers' Professional Responsibilities*.
2. Bantock, *Freedom and Authority*, 22.
3. Palmer, *Courage to Teach*.

thesis in this chapter is that teachers can understand their own authority in ways that will help them sustain an inviting classroom program from year to year if they can distinguish between what is and what is not classroom authority and if they can understand the varieties of soil from which genuine classroom authority grows. I organize the remainder of this chapter to reflect those categories, beginning in the next two sections ("What is Classroom Authority?" and "What Classroom Authority is Not") with what classroom authority is and is not. In the "Nonessential Sources of Teacher Authority"section, I turn to what I call unnecessary sources, the soil from which authority may grow but does not necessarily grow. In the "Sources of the Teacher's Authority" section, I list several kinds of soil from which genuine classroom authority does grow.

What is Classroom Authority?

The confusions I listed in the introduction already make clear the directions this chapter points. I will surprise no one by stipulating a definition of authority that has two aspects: teachers have classroom authority when they possess the formal qualifications to offer a sustained educational program and they have the consent of their students to carry out that program. I explore both formal qualifications and consent later in the chapter but will comment briefly here on the concept of consent.

Consent implies a position or relationship in which failing students willingly join us in the educational program we want to carry out in our classroom. At minimum, consent implies permission. I use the word *minimum* because teachers need much more than minimal permission to execute their educational plans and programs. So I want to suggest a degree of consent or support along the lines of what, at the time of writing, many people have granted Oprah Winfrey or Jon Stewart.[4] When either of these two speaks, millions of people listen; people take their cues from them, read the books they recommend, and attend Rall[ies] to Restore Sanity that they organize. To my point, people do so voluntarily. No one has elected them to rule over us; they are not *in office* in the sense that a nation's president or prime minister takes office. In short, the consent we give people such as Oprah Winfrey and Jon Stewart goes well beyond mere permission. This kind of consent is key to teachers' authority.

---

4. I do not mean that teachers need to be as charismatic, famous, or popular as either of these two figures.

What Classroom Authority is Not

In contrast to the kind of authority apparent in the consent millions of people grant to trusted television personalities, think about the kind of coercion or raw power represented by a military force. Centuries ago, in *Leviathan*, Thomas Hobbes labeled this kind of power as *command*, where a person can expect obedience without having to supply reasons. He distinguished the power to command from what he called *counsel*, where reasons are required.[5] To employ an earthy illustration, the bulldozer does not ask the dirt's permission before moving the dirt. Likewise, Stalin and Hitler sought no one's permission when enacting their respective evil visions. No doubt, some of the confusion surrounding teachers' authority arises when people fail to notice the distinction between power and authority, between command (or coercion) and consent. What I call consent and Hobbes called counsel is a very different property or state from what I call power and Hobbes called command. But some people use the word "authority" without distinguishing these dramatically different senses. To summarize, we need to recognize power as the first thing classroom authority is not.

For decades, social scientists and education scholars have examined power and classroom power. One sharply worded comment from decades back catches the same point Hobbes made centuries ago:

> The stupidity that often inheres in the use of coercive sanctions, by established bearers of authority, in and out of the schoolroom, is not that their use establishes and preserves authority. It is rather that they prevent the establishment of an organic moral order adequate and congenial to the stabilization and guidance of the social process underway—an order morally accepted in some measure as rightful by all participants in the process. In other words, they are to be condemned as defeating rather than serving the development of an adequate authority."[6]

Read this quotation again if you need to because its author has gone beyond the distinction I called for in the previous paragraph. Benne is claiming that the use of power actively undermines the teacher's authority; it sabotages the *organic moral order* required for learning.[7] The one is actually inimical to the other. These are powerful words indeed and an idea to which I will return in my treatment of consent (in the "Sources of the Teacher's Authority" section).

5. Hobbes, *Leviathan*, chapter 25.
6. Benne, *Conception of Authority*, 149.
7. Metz, *Classrooms and Corridors*.

Second, classroom authority is not classroom management. I used this distinction as my third example in the introduction to this chapter. Distinguishing classroom management from the classroom ethos will go a long way toward clearing up some of the confusion about teacher authority. At that, the phrase *classroom management* likely has both an ambient sense and an episodic sense. The teacher wants to create an atmosphere conducive to learning (the ambient sense). Even with that atmosphere generally in place, some students at some points will have bad days or bad moments; teachers will encounter episodes requiring their intervention. But the classroom management mind-set and literature generally do not go far enough.

Consider again the word *ethos*. When I ask us to distinguish classroom ethos from simple classroom management, I want to include curriculum, course, unit, and lesson planning, mastering and employing a wide repertoire of instructional methods appropriate to contents and students' ages and abilities, promoting and assessing student learning, developing record-keeping and paper-flow systems, interacting with students in a friendly yet professional way throughout each work day, and so on. In other words, classroom ethos has to do with our whole program; it goes far beyond simply maintaining order or dealing with misbehaviors and episodes.

To conclude this section, I have identified two things that classroom authority is not. It is not the power to make students do whatever we want. Granted, some learning may occur in authoritarian classrooms where students grant teachers only minimal compliance, but that learning will be characterized only rarely by either joy or flow.[8] Second, teacher authority or classroom authority is not classroom management. In my most Kentopian picture of a classroom, the learning ethos is so positive and powerful that the teacher never needs to make a classroom management intervention. I suspect that few such classrooms exist in the real world.

Nevertheless, I have argued here that the classroom ethos encompasses something much larger and more substantial than classroom management and that in classrooms grounded on the kind of consent I describe here, students want to learn and they engage fully in their teacher's program.

Nonessential Sources of Teacher Authority

Several misconceptions embed themselves in both students' and teachers' thinking about teachers' authority, some of them induced by the images of what I call reel teachers, the teachers we and our students see on screen. We

---

8. I use *flow* as a technical term, based on the work of Csikszentmihalyi, especially *Flow: The Psychology of Optimal Experience*.

begin with charisma.⁹ In our reflections on teacher film clips, my preservice teachers and I discuss our tendency to compare the charismatic reel teachers we see—played by actors such as Meryl Streep, Robin Williams, and Hilary Swank—from the real teachers we know. Even periodic exposure to reel teachers can shape our collective expectation that teachers should be charismatic. In truth, millions of teachers lack charisma. Even if charisma might make classroom time pass more quickly for students or make them want to attend more carefully to their learning, charisma is not necessary. In fact, charisma has the power to distract students from their work if it leads them to focus too much on their teacher. Some have even argued that charismatic teachers, albeit unwittingly, may diminish students' freedom because their students end up wanting to imitate them and become their disciples.[10]

Turning to another widespread mistake and one related to charisma, many teachers and students believe that teachers must be funny. We need to distinguish two senses here. Some teachers are entertainingly funny; they can lace instruction with jokes, quips, and clever asides.

We distinguish that sense of *funny* from having a sense of humor, especially being able to laugh at oneself and at one's own mistakes. The sheer number of successful teachers who do not entertain ought to tell us all we need to know about the necessity of that kind of funny: it is simply not necessary. On the other hand, possessing a sense of humor may be typical of successful teachers and it is always helpful (although it is certainly not sufficient). If a teacher has both a sense of humor and can offer a certain level of entertainment, fine, but funny is not necessary, and can easily backfire.

Related to charisma (and perhaps to humor), some believe that to be successful, teachers must be extroverted. As it happens, many teachers are extroverted but, again, many successful teachers—even amazing teachers—tend toward introversion, forcing us to conclude that extroversion is not necessary, even if it is typical.[11] In fact, researchers have studied teachers' personality types (using the Myers Briggs' type indicator and other such instruments), learning styles (using such scales as those developed by David Kolb or Kenneth and Rita Dunn), and multiple intelligences (using Howard Gardner's categories). Such instruments may help teachers understand more about why they do or do not enjoy teaching and why some students respond more readily than others to different teaching styles. Such mediating instruments also have the power to lead teachers to conclude (wrongly)

---

9. I use *charisma* in its ordinary language sense, not in the sense that Weber used in his *Theory of Social and Economic Organization* or his *Economy and Society*.

10. Finkel and Arney, *Educating for Freedom*.

11. For example, see Eryilmaz, "Perceived Personality Traits."

that their personality or cognitive characteristics actually determine their capabilities as teachers; they thereby lock themselves into a limiting cognitive framework. Thus, not only is being extroverted not necessary but the instrumental means by which some conclude that they should possess this or that characteristic can themselves be disabling.

Some believe that teachers must be enigmatic and mysterious like the Robin Williams character, Mr. Keating, in *Dead Poets Society*.[12] This belief may illustrate that art shapes life as much as it reflects it; in fact, *Dead Poets* may be a major source of this expectation. Again, if thousands of successful teachers are not enigmatic or mysterious, then apparently these qualities are not necessary. And, in fact, thousands of teachers are quite open about their beliefs, their biographies, their children, what they learned on the internet the day before, and what they ate for breakfast. No mysteries there. Being enigmatic is not only not necessary, it may not even be typical.

As I noted in the introduction, beginning teachers often make the mistake of thinking that teachers must become friends with students. They fail to distinguish being friendly with students with being students' friends. Teachers are professionals. Students want their teachers to be professionals. A school or jurisdiction hired us because of our qualifications and those qualifications set us apart from our students. Teachers need to stay set apart, to keep their professional distance from students. Some refer to this as *boundary maintenance*, and teachers who wish to remain in the profession long-term take care to maintain their professional boundaries.[13]

Many induction teachers and veteran teachers, as well as members of the public, believe that teachers must burn themselves out for their students. Again, the movies help perpetuate what some have called the myth of the heroic teacher,[14] who must fight a bean-counting vice principal, obstructionist parents, lazy and stupid colleagues, and the few good students' drug-dealing friends to implement his or her visionary program of studies. These cinematic teachers may work three jobs and sacrifice personal relationships (*Freedom Writers*) or suffer heart attacks (*Stand and Deliver*) because of their nearly pathological dedication to their students.[15] Research on

---

12. In cinema at least, their mysteriousness may contribute to their being fired after one year, as it did in both *Dead Poets* and *Mona Lisa Smile*.

13. For many contemporary teachers, boundary maintenance implies not becoming Facebook friends with students until after graduation.

14. Ayers, "A Teacher Ain't Nothin' but a Hero"; Farber and Holm, "Brotherhood of Heroes."

15. The two films I have named here actually are based on nonfiction sources. See Gruwell, *Freedom Writers Diary*, and Matthews, *Escalante: Best Teacher in America*.

teachers' work patterns points to a typical working week of 55–60 hours.[16] One is tempted, perhaps, to ask if that much work is necessary; many successful teachers do not work these long weeks. But to suggest that all teachers should be able to accomplish all that they do in, say, forty hours, would likely only increase frustration for the dedicated members of a profession who already feel besieged.

To summarize this section, I have tried to correct several misperceptions about what teachers must do or must have to be successful. I included possessing charisma and the ability to entertain. I claimed that teachers need not be extroverted, enigmatic, or mysterious. I warned against becoming friends with students and against the image that successful teachers must become heroes who burn themselves out. Obviously, one could list more misconceptions about successful teaching, but these will do. Obvious as well, many teachers who operate with great authority in their classrooms possess some of the qualities I have named (but likely do not attempt to form friendships with their students). My purpose in presenting this brief inventory is to argue that these qualities and patterns are not necessary for successful teaching, even if they sometimes or even typically characterize successful teachers.

The Sources of the Teacher's Authority

In the introduction, I lumped together expertise, a teaching certificate, and a contract as *three basic necessary conditions* for teaching. Briefly, I want to return to these three basics. I noted that some mistake these necessities for sufficient conditions, that is, thinking that a teacher not only can start teaching but can continue through the school year with these alone. No doubt, in most cases, the teacher needs these three,[17] but they are not sufficient and therefore they warrant our attention. Most school authorities take the certificate issued by a teacher certification agency as evidence of expertise; they assume that those overseeing a teacher education program have seen a pattern of evidence that the preservice teacher possesses the required knowledge, skills, and attitudes desired by the jurisdiction and semi-guaranteed by the program. They

---

16. Search online for "Teachers' Workload Diary Survey" to see the latest available version of this annual British survey. Year-to-year comparisons reveal different numbers, of course, but on average, British teachers work 55–60 hours per week.

17. For reasons including teacher shortages, remote settings, ideology, religion, and budgets, schools hire uncertified teachers, sometimes conditionally and sometimes permanently. Furthermore, teachers in millions of informal (and formal) learning settings share their expertise without a certificate or a contract. I recognize these situations but focus here on the typical teacher formally employed in a K–12 school system that requires certification.

have forwarded this graduate's name to the teacher certification branch of the department of education in their respective jurisdiction and that agency has granted the license or certificate (usually valid for two to three years). With certificate in hand, the new teacher has applied to a school or school authority and has received an offer of employment. Thus, the contract implies certification and certification implies at least a beginning level of expertise. Most schools view the expertise and certificate as necessities before they will issue the contract. That being said, almost every certified teacher with a contract has discovered that, while necessary, these three qualifications are not sufficient to carry on a classroom program month to month and year to year.

In the introduction, I noted that traditional expectations also give teachers a kind of authority. All the places we walk into—elevators, arenas, laundromats, wedding receptions—come with sets of traditional expectations about how we may behave and about who gets to say what. Classrooms also come with traditional, common-sense expectations, and these expectations give teachers a measure of instant authority.

Having listed expertise as the first of the three basic necessities, I want to nuance it a bit further because we need to distinguish two kinds of expertise. Younger students generally extend more grace to their teachers than do older students, but all students begin forming their impression of a new teacher in the opening minutes of the opening day of the school year. On what grounds do they make their judgments? First, the certificate and contract likely do not cross most students' minds. Second, regarding expertise, students' ability to distinguish pedagogical expertise and subject-area expertise increases with age, although even those too young to articulate the distinction or their own educational desires likely want to see both. A teacher's authority rests, in part, on these two kinds of expertise.

Moving beyond this list, students have keen noses for fairness and caring. About the age that they might be able, with a bit of coaching, to pronounce *pedagogical expertise*, they will begin to recognize when their teacher is prepared and when not. In my classes with preservice teachers I regularly ask that we recollect the five qualities of good teachers that almost all researchers identify: caring, fair, prepared, subject-area expertise, and pedagogical expertise. I tell my students that a million researchers have already identified what good teaching entails and that, regardless of the length of the list of qualities those researchers produce, or what other elements appear, these five always appear. In short, they are necessary. But the three that rhyme (caring, fair, and prepared) are sources of authority more than they are forms. Expertise demonstrates authority; experts know what they are doing, so to speak. Care, fairness, and preparation build authority, and I turn now to the kind of authority they build.

Consent

In the "What is Classroom Authority?" section, I distinguished power and coercion from consent or what Hobbes called counsel. Consent occupies a central place in my conception of classroom authority. Without students' consent, the teacher can expect only some form of minimal compliance—likely a begrudging form—from her students (although she might get more than that). In contrast, with students' consent, the teacher can expect to move ahead day by day (at least on most days) with her curriculum plans, with her students and her all aiming at the same educational goals. With students' consent, the teacher can create the kind of teaching and learning space—the classroom ethos—that she wishes to create.

Consent goes by other names. Some call it student goodwill, legitimacy, or moral authority.[18] Retailers call it customer loyalty. Teachers build (or fail to build) this pool of goodwill in a thousand obvious and not-so-obvious moments in every teaching day. Their words (kind? sarcastic?), their response times to student requests, their body language and facial expressions, how often or rarely they exclaim that they simply love coming to class to be with their students, even their periodical appearance in class with snacks.... These are the ways that they demonstrate care and build the pool of goodwill or the moral authority to teach. Note how the items on this list connect to the two concepts of care and fairness; I wrote earlier that caring and fair teachers build student goodwill. The details seem quite simple (but somehow lie beyond the reach of many educators). Many others have explored moral authority and I will not say more here.[19]

Presence

Many treatments of classroom authority ignore teachers' presence. By *presence*, I do not mean that teachers need to project in class what actors such as Jennifer Lawrence and Matt Damon project on screen. I do mean that as teachers we need to demonstrate that we are fully present in our classroom and that we are sure that our classroom is where we belong.[20]

---

18. Arendt saw the roots of authority in communities of people who engaged in discourse and then granted individuals the power to lead them. That is, leaders lead by consent. She defined authority this way with the totalitarian regimes of Hitler and Stalin in mind; that is, they ruled by raw power (coercion) not by the consent of the people. See Arendt, *Human Condition*.

19. Sergiovanni, *Moral Leadership*; Yariv, "Students' Attitudes." See also Dennis's doctoral dissertation, "A Study of how Teachers Show Love in the Classroom."

20. A good introduction to the research on teacher presence appears in Rodgers

The first of those conditions does relate to what we see in Jennifer Lawrence or Matt Damon. They project complete involvement in what they are doing. In fact, one suspects that they can project this because, in fact, they *are* fully involved.[21] They inhabit their roles completely. Teachers can do the same. In fact, we must. We must become fully engaged with our students and the subject at hand. I write those words knowing that teachers have issues in their personal and professional lives that can occupy their attention (and so do actors). But we must focus if we want our students to know that we are fully there with them. Simple to say. Challenging to do.

Obviously, preparation and expertise are ways of saying, "I am fully here, I am not phoning this in." Passion about the subject projects presence. Humble confidence projects presence (and confidence without humility can offend). Even demonstrating humility by periodically admitting that we don't know establishes presence (in part because students usually know when we don't know). Even our physical posture reveals the degree to which we have engaged with the students in our room. Obviously, we could explore presence at much greater length, but that must wait. In the opening paragraph of this sub-section on presence, I noted that we must demonstrate our own confidence that our classroom is where we belong. That discussion is essential to presence, but it also functions importantly in what I call self-authorization, the final source of classroom authority I explore here.

Self-Authorization

The phrase *self-authorization* may be new to some readers but it is a relatively simple concept: we need to permit ourselves to teach. I will highlight two aspects of self-authorization, beginning with the vocational aspect that links back to presence. Many teachers torment themselves with vocational questions, sometimes for good reason. Some families consider the profession of teaching beneath (or above) them and consequently do not support their children's vocational direction. Other teachers end up asking vocational questions because they struggle with the toxic combination of the sheer volume of hard work, the relatively low salaries, and the criticism they regularly face from right-wing politicians and members of the public who apparently believe that teachers should solve all society's ills in about six hours per day. Some question whether teaching is their vocation because

---

and Raider-Roth's article, "Presence in Teaching."

21. For more on what is called *method acting*, search online for information on Konstantin Stanislavsky, the famous teacher of the method that encourages actors to fully inhabit their characters.

they seem unable to make their classroom work (a legitimate concern!). In the face of doubts and criticism, teachers need to authorize themselves, by which I mean they need to say to themselves and to their most trusted friends, "I am going to teach." Current and vernacular versions of that expression run more like, "I've got this," or "You go girl!" In my view, if some form of the Nike slogan "Just do it" gets one out of bed in the morning and to school, then that is precisely what teachers should say.

Teachers who would authorize themselves must rise above family expectations, work load, salary, and public criticism, environmental factors that ultimately form only a kind of persistent backdrop. The most obvious setting in which teachers need to authorize themselves is in the day, to work in their own classrooms with their students. They need to authorize themselves in this second, more direct way every time they start a class. In music and comedy, a *cold start* implies beginning one's song or sketch without an introduction by a host or master of ceremonies. Opera singers have to authorize themselves this way every time they sing; no one introduces them. They muster all the chutzpah or pluck they have, they stand up, they start. Apparently, the decision to start a given *Saturday Night Live* cold open always entails a lot of discussion during the week. The big question at SNL is always whether the audience will go with the performer or performers who begin the show with a cold start. To be quite blunt, teachers do a cold start at the start of their first year in their first school, at the start of their first year in every school after that, at the start of every new school day, and at the start of every class in their career. Obviously, it gets easier, but my point is that they never (or rarely) have the luxury of a principal introducing them after warming the class up with a funny monologue. In the ordinary circumstances in which teachers work every day, they must authorize themselves to teach. Doing that requires chutzpah, moxy, pluck, courage ... call it what you will. I call it self-authorization. Teachers start; it is what they do.

Earlier, I listed Erin Gruwell (portrayed by Hilary Swank in *Freedom Writers*), as an example of a teacher who worked too hard. To its credit, this film also gives viewers a superb view of self-authorization. Gruwell's students made quite clear that they did not care one iota about her credentials, contract, or educational ideals. In their view, she came to their side of town as another white, do-gooder, hero-wannabe, and they planned to cut her no slack whatsoever. She had no choice but to authorize herself to teach them and she did that. Not to be cynical, but of course her story would never have made it to the screen had her students not ultimately authorized her as well, but my point here is that, to begin, she had to authorize herself. As the story unfolds, we learn that her students ultimately authorized her partly because she had authorized herself. Not all teachers face the antipathy she had to overcome, but all teachers do have to authorize themselves. In the clearest possible terms, then, I say that we must consider this a necessary step or condition; no one can teach without self-authorization.

Conclusion

Teachers' authority is essential for the productive functioning of classrooms. It is complex because it overlaps conceptually with power and because it derives from such varied sources, some of them legal and formal (such as certificates and contracts), others informal and almost abstract (such as presence or showing kindness and fairness).

Several sources of the teacher's authority are simply missing from the chapter. For example, what role does age play? Some students grant more authority to the young teacher who is cool; others respect the old teacher who is wise (although these qualities are neither guaranteed in nor restricted to those respective age groups). I have not dealt with how a good reputation developed over years in a single school building increases the authority each new cohort of students grants their teacher. Nor have I talked about how accomplishments outside the classroom—in business, sports, government, or religion and philanthropy, for example—enhance the teacher's classroom authority. Much work remains if we are to understand how the teacher's authority and classroom authority (which I have used interchangeably here) connect. How does authorizing students—making them authorities—affect the teacher's authority? How will students understand teacher expertise as the internet becomes available everywhere? How will teachers frame their own expertise and work with the landscape changes brought by ubiquitous technology? These questions remain.

I have argued that the formal qualifications of certificate and contract and the expertise that they imply may be sufficient to launch a school year but will not carry a teacher through that year. Primary among the many kinds or sources of classroom authority, teachers must have their students' consent or goodwill. Without such legitimacy or moral authority, they will not be able to carry out their program with anything beyond minimal compliance. At that, one does not assemble consent like a piece of Swedish furniture. One earns one's students' consent over time.

Late in the chapter, I argued that being fully present is also necessary if a teacher wishes to carry out his or her classroom program. In explaining the grounds of their classroom cell-phone policies, some professors use the saying, "If you're going to be present, you might as well be present." This clever sentence applies to teacher presence as well, and those teachers desiring student engagement will recognize the necessity that they be engaged themselves. I tied presence to self-authorization by noting that classroom teachers must come to peace about their own vocation as educators. Ultimately, the teacher who will cold start class after class for years on end needs to know that the classroom is, indeed, where he or she belongs. And those thousands of cold starts obviously require both deep courage as well as the pluck to stand up and start each class.

Refection Questions

1. List some ways that teachers in film may have shaped your perceptions of how teachers gain or exercise authority.
2. Revise the "big five" list of basic teacher qualities given here—caring, fair, prepared, subject-area expertise, and pedagogical expertise—to reflect your own understanding of the essential qualities of good teachers.
3. Describe your own understanding of the relationship between power and classroom authority, especially as that relationship connects to the two matters of instruction and classroom management.
4. Many teachers have never considered self-authorization. In what situations in your own teaching context do you typically need to authorize yourself to teach?
5. If teachers do not need to burn out with hard work, or be enigmatic, extroverted, funny, or charismatic, what do they need to be to carry out their teaching program?

Bibliography

Arendt, Hanna. *The Human Condition*. Chicago: University of Chicago Press, 1958.
Ayers, William. "A Teacher Ain't Nothin' but a Hero: Teachers and Teaching in Film." In *Images of Schoolteachers in America*, edited by Pamela Bolotin Joseph and Gail E. Burnaford, 201–9. Mahwah, NJ: Lawrence Erlbaum, 2001.
Bantock, G. H. *Freedom and Authority in Education*. London: Faber & Faber, 1966.
Benne, Kenneth D. *A Conception of Authority: An Introductory Study*. New York: Teachers College Press, 1943.
Csikszentmihalyi, Mihaly. *Flow: The Psychology of Optimal Experience*. New York: Harper and Row, 1990.
Dennis, Mary. "A Study of how Teachers Show Love in the Classroom." PhD diss., George Fox University, 2012. http://digitalcommons.georgefox.edu/edd/13.

Eryilmaz, Ali. "Perceived Personality Traits and Types of Teachers and their Relationship to the Subjective Well-Being and Academic Achievements of Adolescents." *Educational Sciences: Theory and Practice* 14 (2014) 2049–62.

Farber, Paul, and Gunilla Holm. "A Brotherhood of Heroes: The Charismatic Educator in Recent American Movies." In *Schooling in the Light of Popular Culture*, edited by Paul Farber, Eugene Provenzo, and Gunilla Golm, 153–72. Albany: State University of New York Press, 1994.

Finkel, Donald L., and William R. Arney. *Educating for Freedom: The Paradox of Pedagogy*. New Brunswick: Rutgers University Press, 1995.

Gruwell, Erin. *The Freedom Writers Diary: How a Teacher and 150 Teens Used Writing to Change Themselves and the World Around Them*. New York: Broadway Books, 1999.

Hobbes, Thomas. *Leviathan*. New York: Dutton, 1950.

Matthews, Jay. *Escalante: The Best Teacher in America*. New York: Holt, 1986.

Metz, Mary Haywood. *Classrooms and Corridors: The Crisis of Authority in Desegregated Secondary Schools*. Berkeley: University of California Press, 1978.

Palmer, Parker. *The Courage to Teach*. San Francisco: Jossey-Bass, 1998.

Rodgers, Carol, and Miriam B. Raider-Roth. "Presence in Teaching." *Teachers and Teaching: Theory and Practice* 12 (2006) 265–87.

Sergiovanni, Thomas J. *Moral Leadership: Getting to the Heart of School Improvement*. San Francisco, Jossey-Bass, 1992.

Spackman, Frances. *Teachers' Professional Responsibilities*. London: David Fulton, 1991.

Weber, Max. *Economy and Society*. New York: Bedminster, 1968.

———. *Theory of Social and Economic Organization*. London: Collier-Macmillan, 1947.

Yariv, Eliezer. "Students' Attitudes on the Boundaries of Teachers' Authority." *School Psychology International* 30 (2009) 92–111.

PART THREE

Worldview and Story

14

Worldview Inclusion in Public Schooling
John Valk

Introduction

ONE OF THE MOST difficult issues for educators concerns what constitutes an adequate level of knowledge and awareness for graduating students. What should students in general know that prepares them well for responsible civic engagement in the communities in which they live, the areas of employment in which they will find themselves, and the larger global world that now impacts all of us? What skills should public schooling develop in them for a successful, challenging, and robust life? No doubt educators struggle with these questions, and rightly so.

Schools are not, of course, the only places to gain knowledge and awareness of the world around us. Various media, from print to visual to social, also shape our views and opinions on the political, social, and economic issues of the day. But they do not generally develop in students a crucial skill: critical thinking. This skill is vital in discerning the true from the popular, the right from the widespread, and the common good from the feel-good. Schools have laid claim to uniquely developing this skill in students. But how should they do so?

For some time now debates and discussions have focused on providing a balance between content (knowledge) and skills development (abilities): what should students know and what skills should they possess to adequately prepare them for the life ahead of them? Critical thinking requires a certain knowledge level in order for that skill to be meaningfully and beneficially exercised. What, then, should students know to become critical thinkers? What should schooling include that will enhance such skills development?

What is increasingly lacking in debates and discussions of this nature is an essential piece—a foundational piece—and it comes in the form of some meaningful existential questions. Knowledge is used for some purpose, great or small. But what purpose? Skills and abilities are put to some service, great or small. But what service? What purpose will guide one's thinking, as one discerns to what service one will put one's knowledge and skills? Neither knowledge nor skills are neutrally employed. They are guided and directed by some purpose and for some service, which in turn is founded on beliefs and values of some kind.

A neutral stance amidst a sea of beliefs and values is difficult to maintain; everyone is grounded in something, everyone begins from somewhere, everyone comes with some preconceived beliefs and values. Does public schooling sufficiently assist students in coming to better understand what these might be? Does it assist students in coming to understand and deepen the beliefs and values they hold, and broaden or adjust them in light of other beliefs and values? Does it seek to counter these and instill in students some specific beliefs and values?[1]

Critical thinking is central to all of this. In developing this ability in students, schools can assist them in becoming aware of and discerning their own beliefs and values, as well as the beliefs and values of others. Journeying into one's own beliefs and values cannot be done well if one does not journey into the beliefs and values of others, for as Max Mueller stated, "He who knows one; knows none."[2]

Beliefs and values are easily linked to religion. But they should not be linked exclusively to religion—not all people are religious. Yet all people have beliefs and values of some kind. As such, discussions about beliefs and values should encompass both religious and secular perspectives, or worldviews. In fact, it might be more prudent to speak about worldviews, for such a term is more inclusive of all people, religious and secular alike.[3]

Worldviews are *visions of life* and *ways of life*, and everyone has one.[4] To discuss beliefs and values in the context of worldviews, and then various worldviews, would be to take an inclusive approach, and this would be an advance. But to what extent should worldview knowledge and awareness be part of the educational process and curriculum? To what extent might this kind of knowledge and awareness indeed be foundational, that is, the bedrock upon which skills, abilities, and critical thinking should be developed? To what extent can such foundational knowledge and awareness assist students in making decisions that go beyond the popular, the widespread, or

1. Almond, "Education for Tolerance," 132–33.
2. Quoted in Sharpe, *Comparative Religion*, 36.
3. Valk, "Religion or Worldview," 1–16.
4. Sunshine, *Why You Think the Way You Do*, 14.

the feel-good? For the popular, the widespread or the feel-good are as easily passing phases as they are superficial and troublesome.

A Decrease in Worldview Knowledge and Awareness

From time to time I ask students to complete informal questionnaires to test their knowledge and awareness of worldviews, especially religious worldviews. Recently, a group of approximately sixty graduating (fifth year) education students did so. In one question they were asked to identify from a list of four options the religion of which the Dalai Lama is the spiritual leader. The results were quite startling. A large number thought he was Hindu. A few believed he was a Tibetan Deist, an entirely fictitious religion. Only about half identified him correctly as Buddhist.

In another question, students were asked the book from which Martin Luther King Jr. took themes for his most famous speech, "I Have a Dream." Many students know of King, the racism he fought against, and his famous speech; some may even have read it. The list from which they were asked to choose comprised the following: 1) *Black Like Me*; 2) *Isaiah*; 3) *Wild Hope*; and 4) *Long Walk to Freedom*. A significant majority of students picked the book *Long Walk to Freedom*, which is indeed about racism. But *Long Walk to Freedom* was written in 1994—twenty-six years after the assassination of King—by Nelson Mandela, documenting his long struggle against apartheid (racial segregation) in South Africa. Fifth year education students about to graduate from university and spend their lives teaching children to shun racism, among other things, were unaware of the anachronism of their choice.

These students were further unaware of what grounded the foundational beliefs of one of America's most renowned proponents of racial integration. Only a few picked Isaiah as the correct answer. Why is this? Perhaps most were unaware of two crucial facts they had not been taught regarding Martin Luther King Jr. One, that King was a Baptist minister who would naturally resort to the Bible for speech material. Two, that Isaiah was a book in the Hebrew Bible (Old Testament) that spoke about freedom from oppression. They failed to make what should have been an obvious connection had the religious factor been part of their learning about King.

Those who did select Isaiah indicated that they had attended church, mosque, or synagogue when they were younger. Half indicated that they still attend church, mosque, or synagogue and that they had also attended a religiously based school. Only a few took religion courses in public high school; fewer still took them while at university. One might conclude from this that religious knowledge and awareness comes largely from outside the public school system.

Was the question unfair—too obscure for the average university student? Perhaps, but most students are aware of the movements against racial segregation in the United States and South Africa. These have now been taught for a generation or more in the schools. They are also aware of prominent figures involved in those movements, and not least of King and Mandela. Could it be then that what has not been taught in the schools is the role religion played in those social movements?

In general, students did not fair well on the questionnaire. The results corroborate the findings of others and reveal a disturbing trend: a lack of knowledge and awareness of religious worldviews.[5] Should this be of concern for public schooling?

A Disquieting Religious Illiteracy

It could be argued that in an increasingly secular West, where concern for religious matters is waning, disinterest would be understandable. Further, news media, social media, and popular books offer up a steady diet of ecclesiastical scandals, fundamentalist rantings, and declarations that God is a delusion, redundant in the light of advancing science.[6] None of this invites enthusiasm regarding the study or teaching about religion, to be sure. Small wonder.

Much of what students gain in knowledge and awareness of religious worldviews is, however, at best half the story, and the shadow half at that. Hence, not only is there a lack of knowledge and awareness, there is also a distortion. Most come to believe, for example, that wars are caused by religion. They learn about the Crusades, Inquisition, sixteenth and seventeenth century religious wars, Irish Catholic-Protestant struggles, 9/11, and the acts of Islamic terrorists. Small wonder then that so many are of the view that religion poisons everything.[7] But this notion has been thoroughly challenged and refuted by recent scholarship.[8] Further, many students come to believe that science and religion conflict. This, again, is a distortion. For only a very small percentage of fundamentalist believers is this the case, and then largely in regard to evolutionary science. Most scientists who have religious beliefs see no conflict at all, refuting Dawkins' assertions that science inevitably leads to atheism: they simply do not buy this. Most alarming is

---

5. See Prothero, *God is Not One*, and Nord, *Religion in American Education*.
6. See Dawkins, *God Delusion*.
7. See Hitchens, *God is Not Great*.
8. See Armstrong, *Fields of Blood*, and Cavanaugh, *Myth of Religious Violence*.

that students come to believe that religion is little more than fundamentalist beliefs, rigid dogma, forced behaviors, and institutional attendance. Few well-meaning, well-educated, discerning, and astute religious believers see it this way. There appears to be a very large disconnect.

Should it be a concern for public schooling that a large number of students who graduate are, in effect, religiously illiterate? Should it be a concern that students readily learn that religion causes wars, but seldom if ever learn the role played by religion in fighting against conflict and discrimination of various kinds, advocating for peace and harmony throughout the world, and even countering the ravages of capitalism.[9] The media is largely silent on this, but no less the school curriculum. Both appear disinterested in the positive side of religious worldviews, or worse still religious worldviews in general.

Awareness of the rich stories, parables, and teachings of religious traditions that have inspired and impacted people and cultures throughout the ages have waned and appear to become insignificant for most students. But with it, of course, disappears awareness of the spiritual mysteries, philosophical insights, theological discoveries, literary creations, and musical wonderments that have emerged from them. Many of the world's great struggles for human rights, equality, and freedom developed *from* the teachings of the great religious traditions, not in spite of them. This includes the abolition of slavery, human rights, rights for women, rights for the disabled, concern for the environment, and more. Many of these movements are grounded in religious traditions and have gained inspiration from the rich teaching and stories of liberation that are themselves part of larger sacred stories. Unfortunately, much of this has come to be excluded from public education. Why might all of this be important and why should schooling concern itself with such matters? It has to do with two simple yet complex concepts: inclusion and diversity. Ironically, these two concepts are themselves promoted by public educators.

A History of Exclusion

Public schooling began in the nineteenth century as a project to minimize differences so nations with people of diverse perspectives could be united under common national aspirations. Almost two centuries of public schooling in the Western world has integrated many in common social, cultural, and economic aims. To this end education has served Western nations well.

---

9. See, for example, Belshaw et al., *Faith in Development*, and Johnston and Sampson, *Religion*.

But a price has also been paid in all of this. In some cases public schooling sought to eliminate social and cultural differences, as in the case of minority groupings. In other cases it sought to eliminate cultural and spiritual differences, as in the case of Indigenous peoples. In yet other cases, it sought to eliminate religious differences, in the case of religious minorities. The results in most of these initiatives are rather disconcerting, and have led to a certain silencing in the public square. People in general, but leaders in particular, especially in Canada, are discouraged from speaking about their deepest held convictions, most particularly if they are of a religious or spiritual kind. Many fear that when they do, even in a cursory fashion, they may be dismissed or targeted as biased, narrow-minded, even intolerant. Public discussions regarding controversial social issues such as abortion, same-sex marriage, and euthanasia often quite quickly paint "religious types" as opposing change or being anti-choice.

Some argue that purging the public square of religious voices creates a neutral public space, one free from positions based on faith perspectives. An argument is made that the public square, and with it public schooling, should remain secular. Some secular fundamentalists fear that people of faith seek to control society, government, and public schooling; an alarmist fear that we will then all be under the auspices of a theocracy that will create public policy and in turn will straightjacket citizens and eliminate freedom.

For all too many there is also the notion that religion is merely an add-on, something a person can embrace if they so choose, but also something one can easily do without in modern society. If one chooses this add-on, this extra element, this life of faith, it should be something private, for it is not something necessary for public life.

A further assumption is that only religious people have faith. We easily slip into this kind of language, and it is commonplace, expressed in sentiments such as, "I'm not a person of faith." But it does us well to have a closer look at such expressions, for such language has a way of distorting our reality, with the result that it can easily lead to exclusion and minimizing a rich diversity.

It would be much more accurate to say that everyone has faith; everyone has faith of some kind. Everyone places their ultimate certainty in something that orients and grounds them, that gives them assurance and confidence to face the hardships and issues of the day. For some, ultimate certainty continues to be in God. But for others it might simply be in themselves, or in the power of reason, science, and technology, or even in the power of money and material things.

To be sure, that in which one places their ultimate certainty is a private matter, and ought not to be dictated by government or even education, much as it is a private matter regarding the social, political, or economic ideology one embraces. But to be completely unaware of those various ultimate certainties, or of various social, political, or economic ideologies, and to give them no stock, is to applaud a kind of ignorance that is unbecoming of an educated and responsible citizen. Further, to argue that students should be educated about particular kinds of secular certainties or ideologies, but not religious or spiritual ones, does not lend itself well to creating an open society. Instead, it creates one of exclusion—a kind of intolerance of certain perspectives. It is also an affront to a society seeking to be inclusive, tolerant, and multicultural.

To be open and tolerant of perspectives with which one agrees is easy enough. To be open and tolerant regarding differences that are largely superficial is also relatively easy; ethnic or cultural differences, for example, such as dress, food, and music. But we short-change ourselves, and others, when acceptance of differences goes no further than these, for what distinguishes perspectives at a deeper level has a possibility of enriching us all.

Today, that may be of particular importance, as our societies are becoming dominated by particular worldviews, such as consumerism and capitalism. Of course, we are all consumers and capitalists to a degree. To be immersed in contemporary Western society means that one can hardly avoid the impacts, if not the benefits, of these two domineering worldviews. But without other voices and alternative worldviews the inundated messages of these two dominant worldviews leaves us victim to their slow but steady mission/vision creep, and no less in places such as education.

Demands for inclusion come from more than just religious communities. One hears it also from groups whose worldview is defined by distinct spiritualities. First Nations peoples, for example, are demanding the right to be heard, but not just in regard to economic issues. Not long ago they were denied the right to practice their own spirituality, under the pretext that it was pagan and not in their best interest. The educational system of the day sought to eradicate their traditional beliefs and practices, and almost succeeded, as we discover when we learn more about the history of the residential schools system.[10] Today, there is clear recognition that such exclusion and suppression was detrimental to the identity, existence, and survival of First Nations peoples. Even today there is concern that their children feel alienated in public schools—that their way of life is not appreciated, much less understood.[11]

10. See, for example, Benjamin, *Indian School Road*.
11. These were the findings of the "Truth and Reconciliation Commission of Canada: Interim Report."

Today, nonetheless, there is in general more reception and openness to the beliefs and practices of First Nations peoples. Rituals such as prayers, smudgings, and drumming have become more and more part of public events—political proceedings, graduation exercises, school ceremonies—and to the benefit of all. Many nonnative people are becoming aware, as a result, that when they probe further they learn that Native spirituality is rich in ceremony, story, and teachings. They also learn that it is deeply connected to the community and land.

Public educators are now scrambling to develop curriculum that includes First Nations peoples, their traditions, teachings, and spirituality. Educators are now recognizing a shameful exclusion of First Nations' visions of life and ways of life—in essence, their worldview—in public schooling, and they are doing their part to overcome this lacuna. In fact, the Interim Report of the Truth and Reconciliation Commission strongly recommended that medical, nursing, and law students in Canada be taught knowledge and awareness of Canada's Indigenous peoples: their rights, history, teachings, practices, health issues, legacy of the residential schools, and more.[12]

If exclusion, and lack of knowledge and awareness, of First Nations peoples worldviews are unacceptable today in public schooling, is the exclusion of other religious/spiritual worldviews not equally unacceptable? A secular society that insists on neutrality yet teaches little *about* religious worldviews subtly conveys the message to students that such worldviews are not important. Ignoring the worldviews of First Nations peoples was offensive to them. Ignoring the worldviews of Jews, Christians, Muslims, and others is equally offensive to adherents of these worldviews. It communicates that the rich heritage of such worldviews is unimportant, and best left to the privacy of home, church, mosque, or synagogue. It can also lead to alienation and misunderstandings. This has generational impact, of which First Nations peoples became increasingly aware and fought hard against.

An argument often raised is that religion is too controversial. True, in some ways it can be, but politics, history, and economics are no less controversial. There is also fear that educators may lean toward promoting one particular worldview, to the detriment of others. But this holds for all subject matter. Teachers should not promote any particular kind of worldview or ideology in their teachings in the classroom, whether these are political, economic, or religious. Rather, they should teach *about* them, so that students gain knowledge and awareness about them, and can then make their own decisions regarding them.

---

12. "Truth and Reconciliation Commission of Canada: Calls to Action," 3, Articles 24 and 28.

Today, it is unacceptable that students are unaware of political and economic ideologies and their teachings. So, too, should it be unacceptable that students are unaware of religious worldviews and their teachings. Not to know that the Dalai Lama is Buddhist is really not to know anything of significance about him at all. Not to know the source of one of the greatest speeches of all time—"I Have a Dream"—is to fail to know much about Martin Luther King Jr. in general and his vision for an interracial America in particular. It is also to exclude.

That kind of exclusion is all the more disconcerting because it only allows others to be included on terms set by the majority or dominant worldview. Increasingly, language is sanitized of words and phrases, thoughts and ideas, with which others may disagree. A few years ago pressure was placed on the Canadian government to remove the words "recognize the supremacy of God" from its Charter of Rights and Freedoms because it was deemed offensive to atheists. The reciting of the Lord's Prayer in many municipal council meetings has been removed because it is deemed offensive to some, but now largely replaced with nothing more than a secular "getting down to the business at hand." All of these actions do not create an atmosphere of inclusion. Rather, they result in exclusion, with the default position that of a dominant secularism. Lost in all of these measures is the rich diversity that comes with inclusion.

The Value of Inclusion and Diversity

We live in a global world, a world full of social, cultural, political, economic, and philosophical differences. Knowledge of those differences is important for understanding the world around us. We cannot engage with "the other" if we are unaware of who and what they are. Education in general recognizes the importance of developing global awareness, especially as pressure to become global citizens increases as time unfolds. Global citizenship is not a push to eliminate differences, but it does entail becoming conscious of differences, of diversity among us, and coming to understand not only why we are different, but also *that* we are different. Difference and diversity are not to be overcome as much as they are to be celebrated and embraced. As in nature, so with humans, diversity adds to the vast richness of existence. But has public schooling been as successful in including diversity?

In *Becoming Human*, Jean Vanier argues that people with mental and physical disabilities can teach us much about what it means to be human. They, too, rightly have a place in the communities in which we live and should not be isolated in institutions. By isolating them, we so easily narrow our understanding of them and of the nature of the human. Vanier comes to such a conclusion having lived with people with mental and physical disabilities, in L'Arche communities that he initiated and are now spread around the world. He also comes to this conclusion from the particular Christian worldview perspective he embraces, one similar to that of Martin Luther King, Jr.

Vanier, and no less King, argued that all people, regardless of their color, gender, or mental or physical abilities, merit freedom, dignity, and protection by law. Numerous Canadians agree, yet the worldview perspective in which that view of the human is embedded is not always well known. It is also increasingly discredited in the public sphere, largely because it is associated with certain individuals who have acted criminally or disparagingly of others. Others declare religious perspectives as medieval, and that society has progressed far beyond such thinking. But demeaning religious perspectives in this manner easily leads to distortion and to the view that those who embrace nonreligious perspectives are much more enlightened *because* they are not religious. But this is debatable, of course, and becomes apparent when some of the controversial issues of society surface. It is debatable, for example, whether all the inventions and advancements of the twentieth century brought on by secular ideologies proclaiming to create a fair and just society in fact resulted in enlightened societies, for it is a century littered with millions of victims who stood in the way of these ideologies. It is debatable as to whether society has become that much more enlightened and advanced when those with severe mental disabilities are not considered human and can be euthanized.[13] It is debatable as to whether we as humans have become much more enlightened and advanced when, for example, steps are taken in society to ensure that future populations have been sanitized of people with Down syndrome, communicating a not so subtle message that people with certain characteristics are not valued.[14]

The point here is not to argue or debate which perspectives are more laudable or enlightened, for if history teaches us anything it is that all perspectives have their shadow side. Rather, it is to ensure that the educational system sufficiently teaches *about* various perspectives so students become aware of them, develop their critical thinking as a result of that awareness, and then draw their own conclusions. To assume that society has become secular and has moved away from religious worldview perspectives, is to

---

13. Singer, *Practical Ethics*, 179–91.

14. Garland-Thompson, "Case for Conserving Disability," 339–55; Taylor, "A World Without," 4.

make a rather naive assumption.[15] To feel or believe that society *should* move away from religious worldview perspectives is a totally different matter, and is a personal opinion, one those in public educational systems are not privileged to convey to their students. As such, teaching *about* various worldview perspectives (secular and religious) ought to have a central place in public schooling. What, then, are its benefits, and how might this be done? And what does public schooling that is inclusive and open to the voices of those with whom one may not always agree look like?

Worldview Education: An Inclusive Model

Well-known German philosopher Jürgen Habermas has, over the years, warmed up to religious worldviews. Though still an avowed atheist, he has nonetheless come to realize that religious worldview traditions have, over the centuries, developed language to deal with life and death issues that atheists have and will have a difficult time surpassing. That kind of language has a place in the public square, he asserts, but it must be presented in a manner understandable to nonreligious people.[16] Alan de Botton, also an atheist, senses the richness in religious rituals and practices and states that atheists can learn much from them. He emulates some of them as he develops his own secular religion.[17] Even the atheistic pugilist Richard Dawkins reluctantly admits an emotional appreciation for religious ritual, even some nostalgia for the old Christian hymns, and incorporates some rites of passage in his own brand of secular humanism.[18] Auguste Comte, the so-called father of positivism and sociology, considered religion an inferior stage in the progression of humanity yet modeled some of the very religious rituals and practices he despised, and at times eccentrically so, when he developed his own "Religion of Humanity" in Paris in the mid-nineteenth century.

What does all of this say, and why might it be important in assisting public school educators in teaching about different worldview perspectives? First, in regard to rituals, it conveys the notion that they are not the exclusive domain of religious people, but are central to the human situation and hence to a wide variety of worldviews. One may criticize the pomp of certain religious rituals but do they really differ in essence from the pomp that takes place at certain academic events, government proceedings, or even

---

15. Berger, *Desecularization*, 1–18.
16. Habermas, "Religion," 1–25.
17. See de Botton, *Religion for Atheists*.
18. Carter, "Richard Dawkins Admits"; Knapton, "Richard Dawkins: 'I Am a Secular Christian.'"

sporting events? Comparing and contrasting such rituals will communicate to students that ritual is a human activity. Humans by nature participate in rituals of one sort or another. What those rituals intend to convey and what they are grounded in may differ considerably from one worldview to the next.

Second, large ultimate and existential questions regarding, for example, meaning and purpose of life, are also central to the human situation, but responses to such questions vary according to different worldviews, both religious and secular. Jean-Paul Sartre, the twentieth century French existentialist, declared, "It is meaningless that we are born; it is meaningless that we die." For Sartre there was no ultimate meaning to life; there was only the meaning that we individually make. Viktor Frankl, Holocaust survivor and psychiatrist, stated that "one should not search for an abstract meaning of life, but rather the specific meaning of a person's life at any given moment."[19] On the other hand, Desmond Tutu, Anglican bishop and apartheid fighter, believed that there was greater meaning and purpose to life and this was connected to "giving God glory by reflecting his beauty and his love."[20] For Tutu, meaning is connected to a higher power, but not so for Sartre and Frankl, both of whom rejected ultimate meaning as well as the existence of a higher power, at least if that higher power was understood as the God of Christianity. Nonetheless, all three spoke of meaning and purpose of life, even if each does so differently.

Both of these examples illustrate that people of different worldview perspectives may deal with the same questions or issues but respond to them in different ways. They also ground their responses in different sources, whether that is reason, revelation, story, or even science, or a mixture of all four. Each of these serves as sources of truth and certainty. What is common here is that Sartre, Frankl, and Tutu each have sources to which they appeal. Alas, these sources are different, and one places faith in one or another source for their ultimate certainty. Determining which source is ultimately true and trustworthy can only be taken on faith. Not even science can assist us here, even though some argue that scientific truth is superior to all other truths, especially revelation. To argue such, however, is to affirm scientism, which itself is a worldview.

An approach such as this levels the worldview playing field. It recognizes that all worldviews (religious and secular) have similar structures (narratives, myths, rituals, symbols, teachings, and more) but the content or understanding of each can be vastly different. All worldviews, for example,

---

19. Frankl, *Man's Search for Meaning*, 131.
20. Friend, *Meaning of Life*, 13.

have a view regarding the nature of the human, what it means to be human, or even when human life properly begins. These issues are with us today, and people take different positions on them based largely on their worldview beliefs. As such, it is much more of an advance to recognize that people have different worldview perspectives, and as a result take different positions on a variety of issues not because some are more intelligent, enlightened, or scientific but because they take a different worldview perspective. Hence, to engage in belittling or disparaging certain worldviews *as* worldviews ("religion poisons everything") is to engage in vitriol and derision.

More beneficial is to come to a greater understanding of different worldviews: their beliefs, values, teachings, rituals, symbols, narratives, ontologies, epistemologies, and more. In asking questions of other worldviews, one comes to better understand one's own. With greater understanding comes greater dialogue and exchange—we all learn from one another. It also avoids the simplistic notion that some worldviews, especially religious worldviews, are all the same.[21]

Teaching about worldviews both religious and secular in various subject areas can reveal their breadth and depth that is all too often missing in the public school curricula. Reading literature, for example, will reveal that poems and prose are rich with the thoughts and ideas of writers from numerous worldview perspectives. Studying sacred texts as literary texts can assist in exploring their various genres, as well as their teachings.[22] Critically analyzing films and movies can uncover both secular and religious themes that are rife in many of them.[23] Studying social justice movements such as the abolition of slavery and freedom marches will reveal that proponents of both secular and religious worldviews have locked arms, but do so for different reasons. Analyzing current environmental movements will reveal that individuals and groups from different worldview perspectives are heavily involved, each concerned about the ecological predicament of the planet but each for different reasons.[24] Examining various economic and political ideologies will reveal that they emerge from more complex worldview perspectives.[25] Even examining the history and philosophy of education will reveal that numerous worldviews have been at play in the development of public schooling.[26]

---

21. Prothero, *God is Not One*, 3.
22. See, for example, Crain, *Reading the Bible*.
23. See, for example, Godawa, *Hollywood Worldviews*.
24. See, for example, Gottlieb, *Greener Faith*.
25. See, for example, Koyzis, *Political Visions*.
26. See, for example, Reuben, *Making of a Modern University*; Postman, *End of Education*; and Marsden, *Soul of the American University*.

Studying worldviews, especially religious worldviews, need not take place solely within the subject area of religious studies. While much of importance can be done there, to isolate it in this field truncates it and conveys the subtle message that worldviews, whether secular or religious, have little to do with the rest of schooling or even the rest of life. Worldviews, as *visions of life* and *ways of life*, are interwoven into the fabric of life. Becoming aware and knowledgeable about our deeply held beliefs and values, as well as those of others, and how they impact us individually and collectively, is an important aspect of the educational journey.

Conclusion

Religious worldviews have been part of the human story since its beginnings. They continue to influence human thought and action today. As Canada increasingly becomes home to people from various cultures and religious perspectives, and Canadians increasingly travel and live in various places in the world, awareness, knowledge, and understanding of both religious and secular worldviews becomes increasingly important. That awareness, knowledge, and understanding must get beyond reducing religious worldviews to fundamentalist beliefs, inflexible dogmatism, and institutional attendance, for that is only to distort it. That increased understanding must take place also within the context of secular worldviews, for these too are on the increase. Rich stories, teachings, mysteries, philosophical intrigues, literary creations, and musical wonderments are the domain of all worldviews, religious and secular. An increase in knowledge and critical awareness of both of these worldviews will greatly assist students in discerning the true from the popular, the right from the widespread, and the common good from the feel-good.

Reflection Questions

1. What do you do to develop critical awareness in your students?
2. What do you do to open up space for discussions with students about different worldviews, both religious and secular?
3. What do you do to awaken in your students a desire to ask some of life's biggest questions that then lead them to seek responses from their own worldview perspective and those of others?
4. What do you do to be inclusive of a variety of worldview perspectives in your subject area?

Bibliography

Almond, Brenda. "Education for Tolerance: Cultural Difference and Family Values." *Journal of Moral Education* 39 (2010) 131–43.

Armstrong, Karen. *Fields of Blood: Religion and the History of Violence*. Toronto: Knopf, 2014.

Belshaw, Deryke, et al. *Faith in Development: Partnership Between the World Bank and the Churches of Africa*. Oxford: Regnum, 2001.

Benjamin, Chris. *Indian School Road: Legacies of the Schubenacadie Residential School*. Halifax: Nimbus, 2014.

Berger, Peter, ed. *The Desecularization of the World: Resurgent Religion and World Politics*. Grand Rapids: Eerdmans, 1999.

de Botton, Alain. *Religion for Atheists: A Non-believers Guide to the Uses of Religion*. Toronto: Signal, 2013.

Carter, Claire. "Richard Dawkins Admits He is a 'Cultural Anglican.'" *Telegraph*, September 12, 2013. http://www.telegraph.co.uk/news/religion/10303223/Richard-Dawkins-admits-he-is-a-cultural-Anglican.html.

Cavanaugh, William. *The Myth of Religious Violence: Secular Ideology and the Roots of Modern Conflict*. New York: Oxford University Press, 2009.

Crain, Jeanie. *Reading the Bible as Literature*. Cambridge: Polity, 2010.

Dawkins, Richard. *The God Delusion*. Boston: Houghton Mifflin, 2006.

Frankl, Viktor. *Man's Search for Meaning*. New York: Pocket Books, 1985.

Friend, David. *The Meaning of Life: Reflections in Words and Pictures on Why We Are Here*. Boston: Little, Brown, 1991.

Garland-Thomson, Rosemarie. "The Case for Conserving Disability." *Bioethical Inquiry* 9 (2012) 339–55.

Godawa, Brian. *Hollywood Worldviews: Watching Films with Wisdom and Discernment*. Grand Rapids: Eerdmans, 2002.

Gottlieb, Roger. *A Greener Faith: Religious Environmentalism and Our Planet's Future*. New York: Oxford University Press, 2006.

Habermas, Jurgen. "Religion in the Public Square." *European Journal of Philosophy* 14 (2006) 1–25.

Hitchins, Christopher. *God is Not Great: How Religion Poisons Everything*. Toronto: McClelland & Stewart, 2007.

Johnston, Douglas, and Cynthia Sampson, eds. *Religion, The Missing Dimension of Statecraft*. New York: Oxford University Press, 1994.

Knapton, Sarah. "Richard Dawkins: 'I Am a Secular Christian.'" *Telegraph*, May 24, 2014. http://www.telegraph.co.uk/culture/hay-festival/10853648/Richard-Dawkins-I-am-a-secular-Christian.html.

Koyzis, David. *Political Visions and Illusions: A Survey and Christian Critique of Contemporary Ideologies*. Downers Grove, IL: InterVarsity, 2003.

Marsden, George M. *The Soul of the American University: From Protestant Establishment to Established Non-belief*. New York: Oxford University Press, 1994.

Nord, Warren. *Religion in American Education: Rethinking a National Dilemma*. Chapel Hill: University of North Carolina Press, 1995.

Postman, Neil. *The End of Education: Redefining the Value of School*. New York: Vintage, 1995.

Prothero, Stephen. *God is Not One: The Eight Rival Religions that Run the World—and Why their Differences Matter.* New York: HarperOne, 2010.

———. *Religious Illiteracy: What Every American Needs to Know—And Doesn't.* New York: HarperOne, 2007.

Reuben, Julie. *The Making of the Modern University: Intellectual Transformation and the Marginalization of Morality.* Chicago: University of Chicago Press, 1996.

Sharpe, Eric. *Comparative Religion: A History.* London: Duckworth, 1975.

Singer, Peter. *Practical Ethics.* Cambridge: Cambridge University Press, 2011.

Sunshine, Glenn. *Why You Think the Way You Do: The Story of Western Worldviews from Rome to Home.* Grand Rapids: Zondervan, 2009.

Taylor, Daniel. "A World Without the Disabled Will Be the Poorer." *Christian Courier*, September 8, 2014. http://www.christiancourier.ca/columns-op-ed/entry/a-world-without-the-disabled-will-be-the-poorer.

"Truth and Reconciliation Commission of Canada: Calls to Action." Winnipeg: Truth and Reconciliation Commission of Canada, 2015. http://www.trc.ca/websites/trcinstitution/File/2015/Findings/Calls_to_Action_English2.pdf.

"Truth and Reconciliation Commission of Canada: Interim Report." Winnipeg, Truth and Reconciliation Commission of Canada, 2012. http://www.myrobust.com/websites/trcinstitution/File/Interim%20report%20English%20electronic.pdf.

Valk, John. "Religion or Worldview: Enhancing Dialogue in the Public Square." *Marburg Journal of Religion* 14 (May 2009) 1–16.

———. "Worldviews of Today: Teaching for Dialogue and Mutual Understanding." In *Values, Religions and Education in Changing Societies*, edited by Karin Sporre and Jan Mannberg, 103–19. Dordrecht, Netherlands: Springer, 2010.

Vanier, Jean. *Becoming Human.* Toronto: Anansi, 1998.

15

What Teachers Need to Know about Tolerance

Matthew Etherington

Introduction in Conversation

THESE SIMULATED CONVERSATIONS HIGHLIGHT the many different levels of human interaction.

Ayda: I don't believe in God.
Joanna: I tolerate your position, I disagree.

Wayne: I have decided this year to tell my children that Santa Claus is based on the historic person of Saint Nicholas in the fourth century and not the man dressed up today in red.
Peter: I respect this position, I agree.

Shakyra: I cheated on my last exam and will continue to do so; it is okay because I know that some other people do too and the teacher doesn't care.
Susie: I am disappointed, I am intolerant to what you do and will act to stop your behavior.

Aaron: I have McDonald's for breakfast three times a week.
Tomi: That is not good for your health, but I tolerate your eating habits. But if you become unwell, I may change my position.

Kelly: When my mother makes my lunch for school, I throw it away the first chance I get and take a lunch from another child.
Georgia: I am intolerant to what you are doing, this needs to stop.

Sagar: In my culture we show our acceptance of you by sharing and eating a meal together.
Dale: I celebrate with you in this.

Within these brief exchanges we encounter people expressing tolerance, celebration, respect, and potential intolerance at the actions, behaviors, and ideas of others. These imaginary conversations are important because they remind us that conversations like these occur every day on many different levels and within different contexts. Elementary and high schools since the Second World War have been cognizant to these different levels of human interaction and to the diversity of values and beliefs that students bring with them to the classroom. Although some schools have accommodated these differences more effectively than others, most schools are designed to be centers of their communities and as such be accessible, open, inclusive, and welcoming to all who attend.[1]

The progress that schools have made in relation to the implementation of a more inclusive education curriculum, policy, and pedagogy has been facilitated by a commitment to upholding a praxis of tolerance. When understood and implemented, tolerance in the classical sense motivates schools to protect the values and beliefs of others, assist with religious and cultural literary, build upon the skills necessary to know how to disagree respectfully, and generate familiarity for the absorption and reality of cultural and religious difference.[2] This all occurs within the framework of classical tolerance.

One may recall, however, that the concept of tolerance is a fairly recent one. Tolerance was not included in the four classical virtues or in the three Christian virtues.[3] That said, tolerance is often associated with democracy for which citizens and institutions are responsible.[4] A democratic and tolerant classroom upholds the freedom of expression, and a readiness to engage in dialogue with others.[5]

Classical tolerance is the ideal tolerance as it acknowledges the importance and preservation of liberalism, that is, a recognition that there are many good ways to live. Classical tolerance acknowledges identity differences (who I am) and epistemological differences (what I believe). When classical tolerance is lacking, historical precedent conveys a painful story. The residential school system in Canada is an example of Europeans

1. Horvat and Baugh, "Not all Parents," 12.
2. Dooyeweerd, *Roots of Western Culture*, 10.
3. Kilpatrick, *Why Johnny Can't Tell*, 90.
4. Bassiouni, "Toward a Universal Declaration," 18.
5. Beetham, "Democracy," 29.

attempting to destroy and replace Indigenous identity and epistemology with European values, identities, and beliefs."[6]

Classical tolerance accepts and includes the value and worth of every single person. This is identity-based inclusion.[7] In addition, classical tolerance also identifies epistemological-based inclusion. This is a recognition that people have established propositions about reality. Classical tolerance respects and defends the value of people but it does not accept all propositions about reality as correct, only the right of all people to have and live by their beliefs.[8] In this sense, classical tolerance is the bedrock of free, democratic, and just societies.[9]

Although classical tolerance is necessary for a free society it has been modified recently to a view that presupposes tolerance as antithetical to a respect of persons, because tolerance by its very definition presupposes disagreement with certain beliefs, values, and behaviors. Tolerance is viewed as arrogantly standing over people with a condescending attitude of disagreement. Consequently, tolerance has been replaced with a version which promotes the view that all ideas and practices must be accepted and affirmed as equal and true.[10]

This conceptual shift is due to a misleading notion that presents tolerance and respect as at odds with each other. As a consequence, classical tolerance and respect are perceived as mutually exclusive. The school student and teacher is then faced with a (false) dilemma—should I teach tolerance or be respectful and teach respect? If there is one thing that philosophical thought and personal experience has shown us, it is that either/or dilemmas are frequently false. The potential for misunderstanding tolerance, stereotyping, and oversimplification based on ignorance is enormous—and schools have a big part to play in correcting misconceptions.

The argument for what the author believes is a correct understanding of tolerance to be taught in schools, namely classical tolerance, derives from four premises that ought to be stated openly for the sake of transparency: (a) people living, working, and being educated in Western liberal societies do so in increasingly religious and culturally pluralistic societies, (b) the human rights of all people ought to be protected by the state, (c) the best system for accommodating religious, educational, and cultural pluralism while protecting human rights is classical tolerance, and (d) schools can and

---

6. Battiste, *Decolonizing Education*, 56.
7. Ipgrave, "Including the Religious Viewpoints," 5–22.
8. Von Bergen et al., "Authentic Tolerance," 112.
9. Thiessen, *Charge of Fostering Intolerance*, 52.
10. Von Bergen et al., "Authentic Tolerance," 111.

ought to play an important role in preparing students with the knowledge, skills, and dispositions needed for the application of classical tolerance in a pluralistic society.[11]

With those four points, we can then consider how we, as individuals and as a society, are to get along given our deep ideological differences. This question is especially significant as it relates to "schools situated in contemporary pluralist democratic societies, where educators are tasked with fostering in students a shared civic identity while refraining from undermining their cultural and religious commitments."[12]

The following sections of this discussion will consider other assessments and practices of tolerance. The central thesis is that classical tolerance is necessary for individuals and democratic societies to flourish and is reserved for beliefs, values, or behaviors and not persons themselves. Additionally, respect is a necessary condition of classical tolerance—respecting persons as valuable ends in themselves. Consequently, one is tolerant and respectful simultaneously.

Tolerance is a Dirty Word

Regrettably, as previously noted, a contemporary and popular conception of tolerance has resulted in some people demanding its demise. One of these is the accusation that to tolerate someone is to hate them."[13] To judge in this context is to take a privileged and powerful position in other people's lives, determining who is acceptable and who is not. For example, according to one blogger, "We tolerate those we consider inferior. . . . We would find it patronizing, even downright insulting, to be 'tolerated' at someone's dinner table. . . . The word 'tolerance' should be replaced with 'mutual respect.'"[14]

Similarly, in a recent TEDx talk, the speaker opens by claiming that "tolerance is a dirty word" and "we must eliminate it from the American vocabulary."[15] The speaker proclaims that tolerance is inadequate because it implies that the one who tolerates will not allow another to be themselves but only to just exist.

---

11. A similar four-point argument is given by Rosenblith and Bindewald, "Between Mere Tolerance," 593.

12. Ibid.

13. This stems from the misguided use of Yeshua's words, "Judge not, that you be not judged" (Matt 7:1).

14. Malhotra, "Tolerance Isn't Good Enough."

15. Slayer, "Tolerance is a Dirty Word."

It is claimed that if I tolerate you I then make no effort to know you or to develop a caring relationship with you. You exist, I can accept the fact, and that is all. If this is what tolerance is then indeed, I agree, we must replace it with something more compassionate. One cannot truly flourish as a human being by just existing. Moreover, communities could never be places where people reach out to their neighbors in love and care. If this really is tolerance then it is unjust and inhumane, and must be substituted by more adequate concepts, such as respect and celebration.

This view of tolerance is fundamentally mistaken. It is, however, a characteristic of the neoclassical classification of tolerance that demands people to be open-minded and empathetic toward a virtually endless parade of differences.[16] It rejects the view that one can disagree with an idea or reject a behavior as wrong or objectionable. One must be open-minded to everything. Although this might be perceived by some as a modern, progressive, and even loving approach to diversity, it is wrong on a number of levels.

So let us not in haste discard what has been touted a repulsive practice and neglect to carefully investigate the status of true tolerance. The significance of tolerance is best attributed to the French philosopher Voltaire, who argued in favor of tolerating religious belief while reserving the right to argue strenuously against it, which he did. Although there is some doubt as to whether Voltaire actually uttered precisely the following definition of tolerance, he is frequently attributed with the following view regarding tolerance and it is worth repeating here: "I disagree with what you say, but I will defend to the death your right to say it."[17] I disagree with your ideas but not you as a person. In that sense, tolerance frees a person to believe as true something another person might believe to be false, and in some cases even objectionable. I can tolerate your beliefs and at the same time defend your right to believe them. Moreover, I can disagree with you and I can also love you as a human being. For those of us who might question why someone would even need to tolerate something they believe to be wrong, the answer is simple: "You tolerate it because people are more important than beliefs—ethics supersedes epistemology."[18] A person can disagree, which can lead to judging, but having an opinion about something that differs from another person, even to

---

16. Von Bergen et al., "Authentic Tolerance," 113.

17. This quotation was derived from the work of English biographer, Evelyn Beatrice Hall who used this quotation to describe Voltaire's "attitude" in her 1906 biography, *The Friends of Voltaire*.

18. Thiessen, *Charge of Fostering Intolerance*, 47.

vocalize that opinion, isn't hatred.[19] It seems that critics of tolerance are fine with people not looking like them, as long as they think like them.[20]

Tolerance does not interfere with individual freedom. It actually creates the grounds for an autonomous life, a life where people can choose purposefully and individually[21] and others are at the same time free to disagree. While individual liberty is a necessary good for people who crave autonomy and independence, at the same time it is not an absolute good for all people. Absolute autonomy and independence is a very modern and, some might suggest, secular perspective of living out one's life and goals. Many cultures and religions are communitarian, not individualistic, drawing on established and enduring traditions that sometimes limit individual choices for a greater good. Moreover, human beings are not the liberated self-made individuals they sometimes claim to be but are formed and embedded by historical, religious, and cultural knowledge and practices.[22] This presents not a dilemma for teachers and schools but a motivation for teachers to help their students understand the epistemological underpinnings that provide the teachings and guidance for people to direct their lives. With this understanding, individuals can then decide if these beliefs, values, and behaviors are to be tolerated, agreed upon, or in some cases even extinguished.

There are circumstances when intolerance is necessary and right, in other words there are limits to tolerance. This is because classical tolerance is not intrinsically good. That is, classical tolerance is good only if one is tolerating what ought to be tolerated—therefore it has limitations.[23] For example, "Using a ginger-bread-shaped cookie mold to make delicious gingerbread cookies is good, but not if they're used to beat the dog."[24] Moreover, most teachers do not and should not tolerate acts of hate or schoolyard bullying.[25] This is why anti-bullying programs exist and no-tolerance policies are widely implemented in districts, states, and provinces.[26] Intolerance toward behaviors that are psychologically or physically destructive to

---

19. Gilman, "Disagreement Isn't Hate."
20. Kristoff, "Confession of Liberal Intolerance."
21. Afdal, *Tolerance and Curriculum*, 115.
22. Ibid., 98.
23. Stetson and Conti, *Truth About Tolerance*, 139–61.
24. Ibid., 92.
25. Zero-tolerance policies are in some of America's most enlightened schools. Alternative approaches to discipline include other strategies like restorative justice. Anti-bullying programs are also available in an attempt to prevent bullying in both schools and communities.
26. Horvat and Baugh, "Not All Parents," 12.

people is appropriate. With this understanding, classical tolerance respects people but is intolerant to harmful behaviors.

And yet the implications for teaching students a mistaken interpretation of tolerance which ignores beliefs and values and expands the skills of disagreement are enormous if not confusing. This would result in educators asking their students to refrain from disagreeing with any behaviors, values, or beliefs for fear of being intolerant. Without any debate or discussion students would be taught to accept all views and behaviors of people as equally good and correct. Educators would teach their students to not only respect all views and behaviors but also celebrate them, even those they do not consider ethical. Do the values of the Ku Klux Klan or the mafia deserve respect? What about the Colombian cocaine cartels or the pornography industry—surely the answer is no and never.[27] By accommodating a misunderstood and false application of tolerance, teachers would not be fulfilling their legal, ethical, and professional duty to educate young people with opportunities to think critically about competing (and sometimes dangerous) epistemologies and behaviors. When students are given opportunities to think critically about competing ideas, they are in a better place to understand why people behave the way they do rather than just how they behave.[28] The *why* requires students to investigate a person's core beliefs about reality. Critical thinking then aids students to analyze and develop appropriate and careful responses to the origin and conditions surrounding a person's behavior and the conflicting evaluations and opinions about their behavior.[29]

Unfortunately, a misunderstanding of classical tolerance is not only dangerous but is also self-refuting. Are we to respect and celebrate with the child who chooses to taunt his victims and deprive them of their basic rights just because he doesn't like their views? Are we to respect and celebrate with the student who has decided to cheat in all her final examinations? Are we to respect and celebrate with the verbally abusive parent at the school sports carnival? It would be a professional disaster and ethical failure to respect and celebrate such actions and behaviors and yet, if taken to its logical conclusion, an incorrect version of tolerance would allow for these behaviors to flourish.

27. Kilpatrick, *Why Johnny Can't Tell*, 90.
28. Tsai, Chen, Chang, and Chang, "Effects of Prompting," 99.
29. Ibid., 89.

What Teachers Need to Know

Teachers need to know that classical tolerance and respect are not mutually exclusive but should coexist. They need to know that to be tolerant of an idea, belief, or behavior is to always disagree while displaying utmost respect to the person who holds the belief.

In addition, classical tolerance promotes learning and justice. In fact, what stops injustice is opposition and the accountability that stems from other people who disagree with you. The vibrant and preeminent figure John Stuart Mill wrote in his famous essay *On Liberty* that "unpopular, minority opinion ought to be welcomed because they might turn out to be correct and even if such opinions are incorrect the truth is made stronger, richer, and deeper through encounters with opposing arguments."[30]

Teachers also need to know that there are restrictions to tolerance. If someone holds a belief that requires them to physically or psychologically harm another person, then a tolerant stance should not be adopted but rather intolerance applied with the incentive to end the behavior. Some cultures, beliefs and values oppress woman, erode community, legitimize various forms of violence, or destroy the environment.[31] Some beliefs are bound up with patterns of dominance, exploitation, and exclusion of the vulnerable. Tolerance, then, is not complacent to insensitivity or suffering but consists of a mixture of affirmation, resistance, and celebration.[32] This was clarified most eloquently by John Stuart Mill. As Mill argued, tolerance is the basis of a free society and provides individuals the liberty to believe and value what they choose; however, there is one condition—that it does not harm others.[33] Mill is an important voice in any discussion of tolerance because his argument provides a compelling reason for safeguarding a free society where individuals can choose for themselves how to live and what to believe. He believed that the outcome of a tolerant society is that "Mankind (*sic*) are greater gainers by suffering each other to live as seems good to themselves, than by compelling each to live as seems good to the rest."[34]

Schools and educators should not distance themselves from a classical understanding of tolerance and move only to a narrative focused on the respect and celebration of persons. Classical tolerance already promotes the value and respect of persons but allows for disagreement of action, behavior,

---

30. Gill, *Should God Get Tenure*, 3.
31. Smith, *Learning from the Stranger*, 56.
32. Ibid., 57.
33. Mill, *On Liberty*.
34 Ibid., 16.

and claims to certainty. Consequently, classical tolerance encourages critical thinking, dialogue, and debate. If schools and educators do not clearly make the case for classical tolerance, school students are led to believe that the ideas and core beliefs that people use to make sense of the world are insignificant. Students are also left with a false dichotomy of having to choose between tolerance and respect. This dualistic and fragmentary discord "pushes one's posture of life to opposite extremes that cannot be resolved by any true synthesis."[35] To say that tolerance and respect cannot coexist is similar to the proposition that "motion and rest exclude each other. . . . It is not difficult to determine that motion and rest simply make the same temporal reality visible in two different ways. . . . Instead of excluding they presuppose each other"[36] in the same way tolerance and respect are mutually dependent.

Moreover, schools and educators have a civic responsibility not to ignore the epistemological central beliefs and values that people internalize and use to make sense of the world. Every person has an underlying set of fundamental beliefs to which they strongly hold and for which they have the most commitment.[37] A school student must have the necessary background knowledge for understanding and evaluating fundamental beliefs and the behaviors of individuals and groups. The more you know, the more you can understand. Historian Stephen Prothero maintains that the violent clashes we see between religious groups in the Middle East and groups and individuals in the West are largely drawn from ideas and basic beliefs relating to doctrine, ritual, mythology, experience, and law.[38] These beliefs have real effects on the world and individual lives. Unfortunately, our understanding of these ideological differences is not advanced in the least if schools and educators bypass the importance of teaching classical tolerance. Although schools do host multicultural days as a way to display tolerance, respect, and inclusion of various cultural groups, by themselves these events are insufficient if schools ignore the central epistemological principles and claims that impact people's beliefs and behaviors.

Schools as Homogenous Entities

One of the reasons for overlooking epistemological difference and focusing on cultural days is to stop bullying, fighting, and in some circumstances, killing. If schools can package difference into festivals and foods

35. Dooyeweerd, *Roots of Western Culture*, 11.
36. Ibid., 12.
37. De Jong, *Education in the Truth*, 43.
38. Prothero, "A Dangerous Belief."

and pretend that ideological differences about reality do not exist or are of secondary importance compared to the similarities we share as human beings, maybe civility will prevail and everyone will get along together. A similar notion was advanced by the celebrated and influential pragmatist of the twentieth century John Dewey, who believed that the goal of public education was an assimilative progressive one where students would develop from simple ancient beliefs to more complex and useful scientific ones.[39] In the same way Sheldon Chumir was forthright in his hope for public schooling with a declaration that "public schools were designed to mix children of different ethnic and religious groups and eliminate those differences."[40] It is difficult to oppose the vision that Dewey and Chumir had for education if the purpose of schooling is assimilation and homogeneity.[41] Such a prospect, however well-intentioned, is out of touch with the increasing numbers of students and families that attend public education and live out their religions, cultural, and traditional values, and who embrace core beliefs about reality that offer their own diagnosis of the human predicament and their own prescription for a cure. Furthermore, they do not intend to relinquish their beliefs for another belief system any time soon.[42] A professor of culturally sensitive pedagogy, Anna Kirova, argues that assimilation is never in the spirit of unity but rather is aimed to make difference invisible. Kirova continues, "When someone tells me that they see me as the same as everyone else, I tell them that I don't want that. I am different and I am comfortable with my differences."[43]

Unless teachers and schools seek to unleash enormous authority over children, "the dominant values and behavioral norms will be those the children bring with them to school and against . . . competing values and norms of the teachers' will."[44] Similarities are important but so are differences, especially in a world that is increasingly more diverse than it is the same.

---

39. Egan, *Getting it Wrong*, 110.

40. Sheldon Chumir was a prominent member of the Alberta legislature who led a campaign in the 1980s against alternatives in public schools because he held that isolating children in segregated schools would cause intolerance. Quoted in Bateman, "Exploring the Limits of Pluralism."

41. Thiessen, *Charge of Fostering Intolerance*, 49.

42. Prothero, "A Dangerous Belief."

43. These thoughts were communicated to an academic audience by Dr. Anna Kirova at the CSSE Conference in Calgary, Alberta, May 2016. Kirova is a professor at the University of Alberta and presented a paper at the conference titled, "Critical and Emerging Discourses in Multicultural Education Literature: An (Updated) Review."

44. Egan, *Getting it Wrong*, 135.

If schools can maintain knowledgeable, empathetic, and tolerant graduates prepared for living in diverse pluralistic environments, then teachers need to know that their students require an education permeated with classical tolerance. This entails that schools do more than merely host multicultural days once or twice a year. It requires students having the information necessary to understand the values and beliefs of people different to themselves and the skills needed to disagree respectfully. Students and teachers need experience engaging with the unfamiliar beliefs and values of distinct people groups. They also need to know how to match ideas with competing ideas. Without such experience, school graduates are disadvantaged, easily swayed by leaders on the left and right.[45] This is reminiscent of what historian Carter G. Woodson, in 1933, called "miseducation."[46]

Miseducation potentially "imperils our public life, putting citizens in the thrall of talking heads and effectively transferring power from the third estate (the people) to the fourth (the press)."[47] If differences are made invisible young people may never know why particular people groups and individuals think and act the way they do. And ignorance often manifests fear, and fear frequently leads to intolerance. If people are not free to seriously consider all manner of views, this would hardly be an education.[48]

How will schools and teachers help their students comprehend the core values that inspire religious and cultural groups, and which ones do they accept as true and reject as false The answers to such questions will never be forthcoming if schools overlook teaching classical tolerance to their students.

Within heterogeneous classrooms and playgrounds educators need to return to a comprehensive model of tolerance, namely classical tolerance. Classical tolerance maintains the advancement of truth, highlights differences and commonalities, builds cultural and religious literacy, and assists with forming open-minded, educated citizens living within diverse, multicultural and multireligious societies. Classical tolerance best reflects traditional liberalism, which rests upon the idea that there are "multiple and competing 'good lives' and that individuals ought to be allowed to choose among these good lives with little intervention from the State"[49]

---

45. Prothero, *Religious Literacy*, 13.
46. Woodson, *The Mis-Education of the Negro*, 37.
47. Ibid., 13.
48. Sommerville, *Decline of the Secular University*, 95.
49. McAvoy, "There Are No Housewives," 535.

Children's Picture Books and the Teaching of Tolerance

Children's books present young people with perspectives of the world and their role in it.[50] Picture books written specifically for children say to the future generation, this is what we would like you to believe, think, and how to behave.[51] This is significant because there are a number of children's books written specifically about inclusion and tolerance and so these books will have an important role to play in shaping children's attitudes and beliefs about difference.

A number of recent children's picture books have focused exclusively on teaching tolerance and other related topics about inclusion and diversity. As important as this is, these books present their readers with stories and themes centered only on physical or behavioral differences and largely ignore a person's beliefs, values, or worldview.[52] These books are insufficient for teaching classical tolerance because they concentrate only on identity inclusion, which, as previously noted, is concerned with the question of "who am I" but disregards epistemological inclusion and awareness, which is concerned with "how I understand reality."[53] Without any discussion in the text or examples of epistemological inclusion in action these children's picture books fail to educate students with an authentic and broad understanding of difference, tolerance, and inclusion. Differences are related merely to physical particularities such as clothing, family structure, foods, and festivals but ignore epistemological questions.

For example, the *Ezra Jack Keats Foundation* hosts a website intended for teachers selecting children's books related to multicultural issues such as difference, tolerance, and inclusion. These books are well-written and display attractive visuals and interesting story lines. The commitment to diversity is obvious when the *Ezra Jack Keats Foundation* states on its website that "diversity is one of the books' greatest assets, as children learn to navigate the world see characters who *look* [emphasis added] like them, or who look quite different, embarked on the same journey."[54]

The inadequacies of these books is due to the primary importance they give to differences related chiefly to "looks" (i.e., visual differences in people) and a focus on the foods and the festivals which various people maintain. This emphasis, although important, comes at the expense of not

---

50. Van Brummelen, "Faith on the Wane," 51.

51. Ibid., 52.

52. Ipgrave, "Including the Religious Viewpoints," 94.

53. Ibid.

54. For more information, see http://www.ezra-jack-keats.org/h/keats-the-common-core/.

serving young people with the knowledge and skills needed for navigating epistemological diversity within the fundamental beliefs, values, and behaviors of the characters represented in the books. The books themselves offer no examples of characters who state how they understand the world and the way it should be, nor do they make available for their readership any characters in dialogue who share their beliefs and disagreements openly. This is extraordinary considering that the majority of readers will most likely be in schools located in multicultural and multireligious contexts. Surely the authors could provide some basic awareness and skill building for helping children learn how to listen, respond, and respectfully disagree with people's ideas but still value them as valuable human beings.

The first example is a children's picture book written by Jenny Sue Kostecki-Shaw titled *Same, Same but Different*.[55] The book is listed as having received the Ezra Jack Keats book award. The story line consists of two pen pals, a boy called Elliot who lives in America and Kailash a boy who lives in India. They exchange numerous letters and pictures with the goal, it seems, to learn about each other. Elliot likes to climb trees and so does Kailash. Elliot lives with his mother, father, and baby sister, while Kailash lives with his extended family consisting of twenty-three people. They learn the different hand actions for saying hello and the story ends with a picture displayed of them both sleeping in almost identical looking beds with the author raising the question if they do in fact live in different worlds at all; after all, their bedding apparel and sleeping habits are obviously very similar.

While *Same, Same but Different* is a fascinating and intriguing picturesque storybook for school children, it is all too typical of the foods-and-festivals approach to teaching diversity. The book completely overlooks the epistemological differences of the two boys and does not provide readers with any examples of them sharing their central beliefs about life with each other. At the conclusion of the book we know nothing of the basic values that guide their lives, or which ones are ironically the same and different. The reader misses an opportunity to consider and learn from two boys who disagree with each other's values or beliefs and yet still are respectful and good friends. Unfortunately, this is characteristic of the children's books for teaching children about tolerance and diversity. Books like these give students a distorted, superficial-level view of diversity.

Another picture book that also provides young readers with a foods-and-festivals approach for teaching tolerance and diversity is titled *We Can Get Along Together: A Child's Book of Choices* by Lauren Murphy Payne.[56]

---

55. Kostecki-Shaw, *Same, Same but Different*.
56. Payne, *We Can Get Along*, 1–64.

This book is essentially about treating people respectfully. However, the main problem, once again, is its emphasis on difference related only to the activities and behaviors that people engage. Although there is one example of intolerance where the two children in the story speak of hitting and fighting each other, no examples are offered where the children are represented sharing their values and beliefs and then disagreeing respectfully and tolerating. How would a child understand another child who has a vastly different view of the world and acted out their beliefs? Could they disagree but still be friends? Maybe, but children reading this book are given no strategies for responding to such questions.

A third children's book that is more attentive to epistemological difference is titled *I am I*, by Marie-Louise Fitzpatrick.[57] At the beginning of the story the reader is presented with examples of intolerance as the two boys, one red-haired and the other blue-haired, stand on opposite sides of a river challenging each other by declaring their superiority and importance. They take turns hurling words of hate and blame toward each another until finally they come to accept one another as human beings who disagree on certain issues—although we still don't really know what those issues are. While not sufficient by any means, this book does underscore the importance of epistemological diversity and the potential of practicing classical tolerance within the context of diverse ways of thinking. Compared to the two previous books noted earlier, this book does introduce young readers to a more authentic and traditional understanding of classical tolerance. Nevertheless, what is still lacking are the specifics relating to the children's values and beliefs and examples of how the children can disagree respectfully and still remains friends. At the close of the book we still know nothing about their central beliefs or values or how they make sense of the world and their place in it.

What is surprising is that while the authors of these books have provided their readers with the reality of differences related to food, clothing, and interests, all important for living in pluralistic and multicultural contexts, the books by themselves are insufficient for teaching tolerance and difference because the beliefs and values that the characters live by are not present. If educators and schools teach difference as "consisting of a few exotic external behaviors—wearing grass skirts or bowler hats, eating with chopsticks or following baseball—then the education their students could have received regarding epistemological claims about the world is pushed aside."[58]

57. Fitzpatrick, *I am I*, 1–27.
58. Smith, *Learning from the Stranger*, 8.

If this is the best that authors and schools can do to teach tolerance and diversity, students graduating high school would know very little else about people except for the foods they eat and the festivals they participate. The Indigenous scholar Verna St. Denis responds to the foods-and-festivals approach as a "form of participation on the part of those designated as "cultural others" that is limited to the decorative and includes "leisure, entertainment, food, and song and dance."[59] But the most important missing piece is that the approach is both "impractical and inadequate for sorting out the conflicting claims of individuals, minority groups, vested interests, and a centralized state."[60] It is tempting and easy to think about difference in the physical, which are obvious outward markers of difference, but "they are just the tip of the iceberg because the most interesting differences are invisible until we begin to interact."[61]

In the end, an inadequate understanding of diversity and tolerance has the potential to fuel ignorant and intolerant people who are sometimes portrayed in the media as puzzled as to why everyone does not think, act, and value the same things they do.

The Cultural and Religious Reality and the Necessity of Classical Tolerance

An authentic understanding of classical tolerance is critically important because it provides for a range of perspectives from A to Z not just V to A.[62] Second, in terms of demographics, school students attending educational intuitions in Western contexts do so within increasingly multiethnic environments. Because of increasingly high immigration rates to many Western countries, University of London professor Eric Kaufmann projects regions such as Europe, the United States, Canada, and Australia will grow more diverse because people from less developed countries tend to be more religious. Kaufmann notes that "religion is coming to the West on the backs of immigrants."[63] John Sommerville goes even further. He notes that the secular university is becoming increasingly marginal to American society because of its narrow secularism.[64] The central questions about being hu-

---

59. Fleras and Elliot, as cited in St. Denis, "Silencing Aboriginal Curricular Content," 28.

60. Ibid.

61. Smith, *Learning from the Stranger*, 25.

62. Kristof, "Confession of Liberal Intolerance."

63. Todd, "Think Religion is in Decline."

64. Sommerville, *Decline of the Secular University*, 4.

man that might be essential to the university's mission and identity are now too religious and controversial for it to deal with.[65]

This is a concern for the increasing number of immigrants who have relocated to schools and educational institutions located in Western countries and carry deep religious convictions.[66] Their religious principles and values matter to them and they do not intend nor should they be compelled to disregard their core beliefs if and when they choose to become Canadian citizens. In fact, as many employers of immigrant workers have noted, refugees as survivors of war are capable of "ferocious resistance to integration; their traditions live on, often in another geographic location."[67] Classical tolerance is increasingly important for educators to include early in a student's schooling life as Western nations become culturally diverse and religious.

So a core question for schools is to ask how educators who value civic liberalism are preparing their students for contending with epistemological diversity in a way that is at least adequate for living within liberal democracies. Addressing this question will consist of giving teachers and educators the opportunity to consider the necessary reasons for restoring classical tolerance in schools and classrooms.

Classical tolerance is not the problem in schools or society but rather one important solution to understanding epistemological diversity. A further concern to address is when students are presented with false dichotomies of choosing either tolerance or respect. As Western culture becomes progressively religious, a reality we rarely encounter from the media, educators must know how to embrace classical tolerance in the classroom. This is because classical tolerance takes epistemological diversity and disagreement seriously while respecting the person. Unfortunately, with a shifting view of classical tolerance towards a type of neo-tolerance that overlooks the importance of fundamental beliefs and the skills required for respectful disagreement, classical tolerance appears out of date and unnecessary. Students must reflect on the fact that in the West we are (and ought to be) free to live, move, and breath within societies that are more diverse in thought

---

65. Ibid.

66. According to Canadian political scientist Eric Kaufmann, Western nations are increasingly religious because of an increase in immigration and fertility rates. Canada will receive between twenty-five thousand and fifty thousand Syrian refugees in 2016 and in the years following. The reality is that the majority of Syrian refugees are religious, with deeply held religious convictions. Because religious people tend to have more children compared with secular people, Canada will also experience an increase in religion. Moreover, Christian and Jewish fundamentalists are also increasing in the West due to the forces of secular modernism, which are not always sympathetic to so-called religious interference. For more information, see Kauffmann, *Shall the Religious Inherit*.

67. Donkin, *History of Work*, 319.

and practice than they are similar. As such, learners must be cognizant of what people believe and why they believe because "tolerance is an empty virtue until we actually understand whatever it is we are supposed to be tolerating."[68]

Tolerating Ideas, Values, and Behaviors—but Not Persons

It is argued that classical tolerance[69] does not lead to a disrespect of persons but is concerned with the truth claim of a value, action, or belief. A person is free to disagree with a truth claim and yet still respect and value the person who holds to it. This is the "paradox of classical tolerance—what is tolerated is both rejected and accepted—the believer can be accepted even though one rejects his or her beliefs."[70] And this "paradox" occurs on a daily basis in the work place, the classroom, the courts, the health care system, and so on. It is a false contrast to assume tolerance and acceptance or even love for a person cannot be experienced at the same time.

One can easily tolerate (i.e., disagree with) a person's behavior and still appreciate and respect the person. An example is a mother who is tolerant of the decision that her twenty-year-old daughter has made to date a married man thirty years her senior. She disagrees with her daughter's decision for continuing such a relationship, which the mother considers unethical but the mother's tolerance does not mean that she must stop loving her daughter. In fact, the mother tolerates her daughter's behavior and loves her decisively at the same time. Although the behavior is not approved, the person is.

Also, tolerance should not be the ultimate goal, otherwise teachers will have a difficult time squelching any hazardous ideas that students bring to school with them.[71] Furthermore, tolerance is not the only way to measure an idea, belief, or behavior. One can respect, celebrate, or even strive to extinguish ideas, values, and certain behaviors—for example, bullying, lying, hating people, cheating, and so on. Once again, notice that application is always centered on ideas, values, or behaviors and not on persons themselves. Classical tolerance requires having an egalitarian approach toward persons but an elitist with ideas or behaviors that are wrong or harm others. That is, classical tolerance judges some ideas as better than others. In fact, this is

68. Prothero, "A Dangerous Belief."

69. Classical tolerance always entails disagreement and the right for someone to believe in, teach, and live out an idea, value, or behavior (as long as the belief does not lead to physical or psychological trauma).

70. Thiessen, *Charge of Fostering Intolerance*, 47.

71. Sommerville, *Decline of the Secular University*, 89.

exactly what the TEDx speaker does as he seeks to eliminate tolerance from the American vocabulary. In other words, those who claim that tolerance should be eliminated are just as exclusivist in their beliefs as anybody else. If we lose diversity and especially the toleration of diversity of thought, something that has been happening in academia since the 1990s, we all lose.[72]

An incorrect understanding of tolerance falsely claims that a person should accept all values, beliefs, lifestyles, actions, and truth claims as equally valid.[73] A classical definition of tolerance affirms that people have a right to their beliefs and practices (but not those that are psychologically or physically destructive) without others having to accept them as good or equally valid. Moreover, classical tolerance welcomes the view that human beings will always disagree on fundamental issues and "do not have to value the perspectives held by others, but, as a condition of equal citizenship, they must recognize that others do hold these perspectives and that (as equal citizens) they have a right to hold such perspectives and to have their perspectives given due consideration in collective decision-making processes."[74] Classical tolerance teaches individuals to be alert to alternative ways of living, values, and beliefs, so they have the capacity to understand and assess those alternatives without intimidation or force to adopt them as good or true.

Teachers are faced with two alternatives for teaching tolerance in schools. Either they ask too little of students to accept other beliefs or actions and as a result do not make much progress in fostering their civic aims, or they ask too much of students to accept and respect other beliefs and values, which the most orthodox people refuse to do.[75] Although these are important considerations, they divert our attention from the importance of upholding classical tolerance in free democratic classrooms. The toleration, acceptance, and celebration of different views, beliefs, lifestyles, or behaviors are choices that people make based on how they see the world and how they think the world ought to be. And this is drawn from the worldviews that people adopt as their own to make sense of things. To expect someone to change or alter their worldview to comply with another is substantial. The teacher wanting the change conveys to her class that her worldview reflects reality in a more truthful, ethical, or honorable way. This might be asking too much. A worldview, after all, identifies the way the world is and how it ought to be.

72. Kristof, "Confession of Liberal Intolerance."

73. This is said with some reservation. One could make the case that real diversity should include all viewpoints. Yet many educators still think religion is an enemy to diversity and tolerance, so it is easily dismissed.

74. Rosenblith and Bindewald, "Between Mere Tolerance," 594.

75. Ibid., 591.

What about tolerating the behavior of students who opt out of particular school courses, presentations, or teachings that are in conflict with their beliefs and values? It is often claimed that they miss an educational opportunity to engage in ideas, beliefs, and behaviors that are necessary for civic engagement.[76] However, this view shoulders an assumption that these students do not already have a knowledge and understanding of other beliefs and actions. To automatically assume that students who opt out of classes are ignorant is hasty and assumes without evidence that schools are the only places that students can learn about other beliefs and practices, when this is simply not the case.

Conclusion: What Tolerance Should and Should Not Be

A misunderstanding of the differences between identity-based and epistemological-based inclusion is evident among some educators. Identity-based tolerance is about *who* the person is, while epistemological-based tolerance is about what and how a person understands the world and everything in it. The former entails a respect of the person, while the latter entails disagreement with a person's propositions about reality. Schools should be connected to the larger society and educate young citizens about the differences between identity-based and epistemological-based tolerance.

A more inclusive understanding and practice of tolerance prepares young people for a society that is increasingly heterogeneous, and for that reason classical tolerance reinforces the ideals of democracy. Tolerance is reserved only for those you disagree with, and does not require people to "dissolve or weaken their commitment to ancient and honorable beliefs."[77] We must end the hypocrisy, which consists of educators confirming that they are for "democracy in the classroom and all its free institutions and then maintain learning environments where only some of the students are educable for full citizenship and a full human life."[78]

Educators must look for critical learning spaces in their classrooms to include classical tolerance as a necessary prerequisite for coming to know, engage, and compromise with the other.[79] This might require every educator to undertake professional development on classical tolerance in the classroom. Many teachers have been schooled in an education system that focused mainly on respect but ignored the importance of classical tolerance.

76. Ibid., 592.
77. Bennett, *Broken Hearth*, 138.
78. Adler, *Paideia Proposal*, 7
79. Modood, *Multiculturalism*.

Just as there should be attention given by educators to the promotion of an inclusive learning environment, teachers also need to explore how they can implement a comprehensive application of classical tolerance to sustain diversity and liberty of thought. If we neglect to embrace classical tolerance and epistemological diversity in our classrooms, we will all lose.

Reflection Questions

1. How have you experienced the teaching of tolerance in your education? How was the concept presented to you?
2. Political scientist Eric Kaufmann argues that current trends in the world suggests that the world (in particular Western society) is becoming more religious and diverse due to immigration and the higher birth rates of religious people. If this is true, how is a proper understanding of classical tolerance important for K–12 and post-secondary education?
3. In your opinion and experience, are controversial or politically incorrect views allowed in class discussions and school projects?
4. How have the different perspectives, talents, skills, and styles of students awakened critical thinking and broadened classroom discussions?
5. Why do some people claim that tolerance and respect cannot coexist?
6. Draw four columns on a blank piece of paper with the words "tolerate," "respect," "celebrate," and "extinguish" in each column. As a current or future educator, list some ideas and behaviors that might reflect each category. Share them with another person and compare similarities and differences.

Bibliography

Adler, Mortimer J. *The Paideia Proposal: An Educational Manifesto.* New York: Macmillan, 1998.

Afdal, Geir. *Tolerance and Curriculum, Conceptions of Tolerance in the Multicultural Unitary Norwegian Compulsory School.* Berlin: Waxmann Verlag GmbH, 2006.

Bassiouni, Cherif. "Toward a Universal Declaration on the Basic Principles of Democracy: From Principles to Realization." In *Democracy: Its Principles and Achievement*, 1–20. Geneva: Inter-Parliamentary Union, 1998. http://www.ipu.org/PDF/publications/DEMOCRACY_PR_E.pdf.

Bateman, T. "Exploring the Limits of Pluralism." *Catalyst* 12 (1988) 27–39.

Battiste, Marie. *Decolonizing Education: Nourishing the Learning Spirit*. Saskatoon, SK: Purich, 2013.
Beetham, David. "Democracy: Key Principles, Institutions and Problems." In *Democracy: Its Principles and Achievement*, 21–30. Geneva: Inter-Parliamentary Union, 1998. http://www.ipu.org/PDF/publications/DEMOCRACY_PR_E.pdf.
Bennett, William J. *The Broken Hearth*. New York: Doubleday, 2001.
De Jong, Norman. *Education in the Truth*. Lansing, IL: Redeemer, 1989.
Donkin, Richard. *The History of Work*. New York: Palgrave Macmillan, 2010.
Dooyeweerd, Herman. *Roots of Western Culture: Pagan, Secular and Christian Options*. Toronto: Wedge, 1979.
Egan, Kieran. *Getting it Wrong from the Beginning: Our Progressive Inheritance from Herbert Spencer, John Dewey and Jean Piaget*. London: Yale University Press, 2002.
Fitzpatrick, Marie-Louise. *I am I*. New Milford, CT: Roaring Brook, 2006.
Gill, David, ed. *Should God Get Tenure: Essays on Religion and Higher Education*. Grand Rapids: Eerdmans, 1997.
Gilman, Alan. "Disagreement Isn't Hate." *Alan Gilman—Bible Teacher*, blog, June 7, 2016. http://blog.alangilman.ca/2016/06/07/boldness02/.
Glanzer, Perry. "Finding the Gods in Public School: A Christian Deconstruction of Character Education." *Journal of Education and Christian Belief* 4 (2000) 115–30.
Hall, Evelyn B. *The Friends of Voltaire*. London: Cornell University Library, 1906.
Horvat, Erin McNamara, and David E. Baugh. "Not All Parents Make the Grade in Today's Schools." *Phi Delta Kappan* 96 (2015) 8–13.
Ipgrave, Julia. "Including the Religious Viewpoints and Experiences of Muslim Students in an Environment that is Both Plural and Secular." *Journal of International Migration and Integration* 11 (2010) 5–22.
Kaufmann, Eric. *Shall the Religious Inherit the Earth: Demography and Politics in the Twenty-First Century*. London: Profile Books, 2010.
Kilpatrick, William. *Why Johnny Can't Tell Right from Wrong and What We Can Do About It*. New York: Touchstone, 1992.
Kostecki-Shaw, Jenny Sue. *Same, Same but Different*. New York: Henry Holt, 2011.
Kristof, Nicholas. "A Confession of Liberal Intolerance." *New York Times*, May 7, 2016. http://www.nytimes.com/2016/05/08/opinion/sunday/a-confession-of-liberal-intolerance.html?emc=eta1&_r=1.
Malhotra, Rajiv. "Tolerance Isn't Good Enough: The Need for Mutual Respect in Interfaith Relations." *Huffington Post*, May 25, 2011. http://www.huffingtonpost.com/rajiv-malhotra/hypocrisy-of-tolerance_b_792239.html.
McAvoy, Paula. "There Are No Housewives on 'Star Trek': A Reexamination of Exit Rights for the Children of Insular Fundamentalist Parents." *Educational Theory* 62 (2012) 535–52.
McDowell, Josh, and Bob Hostetler. *The New Tolerance: How a Cultural Movement Threatens to Destroy You, Your Faith, and Your Children*. Carol Stream, IL: Tyndale, 1998.
Mill, John Stuart. *On Liberty*. Kitchener, ON: Batoche, 1859.
Modood, Tariq. *Multiculturalism: A Civic Idea*. Cambridge: Polity, 2007.
Payne, Lauren Murphy. *We Can Get Along Together: A Child's Book of Choices*. Minneapolis: Free Spirit, 1997.
Prothero, Stephen. "A Dangerous Belief." *Wall Street Journal*, April 23, 2010. http://www.wsj.com/articles/SB10001424052748703709804575202261474208230.

———. *Religious Literacy.* New York: HarperOne, 2008.

Rosenblith, Suzanne, and Benjamin Bindewald. "Between Mere Tolerance and Robust Respect: Mutuality as a Basis for Civic Education in Pluralist Democracies." *Educational Theory* 64 (2014) 589–606.

Slayer, Andrew. "Tolerance is a Dirty Word." TEDx Semester At Sea, November 5, 2014. https://www.youtube.com/watch?v=UyQIKwSPZGM.

Smith, David. *Learning from the Stranger.* Grand Rapids: Eerdmans, 2009.

Sommerville, John. *The Decline of the Secular University.* New York: Oxford University Press, 2006.

St. Denis, Verna. "Silencing Aboriginal Curricular Content and Perspectives through Multiculturalism: There Are Other Children Here." In *Approaches to Aboriginal Education in Canada: Searching for Solutions,* edited by Frances Widdowson and Albert Howard, 26–37. Alberta: Brush Education, 2013.

Stetson, Brad, and Joseph Conti. *The Truth About Tolerance.* Downers Grove, IL: InterVarsity, 2005.

Thiessen, Elmer. *The Charge of Fostering Intolerance: In Defence of Religious Schools and Colleges.* Montreal: McGill-Queens University Press, 2001.

Todd, Douglas. "Think Religion is in Decline? Look at Who is 'Going Forth and Multiplying.'" *Vancouver Sun,* October 12, 2014. http://blogs.vancouversun.com/2014/10/12/think-religion-is-declining-look-at-who-is-going-forth-and-multiplying/.

Tsai, Pei-Ying, Sufen Chen, Huey-Por Chang, and Wen-Hua Chang. "Effects of Prompting Critical Reading of Science News on Seventh Graders' Cognitive Achievement." *International Journal of Environmental and Science* 8 (2013) 85–107. http://files.eric.ed.gov/fulltext/EJ1008596.pdf.

Van Brummelen, Harro. "Faith on the Wane: A Documentary Analysis of Shifting Worldviews in Canadian Textbooks." *Journal of Research on Christian Education* 3 (1994) 51–77.

Von Bergen, C. W., et al. "Authentic Tolerance: Between Forbearance and Acceptance." *Journal of Cultural Diversity* 19 (2012) 111–17.

Woodson, Carter. *The Mis-Education of the Negro.* San Diego: Book Tree, 2006.

16

Experience, Education, and Story: A Transcultural Teacher Narrative

Edward R. Howe

Introduction

EXPERIENCE, EDUCATION, AND STORY are an integral part of my curriculum, teaching, and learning. From my experiences first as a secondary teacher and then as a teacher educator and researcher, I have found that teachers are naturally great storytellers.[1] Of course, going back thousands of years, well before the first universities were established, Indigenous peoples have traditionally relied on storytelling as an integral part of teaching.[2] Therefore, it is not surprising I draw from reflexive ethnography and narrative inquiry in both my teaching and research.[3] My research includes journals, reflections, letters, and *teacher-to-teacher conversations*,[4] for teacher knowledge is a tacit and narrative construct drawing from personal practical knowledge, gained from formal and informal educational experience.[5] Thus, I have recovered and reconstructed personal practical knowledge through an exploration of images, personal philosophies, metaphors, and other artifacts.

Interest in narrative pedagogies has grown significantly in recent years across many disciplines, including teacher education.[6] Most notably, John

---

1. Howe, "Narrative of Teacher Education."

2. Archibald, *Indigenous Storywork*; Masemann, "Ways of Knowing."

3. Howe, "Comparative Ethnographic Narrative"; Howe and Arimoto, "Narrative Teacher Education."

4. Howe, "Japan's Teacher Acculturation: Critical Analysis"; Yonemura, "Teacher Conversations."

5. Clandinin and Connelly, *Narrative Inquiry*.

6. Adler, "Teacher Epistemology"; Beattie, "New Prospects"; Ciuffetelli Parker,

Dewey, Schwab, Freema Elbaz-Luwisch and the groundbreaking work of D. Jean Clandinin and F. Michael Connelly have advanced the acceptance of narrative approaches.[7] An excellent summary of the origins of narrative inquiry and the significance to teacher education can be found in Cheryl Craig's recent contribution to the field.[8] However, few studies have been conducted outside of Western contexts.[9] Moreover, there remains a paucity of narrative research published by Japanese scholars, despite a pervasive culture of *teacher-to-teacher conversations*, storytelling, reflection, and action-research by teachers in Japan.[10] Thus, the research reported here fills an important gap in the literature.

This chapter evolved from twenty-five years of personal and professional cross-cultural experiences in Canada and Japan. In my doctoral research, I used a *comparative ethnographic narrative* to capture the essence of Japan's teacher acculturation, while chronicling my educational journey as a learner, teacher, and researcher.[11] The narrative text is filled with intriguing and heart-warming teachers' stories based on lived experiences—connected through the common thread of learning to teach. The rich, descriptive narratives show that much of what teachers do is learned implicitly through years of schooling and is culturally embedded. Significant teacher issues that until now have remained hidden have been unearthed in these compelling stories spanning five decades. However, there is only room for a small portion of teacher stories here. Thus, I begin with a brief overview of teacher acculturation in Japan, followed by three exemplary stories, and finally a brief summary of what teachers and teacher educators can learn from it all.

Japan's Teacher Acculturation

Beginning teachers in Canada and the United States are largely required to work in isolation, to learn their practice through trial and error—left to *sink or swim*.[12] There is little provision for mentorship and insufficient time to re-

---

"Related Literacy Narratives"; Xu and Connelly, "Narrative Inquiry."

7. Clandinin and Connelly, *Narrative Inquiry*; Craig, "Joseph Schwab"; Dewey, *Experience and Education*; Elbaz-Luwisch, *Teacher Thinking*.

8. Craig, "Narrative Inquiry."

9. Howe and Xu, "Transcultural Teacher Development."

10. Howe, "Japan's Teacher Acculturation: A Comparative Ethongraphic"; Yonemura, "Teacher Conversations."

11. Howe, "Japan's Teacher Acculturation: A Comparative Ethongraphic Narrative of Teacher Induction."

12. Howe, "Exemplary Teacher Induction"; Howe, "Teacher Induction."

flect on teaching practices. In contrast, Japan's teacher induction programs facilitate collegiality and collaboration between novice and experienced teachers. Moreover, teachers are both life-long learners and researchers and thus contribute greatly to the profession. Effective induction practices in Japan have evolved gradually, becoming a tacit part of the teaching culture. Japan's teacher acculturation is characterized by significant teacher relationships, built on mutual understanding and trust; an apprenticeship model of teacher development; leadership and guidance; and it is further cultivated through collaboration and professional development. Relationships with colleagues, students, and parents are critical to the socialization of Japan's teachers.

While Japanese teacher induction programs are outstanding in many ways, there remain issues that need attention. A pervasive top-down hierarchy in Japanese schooling makes it difficult for new teaching strategies to be disseminated from universities through new teachers to veterans. One-way pedagogical exchanges can lead to stagnation and a continuation of the status quo. Furthermore, the induction program, introduced in 1989, adds a great deal more to the burden of first-year teachers. New teachers need reduced responsibilities and duties to fully absorb their training in the first year of teaching. The induction of Japanese first-year teachers is simply too much, too late. This is especially germane since most new teachers in Japan now spend considerable time initially as part-time assistant teachers before receiving the professional development in-service training in their first year as a regular employee. Some of the essential induction lessons, such as classroom management and student guidance, should be learned prior to first-year teaching. Japanese teacher education programs must provide a better link between theory and practice, universities and schools, preservice and in-service. Extended practica and enhanced preservice education programs would help to narrow this gap and to better prepare teacher candidates. University teacher preparation programs must be improved so that potential teachers can acquire a vision of their mission as a professional teacher. However, none of these suggestions will be possible unless classroom teachers support these initiatives and provide the same level of assistance to student teachers that is afforded to first-year teachers. Finally, one of my strongest criticisms of Japanese teacher induction practices has to do with the selection of school-based mentors. Mentors should be more carefully selected, based on appropriate criteria including their leadership potential and teaching quality, rather than seniority. Moreover, mentors need specific leadership and mentorship training in their enhanced role. Retired teachers seem to be better able to fulfill the demands of a mentor; however, they are not widely used at all levels of schooling in this capacity and may be out of touch with current practices.

Despite these weaknesses, Japanese teacher induction is exemplary. The *sink or swim* metaphor, so prevalent in North American teaching culture, has no equivalent in Japanese teacher education. First-year teachers are provided with extensive support and assistance. Toward the end of their first year, Japanese teachers are well on their way to becoming professionals. There is much to be gained from studying how one becomes a teacher in Japan. Cultural context is important when considering how induction programs from abroad could be borrowed and adapted for use at home. The role of Japan's teachers is broader and more diverse as teaching is much more than just time spent in the classroom. Japanese teachers act as facilitators, councilors, coaches, and much more. Nevertheless, while some foreign practices might not be appropriate, they challenge us to think *outside the box*, about what we tend to ignore or leave unexamined. The focus should be on what works well and why and how to incorporate innovative practices. Just as teachers must get out of their classrooms, educators shouldn't hesitate to venture beyond their borders to share lessons with colleagues.

This book chapter provides a behind-the-scenes glimpse of the lived experiences of teachers and offers a mirror for us to reflect on current teacher induction practices. The three thought-provoking stories that follow illustrate a number of key features of Japanese teacher acculturation, including strength of relationships, collegiality, collaboration, mentoring, and emphasis on the peer group. In addition, I demonstrate how narrative pedagogies relate to three significant Japanese cultural practices: *kankei* (inter-relationships), *kizuna* (bonds), and *kizuki* (with-it-ness).[13] Moreover, these stories show how Japan successfully prepares individuals to gradually become acculturated into the teaching profession. Effective teacher induction is critical, for any effort to reform education ultimately depends on the effectiveness of teachers. So, let us now turn our attention to the three narratives, from a novice teacher to a veteran and in between.

Three Teacher Narratives of Experience, Education, and Story

Narrative of Miss Sakaguchi, Novice Teacher

At the time of this research, back in 2002–2003, Miss Sakaguchi was in her second year of teaching English and her first year teaching band at Sakura High School in Tochigi. She is a highly competent and dedicated professional who spends long hours at school devoting most of her energy and

13. Howe and Arimoto, "Narrative Teacher Education."

free time to her work. Sakaguchi is an outstanding example of young teachers in Japan. Her story, while unique, captures the atmosphere of Japan's teacher acculturation in a rural setting.

Sakaguchi was born in Yokohama in October 1978 but is a long-time resident of Tochigi prefecture. She moved to Tochigi at age seven where she grew up in a mid-sized city of about 83,000 people, living just fifteen meters away from the local elementary school. At the age of three, her mother bought an English picture book, which she cherished. From an early age, Sakaguchi showed an interest in English. At five, she began to play the piano. It was obvious that Sakaguchi had a gift in the area of music, as she excelled in her piano lessons. Later, she learned that she had perfect pitch and could easily imitate sounds and melodies she heard. This talent carried over to her ability to speak and comprehend English.

In elementary school, Sakaguchi had lots of friends but most of them were boys. This is unusual in Japan where gender segregation is ubiquitous from early on. For a short time, the other girls bullied her. This was likely out of jealousy, as she was one of the top students. While this experience was unpleasant, it made her a stronger person and gave her more self-confidence, as she was able to transcend the immature behavior of her peers. Moreover, this gave her empathy for others, which in later years would prove invaluable in her teaching. While Sakaguchi doesn't recall any specific teachers or moments of inspiration, she indicated that as a young girl she wanted to be an elementary school teacher. In grade four she joined the school band and learned to play the flute.

In junior high school, Sakaguchi continued to excel and was again one of the top students. She was good at all her subjects but enjoyed English and band most. She continued to play the flute, eventually becoming a club leader of the junior and senior high school orchestra. This is quite an honor and distinction, as club leaders are nominated by student members and elected by popular consensus. Sakaguchi liked listening to English pop music and this motivated her to learn more English informally on her own. A critical moment for her at this age was her participation in the annual speech contest. In two years of both junior and senior high school she was chosen as the sole representative of her school in Tochigi's speech contest. The intense preparation for these competitions, with the support and guidance of her English teacher and the assistant English teacher (AET or ALT), helped to further hone her English communication and natural pronunciation. In high school she continued to develop her English to a much higher level. She credits her hard work and natural ability combined with the support from teachers for her success. These characteristics carry over to her teaching philosophy.

Sakaguchi believes that an effective teacher must have a good understanding of students while providing feedback and positive reinforcement to facilitate learning. She sees teaching as a continuous learning process but she indicated that it is a talent or gift that some will have and others will not. This notion of teaching being a natural ability is contrary to the typical Japanese belief that teaching is a craft that has to be learned through practice. However, she indicated that if someone has the essential qualities, effective teaching could be further developed through study and practice. Sakaguchi believes that her interest and ability in music, in particular her good ear and time spent listening to English pop music as a teenager, helped her to develop her English skills. The intense preparation and daily practice for the speech contest was seminal to her future career as an English teacher. While she admits to wanting to be a junior high school teacher, at this point in time she hadn't thought about which subjects she would teach. However, she noted that teaching "seemed like an easy job" and something she thought she was familiar with as a student.

Another important life event for Sakaguchi was her experience as a participant in an exchange program with the United States. In both junior high and high school she spent two weeks abroad. Her home-stay experiences in Pennsylvania and Indiana, as well as her travel around the United States, put her English to the test. She quickly learned that her English skills would have to be improved considerably in order for her to communicate effectively with native speakers. Sakaguchi still keeps in touch with the host family from her visit as a high school student at the age of seventeen. As a result of these experiences abroad, she decided that she would like to live in a foreign country.

After graduation from a prestigious girl's public high school in Tochigi, Sakaguchi attended Sophia University in Tokyo. This is an elite private institution specializing in English and international affairs with more than half the courses taught in English. The faculty comes from all over the world. This prompted her to travel to San Francisco where she studied for nine months earning credits toward her Bachelor of Art from Sophia University. However, she was more interested in sociology, psychology, and general education rather than teaching English grammar. Her experience as a university student in the United States provided her with an opportunity to pursue greater diversity in courses. This liberal arts education appealed to her since it allowed greater flexibility in course selection than was available in her Japanese university. By age twenty she had decided to become a teacher as she had thoroughly enjoyed her experience teaching at a *juku* (cram school) in Tokyo and tutoring Japanese to foreign students while in San Francisco.

Sakaguchi's brief two-week practicum experience in June of her fourth year was perhaps the most significant formal education event along her teaching journey. Her sponsor teacher proved to be highly enthusiastic and full of creativity. While Sakaguchi had to work extremely hard during these two weeks, she credits her sponsor teacher for providing her with inspiration to use a variety of teaching strategies. He was most influential in her teacher induction—significantly more so than her designated mentor teacher in first year or any other teacher in her experience as a beginning teacher.

Sakaguchi cares a great deal about her teaching—placing her job as English and band teacher at Sakura High above all else. This became evident in conversations with colleagues but the most significant indicator was her recent choice of career over marriage. Sakaguchi was to be married in December of her second year of teaching but broke off the engagement one month prior in order to pursue her teaching. Her fiancé, also a Tochigi teacher, ten years her senior, had insisted she become a traditional wife (bear children, give up her position at Sakura, move to a school closer to his home in order to take care of the family and household) but she couldn't bear the thought of leaving her teaching job at Sakura. In her first year of teaching this seemed a reasonable prospect but in her second year she began to really appreciate her role and got a great deal of personal satisfaction out of her teaching. In particular, Sakaguchi is proud that she has been credited for bringing the school band back into the spotlight, having earned the first gold medal in recent years in the annual Tochigi competition. Sakura has a long-standing tradition of excellence in music that had waned in recent years due to the lack of interest her predecessor had in instructing the band. If she were to leave Sakura, she wonders what would happen to the band program. Finally, Sakaguchi also enjoys helping students with the speech contest and those who wish to go on exchanges abroad. In her job she has the chance to help students succeed in the same way her teachers helped her. Perhaps this is the most powerful lesson of all.

Insights from a Veteran Teacher, Kojima-sensei

The interview with Kojima-sensei (sponsor of the English club at Sakura High School in the 1980s) provided another unique perspective. We spoke in English and Japanese for over two hours at his place one night. He has a son (33) who is a Tokyo University graduate and researcher at Columbia University for Meiji Pharmaceuticals, and a daughter (30) who is an art teacher in Ibaraki. His wife sat at the next table, served us tea, and spoke in

Japanese but remained quiet for most of the *teacher-to-teacher conversation*, which was conducted largely in English. They live in a comfortable home in a rural part of Sakura. They exude a youthful appearance that betrays their years.

Kojima-sensei spoke at length about his teaching philosophy. He felt that learning alongside the students was critical to developing his teaching. However, Kojima-sensei did mention one influential *sempai* (senior) in his first year of teaching, but this was only after I asked him about *zatsudan* (informal teacher-to-teacher conversations) and if he had a mentor. I recorded our conversation in an educational chronicle. It was helpful to get the ball rolling and in providing a framework for the conversation that followed but our conversation tended to focus on themes and incidents rather than a chronology of events.

We were provided with one or two contacts worth pursuing. He arranged to personally introduce me to the former head of the Tochigi Education Center who is a good friend of his. I was impressed at how well both he and his wife knew other teachers and former students. The names and contact information, like where people are working now and so on, seemed readily available. He even phoned his friend right then and there to introduce me. We spoke to Mr. Fuji and made an appointment to see him.

Kojima-sensei has lived in Tochigi-ken all his life. He began teaching high school English almost by chance. His choices were limited to the two courses of study offered at Utsunomiya University: education or agriculture. While completing his application form his older brother, a math major, persuaded him to choose English rather than math, which was his first choice as he was interested in architecture. Ultimately, he has no regrets and feels this was the best choice for him. While trained to teach elementary and junior high school, he passed the exams to teach secondary school as well. The first opportunity came at Sakura High School where he spent twenty years as an English teacher.

The most interesting story told by Kojima-sensei was about his first- and second-year experience at Sakura High School in 1962. He admitted to being a "poor teacher" at first but became motivated at an early stage in his career to improve. He had an outstanding and dedicated student, whose enthusiasm acted as a catalyst for him to work extremely hard, staying up late studying English in order to be better prepared for their weekly tutorials and frequent discussions. "He had difficult questions but he trusted me." The trust placed in Kojima's hands by this young man was immense and the bond they formed was considerable. Later, his star pupil returned to work with Kojima as a student teacher (but gave up teaching to go abroad and to work for a company). Kojima-sensei is looking forward with much anticipation to the upcoming class reunion in a couple of weeks when they have the opportunity to meet again.

Kojima-sensei also mentioned his experience coaching the judo team. Again, he focused on what the students taught him rather than what he did. These became mutually beneficial relationships. The students' hard work motivated him in turn to be the best teacher he could be. This experience helped him to see students' growth leading to well-tempered and good character. His motto became, "You never fail to succeed if you practice very hard" (quote from a judo master). Other parts of his teaching philosophy are exemplified by these quotes: "Good teachers are trustworthy and are respected as leaders. . . . Studying with students is a great enjoyment to me. . . . Teachers learn from students." Finally, he mentioned his English department head and *sempai* (who at the time was twice his age of twenty-two) who taught him teaching pedagogy and passed down practical lessons.

A Tribute to Hiro-sensei, a Mid-Career Teacher

Imagine living through a 9.0 magnitude earthquake, a ten-meter tsunami, threat of nuclear radiation, and hundreds of terrifying aftershocks. Then, picture, if you will, someone so dedicated to work that rather than fleeing to the nearest safe haven or calling in sick this individual heads to school because classes are in session and education of young children is the highest priority. This is a true story of what transpired at my son's school in Saitama following the Sendai Earthquake of Friday, March 11, 2011. It is a tribute to Hiro-sensei and other teachers here.

On Monday morning, Hiro-sensei awoke at 4 a.m. and caught the first train from his home in Adachi-ku, Tokyo, heading northwest toward Saitama. However, the Japan Rail (JR) train only went as far as Akabane, Tokyo, as train service was severely disrupted after the great earthquake and ongoing tremors. While waiting patiently in a long line of distraught commuters to ask the conductor what to do next, the man in front of Hiro-sensei became furious when he learned there were no further trains beyond Akabane. However, Hiro-sensei kept calm. He waited in another long line and boarded a bus bound for Kawaguchi, on the other side of the river. Hours later, he arrived at Kawaguchi, Saitama. Then he set out on the long journey that lay ahead on foot. Hiro-sensei walked an arduous eighteen kilometers from Kawaguchi to our elementary school in Omiya. It took over three hours! Hiro-sensei finally arrived at school around 11:40 a.m. and went straight to the gym to join his colleagues who had been supervising his students since 8:30. All grade six students were busy preparing for next week's graduation ceremony.

As a result of the threat of nuclear radiation and scientists' ominous predictions of a greater than 70 percent chance of a 7.0 magnitude earthquake, school officials dismissed children early Monday and declared Tuesday a school holiday. Wednesday through Friday were half-days at school as a result of scheduled rotating three-hour blackouts. Hiro-sensei decided to stay overnight at the school rather than attempt to return home. He joined the principal, vice-principal, and other teachers in the gym for a round-the-clock vigil. In the event of emergency evacuations, it is the responsibility of administrators to remain at school, as a safety mechanism to help the community. Teachers often share this burden and other significant administrative duties. Another example of the incredible dedication and sense of duty teachers exemplify can be found in the story of a teacher I know who lives just twenty-five kilometers from the Fukushima nuclear plant. While government officials ordered the evacuation of all residents within a twenty-kilometer radius and told others within a thirty-kilometer radius to remain indoors, this woman and other teachers in the vicinity continued to teach and carry on other extended duties in spite of the personal health risk to themselves and their families.

During the week following the disaster in Japan, many people chose to stay indoors or to flee the Kanto area altogether. Those that remained lined up to fill their cars with gas and stock up on essentials. The panic-ridden public feared the worst in the wake of earthquakes, tsunamis, and threat of nuclear fallout—a tragedy described by the prime minister as "the biggest challenge facing Japan since World War II." Foreigners were told to leave the country. Worried housewives donned masks and covered themselves from head to foot as they ventured outside to brave the frenzied crowds to buy batteries, emergency gear, food, and other essentials. Meanwhile, people in the Tohoku region were coping with the aftermath of a major catastrophe. Lack of food, water, adequate shelter, and communication with loved ones continued to test the strength and determination of survivors in Sendai, Fukushima, and other areas hardest hit.

Tokyoites had different challenges to face, however—train service continued to be troublesome throughout the week with severe disruptions, convenience stores were closed at odd hours, and shelves were stripped bare. People were stressed. The situation appeared increasingly grim as NHK news reports and video clips circulated, highlighting the massive devastation and aftermath of the disaster unfolding.

Despite all this, my son's teacher continued to do his duties to his utmost. It is unbelievable that this teacher would travel such a great distance on foot to reach the school and then choose to stay there rather than retreat to the comfort of home. Nevertheless, I'm convinced that many teachers would have done exactly the same thing because they care deeply for their students. It is time the public recognized the enduring efforts of teachers, their professionalism and dedication. In these difficult times, please do not forget to acknowledge the amazing work done by teachers.

Conclusion:
What We Can Learn from These Teacher Stories

Teachers must care deeply for children. It is all about nurturing caring, trusting relationships and creating lasting bonds through *kizuna, kankei* and *kizuki*. In the words of a first year teacher in my doctoral research, it means:

> [T]o trust each other [teachers, students, and others] and to do things for each other and the class as a whole. . . . Children are dear to us. They may be noisy at times and some are difficult, but they are cute. If other teachers compliment or praise my students it make me happy.[14]

My research into Japan's teacher acculturation has enabled me to identify a number of key features that I believe are essential elements to effective teaching. In particular, the following attributes are noteworthy: strength of relationships, collegiality, collaboration, mentoring, and emphasis on the peer group. In addition, other research has identified lesson study[15] and communities of learning[16] as seminal to the success of Japanese education. Narrative pedagogies relate to many Japanese cultural practices including *kankei* (inter-relationships), *kizuna* (bonds), and *kizuki* (with-it-ness).[17] These are important, integral, and tacit elements of Japanese teachers' practices because they embody mind and heart. Japanese society values *kankei* and access to networks of trusted people.[18] The significant bonds or *kizuna* formed between teachers and students and amongst peers in Japan is noteworthy. I experienced this phenomenon of *kizuna* with my teacher education students during my decade in Japanese higher education. Finally, the concept of *kizuki* is something that is difficult to define but most teachers can identify this important tacit classroom skill in observations of other

14. Conversation with Sachie and four other novice teachers, January 28, 2003.
15. Lewis, *Lesson Study*.
16. Howe, "Nurturing a Culture of Kizuki."
17. Sakamoto, "Professional Development."
18. Howe and Arimoto, "Narrative Teacher Education."

teachers. This is something it takes years to obtain but through the practice of lesson study it is readily observed, learned, practiced, and mastered.

Extended time in a foreign culture has given me a profound understanding of what it means to be treated as an Other. This in turn has fostered transcultural teaching and empathy for others. This is very important, given Canada's immigration policies attracting more and more international students, forming increasingly larger proportions of our Canadian classrooms. Furthermore, my experience outside my own culture has helped me to see the significance of *kankei*, *kizuna*, and *kizuki*, as these Japanese teacher qualities all involve placing other people's needs before one's own. These are essential skills for global citizens of the twenty-first century. I believe these practices, combined with narrative pedagogies, show great promise in providing much needed empathy for others within our ever-more interconnected world.

Reflection Questions

1. In reflecting on your own education and experience, are there any noteworthy stories that come to mind?
2. What personal practical knowledge do you hold as a teacher or teacher educator?
3. How might you use transcultural experiences in your own teaching?
4. Have you ever used an electronic journal or diary? Why or why not?
5. How could you use letter writing in your curriculum, teaching, and learning?

Bibliography

Adler, Susan Matoba. "Teacher Epistemology and Collective Narratives: Interrogating Teaching and Diversity." *Teaching and Teacher Education* 27 (2011) 609–18.

Archibald, Jo-ann. *Indigenous Storywork: Educating the Heart, Mind, Body, and Spirit*. Vancouver: University of British Columbia Press, 2008.

Beattie, Mary. "New Prospects for Teacher Education: Narrative Ways of Knowing Teaching and Teacher Learning." *Educational Research* 37 (1995) 53–78.

Ciuffetelli Parker, Darlene. "Related Literacy Narratives: Letters as a Narrative Inquiry Method in Teacher Education." In *Narrative Inquiries into Curriculum Making in Teacher Education*, edited by Julian Kitchen, Darlene Ciuffetelli Parker, and Debbie Pushor, 131–49. Advances in Research on Teaching 13. New York: Emerald Group, 2011.

Clandinin, D. Jean, and F. Michael Connelly. *Narrative Inquiry: Experience and Story in Qualitative Research*. San Francisco: Jossey-Bass, 2000.

———. *Teachers as Curriculum Planners: Narratives of Experience*. New York: Teachers College, Columbia University, 1988.

Craig, Cheryl J. "Joseph Schwab, Self-Study of Teaching and Teacher Education Practices Proponent: A Personal Perspective." *Teaching and Teacher Education* 24 (2008) 1993–2001.

———. "Narrative Inquiry in Teaching and Teacher Education." In *Narrative Inquiries into Curriculum Making in Teacher Education*, edited by Julian Kitchen, Darlene Ciuffetelli Parker, and Debbie Pushor, 19–42. Advances in Research on Teaching 13. New York: Emerald Group, 2011.

Dewey, John. *Experience and Education*. New York: Collier, 1938.

Elbaz-Luwisch, Freema. *Teacher Thinking: A Study of Practical Knowledge*. New York: Croom Helm, 1983.

———. "Writing and Professional Learning: The Uses of Autobiography in Graduate Studies in Education." *Teachers and Teaching: Theory and Practice* 16 (2010) 307–27.

Howe, Edward R. "A Comparative Ethnographic Narrative Approach to Studying Teacher Acculturation." In *Papers in Memory of David N. Wilson: Clamouring for a Better World*, edited by Vandra L. Masemman et al., 121–36. Rotterdam: Sense, 2010.

———. "Exemplary Teacher Induction: An International Review." *Educational Philosophy and Theory* 38 (2006) 287–97.

———. "Japan's Teacher Acculturation: A Comparative Ethongraphic Narrative of Teacher Induction." PhD diss., University of Toronto, 2005.

———. "Japan's Teacher Acculturation: Critical Analysis Through Comparative Ethnographic Narrative." *Journal of Education for Teaching* 31 (2005) 121–31.

———. "A Narrative of Teacher Education in Canada: Multiculturalism, Global Citizenship Education, and Bridging the Theory/Practice Divide." *Journal of Education for Teaching: International Research and Pedagogy* 40 (2014) 588–99.

———. "Nurturing a Culture of Kizuki: A Narrative Inquiry of Communities of Learning in Rural Japan." Paper presented at the Canadian Association of Teacher Educators, Annual Meeting for the Canadian Society for the Study of Education, University of Victoria, 2013.

———. "Teacher Induction Across the Pacific: A Comparative Study of Canada and Japan." *Journal of Education for Teaching: International Research and Pedagogy* 34 (2008) 333–46.

Howe, Edward R., and Masahiro Arimoto. "Narrative Teacher Education Pedagogies from Across the Pacific." In *International Teacher Education: Promising Pedagogies*, edited by Cheryl Craig and Lily Orland-Barak, 212–32. Advances in Research on Teaching 22(A). New York: Emerald Group, 2014.

Howe, Edward R., and Shijing Xu. "Transcultural Teacher Development Within the Dialectic of the Global and Local: Bridging Gaps Between East and West." *Teaching and Teacher Education* 36 (2013) 33–43.

Lewis, Catherine. *Lesson Study: A Handbook of Teacher-Led Instructional Improvement*. Philadelphia: Research for Better Schools, 2002.

Masemann, Vandra Lea. "Ways of Knowing: Implications for Comparative Education." *Comparative Education Review* 34 (1990) 465–73.

Sakamoto, Nami. "Professional Development Through *Kizuki*—Cognitive, Emotional and Collegial Awareness." *Teacher Development* 15 (2011) 187–203.

Xu, Shijing J., and F. Michael Connelly. "Narrative Inquiry for Teacher Education and Development: Focus on English as a Foreign Language in China." *Teaching and Teacher Education* 25 (2009) 219–27.

Yonemura, Margaret. "Teacher Conversations: A Potential Source for Their Own Professional Growth." *Curriculum Inquiry* 12 (1982) 239–56.

17

Considering the Nature of Science and Religion in Science Education

Adam Forsyth

Introduction

TEACHING STUDENTS ABOUT THE nature of science (NOS) is a central aim of contemporary science education; consequently, an emphasis on student understanding about the NOS is predominant in many current science education standards and results from the NOS being regarded as a key component of scientific literacy.[1] Given the emphasis on the NOS in national science education standards worldwide a growing body of research by science educators is focused on various aspects of the teaching and learning of the NOS; for example, these include NOS understanding by teachers[2] and students,[3] and the impacts of different instructional approaches on student understanding of the NOS.[4] The importance of emphasizing the explicit teaching of the NOS has gained additional traction with widespread concerns being raised by governments, industry groups, and scientists at the number of students who are not choosing to study science beyond the compulsory level (typically around the age of 15–16).[5] The teaching of the NOS is thus considered a critical component of many national science curricula, as it is deemed essential that students are given meaningful exposure to key NOS concepts during their compulsory years of science education

---

1. Bell, Matkins, and Gansneder, "Impacts," 414–36.
2. Abd-El-Khalick and BouJaoude, "An Exploratory," 89–133; Lunn, "What We Think," 649–72; Van Driel and Verloop, "Experienced," 1255–72.
3. Solomon, Duveen, and Scott, "Pupils' Images," 361–73.
4. Deng et al., "Students," 961–99.
5. Hanley, Bennett, and Ratcliffe, "The Inter–relationship," 1210–29.

so that they can enter their post-school lives equipped with some knowledge and appreciation of how science works. This decline has also focused research attention on various aspects of the teaching and learning of science up to this age, and one important area of investigation is an attempt to understand the influence that students' religious beliefs, and their view of the relationship between religion and science, has on their learning of science. Unfortunately, in recent times especially, the notion that religion and science are in conflict has received a lot of attention in the mass media; much of this has stemmed from the attention paid to people like Richard Dawkins who have vigorously proclaimed the triumph of rational science over religious "delusion"—or, as Cobern notes, "rational knowledge *versus* irrational belief."[6] Unfortunately, such a view of conflict has dominated the commentary around this issue and has drowned out the views of many religious scientists and scientific theologians who promote a range of positions on the interactions between science and religion.

The interrogation of these views is rarely attempted in science classrooms—where the push to deliver content-laden curricula limits opportunities for the exploration of various aspects of the nature of science (of which this is just one facet), and so many students studying compulsory science are left with questions unanswered and prejudices left unchallenged, the result of which is a skewed, one-dimensional view of the relationship between science and religion. It is not hard to imagine that students who come to the science classroom with a view of conflict between science and religion, and who don't have these understandings and beliefs challenged or have the opportunity to discuss alternative views, could find the learning of some aspects of science uncomfortable and may, as a result of this experience, choose to avoid the study of science beyond the compulsory level.[7]

The aim of this chapter is to provide an overview from the literature of the challenges facing science education with respect to the relationship/s between science and religion and the opportunities (and resources) available for teachers who wish to overcome these challenges and provide their students with a range of possible views and, in doing so, arrive at their own decision about the relationship between science and religion and, through this, improve their understanding of the nature of science.

---

6. Cobern, "Nature of Science," 219–46.

7. Esbenshade, "Student," 334–38; Koul, "Religious," 251–67; Hanley, Bennett, and Ratcliffe, "The Inter-relationship," 1210–29.

Challenges Facing Science Educators Concerning the Relationships Between Science and Religion

It is well established that the prevailing knowledge and ideas a learner brings to the classroom need to be taken into account by the teacher if the most effective exchange of teaching and learning is to occur.[8] The outcomes from the interactions students' underlying knowledge can have with teaching were explored by Gilbert, Osborne, and Fensham who sought to identify the consequences from interactions between children's and curriculum science; not surprisingly, a range of possible outcomes were identified.

i. *Undisturbed* outcome—where the preexisting knowledge is unchanged by science teaching;

ii. *Unified scientific* outcome—where the intended and actual learning outcomes were closely matched;

iii. *Two perspectives* outcome—where the intended learning outcomes run "alongside" the preexisting knowledge;

iv. *Reinforced* outcome—where the prevailing knowledge is reinforced by learning of presented material that has been misinterpreted by the student;

v. *Mixed* outcome – where only some of the presented material is learned.[9]

From such an array of outcomes one would expect a similar spectrum from any given science class; so while some students will successfully learn the intended scientific material despite their (possibly erroneous) prior ideas and knowledge, others will take away varying degrees of the intended learning in a diminishing standard ranging from a version of the intended learning, which doesn't displace the prior ideas but runs alongside them, to a view of knowledge which, through confusion and/or misunderstanding, reinforces the previously held erroneous view.[10] Such barriers to effective learning can occur for any topic in any subject area, but science is most at risk of such outcomes as an attempt to understand and explain the way the world works cuts right to the very heart of the subject and also cuts to the very heart of what it is to be a human who, from birth, strives to understand and interpret the world.

A growing area of research in science education is focused on trying to understand the views on the relationship between science and religion that students hold and how these views influence certain aspects and processes

---

8. Taber, *Progressing Science Education*, 134–36.
9. Gilbert, Osborne, and Fensham, "Children's Science," 628–31.
10. Taber, *Progressing Science Education*, 135–36.

in the learning of science content and also learning about the nature of science.[11] As Stolberg reminds us, an individual will commonly seek to employ both science and religion when trying to interpret and understand the world around them and indeed the universe.[12] The aspect of "origins" (namely, the origins of the universe, the origin of different living species) in particular has provided a focus of much of the concern in science education; however, less obvious "accounts of science make claims such as that there is no supernatural phenomena (such as a spiritual realm beyond the physical world), and that the laws of science are not just observed regularities but irrevocable accounts of what is possible (i.e., excluding any kind of miracle that might be understood as an interruption or overrule of the laws of nature)."[13] The question of "origins," however, has drawn the most attention, not just in science education but in a society fuelled by a mass media that thrives on conflicts and delights in the sparring of extreme opposites; such as the debates in 2012 and 2013 between Richard Dawkins (who held the position of the University of Oxford's professor for public understanding of science from 1995 until 2008) and the former Archbishop of Canterbury Rowan Williams; consequently, interest in debates about the origin of the universe and the evolution of life on earth has, for many people (and thus students), positioned science and religion in conflict.

Some examples of the effect that attitudes and perceptions about "origins" can have on students and their learning of science are McKeachie, Lin, and Strayer who demonstrated that students who rejected evolution also demonstrated lower interest and intrinsic motivation toward learning science along with elevated anxiety when learning about evolution.[14] In other studies, students who rejected evolution either completely disengaged with the learning or only engaged with the learning in an attempt to falsify the theory.[15] For science teachers to best meet the needs of their students, an appreciation of the spectrum of possible views held of the relationship between religion and science is necessary. A summary considering the major categories (taxonomies) of this relationship from the literature is presented here as a guide—it is a brief overview and the bibliography includes some recommended readings that will provide much greater breadth and depth.

---

11. Yasri and Mancy, "Understanding Student," 24–45.
12. Stolberg, "The Religio-Scientific," 909–30.
13. Taber et al., "Secondary Students," 1001.
14. McKeachie, Lin, and Strayer, "Creationist vs. Evolutionary," 189–92.
15. Meadows, Doster, and Jackson, "Managing the Conflict," 102–7; Yasri and Mancy, "Understanding Student," 24–45.

An extensive range of the views of the relationship between religion and science exists in the philosophical and educational literature, typically presented in the form of categories, and are referred to both here and in the literature as taxonomies. As part of their effort to develop a tool for eliciting individual students' views on the relationship between science and religion, Yasri, Arthur, Smith, and Mancy completed an extensive review of this literature with the aim of organizing the many different taxonomies according to their similarities and differences;[16] they identified five taxonomies from the philosophical literature (which are summarized in Table 1): Polkinghorne,[17] a theoretical physicist who became an Anglican minister; Barbour,[18] a professor of religion; Haught,[19] a Roman Catholic theologian; Nord,[20] a philosopher; and Alexander,[21] a biologist. They also identified four taxonomies from the educational literature: Shipman, Dagher, and Letts;[22] Hokayem and BouJaoude;[23] Taber et al.;[24] and Yasri and Mancy.[25] They sought to describe the relationship of each in terms of their epistemology (characteristics of inquiry and knowledge) and metaphysics (characteristics of reality). This summary was then organized by Yasri et al. to develop a framework showing the relationship of different views—an example from this framework, the view provided by Haught, will serve to provide an example of the kind of grouping considered by the authors. Haught's view provides four positions of the view of the relationship between science and religion: *conflict*, *contrast*, *contact*, and *confirmation*. *Conflict* positions the two as fundamentally incompatible, with the significant differences for this position being based on method, the falsifiability of scientific theories compared to the non-falsifiability of religious theories, and epistemology. The position of *contrast*, considered by Haught to be the "safest" position, acknowledges the differences between the two realms and that conflict between them is impossible as they "have no business meddling in each other's affairs in the first place."[26] *Contact* acknowledges that although the two are separate they can effect one another; for example, a more

16. Yasri et al., "Relating Science," 2679–707.
17. Polkinghorne, *One World*.
18. Barbour, *Religion in an Age of Science*.
19. Haught, *Science and Religion*.
20. Nord, "Science, Religion," 28–33.
21. Alexander, "Models for Relating," 1–4.
22. Shipman et al., "Changes," 526–47.
23. Hokayem and BouJaoude, "College Students," 395–419.
24. Taber et al., "Secondary Students," 1000–25.
25. Yasri and Mancy, "Understanding Student," 24–45.
26. Haught, *Science and Religion*, 10–22.

intense appreciation of the universe can be gained through religious faith. The position of *confirmation* holds that science is supported by religion, as Koul puts it, a view "of a coherent, rational, and ordered universe, filled with promise."[27] This view is Haught's favored position—a position where religion supports and reinforces science; for Haught, religion claims "the universe is a finite, coherent, rational ordered totality, grounded in an ultimate love and promise" and "provides a general vision of things that consistently nurtures the scientific quest for knowledge."[28]

Authors	View names	Descriptions
Polkinghorne	Conflict	Science and religion make (at times) contradictory assertions about a single reality.
	Natural theology	Science and religion make the same claims about a single reality and science helps to explain the nature of God.
	Modes of thought	Science and religion deal with two different kinds of subject matter (physical and objective versus spiritual and subjective).
	One world	Science and religion consider different aspects of a single reality to create a richer understanding.
Barbour	Conflict	Two forms: either matter is the only form of reality and knowledge is gained only through the scientific method, or alternatively, religious knowledge is the only true source of knowledge.
	Independence	Science and religion differ in two ways: their approaches to arrive at knowledge and their communicational functions.
	Dialogue	Science and religion are mutually supportive in directing and underpinning the human quest for knowledge.
	Integration	Three ways of integrating science and religion to form a single explanation of the world: natural theology, theology of nature, and systematic synthesis.

---

27. Koul, "Revivalist Thinking," 104.
28. Haught, *Science and Religion*, 10–22.

Authors	View names	Descriptions
Haught	Conflict	Science and religion are fundamentally incompatible and one makes claims that are positively or normatively "wrong."
	Contrast	Science and religion focus on different kinds of questions and each is valid in its own realm.
	Contact	Science and religion interact indirectly through conversations among scientists and theologians.
	Confirmation	Religion undergirds science by providing a rationale for the scientific assumption of a coherent and ordered universe.
Nord	Science trumps religion	When science and religion are in conflict, only religion is correct.
	Religion trumps science	When science and religion are in conflict, only science is correct.
	Independence	Science and religion have their own methods and domains of application.
	Integration	Science and religion both contribute knowledge and a full understanding of reality relies on understandings from both.
Alexander	Conflict	Science and religion are fundamentally contradictory.
	NOMA	Science and religion consider two separate aspects of reality that do not overlap.
	Complementary	Science and religion consider different aspects of the same reality that must be combined to understand the richness of reality.
	Fusion	Science and religion are completely integrated into a united reality.

Table 1: Summary of views discussed in the philosophical literature, with descriptions from Yasri.[29]

The framework presented by Yasri et al. houses a range of views of the relationships between science and religion, and exploring the range of views, or picking out just one, in a classroom could give students an opportunity to gain a more balanced understanding of the positions that exist outside of the commonly held position of conflict; the complete set of views and descriptions set out by Yasri are provided in Table 2. One difficulty in attempting to expose students to different perceptions or trying to mesh the views of students on religion and science to frameworks developed by

29. Yasri, "Views of the Relationship," 67.

philosophers and theologians is the discrepancy in knowledge between the two used in establishing the relationship. Taber et al., who recognized that the range of student positions "superficially reflect the range of opinions discussed in academic scholarship," noted that the students' "positions were generally supported by limited (indeed sometimes clearly inaccurate) knowledge of what the canonical scientific and religious positions on different topics might be."[30] Taber et al. acknowledge that these difficulties might well be a manifestation of the cognitive development stage of the students in their study and, in later work, assert that thinking about the relationship between science and religion is likely to require, for many school-aged students, a considerable "learning demand": "research into intellectual development suggests that secondary age learners will likely face a large learning demand (Leach and Scott, 2002) when asked to engage with aspects of the NOS (such as the status of scientific knowledge), or socioscientifc issues (such as why people will take such diverse views on the compatibility of science and religion)."[31]

Student difficulties with the nature of scientific knowledge and aspects of the NOS have been highlighted in the literature and emphasise the limitations and naivety of student understanding and their simplistic epistemologies.[32] Such difficulties need to be embraced by teachers and strategies developed to help students to connect with these important aspects of the NOS.

View	Description
Compartment	Some aspects of science appear to conflict with religion but I do not really understand the conflicts.
Conflict (science trumps religion)	Some aspects of science appear to conflict with religion. When there are different answers to the same questions, I think only science provides true answers.
Conflict (religion trumps science)	Some aspects of science appear to conflict with religion. When there are different answers to the same questions, I think only religion provides true answers.
Contrast (Questions)	Science and religion do not conflict because their role is to answer different questions (e.g., science deals with questions about the physical universe, while religion addresses questions of ethics, value, and purpose).

---

30. Taber et al., "Secondary Students," 1018.

31. Taber et al., "English Secondary," 394.

32. Carey and Smith, "On Understanding," 235–51; Taber et al., "English Secondary," 370–403.

View	Description
Contrast (Methods)	Science and religion do not conflict because they construct knowledge in different ways (e.g., scientific knowledge is constructed through testing explanations, while religious knowledge is constructed by interpreting religious texts).
Coalescence	It must be possible to combine science and religion together because they provide the same answers to the same questions.
Complementary	Science and religion are complementary. Both are useful to understand all aspects of life.

Table 2: Summary of selected view labels in the proposed empirically oriented taxonomy, with descriptions from Yasri.[33]

With respect to the relationships between science and religion, an especially important aspect of the NOS is providing opportunities for students to discover the wide ranging positions scientists have. As mentioned earlier, a prevailing view in Western society is that science, and thus scientists, is and are opposed to religion; a view reinforced in recent times with high profile scientists, such as Richard Dawkins, receiving considerable coverage in the mass media. This view, not surprisingly, has been reported in the literature among school students who commonly perceive science and religion to be in opposition to science;[34] this view can also be reinforced by ethnic and cultural influences. An adequate exploration of the influence of the relationships between different "worldviews" and science is beyond the scope of this chapter, and what follows is but a brief outline of the difficulties that can arise when different knowledge domains, namely Indigenous knowledge and scientific knowledge, meet.

The development of science—from origins in ancient Greek thought, nurtured and enriched over time through the Islamic world, and then the later "rediscovery" of this knowledge by Europeans and the subsequent further development during the Renaissance—has resulted in a "Western tradition" of what the very nature of science is.[35] The resultant view of the world from this position is very different from how many cultures view and think about the world and could explain why some students from non-Western cultures encounter difficulties with science.[36] The influence of cul-

33. Yasri, "Views of the Relationship," 78.

34 Fulljames, Gibson, and Francis, "Creationism, Scientism," 171–90; Taber et al., "Secondary Students," 1000–25.

35. Cobern, "Nature, of Science" 219–46.

36. Taber et al., "Secondary Students," 1002.

tural values and Indigenous worldviews are significant and can conflict with the (Western) science taught in the classroom; for example, Jegede states: "the non-Western learner uses the anthropomorphic worldview to build enabling structures and to understand nature, including school science. This is quite different from the way the Western learner would builds his/her own structures through the mechanistic worldview."[37] Jegede cites the example of the worldview commonly held by traditional African societies, a view which would make it very difficult for students to attempt to try and adopt a Western scientific view of the physical world as for them physical and mental entities are not separate. Jegede suggests that students from these, and similar, traditional societies might only succeed in science if they can substitute a monistic worldview with a Cartesian dualist view.[38] Beyond the potential difficulties the philosophical foundations of Western science present, Jegede laments the nature of Western science being presented as the foremost *way of knowing*—a view that belittles Indigenous knowledge and creates significant obstacles to the "thought processes of African learners."[39] Additionally, Western science, Semali and Kincheloe argue, produces "universal histories, defines civilization, and determines reality," and in doing so sweeps aside different forms of Indigenous knowledge and renders it "inadequate and inferior."[40]

Implications for Science Educators and Resources to Meet the Challenge

The educational literature indicates that science educators will be working with many students who see science and religion in opposition, for example, many Christian students whose view of "origins" will include a strong commitment to the six-day creation of the world, and many students from non-Western backgrounds whose cultural worldview may have some significant overlaps but also some significant differences. The challenge facing science educators is considerable—the provision of lessons that instill a solid foundation of scientific ideas that allow students to build their own ideas about how science and religion interact. What follows are a range of recommended resources gleaned from the literature that science educators can use

---

37. Jegede, "Worldview," 78.
38. Jegede, "Toward a Philosophical Basis," 185–98; Koul, "Revivalist Thinking," 104.
39. Jegede, "Collateral Learning," 97.
40. Semali and Kincheloe, *What is Indigenous Knowledge*, 29.

CONSIDERING THE NATURE OF SCIENCE AND RELIGION   295

to help build their own knowledge of the relationships between science and religion, and tools to help support their students develop their own views.

Published research papers and teaching resources from the Learning about Science and Religion (LASAR) research project. The LASAR project was a collaboration between the universities of Reading and Cambridge, which sought to try and better understand how students perceive the relationships between science and religion and how this then impacts their thinking and learning in the science classroom. The project was led by Dr. Berry Billingsley at the University of Reading. Full details of key research papers, listed below, from the LASAR project,[41] which are highly recommended to science teachers, are given in the bibliography:

(i) Billingsley, Berry, et al. "Secondary School Students' Epistemic Insight into the Relationships Between Science and Religion—A Preliminary Enquiry." *Research in Science Education* 43 (2013) 1715–32;

(ii) Billingsley, Berry, et al. "Secondary School Teachers' Perspectives on Teaching About Topics that Bridge Science and Religion" *Curriculum Journal* 25 (2014) 372–95;

(iii) Taber, Keith S., et al. "English Secondary Students' Thinking About the Status of Scientific Theories: Consistent, Comprehensive, Coherent, and Extensively Evidenced Explanations of Aspects of the Natural World— or Just 'an Idea Someone Has.'" *Curriculum Journal* 26 (2015) 370–403.

Teachers wanting a starting point for developing a deeper understanding of the nature and scope of the relationships between science and religion alongside a consideration of the implications for science educators should also consult "The Relationship Between Science and Religion—a Contentious and Complex Issue Facing Science Education" by Keith Taber (a member of the LASAR project team). This paper was published in 2013 in the book *Science Education: A Global Perspective* (pp. 39–64), edited by Ben Akpan.

Science teachers face a significant challenge in attempting to ascertain the views held by their students on the relationships between science and religion, and then creating a successful and supportive connection with them to help students to improve their understanding. The 2014 article, "The

---

41. The LASAR project website may be of interest to some science teachers (https://sites.google.com/site/lasarproject/) as it provides a useful summary of research findings. But what is likely to be of more use is the website of teaching resources, which has been developed through the findings from the LASAR project (http://www.faradayschools.com/). This website is brimming with an excellent range of text and video resources for primary and secondary students and teachers.

Inter-relationship of Science and Religion: A Typology of Engagement," by Pam Hanley, Judith Bennett, and Mary Ratcliffe, is recommended to science teachers to help them gain an understanding of the influence different pedagogic approaches toward engaging with "controversial" issues concerning science and religion can have on students. The article also highlights the importance of a teacher gaining an appreciation of the heterogeneity of views held by students in their class so as to effectively support each student. Another excellent article that considers the effect of student worldviews on their learning science that I would recommend to teachers is "Revivalist Thinking and Student Conceptualizations of Science/Religion" by Ravinder Koul.

The desire to better identify the range of views held by students on science and religion has seen the development of a standardized questionnaire: the *Science-Religion Self-Identification Inventory* (SRSII) by Pratchayapong Yasri, Shagufta Arthur, Mike Smith, and Rebecca Mancy. A full overview on the development of the questionnaire and its potential use by teachers is provided in the 2013 article, "Relating Science and Religion: An Ontology of Taxonomies and Development of a Research Tool for Identifying Individual Views." Additionally, the PhD dissertation by Yasri, "Views of the Relationship Between Science and Religion and Their Implications for Student Learning of Evolutionary Biology," is well worth reading; it provides a full and thorough outline of how the SRSII instrument was developed and contains an excellent review of the relevant literature.

Considering the relationships between science and religion in the science classroom provides an opportunity to examine the nature of science through the lens of the nature and meaning of science knowledge, and "this cannot be done . . . without acknowledging students' *other* beliefs and *other* beliefs held by scientists and science teachers. Rather than fearing such a situation as an unpalatable intrusion on the science classroom, it should be welcomed as an opportunity to discuss how reason operates in different disciplines and in different areas of life."[42]

The article by William Cobern, "The Nature of Science and the Role of Knowledge and Belief," provides a useful summary of the historical development of knowledge and belief and would benefit science classroom teachers who wish to improve their knowledge on how scientific knowledge interacts with belief and other forms of knowledge. Another useful resource which could assist science teachers in giving their students insight into how scientific knowledge and religious belief interact is the 2009 article by Richard Coll, Neil Taylor, and Mark Lay, "Scientists' Habits of Mind as

---

42. Cobern, "Nature of Science," 241.

Evidenced by the Interaction Between Their Science Training and Religious Beliefs." Articles such as this would be useful to teachers, especially when used alongside some of the resources from the aforementioned Faraday Schools website (for example, an interview with physicist Dr. Ard Louis, reader in theoretical physics at the University of Oxford, who is a Christian) as they can equip science teachers with an understanding of the range of views on religion held by scientists—they can also be a comfort to students as so much of modern science grew out of an attempt get closer to God; as Douglas Allchin reminds us:

> James Hutton's theological views about the habitability of the earth prompted his reflections on soil for farming and on food and energy, and led to his observations and conclusions about geological uplift, "deep time," the formation of coal, and what we would call energy flow in an ecosystem. . . . Likewise, assumptions about a Noachian flood shaped William Buckland's landmark work on fossil assemblages in caves, recognized by the Royal Society's prestigious Copley Medal. Other diluvialists drew attention to the anomalous locations of huge boulders, remote from the bedrock of which they were composed. (While they concluded that the rocks were moved by turbulent floodwaters, we now interpret them as glacial erratics.) These discoveries all had origins that cannot be separated from the religious concepts and motivations that made the observations possible.[43]

Reflection Questions

In addition to the resources and literature presented here it is useful for science teachers to take the time to *think* about the issues touched on, and as part of this the following questions may help as a starting point with any reflection.

1. How would you respond in your science class if a student asked if you believe in God?
2. What is your view of the relationship between science and religion? How many other views are you aware of?
3. In what ways do science and religion fit together?
4. How could a discussion on the relationships between science and religion benefit students in your classroom? What aspects of the nature of science could be explored by such a discussion?

43. Allchin, "Values in Science," 6–7.

Bibliography

Abd-El-Khalick, Fouad S., and Saouma BouJaoude. "An Exploratory Study of the Disciplinary Knowledge of Science Teachers." In *Proceedings of the 1997 Annual International Conference of the Association for the Education of Science Teachers*. Pensacola, FL: Association for the Education of Teachers in Science (ERIC Document Reproduction Service 405 220), 1997.

Alexander, Denis R. "Models for Relating Science and Religion." *Faraday Paper* 3 (2007) 1–4. https://www.faraday.st-edmunds.cam.ac.uk/resources/Faraday%20Papers/Faraday%20Paper%203%20Alexander_EN.pdf.

Allchin, Douglas. "Values in Science: An Educational Perspective." *Science and Education* 8 (1999) 1–12.

Barbour, Ian G. *Religion in an Age of Science*. London: SCM Press, 1990.

Bell, Randy L., Juanita Jo Matkins, and Bruce M. Gansneder. "Impacts of Contextual and Explicit Instruction on Preservice Elementary Teachers' Understandings of the Nature of Science." *Journal of Research in Science Teaching* 48 (2011) 414–36.

Billingsley, Berry, et al. "Secondary School Students' Epistemic Insight into the Relationships Between Science and Religion—a Preliminary Enquiry." *Research in Science Education* 43 (2013) 1715–32.

———. "Secondary School Teachers' Perspectives on Teaching About Topics that Bridge Science and Religion." *Curriculum Journal* 25 (2014) 372–95.

Carey, Susan, and Carol Smith. "On Understanding the Nature of Scientific Knowledge." *Educational Psychologist* 28 (1993) 235–51.

Cobern, William W. "The Nature of Science and the Role of Knowledge and Belief." *Science and Education* 9 (2000) 219–46.

Coll, Richard K., Neil Taylor, and Mark C. Lay. "Scientists' Habits of Mind as Evidenced by the Interaction Between Their Science Training and Religious Beliefs." *International Journal of Science Education* 31 (2009) 725–55.

Deng, Feng, et al. "Students' Views of the Nature of Science: A Critical Review of Research." *Science Education* 95 (2011) 961–99.

Esbenshade, Donald H., Jr. "Student Perceptions About Science and Religion." *The American Biology Teacher* 55 (1993) 334–38.

Fulljames, Peter, Harry M. Gibson, and Leslie J. Francis. "Creationism, Scientism, Christianity and Science: A Study in Adolescent Attitudes." *British Educational Research Journal* 17 (1991) 171–90.

Gilbert, John K., Roger J. Osborne, and Peter J. Fensham. "Children's Science and its Consequences for Teaching." *Science Education* 66 (1982) 623–33.

Hanley, Pam, Judith Bennett, and Mary Ratcliffe. "The Inter-relationship of Science and Religion: A Typology of Engagement." *International Journal of Science Education* 36 (2014) 1210–29.

Haught, John F. *Science and Religion: From Conflict to Conversation*. Mahwah, NJ: Paulist, 1995.

Hokayem, Hayat, and Saouma BouJaoude. "College Students' Perceptions of the Theory of Evolution." *Journal of Research in Science Teaching* 45 (2008) 395–419.

Jegede, Olugbemiro. "Collateral Learning and the Eco-Cultural Paradigm in Science and Mathematics Education in Africa." *Studies in Science Education* 25 (1995) 97–137.

———. "Toward a Philosophical Basis for Science Education of the 1990s: An African View-Point." In *The History and Philosophy of Science in Science Teaching*, edited by Don Emil Herget, 185–98. Tallahassee: Science Education and Department of Philosophy, Florida State University, 1989.

———. "Worldview Presuppositions and Science and Technology Education." *Science and Technology, Education and Ethnicity: An Aotearoa/New Zealand Perspective*, edited by Beverley Bell and D. Hodson, 76–88. Wellington: Royal Society of New Zealand, 1998.

Koul, Ravinder. "Religious Outlook and Students' Attitudes Towards School Science." *Journal of Beliefs and Values* 27 (2006) 251–67.

———. "Revivalist Thinking and Student Conceptualizations of Science/Religion." *Studies in Science Education* 39 (2003) 103–24.

Leach, John, and Phil Scott. "Designing and Evaluating Science Teaching Sequences: An Approach Drawing Upon the Concept of Learning Demand and a Social Constructivist Perspective on Learning." *Studies in Science Education* 38 (2002) 115–42.

Lunn, Stephen. "'What We Think We Can Safely Say. . .': Primary Teachers' Views of the Nature of Science." *British Educational Research Journal* 28 (2002) 649–72.

McKeachie, Wilbert J., Yi-Guang Lin, and James Strayer. "Creationist vs. Evolutionary Beliefs: Effects on Learning Biology." *The American Biology Teacher* 64 (2002) 189–92.

Meadows, Lee, Elizabeth Doster, and David F. Jackson. "Managing the Conflict Between Evolution and Religion." *The American Biology Teacher* 62 (2000) 102–7.

Nord, Warren A. "Science, Religion and Education." *Religion and Education* 26 (1999) 55–66.

Polkinghorne, John C. *One World: The Interaction of Science and Theology*. West Conshohocken, PA: Templeton Foundation, 2010.

Semali, Ladislaus M., and Joe L. Kincheloe. *What is Indigenous Knowledge? Voices from the Academy*. New York: Routledge, 2002.

Shipman, Harry L., et al. "Changes in Student Views of Religion and Science in a College Astronomy Course." *Science Education* 86 (2002) 526–47.

Solomon, Joan, Jon Duveen, and Linda Scott. "Pupils' Images of Scientific Epistemology." *International Journal of Science Education* 16 (1994) 361–73.

Stolberg, Tonie. "The Religio-Scientific Frameworks of Pre-service Primary Teachers: An Analysis of Their Influence on Their Teaching of Science." *International Journal of Science Education* 29 (2007) 909–30.

Taber, Keith S., ed. *Progressing Science Education: Constructing the Scientific Research Programme into the Contingent Nature of Learning Science*. New York: Springer, 2009.

———. "The Relationship Between Science and Religion: A Contentious and Complex Issue Facing Science Education." In *Science Education: A Global Perspective*, edited by Ben Akpan, 65–91. New York: Springer, 2013.

Taber, Keith S., et al. "English Secondary Students' Thinking about the Status of Scientific Theories: Consistent, Comprehensive, Coherent, and Extensively Evidenced Explanations of Aspects of the Natural World—or Just 'an Idea Someone Has.'" *Curriculum Journal* 26 (2015) 370–403.

———. "Secondary Students' Responses to Perceptions of the Relationship Between Science and Religion: Stances Identified from an Interview Study." *Science Education* 95 (2011) 1000–25.

Van Driel, Jan H., and Nico Verloop. "Experienced Teachers' Knowledge of Teaching and Learning of Models and Modelling in Science Education." *International Journal of Science Education* 24 (2002) 1255–72.

Yasri, Pratchayapong. "Views of the Relationship Between Science and Religion and Their Implications for Student Learning of Evolutionary Biology." PhD diss., University of Glasgow, 2014.

Yasri, Pratchayapong, et al. "Relating Science and Religion: An Ontology of Taxonomies and Development of a Research Tool for Identifying Individual Views." *Science and Education* 22 (2013) 2679–707.

Yasri, Pratchayapong, and Rebecca Mancy. "Understanding Student Approaches to Learning Evolution in the Context of Their Perceptions of the Relationship Between Science and Religion." *International Journal of Science Education* 36 (2014) 24–45.

18

Epistemology, Religion, and the Politics of Inclusion in Ontario Public Education

Leo Van Arragon

Introduction

INCLUSIVITY HAS EMERGED AS an important value in education. The Ontario public school system has identified it as a key identifying feature of state-funded public education, with numerous documents outlining common goals and strategies designed to achieve an inclusive educational environment.[1] Schools across the spectrum in Ontario are working to diversify their programs and program delivery to meet the needs of students whose needs once remained unrecognized.

However, the goal of inclusivity is an elusive one and can include various categories of identity and learning characteristics important to students and their parents. In this chapter, I examine the role of epistemology and epistemological diversity in setting the parameters for inclusion within schools and among school systems within jurisdictions, using Ontario public education as my case study.[2] I argue that respect for epistemological diversity is important for three reasons. The first is that no school or school system can legitimately claim ownership of universal values and ways of knowing. The second is that respect for epistemological diversity is important for humility in relationship between teachers and students but also among groups in a society. The third reason is that the humble recognition of the limitations of one's own epistemology can address the risks of

---

1. Ontario Ministry of Education, search results, nos. 1–28, for "Inclusivity." http://find.gov.on.ca/index.php?page=1&owner=edu&q=Inclusivity&Lang=EN.

2. This chapter draws on doctoral research summarized in Van Arragon, "We Educate."

the abuses of educational power, particularly in the forms of coercion and indoctrination.

The chapter foregrounds the nexus of epistemology and religion. The first is that religion has emerged as an important social fault line with an ambiguous role in liberal societies which, on the one hand, promote the value of religious freedom while, at the same time, being anxious about the socially disruptive potential of religious diversity. The second is that religion raises important epistemological questions, particularly around the construction of boundaries between forms of knowledge, which can be included in public discourse and which forms of knowledge are marginalized. Religion and religious diversity are hot topics in liberal societies because religion is often linked with "illiberal" modes of educational thought and practices, while being a barrier to critical thought by being inherently prone to indoctrination of students.[3] However, liberalism claiming to speak in a secular voice has its own limitations, blind spots, and coercive and indoctrinational impulses. This chapter invites the readers to step back from their contexts, and reflect critically on their epistemologies and on the role they play in constructing boundaries of inclusivity, which may well have become normalized to the point where they are invisible.

Public, Separate, and Private Schools in Ontario: Regulatory Categories

The regulation of religion and religious diversity in Ontario public education reflects the ambiguous role of religion common to liberal societies but is contested and structured in ways that reflect Ontario's political and social history within the Canadian federation. The Constitution Act of 1867 is based on a division of jurisdictional powers between the central and provincial governments, with Section 93 identifying education as a matter of provincial jurisdiction. As a result, there is not a unified Canadian education system but rather a highly diverse educational polyglot reflecting social and political conditions unique to each province and territory.

Throughout its history, Ontario has recognized three categories of schools as a way of addressing religious diversity at the time of the Canadian Confederation in 1867. The Ontario public school system was established after 1850 largely through the efforts of Egerton Ryerson as a way of centralizing the decentralized system in existence at the time and bringing

---

3. Asad et al., *Is Critique Secular*. See also Richardson, "Cult/Brainwashing," and Richardson, "'Brainwashing' Claims," for critical examination of brainwashing and indoctrination.

education under state control. However, out of political necessity, publicly funded "separate" school systems were also established to accommodate groups in conflict with two principles on which the common school system was based. The first of these principles was that the common school system was a social microcosm to establish common civic values, until 1990 expressed in terms of a form of Protestant Christianity. The second principle was that the common school system was a state instrument to deliver public education as a way of achieving a unified citizenry.

There were three "separate" school systems in the nineteenth century; Roman Catholic, Protestant, and "colored," of which the Roman Catholic system has had the longest and greatest impact. "Private school" is the third category, including a wide range of school options based on religion, educational philosophy, and other interests.

School Categories and Regulation of Epistemological Diversity

Although the categories "public," "separate," and "private" are commonly accepted, they are more than convenient labels. Besides being creations for legal and regulatory purposes, school categories indicate standards of epistemological legitimacy. In other words, school categories reflect assumptions about the nature of the knowledge and which forms of knowledge can be included in public discourse. Designation of schools as "public" is an extension of the original term "common," and the idea that the schools thus categorized represent educational interests which Ontarians hold in common. In addition, public schools are assumed to speak in a common language of secular rationality and other civic values, among which tolerance of diversity is one of the most important.

Epistemological diversity has been the focus of much concern and examination throughout the history of Ontario, lying at the dynamic nexus between freedom and social order but the debates take on additional energy when they occur in public education.[4] The reason is that public education is designed to deliver good citizens with a fundamental commitment to values considered essential to social harmony. Wrong modes of thought are a matter of state interest in Ontario to be addressed by the public school system, which is an important state actor.

---

4. See Hope, *Report of the Royal Commission on Education in Ontario,* for a summary of the nineteenth and early twentieth century debates over epistemological diversity between advocates for the common school movement and advocates for Roman Catholic separate schools. The "Minority Report" is particularly instructive.

The Mackay Report: Indoctrination Becomes a Problem

Epistemology was an important issue in the report titled "Religious Information and Moral Development" (hereafter the *Mackay Report*), tabled in 1969 by the "Committee on Religious Education in the Public Schools of the Province of Ontario," chaired by the Honorable John Keiller Mackay. The committee's mandate was to review educational programs and practices involving religion, moral development, and ethics, and it recommended, among other things, replacing what it identified as Protestant Christian religious indoctrination with "character development" and "moral reasoning" as the basis for public education. "Moral education" and "religious information" would replace Christian religious instruction in the elementary schools while world religions would be included in the high school program. It identified religion as a source of educational harm and equated religious ways of knowing as "emotion" and as out of step with the modern world. The committee indicated its epistemological bias toward scientific reasoning in its distinction between "emotion" and logical thinking when it said:

> To reason morally is to think logically, not emotionally. To think emotionally is not to reason at all.... Religious information was to be presented in a "scholarly and objective fashion and every effort should be made to avoid either giving undue emphasis to a particular form of religious practice or to minimizing the contributions of a particular creed or religion.[5]

Courts as Adjudicators of Epistemology

The *Mackay Report* reemerged in the 1980s as courts considered constitutional challenges by religious minorities to the practice of Protestant Christian school opening exercises and religious instruction, which had provided the language for public discourse and inclusion since the nineteenth century founding of the public school movement. The courts in *Zylberberg v Sudbury Board of Education* (1988) (hereafter *Zylberberg*) and in the *Canadian Civil Liberties Association v Ontario* (Minister of Education) (1990) (hereafter Elgin County) agreed with the plaintiffs that Christian school opening exercises and religious instruction represented a violation of their religious freedom and equality rights. However, the court in Elgin County went further, outlining the kind of knowing appropriate in the public school system, saying:

---

5. Mackay, *Religious Information*, 67, 72.

- The school may sponsor the *study* of religion, but may not sponsor the *practice* of religion.
- The school may *expose* students to all religious views, but may not *impose* any particular view.
- The school's approach to religion is one of *instruction*, not one of *indoctrination*.
- The function of the school is to *educate* about all religions, not to *convert* to any one religion.
- The school's approach is *academic*, not *devotional*.
- The school should *study* what all people believe, but should not teach a student *what* to believe.
- The school should strive for student *awareness* of all religions, but should not press for student *acceptance* of any one religion.
- The school should seek to *inform* the student about various beliefs, but should not seek to *conform* him or her to any one belief.[6]

The court essentially separated religion from education, saying that while religion might be an appropriate subject for academic investigation, it could not be a source of academic imagination or inspiration. In response, the Ministry of Education issued Memorandum 112 (1991), which instructed public boards of education to cease any forms of religious instruction or accommodations and which could be interpreted as being coercive or indoctrinational. Memorandum 112 was subsequently challenged in two cases launched by religious minorities who had been advocating for public recognition for their schools or who had made arrangements with boards of education to allow accommodations for their religious needs.[7] They argued that secularism is not religiously neutral, has its own epistemological perspectives and, as such, its own indoctrinational and coercive impulses which represented violations of the religious freedoms of religious minorities. In addition, Ontario's funding of the Roman Catholic separate school system (and one Protestant school operating in Penetanguishene) while refusing public recognition to other faith-based schools represented a violation of their religious equality rights. However, the courts rejected their arguments saying:

> In Zylberberg and Elgin County there was indirect coercion compelling those children who held different beliefs from the majority to be indoctrinated with the majoritarian views. The

---

6. Canadian Civil Liberties Association v. Ontario. Emphasis included in the original.
7. Adler v. Ontario, 1994, 1996; Bal v. Ontario, 1994, 1997.

public school system is now secular. Its goal is to educate, not indoctrinate. This is very different from the goal in place at the time that Zylberberg and Elgin County were decided. Secularism is not coercive, it is neutral.[8]

While law is often seen to be a neutral adjudicator of social conflict or the benign "curator" of cultural pluralism,[9] examination of the case law on religion and education between 1985 and 1997 shows that the courts were social actors with their own presuppositions of the role of religion in a modern society. The court in *Zylberberg* said:

> In an earlier time, when people believed in the collective responsibility of the community toward some deity, the enforcement of religious conformity may have been a legitimate object of government, but since the Charter, it is no longer legitimate. With the Charter, it has become the right of every Canadian to work out for himself or herself what his or her religious obligations, if any, should be and it is not for the State to dictate otherwise.[10]

In this statement the court shifted the meaning of religion in public life, marginalizing the knowledge base of people with a collective or traditional mode of knowing. Benjamin Berger has observed a tension between the law as a state actor and religious minorities who lose their voices in interaction with state actors, finding "discontent in many quarters on the state of this relationship and a sense the experience of legal regulation is not as benignly curatorial as the orthodox political and juridical stories would suggest."[11] In the case law on religion and education, the courts played an active role in marginalizing some forms of knowing in what Talal Asad had identified as a "project of modernity"[12] in the achievement of an "imagined community."[13]

Religion as a Source of Harm: A Dominant Discourse in Ontario Public Education

The idea that religion and education exist in two distinct and separate epistemological worlds is widely accepted in Ontario society. In 2001, the

8. Bal v. Ontario, 1994.

9. Berger, *Law's Religion*, 13.

10. The court was quoting R v Big M Drug Mart, in which Sunday observance laws were ruled unconstitutional.

11. Berger, *Law's Religion*, 16.

12. Asad, *Formations of the Secular*, 13.

13. Anderson, *Imagined Communities*.

progressive conservative government under Premier Mike Harris introduced the Equity in Education Tax Credit (hereafter the EETC) designed to address the financial pressures for parents choosing privately funded schools as an educational alternative for their children.[14] While there was support, the opposition was intense, based on the belief that the public school system is the one institution able to deliver public education. Among the concerns was that private schools' modes of thought were out of step with a modern diverse society. In the opinion of Martha Jackman (Faculty of Law, University of Ottawa) the EETC was objectionable because it included parents who chose religious schools where "the religious, cultural and social norms which underlie much private religious schooling perpetuate stereotypical discriminatory ideas about the role of women—the fact that they should be confined to the private rather than the public sphere—and also discriminatory attitudes around issues, for example, of reproductive choice for women." For the same reason, in Professor Jackman's view, the EETC discriminated on the basis of gender orientation, since "many of the religious and cultural private schools—hold as a fundamental tenet that sexual orientation is morally reprehensible."[15]

Professor Jackman objected not only to the EETC itself but to the very existence of private and faith-based schools in Ontario since they are, in her view, inherently harmful to the social fabric of Ontario. They are "morally reprehensible" because they perpetuate values and norms that are inherently in conflict with the Canadian values underlying the Charter of Rights and Freedoms. She did grant, however reluctantly, the rights of parents to choose private schools guaranteed by section 2 of the Charter of Rights and Freedoms and other international covenants but, based on her interpretation of section 15, they have no right to equal treatment with the public school system, represented as the one institution that can deliver public education in a way that satisfies the section 15 equality guarantees.

In 2007, the Ontario provincial election unexpectedly became a referendum on the role of religion in public education when John Tory, leader of the Progressive Conservative Party, announced that consideration of some form of financial support for non-Catholic faith-based schools as part of his party's platform in his bid for electoral success. He quickly lost control of the debate as politicians and commentators reacted to, among other things, religion as a disruptive force in public education and in Ontario society.

One way in which faith-based schools were seen as forces of fragmentation was in the education they offer which, based on religion, was

14. Ontario Ministry of Finance, "Equity in Education."
15. Hope, *Report of the Royal Commission*, F-374.

understood to be inherently harmful to children. The role of religion in education was an explicit theme during the election with fears of indoctrination and the perpetuation of an imagination out of step with modern, scientific thought. The following letter made explicit reference to the link between education and religion as a threat to Ontario as a modern society:

> Faith-based education segregates students based on their parents' religious worldview, thus partitioning children into "silos" where they have little contact with others outside the religious group into which they were born. Because a vast body of empirical scientific evidence from sociology and psychology has shown that such segregation increases the frequency of prejudice and inter-group mistrust, such education cannot in good conscience be financially supported by a multicultural and pluralistic country like Canada. In addition, because many religions advocate beliefs and practices that are contrary to the Canadian Charter of Rights and Freedoms, government funding of religious schools puts Canada in the dangerous position of financially supporting the indoctrination of future citizens against its own liberal-democratic values.[16]

The idea that religion is a private matter is pervasive throughout public education discourse, with the "secular" being deployed as a way of limiting the reach of religion into public spaces to which it does not have a legitimate claim. Further, the Canadian Secular Alliance distinguished between the education offered in a secular environment and the indoctrination offered in faith based schools.

The identification of religion with extremist, reactionary discrimination in contrast with secular progressive inclusivity was evident in an opinion piece in which funding for faith-based schools was seen in stark contrast to John Tory's support for same-sex marriage. Quoting the Canadian Civil Liberties Association in arguing for one secular school system, it said:

> In the event of public funding (of religious schools) there may well be no legitimate or effective way to control any hateful or discriminatory messages espoused by particular religious schools. Although our democracy may defend the right of any groups to hold and attempt to spread such views, it is repugnant for the public purse to subsidize the exercise.[17]

---

16. Canadian Secular Alliance, "Public Financing," 2.
17. Bourassa and Varnell, "John Tory's."

The assumption that religion is inherently a source of harm for both individuals and society was common, along with the idea that, although the harmful modes of thought associated with religion must be tolerated in a democratic society, they must never be given public recognition. Religion, while it may be tolerated and even protected as a private matter, must be confined to the private while the boundaries between public and private space must be carefully guarded

However, religion as a matter of personal belief is a more typically Western Christian and secularized Protestant view of religion. While it was so defined in the context of the election, it is also the way religion was characterized in the case law about the role of religion in Ontario public education between 1985 and 1997. Given that view, this opinion that religious activities, by their nature, must never be funded by taxpayer dollars suggests that religion practiced outside its boundaries is harmful to society, in turn promoting segregation and hateful ideas, which goes beyond the limits of what can be tolerated in a multicultural society.

However, although this dominant view of religion claims to be inclusive, it can marginalize other forms of religion that foreground bodily practice and ritual or those epistemologies with a more comprehensive view of religion and in which the distinction between the religious and the secular does not fit. Winnifred Sullivan describes "Protestantism" in this secularized sense:

> Religion—"true" religion some would say—on this modern protestant reading, came to be understood as being private, voluntary, individual, textual, and believed. Public, coercive, communal, oral, and enacted religion . . . was seen to be "false," . . . iconically represented historically in the United States, for the most part by the Roman Catholic Church (and by Islam today) [which] was and perhaps still is, the religion of most of the world.[18]

The view, expressed in opposition to faith-based schools during the Ontario election of 2007, that religion is incompatible with education and was living in a separate epistemological world, was echoed in the *Economist,* citing research demonstrating that adherence to religion decreases with education. It said,

> Just one extra year of schooling makes someone 10 percent less likely to attend a church, mosque or temple, pray alone or describe himself as religious, concludes a paper published on

---

18. Sullivan, *Impossibility*, 8.

October 6th that looks at the relationship between religiosity and the length of time spent in school. It uses changes in the compulsory school-leaving age in 11 European countries between 1960 and 1985 to tease out the impact of time spent in school on belief and practice among respondents to the European Social Survey, a long-running research project.[19]

However, the Economist did something more than report the research findings by linking religion with "superstition", in its byline "How education makes people less religious – and less superstitious too". "Superstition" is a term loaded with meaning and, linked with religion, constructs a way of marginalizing religion as a legitimate mode of human knowing. In addition, education is linked with modernity while religion is identified as an anachronism associated with less advanced societies and periods in human history.

The point is that epistemology, while usually unexamined, plays an important role in deciding what forms of knowledge are identified as publicly legitimate and which are harmful to the development of good citizenship. The dominant view in Ontario includes the idea that public knowledge is secular and rational while religion and other forms of knowledge considered "non-rational" are private. In this view, the public school system as a state actor is uniquely able to deliver education.

Separate and Private Schools: Resistant Voices in Ontario Public Education

However, out of political necessity Ontario included separate schools in its public funding mechanism as a way of tolerating and managing religious diversity.[20] "Separate" is a designation which implies that these schools serve narrow sectarian interests while the schools categorized as "private" are thought to serve a clientele motivated by private rather than public interests. A confusing feature in Ontario public policy is that "separate schools" are publicly funded, existing alongside "public schools" as a parallel school system protected by section 93 of the Constitution Act of 1867. Separate schools are, therefore, publicly funded faith-based schools. However, their constitutional protection and public funding expose separate schools to questions by critics about their religious practices which reflect their sectarian purposes. Separate schools, therefore, exist in a socially ambiguous

---

19. "Falling Away."
20. See Brown, *Regulating Aversion*, for a detailed analysis of tolerance.

place in Ontario, most recently evident when their way of addressing the needs of LGBT students have become a matter of public scrutiny. The issue of gender diversity has become more prominent as gender inclusivity is defined in liberal secular terms and religious language around gender and gender diversity become increasingly suspect. However, and somewhat paradoxically, Roman Catholic separate schools, along with First Nations voices were seamlessly included in the Character Development Initiative, launched in 2006 by the Ministry of Education as a way of establishing "common ground" for state funded school systems.[21]

The status of private schools is clearer, their designation making them ineligible for any form of public funding. However, their right to grant Ministry of Education academic credits leading to a high school diploma has long been recognized and they serve Ontario citizens alongside their separate and public school colleagues, preparing them for post-secondary institutions and the workplace. Their graduates demonstrate respect for commonly held values of respect for diversity, democratic institutions and processes, and productive work, suggesting that the differences between public, separate, and private schools, from the perspective of civic and academic outcomes, are actually not that great. Therefore, while the school categories used in Ontario suggest very clear and oppositional distinctions between which schools are and are not included in the broad tent of public recognition, the actual picture is much more nuanced and contested.[22]

Privately funded and separate schools include a wide variety of philosophies of education, religious orientations, and governance structures. However, they share two characteristics that distinguish them from public schools in Ontario. First, they agree that ownership of the educational process rests with multiple non-state actors. While they identify the primary stakeholders in a variety of ways, the state plays a supportive rather than a leading role in the delivery of education. Equally important, however, they agree that education, in order to reflect the diversity in Ontario society, should express multiple epistemologies, not as a matter of tolerance but as a valuable contribution to a truly diverse, modern society. In particular, faith-based schools see religion and education as intertwined in a mutually

---

21. Ontario Ministry of Education, *Finding Common Ground*, 3.

22. Since 1985, the most recent surveys of private school achievement were the 2012 research projects, titled "Cardus Education Survey," conducted by Donald Sikkink of Notre Dame University, who served as principal researcher, and Cardus, a Christian research organization based in Hamilton, Ontario. It examined the long-term impact of Christian schools in Canada and the United States on alumni, specifically as regards their academic trajectories, their professional status, and their civic involvement. The research project is available at https://www.cardus.ca/research/education/.

supportive partnership rather than existing as separate, hostile epistemological worlds.

Roman Catholic separate schools identify parents as the key stakeholders but, along with parents, the Roman Catholic church plays an important role in the religious purposes of education. In fact, bishops and others in the church hierarchy have been leading advocates for Roman Catholic education. The reason is that education is seen as an important religious practice and educational outcomes are framed within a religious context. The Roman Catholic Board of Eastern Ontario identifies its vision, "Inspired by the teachings of Jesus Christ, we transform the world with justice and peace through Catholic education." Its mission statement is, "We proclaim our Catholic faith by: Nurturing and celebrating the hearts, minds, bodies and souls of our students. Learning through faith, living with hope, loving in Christ. Teaching wisdom, teaching love . . . creating a world in God's Image. Learning and Growing Together in Christ."[23]

The Ottawa Islamic School says:

> The mission (goals) of the Ottawa Islamic School, henceforth frequently referred to as the OIS throughout this document, is to provide the students with excellent academic skills, while instilling a sound knowledge of the Islamic faith. The school fosters in them the characteristics that will enable them to acquire the necessary tools that will better prepare them to face future life challenges as self-confident, strong, and caring Muslim Canadian citizens. To attain these objectives, the school follows the guidelines for the expectations and requirements of the Ontario Ministry of Education. In addition, the school also offers students courses in the Arabic language and Islamic Studies. With this philosophy of academic excellence coupled with religious studies, the school hopes to culture, motivate, and inspire the students toward becoming productive, educated, and caring citizens.[24]

In similar ways, in Ottawa Christian School's statement of mission and core values, academic, social, and religious outcomes are seamlessly intertwined. Its mission is "to educate children, equipping them for a life of faithful Christian discipleship and service." Its core values state:

> The Bible is foundational to how we grow in learning, understanding and living in God's world. Our educational program recognizes and develops the student as a whole person—intellectual,

---

23. Catholic District School Board of Eastern Ontario. http://www.cdsbeo.on.ca/our-board/mission-vision-theme/.

24. Ottawa Islamic School. http://www.ottawaislamicschool.org/.

spiritual, emotional and physical. We embrace the diverse God-given abilities of each student and provide a nurturing environment for them to reach their individual potential. We are committed to providing a strong administrative and financial foundation for the on-going stability and growth of the school.

The Ottowa Christian School identifies its stakeholders as, "Our community, consisting of staff, parents, non-parent members, supporters and churches, is committed to helping students grow in their individual development for Christ's purpose."[25]

For these schools and their supporters, education is a religious practice, and religion is a more comprehensive category of human knowing that cannot easily be confined to a "private" compartment of life. Religion may include belief but equally includes practice. Rational thought has a role as a source of knowledge but it exists alongside intuition, tradition, revelation and community, intertwined in a way that creates a much more nuanced picture of the role of religion in human life.

Conclusions

There is an important fault line over epistemology between supporters of a single state operated school system and supporters of a system that encourages multiple sites on which education can be delivered. Multiple epistemologies can be seen as a threat to orderly public space while, on the other hand, they are can be seen as evidence of a flourishing epistemological democracy. Part of the purpose of a "common" school system is the delivery of a common epistemology, something identified as a threat to democracy in testimony by Paul Triemstra, principal of Ottawa Christian School, in parliamentary hearings over the EETC. Triemstra placed himself in a Western tradition of liberal thought, citing John Stuart Mill who "warns against monopolistic education in the hands of the government," saying, "a general state education is a mere contrivance for molding people to be exactly like one another."[26]

Jasmin Zine also argues for multiple ways of knowing in the educational process, suggesting that Muslim parents and students who opt out of public schools in favor of Islamic schools do so out of concern that Western rationalist epistemologies have their own limitations to freedom by neglecting the "position of the heart." She refers to Sharifi (1979) who argued that

---

25. Ottawa Christian School. http://ocschool.org/about-ocs/mission.
26. Hope, *Report of the Royal Commission*, F-385.

Islamic educational epistemology is based on "revelation" and intuition, which are neglected in Western educational epistemologies. Sharifi argued:

> When this dimension of the self is neglected, the very center of the human being, that which can realize the truth in education, amounts to the forgetfulness of the transcendental dimension of human life, to imprisonment in our limited sense perceptions and our worldly being forever, to confinement in areas which are by no means appropriate to our Intellect and real nature (*fitrah*). This aspect of spiritual knowing is also referred to as intuition.[27]

Where some see epistemological chaos, others see the opposite dangers of excessive state control over epistemological diversity in public institutions. Much of the debate over what can and what cannot be included in public education can be traced to this fault line. However, the common factor, which is sometimes overlooked in debates in which differences and fault lines are foregrounded, is the teacher in relationship to her students. This volume addresses questions of what teachers need to know about epistemology and inclusion, and the focus of the essays is on the experience of teachers in their classrooms. This is appropriate because teachers are, by nature, deeply committed to the ethical treatment of all students who sit (and stand, play, run, talk) under their professional guidance.

However, teachers also need to be sensitive to the context in which they work for three reasons. First, they must make professional judgments in how they navigate the parameters that define their schools and their school systems. All schools have both explicit and implicit parameters that define what can be included in their educational programs and practices. All schools have boundaries between what is included and what is excluded, which has important implications for teacher practice, parent expectations, and the story into which students are drawn through school practices and programs.[28] This is clear in the mission and vision statements of faith-based schools but equally true of the Ontario public school system. The Ministry of Education, introducing the Character Development Initiative, said:

> Character development is the deliberate effort to nurture the universal attributes upon which schools and communities find consensus. These attributes provide a standard for behavior against which we hold ourselves accountable. They permeate all that happens in schools. They bind us together across the lines that often

---

27. Zine, *Canadian Islamic Schools*, 27. For more on epistemology, see also, Mahmood, *Politics of Piety*, and Mahmood, "Religious Reason."

28. For more on the power of story, see Bolt, *Christian Story,* and Chamberlin, *If This is Your Land*.

divide us in society. They form the basis of our relationships and of responsible citizenship. They are a foundation for excellence and equity in education and for our vision of learning cultures and school communities that are respectful, safe, caring, and inclusive. Excellence in education includes character development. Through character we find common ground.[29]

In addition, the Character Development Initiative is mandatory to be delivered across the curriculum and throughout the public school system, saying that the practice of civic and character skills is essential to an effective educational process. It includes templates from public and separate schools along with models based on First Nations spirituality and tradition. Examination of the initiative suggests that the binary opposition between study and practice, exposure and imposition, instruction and indoctrination, education and conversion, awareness and acceptance, and information and conformity is much more porous than suggested by the court in Elgin County (1990). This is not to argue for or against any particular epistemology or to fault the public school system for having a preferred epistemology. Rather, the point is that all school systems, which operate on the basis of a "big story" into which they want to draw their students and teachers in order to exercise professional judgement, must be aware of the story energizing the school in which they interact with their students.

The second reason teachers should be sensitive to the epistemological context in which they work is to recognize its limitations. Any claim to ownership of "universal values" or some other expression of truth creates blind spots which may be obvious to outsiders but less so to believers in the system. Bernard Shapiro, in the *Report of the Commission on Private Schools,* asserting the value of common values, placed the emphasis in its public policy considerations on the protection of a "common public school." However, while the common schools "represent the priority" they should, at the same time, not necessarily be "the exclusive public investment in education." The danger of the arguments in favor of a public policy making the public school system the "exclusive public investment" of the government in order to achieve a common acculturation experience can be "overstated so that all dissent and variation is suppressed in favor of some single, necessarily imperfect vision, and it is an unfortunate truth that the public school community has not always avoided this pitfall."[30]

An unexamined "single, necessarily imperfect vision" increases the risk of the abuse of educational power, particularly in the forms of

---

29. Ontario Ministry of Education, *Finding Common Ground,* 3.
30. Shapiro, *Report of the Commission,* 40.

indoctrination which deny students access to visions of life other than their own. The Mackay Report (1969) recognized abuses of educational power, particularly through the intervention of the Canadian Jewish Congress, with notable effect on its recommendations regarding religious instruction and school opening exercises. The reasoning of courts in adjudicating religious freedom cases after 1982 linked religion with abuses of educational power while remaining uncritical of the possibilities that a secular state school system can be equally prone to coercion and indoctrination.[31] My argument is that educational professionals in any setting must be alert to abuses of educational power and that awareness of one's own epistemological context can equip practitioners with a sense of humility even about commitments that are important to them.

Third, humility can contribute to respectful openness to epistemologies exercised in other communities but also to the diversity within the community in which one serves. Teachers in faith-based schools, like public schools, serve students who come to their classrooms with a wide range of perspectives and experiences. A sense of humility is essential to creating a truly safe, inclusive classroom in which students can engage in their own developmental journeys toward adulthood. Jasmin Zine argues that, rather than being isolationist ghettos, faith-based schools can provide a safe space for students to integrate into a diverse society. The challenge for schools who identify themselves within a particular faith tradition is to allow students the freedom to develop critical awareness of that tradition. However, the same challenge exists for the state public school system, which claims ownership of universal values and a place of privilege in the delivery of public education.

In conclusion, all teachers and schools are storytellers with stories they want their students to absorb about how the world works, how to live a good life in it and the meaning and purpose of all that is. No one story and no one story teller can tell the whole story of the human journey in time and space but they do add to our shared sense of humanity. The differences in how we see the world is endlessly fascinating and can enrich us when we take time to listen to each other.

---

31. Canada adopted the Constitution Act of 1982, or the Charter of Rights and Freedoms, of which sections 2 and 15 protect religious freedom and equality rights. This leads to important cases relating to education, including Zylberberg v. Sudbury Board of Education, 1985, 1988; Canadian Civil Liberties Association v. Ontario, 1985, 1990; Adler v. Ontario, 1994, 1996; Bal v. Ontario, 1994, 1997.

Reflection Questions

Epistemology can be seen as an abstract philosophical category far removed from your classroom of grade 2, 6, or 10 students. However, your students come to you with their own frameworks of knowing, which they have absorbed from their families and communities and are shaped by their experience of the world. To complicate matters, you have your own preferred ways of knowing and processing the world, most of which is unexamined. The questions below encourage you to think about your epistemology, meeting those of your students in dynamic interaction, and self-critical awareness of which will allow you to manage the power dynamics inherent in the relationship between teachers and their students.

1. What kinds of epistemological diversity do you see among your students? What are the factors contributing to that diversity? How do you find yourself responding to accommodate to the diversity you see?

2. What are your preferred ways of knowing and processing information, and how do they affect your professional practice?

3. Which ways of knowing are privileged and which ones are marginalized in your school?

4. What about your school system? Is there a good "fit" between you and the context in which you work? Is there anything in the relationship between you, your school, and your colleagues that is stressful and uncomfortable?

5. Is the issue of epistemology (or whatever term is used) a topic of conversation in your school? Among your colleagues? In your community?

Bibliography

Adler v. Ontario. (1994) 19 O. R. (3d) 1. http://www.canlii.org/en/on/onca/doc/1994/1994canlii1451/1994canlii1451.html.
Adler v. Ontario. (1996) 3 S. C. R. 609. http://scc-csc.lexum.com/scc-csc/scc-csc/en/1446/1/document.do.
Anderson, Benedict. *Imagined Communities: Reflections on the Origins and Spread of Nationalism.* London: Verso, 2006.
Asad, Talal. *Formations of the Secular: Christianity, Islam, Modernity.* Stanford: Stanford University Press, 2003.
Asad, Talal, et al. *Is Critique Secular? Blasphemy, Injury and Free Speech.* Berkeley: Townsend Center for the Humanities, University of California, 2009.
Bal v. Attorney General of Ontario. (1994) 21 O. R. (3d) 681 [1994] O. J. No. 2814 Action No. RE 722/92. Retrieved from Ontario Court (General Division).

Bal v. Attorney General of Ontario. (1997) Re Bal, et al. and Attorney General for Ontario, et al. [Indexed as: Bal v. Ontario (Attorney General)] 34 O. R. (3d) 484 [1997] O. J. No. 2597 Docket No. C20558. Ontario Court of Appeal. http://www.canlii.org/en/on/onca/doc/1997/1997canlii4473/1997canlii4473.html.

Bayefsky, Anne, and Arieh Waldman. *State Support for Religious Education: Canada versus the United Nations*. Leiden: Brill, 2007.

Berger, Benjamin L. *Law's Religion: Religious Difference and the Claims of Constitutionalism*. Toronto: University of Toronto Press, 2015.

Bolt, John. *The Christian Story and the Christian School*. Grand Rapids: Christian Schools International, 1993.

Bourassa, Kevin, and Joe Varnell. "John Tory's Faith-Based Funding Is a Loser: One School System Network Grows in Opposition." *Equal Marriage*, September 28, 2007. http://www.samesexmarriage.ca/advocacy/00s280907.htm.

Brown, Wendy. *Regulating Aversion: Tolerance in the Age of Identity and Empire*. Princeton: Princeton University Press, 2006.

Canadian Civil Liberties Association v. Ontario (Minister of Education). (1990) 71 O. R. (2nd) 341, 46 C. R. R. 316 (C. A.) 30 January 1990. Ontario Court of Appeal. Retrieved from Anne Bayefsky and Arieh Waldman, 2007.

Canadian Jewish Congress. *Brief of the Canadian Jewish Congress, Central Region to the Committee on Religious Education in the Public Schools of Ontario*. Toronto: Region, 1967.

Canadian Secular Alliance. "Public Financing of Religious Schools: The Policy of Canadian Secular Alliance." September 28, 2009. http://www.secularalliance.ca/wp-content/uploads/2009/10/csa-policy-on-public-financing-of-religious-schools.pdf.

Cavanaugh, William T. *The Myth of Religious Violence: Secular Ideology and the Roots of Modern Conflict*. Oxford: University of Oxford Press, 2009.

Chamberlin, J. Edward. *If This Is Your Land, Where Are Your Stories? Reimagining Home and Sacred Space*. Cleveland: Pilgrim, 2003.

Connolly, William. *Pluralism*. Durham: Duke University Press, 2005.

"Falling Away: How Education Makes People Less Religious—and Less Superstitious, Too." *The Economist*, October 11, 2014. http://www.economist.com/news/international/21623712-how-education-makes-people-less-religiousand-less-superstitious-too-falling-away.

Glenn, Charles L. *The Myth of the Common School*. Amherst: University of Massachusetts Press, 1988.

Hervieu-Léger, Danièle. *Religion as a Chain of Memory*. Translated by Simon Lee. New Brunswick: Rutgers University Press, 2000.

Hiemstra, John L. "Calvinist Pluriformity Challenges Liberal Assimilation: A Novel Case for Publicly Funding Alberta's Private Schools, 1953–1967." *Journal of Canadian Studies* 39 (2005) 146–73.

Hope, John. *Report of the Royal Commission on Education in Ontario*. Legislative Assembly of Ontario. Toronto: Baptist Johnston, 1950. http://www.ontla.on.ca/web/committee-proceedings/committee_transcripts_details.do?locale=en&Date=2001%E2%80%9306-.19&ParlCommID=7&BillID=1003&Business=Bill+45%2C+Responsible+Choices+for+Growth+.

Mackay, Keiller. *Religious Information and Moral Development: The Report of the Committee on Religious Education in the Public Schools of the Province of Ontario.* Toronto: Ontario Department of Education, 1969.

Mahmood, Saba. *The Politics of Piety: The Islamic Revival and the Feminist Subject.* Princeton: Princeton University Press, 2005.

———. "Religious Reason and Secular Affect: An Incommensurable Divide?" In *Is Critique Secular? Blasphemy, Injury and Free Speech*, edited by Talal Asad et al., 64–100. Berkeley: Townsend Center for the Humanities, University of California, 2009.

Nisbet, Robert. *The Quest for Community: A Study in the Ethics of Order and Freedom.* London: Oxford University Press, 1976.

Ontario Ministry of Education. *Finding Common Ground: Character Development in Ontario Schools, K–12.* June 2008. http://www.edu.gov.on.ca/eng/policyfunding/memos/june2008/FindingCommonGroundEng.pdf.

Ontario Ministry of Finance. "Equity in Education Tax Credit: Discussion Paper." August 30, 2001. http://www.fin.gov.on.ca/en/publications/2001/edeq.html.

R v. Big M Drug Mart Ltd. (1985) 1 S. C. R. 295. http://scc.lexum.org/decisia-scc-csc/scc-csc/scc-csc/en/item/43/index.do.

Richardson, James T. "'Brainwashing' Claims and Minority Religions Outside the United States: Cultural Diffusion of a Questionable Concept in the Legal Arena." *Brigham Young University Law Review* 4 (1996) 873–904.

———. "Cult/Brainwashing Cases and Freedom of Religion." *Journal of Church and State* 33 (1991) 55–75.

Shapiro, Bernard. *Report of the Commission on Private Schools in Ontario.* Toronto: Government of Ontario, 1985.

Sullivan, Winnifred Fallers. *The Impossibility of Religious Freedom.* Princeton: Princeton University Press, 2005.

Van Arragon, Leo. "We Educate, They Indoctrinate: Religion and the Politics of Togetherness in Ontario Public Education." PhD diss., University of Ottawa, 2015.

Van Brummelen, Harro. *Telling the Next Generation: Educational Development in North American Calvinist Christian schools.* Lanham, MD: University Press of America, 1986.

Zine, Jasmin. *Canadian Islamic Schools: Unravelling the Politics of Faith, Gender, Knowledge, and Identity.* Toronto: University of Toronto Press, 2008.

Zylberberg v. Sudbury Board of Education. (1988) CanLII 189 (ON CA) http://canlii.ca/t/1p77t.

19

The Reconception of Story in Children's Picture Books: Will Any Story Do?

Christina Belcher

Introduction

WHILE SWEET MEMORIES OF being read to in an easy chair are priceless, stories do more than comfort. They influence what young readers will become and believe. They act as a mirror and a compass, informing the worldview of a child. Nicholas T. Wright reminds us that "stories create worlds. Tell the story differently and you change the world."[1] Stories not only record changes over time in society, but also have the power to endure within society. Stories provide readers, listeners, and viewers with many things, but never neutrality; no author writes without a purpose. Story functions as a social and individual meaning-making vehicle. Picture books have a social function.

Picture books have long provided a platform from which young children discover a love of reading. Reading with children is significant in the formation of the child.[2] Literacy educators are currently concerned that the act of reading with children (different from watching a book being read online) is in decline, which may result in declining literacy skills.[3] For any audience of readers, story provides a cultural replay of what society values over time. Reading becomes an act of not only understanding what is in a story, but also recognizing what has been omitted. In a culture that is rapidly becoming visual-centric and technology-dependent, picture books provide

---

1. Wright, *Original Jesus*, 36.
2. Heath, "What No Bedtime Story Means," 49–76.
3. The demise of literacy skill is frequently noted in discourse regarding elementary education since the rise of technology, in both peer-reviewed journals and the popular press.

a looking glass through which society may see social reading preferences and prerogatives more clearly. Picture books have a teaching function.

Although literacy skill is significant in retaining the beauty of language, the worldview underlying the *purpose* for story has an acute impact on the reader, even if it only becomes visible over time. What happens when words are less significant than visual representations? Harry Blamires reminds us that "the battle for morality and reason is often lost or won when a new verbal usage is accepted or rejected."[4] Do different decades of books portray different perspectives on personhood and identity? Kenneth Gergen believes that since the rise of post-modernity, the answer to the question *who am I?* becomes a provisional possibility, borrowing pieces of identity from whatever sources are available for use in any immediate circumstance as individually desired by one's appetite.[5] Neil Postman advises us that such questions regarding identity and culture are significant ones. He notes that our use of language is used to "create the world" in which we dwell, and it does so to both positive and negative ends.[6] Picture books have an identity-forming function.

This chapter explores fifty-three Caldecott Medal and Honor picture books from 1970 to 2016.[7] The Caldecott Medal Seal, named for nineteenth-century English illustrator Randolph J. Caldecott, is awarded to the most distinguished picture book of the year. Caldecott Honor Seals are given to award-worthy books that did not achieve the final award. It is significant that all of the books examined in this chapter were deemed to achieve a particular standard of excellence for early readers. Even though the Caldecott award is given for illustration rather than narrative, Caldecott winners have been studied for their numerous social connotations.[8] It is possible to study the balance of print and illustration and consider how this relationship may affect the reader. Books mirror society, portraying ways of engaging life in a specific time and place. Picture books have a cultural and worldview function.

The power of story as narrative imparts social awareness, literacy skill, and meaning making within the context of a worldview.

---

4 Blamires, *Post-Christian Mind*, 33.

5 Gergen, *Saturated Self*, 139, 150.

6. Postman, *End of Education*, 81–85.

7. A full list of Caldecott Medal winners and Honor Books can be found online at http://www.ala.org/alsc/awardsgrants/bookmedia/caldecottmedal/caldecotthonors/caldecottmedal.

8. Williams et al., "Human-Environment; Belcher and Maich, "Autism Spectrum Disorder"; Belcher, "Between the Covers."

Change Over Time in Picture Books

Across five and a half decades of Caldecott picture books examined from 1970 to 2016, key themes, messages, narrative styles, and audiences have changed. The books used in this chapter were randomly selected from the award-winning lists according to availability in a local Hamilton, Ontario, library and my own professional teaching library. Books are grouped into cohorts according to decades. Both medal and honor books are included. Each grouping is followed by general story analysis intended to illustrate changes over time in themes and messages, narrative and illustrative styles, and attitudes toward audience.

1970s   4 books

Year	Book	Description	Narrative style	Audience	Key themes/messages
1970 Winner	*Sylvester and the Magic Pebble*	Imaginative fiction about wishing	Traditional story map	Child and parent	All you could wish for is in relationships and love; people are more important than things; a moral lesson
1973 Honor	*Anansi the Spider*	Cultural tale from Ashanti	Traditional story map	Child and parent	Every child of the family is of equal value; a moral lesson
1976 Winner	*Why Mosquitoes Buzz in People's Ears*	West African tale	Traditional story map	Child and parent	Know the facts before assuming; there are consequences for behavior; a moral lesson
1977 Winner	*Ashanti to Zulu: African Traditions*	Alphabet book of African traditions	Traditional alphabetical information	Family; broader audience	Useful for cultural knowledge; an introduction to African culture

Cohort 1: 1970–1979

Since children's picture books have a short publication life and are frequently pruned in library sales when tattered or torn, only four books were available to me in hard copy form in the 1970s selection. All of these picture books presented a traditional story narrative with a clearly defined story map of beginning, middle, and end. Stories had conclusions, and conclusions had consequences. They all had a moral lesson or a *learning for life* theme. Stories were not just entertaining. They were useful for social reflection, moral awareness, and cultural knowledge. Following the post–World War Two era as they did, they were most often assumed to be read by a parent and child.

Key themes in cohort 1 included the premises that people are more important than things, family is precious, there are consequences for behavior, and there is a need both to live from the land and to learn about the lands we cannot visit. Being thankful for what you had was more significant than dreaming about what you wished for. Stories were shared, retold, and held dear as ways of leading children into the future. There was a respect for authority, parenting, and self-governance. Also evident was an overarching cultural worldview which saw family, tradition, and the land as things to be cherished. Story was inclusive and represented the life values of the society reading these books.

1980s   12 books

Year	Book	Description	Narrative style	Audience	Key themes/ messages
1980 Winner	*The Ox-Cart Man*	A description of living off the land	Traditional story map with a cumulative pattern	Family	Hard work brings satisfaction; the value of living off the land
1981 Winner	*Fables*	A collection of fables	Traditional story map	Family	Proper behavior brings rewards; life lessons
1982 Winner	*Jumanji*	An imaginative adventure	Postmodern story with nontraditional story map	Child as central meaning maker	Imagination; consequences of behavior; curiosity without thought leads to trouble
1983 Honor	*A Chair for my Mother*	After a fire, a family saves money for a big, comfy chair	Traditional story	Family	Saving and work brings rewards; lesson of life and loss
1985 Honor	*The Story of Jumping Mouse*	Native American legend	Traditional story map	Family	The need for hope to overcome hardships; persevere and you will live your dream

1980s 12 books

Year	Book	Description	Narrative style	Audience	Key themes/messages
1986 Honor	The Relatives Came	Patterned story about extended family coming to visit	Traditional story map	Family	The love and connection of family; memory making
1986 Winner	The Polar Express	A child takes a train to the North Pole	Postmodern story with traditional mix	Child as central meaning maker	Traditional celebrations; the mystery of belief; what is real and how do we know?
1987 Winner	Hey Al!	A janitor and his dog try to escape their difficult lives; fantasy	Traditional story	Individual	"Paradise lost is sometimes heaven found"; be content in your work; a moral lesson
1988 Winner	Owl Moon	Father and child engage in tradition of going owling	Traditional story map with an illustrative twist	Father and daughter	All children should be treated equally; gender; tradition
1988 Honor	Mufaro's Beautiful Daughters	African version of Cinderella	Traditional story map	Father and daughter	Beauty lies in how you treat others; internal beauty vs. appearance
1989 Winner	Song and Dance Man	A former vaudeville performer dances for his grandchildren	Traditional story map	Grandfather and grandchildren	Reliving youth; youth is about more than age
1989 Honor	Free Fall	Nonspecific visual story	Nontraditional story map; wordless book	Individual	Dreams are stories of our own

Cohort 2: 1980–1989

In cohort 2, twelve picture books were available for examination. The majority of the books continued the traditional story map, following the pattern of the 1970s. This cohort also introduced the postmodern story.

Stories began to incorporate distinctly new themes of gender inclusion and imaginative preferences. There were more illustrations in the text than in those of the same genre in the 1970s selection. The mythical element of magic and belief emerged. The 1989 *Free Fall* was the first wordless book in this cohort to win an award. In a wordless book, there are no—or very few—words. The reader imagines and interprets his or her own story through the images, omitting the relational aspect of oral reading. Family portrayal was changing from gendered visual portrayals of mothers and grandmothers spending time with children to include fathers and grandfathers.

Across the social landscape of the 1980s, women were entering the workforce in greater numbers, families were more mobile, extended family lifestyle was on the wane, and the traditional depiction of story was changing. Traditional reading was creeping from a modern variation of story as *shared telling* to a postmodern variation within wordless books as *independently constructing* a story not formerly known. Postmodern stories need not be linear, conclusive, or singular in focus. Neither do they require a moral component or happy ending; sometimes they have no ending at all. They can be dark or revolutionary in theme and often contain multiple stories rather than one clear path from beginning to end. They often contain adult or social issues, or remain mute or open ended in conclusions.

In this cohort of books, voice was represented more by children, and their perceptions became more authoritative and central to the story. The larger culture was embracing postmodern visions of story, valuing *content information* as well as *individual emancipation*. Communal beliefs were secondary to individualized choice and relative to the person doing the reading.

1990s   11 books

Year	Book	Description	Narrative style	Audience	Key themes/ messages
1990 Winner	*Lon Po Po: A Red-Riding Hood Story from China*	Chinese revision of Little Red Riding Hood	Revised traditional story map	Family	You can win by being intelligent and outsmarting danger; children are the heroes

1990s					11 books
Year	Book	Description	Narrative style	Audience	Key themes/ messages
1991 Winner	Black and White	A story about parents, cows, trains, and a train station	Postmodern story map; four stories in one	Individual; reader as meaning maker	Reinventing chaos; demonstrates emergence of multi-plot reading
1991 Honor	More More More, Said the Baby	Three babies and their parents living in different cultures; each baby wants more playtime with parents	Traditional story map	Family; parent or grandparent and baby	Culture and family awareness; we all love our children in the same way
1992 Honor	Tar Beach	Child's memory of parent facing discrimination	Nontraditional story map; imaginative memoir	Child; family	Racial discrimination in America
1992 Winner	Tuesday	Animals fly at night when people sleep	Nontraditional story map; wordless book	Individual	Draw your own conclusions; focus on time
1993 Winner	Mirette on the High Wire	Child meets an intriguing man who was once a famous tight-rope walker	Nontraditional story map; mentor reversal	Child and adult	Follow your dreams; believe you can overcome fears
1994 Winner	Grandfather's Journey	A child recounts and repeats his grandfather's cross-cultural experience	Traditional story map; memoir	Extended family	Living in two countries; homesickness for both homes
1996 Honor	Alphabet City	Shapes of letters can be found in architecture around you	Alphabet book	Child	Alphabetical symbols are all around us

1990s — 11 books

Year	Book	Description	Narrative style	Audience	Key themes/messages
1997 Honor	*The Graphic Alphabet*	Graphic representations of letters symbolized through shapes	Alphabet book	Child	Symbols represent actions
1998 Honor	*The Gardener*	A child is sent to live with her uncle during the Great Depression	Traditional story map	Child	Making beauty out of hardships; social issue of relocation and hardship
1999 Winner	*Snowflake Bentley*	Biography of the famous child who became the first person to photograph snowflakes	Traditional story map	Child	Recognizing the beauty in snowflakes as unique structures; follow your interests

Cohort 3: 1990–1999

From 1990 to 1999, eleven picture books demonstrated not only change in story *form* and *audience*, but also change in *what a story was for*. Picture books were becoming more inclusive. One tale in this cohort, *Lon Po Po*, is told from the perspective of Chinese culture. This tale about learning from elders and having courage to face fears was geared to promoting *belief in yourself* as an intelligent child. New immigrant beliefs and customs from further shores were making an entrance in picture books, not just in school curriculum for social studies. Embracing multiculturalism, African and Asian stories were becoming more prevalent, as were themes of ecology in scientific study and architecture in mathematics. The photography of snowflakes, rather than the drawing of them, made an entrance in *Snowflake Bentley*. *Alphabet City* and *The Graphic Alphabet*, two wordless, minimal-narrative books, focused on the architecture within alphabetical shapes in the natural world around us. These two books were dependent almost entirely on image, with print functioning more as a bitstrip or signpost to navigate one's own interpretation. Finally, the postmodern book *Black and White* introduced a chaotic reading of multiple interacting stories occurring at the same time, with no evident story map. Individuals (children) were supposed to figure out the stories for themselves in a book-becomes-toy venue. Chaos theory was making an entrance in the form, speed, and complexity of story. *Mirette on the High Wire* signals a cultural shift wherein adults are portrayed less often as role models or authority figures of courage and consistency. Story was becoming a way of introducing adult issues to a younger audience. Children and social issues were the key focus in this cohort's view of society.

Academically, the literary value of words was on the wane. One no longer read to become a writer or to acquire language skills. One no longer even required words to be deemed a reader. Audience perspective was becoming more individual and multilayered with adult overtones. Reading was becoming less shared, with the children being the solo meaning makers of image. Books were more often tools for inquiry, amusement, or viewing illustrations rather than reading the text. Biblically informed *spirituality*, inherent in Canadian education until the late 1960s, was becoming less prominent in reading material. In its place emerged a rise of interest in a religious, collective form of *social spiritism*. Readers were gradually becoming more exposed to thinking with their eyes. The purpose of the author was not often considered. Worldview was no longer one commonly shared view of the world. But would just any story do? And *what* would it do?

2000s   15 books

Year	Book	Description	Narrative style	Audience	Key themes/ messages
2000 Winner	*Joseph Had a Little Overcoat*	A retelling of a traditional Jewish tale	Traditional story map; simple story pattern	Child and adult	Waste not, want not; a moral lesson; social issue of recycling and nonconsumerism
2001 Honor	*Click, Clack, Moo*	Cows make demands to the farmer	Postmodern story map; parody	Dual audience	Getting your own way through political action; social issue of civil action
2002 Honor	*Martin's Big Words*	A biography of Dr. Martin Luther King, Jr.	Traditional	Child and adult	Dreams matter; one person can make a difference; social issue of discrimination

RECONCEPTION OF STORY IN CHILDREN'S PICTURE BOOKS 329

2000s   15 books

Year	Book	Description	Narrative style	Audience	Key themes/messages
2002 Winner	The Three Pigs	Postmodern rewrite of the Three Little Pigs	Postmodern revision	Child and adult	One can subvert original tales
2004 Honor	Don't Let the Pigeon Drive the Bus	A pigeon uses every tactic possible to drive a forbidden bus	Postmodern story map; few words; some bitstrips	Dual audience	Subversive; disobedience is presented as a skill for the child to learn
2005 Honor	The Red Book	Child creates own story from pictures	Wordless book	Individual	Any story will do; you make the story
2006 Honor	Zen Shorts	Zen philosophy in three short life lessons	Postmodern story map	Adult and child	Learn to be still, accept fate, and don't hold anger; social issue of spirituality
2006 Honor	Rosa	The story of Rosa Parks; historical biography	Traditional story map	Adult and child	Stand up for what is right so things can change; social issue of racial discrimination
2007 Honor	Gone Wild	Alphabet book about endangered species	Postmodern story map	Anyone	Endangered species need protection and an environment of care; social issue of ecology
2007 Winner	Flotsam	A boy finds a camera on a beach	Postmodern elements; wordless book	Individual interpretation; reader as meaning maker	Stories continue and are changed or extended
2008 Winner	The Invention of Hugo Cabret	A boy tries to solve a mystery with some science/technology underpinnings	Graphic novel/picture book/movie blend	Individual or group	Technology holds a magic of its own

2000s   15 books

Year	Book	Description	Narrative style	Audience	Key themes/messages
2008 Honor	*Henry's Freedom Box*	A slave's journey to freedom; a true story of the Underground Railroad	Traditional story map	Individual or group	Everyone deserves freedom; people are not things; social issue of justice
2009 Honor	*A River of Words*	The true story of William Carlos Williams, doctor and poet	Traditional story map	Anyone	Observation is the key to good writing
2009 Winner	*The House in the Night*	A bedtime poem about the lights in a home during the night	Poem with a cumulative pattern; repeating story elements	Parent and child	Shows the binary opposites and similarities of light and darkness

Cohort 4: 2000–2009

Picture books from 2000 to 2009 consisted of fifteen samples, making it the largest cohort. Two tales and one parody were present. A traditional Jewish tale, *Joseph Had a Little Overcoat,* focused on consumerism, stressing minimal ownership of things. *The Three Pigs*, a postmodern rewrite of a well-known tale, subverted the original story. Tales were also giving way to parody. In *Click, Clack, Moo,* political correctness paved the way for a perception of what I would term *dual audience*: a child reading this story would find it funny that cows could type, while an adult would read cows going on strike as being loaded with political innuendo.[9] This tale had no ending but displayed a clear postmodern map—with some foreboding concern about future events. The reader controlled the ending. All of these traits are *metafictive*—the reader knows these stories are fictional in new ways.

Identity as *form* became evident. Caricatures became more prevalent than fully formed, realistic characters. Children and animals were often represented as having power over authorities or adults. Both caricature and power themes converged in *Don't Let the Pigeon Drive the Bus*. In this text,

---

9. This *double entendre* is also notable in current animated movies, where the parents identify the satire or irony delivered in the wit of words, and the children "see" something else.

nagging and wearing down authority will hopefully get you what you want in the end. Civil disobedience and rebellion are portrayed as humorous but admirable skills for a child. Biography in this cohort tends to deal with social justice and civil unrest, as in *Martin's Big Words*, *Rosa*, and *Henry's Freedom Box*, or to stress scientific skill and observation, like *A River of Words*, the biography of poet and doctor William Carlos Williams. Biography is of interest not for the characters represented as much as for the issues the stories contain. Even an alphabet book, *Gone Wild*, brings current issues of animal extinction to the fore. Life is more serious.

The first graphic novel picture book to win an award, *The Invention of Hugo Cabret,* contains a balance of picture and text. It is a mystery concerning an automaton, with a link to the real life of an early movie producer as its root. Technology holds a magic and mystery that will solve our problems. The wordless books *Flotsam* and *The Red Book* encourage children to solve problems independently, interpreting pictures to create their own stories. Since story can be an individual construction, if read alone, any story and any solution will do. Gergen's formerly mentioned view of the construction of the *pastiche personality* is emerging.

Life in general is presented as being individual, busy, chaotic, serious, aggressive, sad, lonely, and fast. *Zen Shorts* is in many ways an anomaly to this view, portraying the spiritual components of a Buddhist perspective on life. *The House in the Night* shows the interconnectedness of light and darkness in mystic and poetic nuance. Worldview is reduced to a way of rearranging individual preferences or prejudices. But is that really a worldview, or is it the subversion of one? Will any worldview of our own making satisfy us? If not, we may be on the cusp of a return to the more hopeful life and larger faith reason to live it.

2010S 11 books

Year	Book	Description	Narrative style	Audience	Key themes/ messages
2010 Honor	*All the World*	A collection of information and perceptions about various countries	Alphabet book style	Anyone	The world is reduced to individual ownership; all the world is you and me
2011 Honor	*Interrupting Chicken*	Bedtime story; focus on talking and listening	Postmodern story map; interactive narrative	Adult and child	Role reversal; child reads adult to sleep

2010s — 11 books

Year	Book	Description	Narrative style	Audience	Key themes/messages
2011 Winner	*A Sick Day for Amos McGee*	A zoo keeper is kind to animals, and they reciprocate when he becomes ill	Postmodern story map with a cumulative pattern	Anyone	Cumulative deeds repeat; animals care for human
2012 Honor	*Blackout*	Everyone in a family is too busy until a blackout occurs	Wordless book with minimal bitstrip	Family	Family discovers things to do without technology
2012 Honor	*Grandpa Green*	A book about love, horticulture, and aging	Wordless book with minimal text lines	Anyone	Memory of grandparents endure
2013 Winner	*This is Not My Hat*	A book about stealing; the consequences are seen by the reader, not the thief	Postmodern elements; part wordless, part text; illustrations often in opposition to text	Anyone	Consequences of theft can be violent
2014 Honor	*Mr. Wuffles!*	A cat attacks a tiny alien spaceship; the aliens are aided by insects	Wordless book; one bitstrip	Individual reader as meaning maker	The universality of communication without language; friendship
2014 Honor	*Journey*	About loneliness and needing a friend	Wordless book	Individual reader as meaning maker	Searching for friendship when lonely; imagination takes you away
2015 Honor	*Viva Frida*	About Frida Kahlo; style of biography in bit-strip	Wordless; minimal text: two or three words per page	Individual reader as meaning maker	Artists live to create and create to live
2015 Honor	*Sam and Dave Dig a Hole*	Sam and Dave decide to dig until they find something spectacular	Minimal text; mostly illustration	Individual	The spectacular is all around you even if you don't notice it

Cohort 5: 2010–2016

The remaining books in this study consist of eleven picture books covering the partial decade 2010–2016. A traditionally written book, *Finding Winnie* (about the Canadian bear that inspired the creation of Winnie the Pooh) falls into historical biography, as does *Viva Frida,* which exists in more animated form, similar to a Pixar film. The story *Blackout* is reminiscent of a time when families spent time with each other rather than technological devices, and it shows a child's longing for companionship. Of the remaining books in this cohort, *All the World* represents a multicultural and global theme, but its message is that the world can be reduced to you and me.

The majority of the books are wordless and postmodern, and even traditional stories have some postmodern elements. These books include interactive narrative, cumulative patterns, minimal text, bitstrips, and themes of loneliness, hardship, and loss. Stories embody characters that are whimsical, and literary vocabulary is often simple or sparse. Stories concerning real people are less frequently taken seriously as mentoring vehicles. Illustrations are cartoon or avatar-ish, even if the themes are serious. Role reversal and imagination cloud reality. Stories may be simple, lacking literary quality. The social role of the family has changed. The role of the parent has been filled by other members of a social circle or by amusements in the larger virtual world. Childhood is disappearing for children while being reclaimed by adults. As Postman predicted, we are entering the disappearance of childhood, or perhaps something more sinister.[10] Cultural change promotes a different version of what an author or society wants a child to know and to be as society changes. These books reveal not only evolving forms of narrative, literary standards, representations of meaning making, and story preferences, but they also present a *different desired social impact* and communal target audience.

Worldview is unravelling at the edges. Individual preferences are prolific. And a small voice raises the question of whether or not childhood or adulthood as social concepts are coming to an end in the modern understanding of how we once knew them.

Moving Forward

It is true that educators could choose to bemoan what has been lost in relational aspects and the use of beautiful language, as print gives way to viewing in children's picture books. The language in books is not as challenging, nor are the intricacies of some illustrations. The opportunity for the reader to choose wisely and think deeply is no longer voiced in the text. Can the

10. Postman, *Disappearance of Childhood*, vii-ix.

beauty of language be lost as words in print become diminished? Do teachers still cherish the beauty of reading aloud and studying good poetry? Do parents still read quality bedtime stories with children? Has the availability of digital story reading helped or hindered a love of reading? What opportunity for discussion and deeper thinking are open to engagement?

Picture book availability is increasing. Stories still matter. Stories do create worlds. Stories still have a social, educational, and worldview influence. We are influenced by the stories we read, tell, see, and experience, even if that influence remains unexamined. That's why it's important to ask what is good about current story and what is lacking? What stories are worth telling again and again, and why?

This chapter suggests that there is opportunity to compare stories to real life and to what the heart values. Reading more is an option to reading less. Is reading a wordless book alone as fulfilling as engaging and discussing it? Does engagement in reading teach us more about story and our preferences, or cause us to wonder? Do children still need and want to have time for parent/child interaction? Will the thrill of technological devices last?

We need to help children in a digital age to engage real world conversations about what is significant in life, apart from the social experience of virtual life. In sharing our life stories, we can explore the full orb of meaning making as a heart, body, and soul event—and once again ask the philosophical questions at the heart of our spiritual core. Do morality and ethics matter? Is the individual really the center of the universe? What makes a person feel fulfilled; is it power, wealth, self-indulgence? Or is it service, faith, work, and reverence? As we seek a worldview we truthfully cherish—not just the worldview to which we assent—we may find ourselves creating new stories.

Conclusions: Will Any Story Do?

"Tell the story differently and you change the world." Wright reminds us that life-changing stories last because they are stories that continue to engage our society. They do not just amuse. They do not just inform. Rather, they involve us over time, even as they transcend time. They promote inclusivity, faith, and a sense of place, and they nourish love and hope for the future.

Story provides a way to learn to be "lovingly dissatisfied with life" in all of its beauty.[11] It's essential to understand the importance and power of words, story, illustration, print, and media. Reading the stories of our culture develops our powers of thought and vision, enabling us to imagine what we can understand about and offer to a world often filled with fear,

11. Belcher and Parr, "Commonness, Diversity," 13.

brokenness, loneliness, and despair. Examining children's stories over the past number of decades, for example, reflectively assists us in understanding how technology has provided new ways of engaging story, as well as showing us what we have lost along the way.

Story traces the values of a culture. T. S. Eliot wrote about Christianity and culture in 1939, when many western countries, including Canada, were considered to be rooted in faith as Christian countries. His concerns then provide fuel for thought today: while "a society has ceased to be Christian when religious practices have been abandoned," it also has ceased to be Christian "when behavior ceases to be regulated by reference to Christian principle, and when, in effect, prosperity in this world for the individual or for the group has become the sole conscious aim."[12] Eliot would suggest that "any story" will *not* do. A story with no cohesion or moral center is problematic. The philosophic worldview of the reader is embodied in story.

Humans will always require faith, hope, and a story. We become the stories we tell and read and share. And that matters. That is why not any story will do.

Reflection Questions

1. Do words, or the lack of them, in picture books have different impacts on our reading relationships? In what ways and to what ends? What are the pros and cons? Does the act of viewing books online have the same impact on our reading processes?

2. Why is it important to read a story not only for what it says but also for what it does not say?

3. What have we lost in our humanity as story has changed, what is not being said, and what questions and inquiry could be revived for new considerations?

4. Are picture books over time creating a different kind of story, or a different kind of person, for both adult and child?

Bibliography

Belcher, Christina. "Between the Covers: Suffering, Trauma and Cultural Perspectives in Children's Picture Books." *Journal of Christian Education* 51 (2008) 41–57.

---

12 Eliot, *Idea of a Christian Society*, 9–10.

Belcher, Christina, and Kimberly Maich. "Autism Spectrum Disorder in Popular Media: Storied Reflections of Societal Views." *Brock Education* 23 (2014) 97–115.

Belcher, Christina, and Graham Parr. "Commonness, Diversity, and Disequilibrium in Christian Higher Education: Narratives of and in Institutional Worldviews." *Journal of Christian Education* 53(2010) 7–17.

Blamires, Harry. *The Post-Christian Mind: Exposing Its Destructive Agenda*. Ann Arbor, MI: Vine, 1999.

Eliot, T. S. *The Idea of a Christian Society*. In *Christianity and Culture*, 1–77. New York: Harcourt, Brace, 1949.

Gergen, Kenneth. *The Saturated Self: Dilemmas of Identity in Contemporary Life*. New York: Basic Books, 1991.

Heath, Shirley Brice. "What No Bedtime Story Means: Narrative Skills at Home and School." *Language in Society* 11 (1982) 49–76.

Postman, Neil. *The Disappearance of Childhood*. New York: Random House, 1994.

———. *The End of Education: Redefining the Value of School*. New York: Knopf, 1995.

Serafini, Frank. "Exploring Wordless Picture Books." *The Reading Teacher* 68 (2014) 24–26.

Williams, J. Allen, Jr., et al. "The Human-Environment Dialog in Award-Winning Children's Picture Books." *Sociological Inquiry* 82 (2012) 145–59.

Wright, Nicholas T. *The Original Jesus: The Life and Vision of a Revolutionary*. Grand Rapids: Eerdmans, 1996.

List of Children's Picture Books

Aardema, Verna. *Why Mosquitoes Buzz in People's Ears*. New York: Scholastic, 1975.
Ackerman, Karen. *Song and Dance Man*. New York: Alfred A. Knopf, 1988.
Barnett, Mac. *Sam and Dave Dig a Hole*. Somerville, MA: Candlewick, 2014.
Becker, Aaron. *Journey*. Somerville, MA: Candlewick, 2013.
Bryant, Jen. *The Right Word: Roget and His Thesaurus*. Grand Rapids: Eerdmans, 2014.
———. *A River of Words: The Story of William Carlos Williams*. Grand Rapids: Eerdmans, 2008.
Cronin, Doreen. *Click, Clack, Moo: Cows That Type*. New York: Simon & Schuster, 2000.
Giovanni, Nikki. *Rosa*. New York: Henry Holt, 2005.
Hall, Donald. *The Ox-Cart Man*. New York: Viking, 1979.
Johnson, Stephen T. *Alphabet City*. New York: Viking, 1995.
Klassen, Jon. *This Is Not My Hat*. Somerville, MA: Candlewick, 2013.
Lehman, Barbara. *The Red Book*. New York: Houghton Mifflin, 2004.
Levine, Ellen. *Henry's Freedom Box*. Chicago: Johnson, 2007.
Lobel, Arnold. *Fables*. New York: HarperCollins, 1980.
Macaulay, David. *Black and White*. Boston: Houghton Mifflin, 1990.
Martin, Jacqueline Briggs. *Snowflake Bentley*. Boston: Houghton Mifflin, 1998.
Mattick, Lindsay. *Finding Winnie*. New York: HarperCollins, 2015.
McCully, Emily Arnold. *Mirette on the High Wire*. New York: Scholastic, 1992.
McDermott, Gerald. *Anansi the Spider: A Tale from Ashanti*. New York: Henry Holt, 1972.
McLimans, David. *Gone Wild: An Endangered Animal Alphabet*. New York: Walker, 2006.
Morales, Yuyi. *Viva Frida*. New York: Roaring Brook, 2014.
Musgrove, Margaret. *Ashanti to Zulu: African Traditions*. New York: Puffin, 1976.

Muth, Jon J. *Zen Shorts*. New York: Scholastic, 2005.
Pelletier, David. *The Graphic Alphabet*. New York: Orchard, 1996.
Rappaport, Doreen. *Martin's Big Words: The Life of Dr. Martin Luther King, Jr.* New York: Hyperion, 2001.
Ringgold, Faith. *Tar Beach*. New York: Scholastic, 1991.
Rocco, John. *Blackout*. New York: Hyperion, 2011.
Rylant, Cynthia. *The Relatives Came*. New York: Scholastic, 1985.
Say, Allen. *Grandfather's Journey*. Boston: Houghton Mifflin, 1993.
Scanlon, Liz Garton. *All the World*. New York: Beach Lane Books, 2009.
Selznick, Brian. *The Invention of Hugo Cabret*. New York: Scholastic, 2008.
Smith, Lane. *Grandpa Green*. New York: Roaring Brook, 2011.
Stead, Philip C. *A Sick Day for Amos McGee*. New York: Roaring Brook, 2010.
Steig, William. *Sylvester and the Magic Pebble*. New York: Prentice-Hall, 1969.
Stein, David Ezra. *The Interrupting Chicken*. Sommerville, MA: Candlewick, 2010.
Steptoe, John. *Mufaro's Beautiful Daughters*. New York: Scholastic, 1987.
———. *The Story of Jumping Mouse*. New York: Scholastic, 1972.
Stewart, Sarah. *The Gardener*. New York: Square Fish, 2010.
Swanson, Susan Marie. *The House In the Night*. Boston: Houghton Mifflin, 2008.
Taback, Simms. *Joseph Had a Little Overcoat*. New York: Viking, 1977.
Van Allsburg, Chris. *Jumanji*. New York: Houghton Mifflin, 1981.
———. *The Polar Express*. Boston: Houghton Mifflin, 1985.
Weisner, David. *Flotsam*. New York: Clarion, 2006.
———. *Free Fall*. New York: HarperCollins, 1989.
———. *Mr. Wuffles*. New York: Clarion, 2013.
———. *The Three Pigs*. New York: Clarion, 2001.
———. *Tuesday*. New York: Clarion, 1991.
Willems, Mo. *Don't Let the Pigeon Drive the Bus!* New York: Hyperion, 2003.
Williams, Vera B. *A Chair for My Mother*. New York: Scholastic, 1982.
———. *More More More, Said the Baby*. New York: Greenwillow, 1990.
Yolen, Jane. *Owl Moon*. New York: Scholastic, 1987.
Yorinks, Arthur. *Hey, Al*. New York: Farrar, Straus, and Giroux, 1989.
Young, Ed. *Lon Po Po: A Red-Riding Hood Story*. New York: Putnam and Grosset, 1989.

20

Inclusion and Playing in the In-Between
Cynthia à Beckett

Introduction

ISSUES OF INCLUSION ARE a priority for educational settings in many counties around the world. This focus has been supported by the United Nations through the initial Universal Declaration of Human Rights.[1] When the declaration was adopted by the United Nations General Assembly in 1948, it was the first time that countries agreed on a comprehensive statement of inalienable human rights. Inclusion as it is currently understood is about those inalienable human rights, and concerns the way individual differences in gender, ability, socioeconomics, and cultural diversity are accommodated in equitable ways in educational settings. While much progress has been made there are still many in educational settings that strive to improve inclusive practices. The theories of Georg Wilhelm Friedrich Hegel and Martin Buber and explanations of the "playing in the in-between" theory provide innovative ideas to support inclusion in current educational contexts. These ideas and explanations of the way relations form are presented here as a way to extend current approaches in order to support and extend effective inclusive practices.

The terminology of educational settings and children used in this chapter is designed to be consistent and inclusive. Educational settings refers to settings that cater to children from birth to twelve years of age. For children from birth to five years of age, the settings are known as "early childhood settings," and this includes long day care, kindergartens, and preschools. The term also includes settings that provide compulsory schooling up to the age of twelve years, referred to in a number of countries as elementary or primary

---

1. United Nations General Assembly, "Universal Declaration of Human Rights."

education. The terms "child" and "children" are used rather than "student" so that all in the birth-to-twelve age range attending these settings are included.

Inclusion: Hegel and Buber

In order to respond in a suitable inclusive manner to all in educational settings, teachers and children must recognize the other as a person to be respected, appreciated, and accommodated. These explanations present self and other as discrete entities. Such arguments draw on the work of Hegel.[2] Many daily activities can be explained in terms of Hegel's explanation of subject-object situations. These are times in which self has an instrumental relationship to others.[3] The self acts as a separate entity from the objects that are being observed and used. These objects include all that is not the self and can include other selves. The other is not so much another active person but rather is an object that is needed for the self, and the interaction is, as Hegel argues, based on the negation of difference, even if it is, for example, characterized by praise.[4] This lack of relating, this blasé or negative relation, does not stop the many necessary social activities that transpire.

Activities in educational settings may operate in the subject-object situation, and mealtimes provided by the school can be an example of this. This can happen when there is no real acknowledgement on the part of the child eating lunch or the person providing the food. Each performs a task for the other, and each is an object for the other. Each needs the other to perform instrumental tasks and act in an expected manner but not as another being who requires acknowledgement.[5]

Interactions such as those identified in the lunchtime example are subject-object situations that involve an imposition of one on the other, although this form of imposition does not necessarily generate a consciousness of domination. Imposition in this context need not cause problems for either person, as this is part of the socially required actions that constitute subject-object interactions.[6] A number of features of the way inclusion operates depend on expected subject-object interactions. Teachers are aware of special requirements due to individual differences. If the educational setting operates in an inclusive way then there is an expectation on the part of the child that interactions will be suitable and supportive. The teacher

---

2. Hegel, *Phenomenology of Spirit*, 37–39.
3. á Beckett, "Playing in the In-Between," 67.
4. Hegel, *Phenomenology of Spirit*, 37–39.
5. á Beckett, "Playing in the In-Between," 67.
6. Ibid., 68–69.

and the child will reflect subject-object interactions as the each act out the required responses, and the outcomes will be positive.

Martin Buber (1878–1965) also explains a type of subject-object of interactions and uses his own term I-It.[7] He details the way I-It has a focus on time, space, and boundaries, and through this is an important part of social life. We are aware of the other as an object, something that we must act on. I-It is content filled with a focus on time and space. The It creates for the I a necessary finite quality. This is a dominant feature of the world of things. This is a world of material objects that are prized and sought after, a world where the subject, or I, is sought after.[8] "It is also about the world of knowledge and skill that allows us to function in a knowing capable manner.... When features of linear time and Euclidean space are clear as they are during I-It, interactions can be planned and organized. Such activities are important as they help to sustain and organize the routines of daily life. These actions represent times that can be directed and maintained."[9] Such directions are evident in the guidelines and policies that support inclusive practices in educational settings. Planned events and programs are often designed to support certain children in specific ways so that they can access things in an equivalent manner to others. This ensures that equitable practices are sustained and consistent. All of these actions are supported through times of I-It interactions.

The I-It of Buber and the subject-object of Hegel provide key explanations about the provision of essential requirements in education settings that ensure that no one is discriminated against because of their gender, ability, socioeconomics, or cultural diversity. The ideas are embedded in the policies and guidelines provided, to ensure that all practices are inclusive. While this can appear to answer many issues that can arise, there is a limitation in these arguments as they do not explain all the ways that relations form. There will be times when the best systems established, to ensure inclusion for all, will not succeed. Both Hegel and Buber provide ways to extend their subject-object and I-It arguments in order to explain the way relations form and through this help to clarify the limitations of both subject-object and I-It models.

Hegel argues that while subject-object relation, has "immediate certainty"[10] and is useful in many circumstances, it is not an explanation that can cover all situations of personal interaction. The concept is limited and cannot account for all that can happen during individual exchanges.

---

7. Buber, *I and Thou*, 25.
8. á Beckett, "Playing in the In-Between," 117–18.
9. Ibid., 115.
10. Hegel, *Phenomenology of Spirit*, 67.

The difference is to do with recognition. The subject-object model becomes something else when the other is not just another object. Suddenly, this state of what Hegel presents as consciousness becomes a situation of self-consciousness. The subject-object idea no longer applies as the other moves from object to subject. This means that the act of recognition has turned this interaction into a subject-subject process. At first this can be described as a reciprocal acknowledgment. Each subject regards and acknowledges the other as another subject, another independent self. One cannot be that other, so each needs the other. Each acts in a reciprocal way on the other.[11] This means that both children and teachers will be aware of each other and will understand more about their required actions to one another generally, and this process is critical with regard to the provision of inclusive practices.

Consciousness in Hegel's terms is about an "immediate" knowledge of things as objects rather than a "mediated," considered understanding. Recognition of others as more than objects places them outside their original condition as objects. The object that was being used and was useful suddenly loses its status as an object. This then changes the way it is understood. When things and people are no longer considered as objects they then become subjects that can respond and reflect. This means that one is no longer a single subject alone with an object but one is now a subject with another subject. The original self is no longer the only one in the center of things. This recognition of one for the other is what Hegel calls the double reflection.[12] Inclusion requires this double reflection and recognition of the other in order to achieve ongoing success with inclusive practices. It will be more effective if there is a subject-subject interaction, where each regards and responds to the other, rather than the subject-object interaction described in the lunchtime example.

While the analysis provided by Hegel through the subject-subject process is valuable, there are situations when the mutual recognition and self-assertion, part of the double reflection, do not balance. The necessary tension between recognition and assertion breaks down and conflict follows. These are the times where the Hegelian desire for recognition becomes a battle, leading to the submission and domination of one over the other. This means that inclusive practices will fail and it will be difficult for those involved to understand how and why this has happened. This can cause great distress to both the teachers who are responsible for ensuring that settings are inclusive and the children who may require extra support though the process of inclusion.

The ideas of Hegel's subject-subject can be extended by comparing Buber's explanations of I-Thou. Rather than considering the Hegelian

---

11. á Beckett, "Imaginative Education," 193.
12. á Beckett, "Playing in the In-Between," 69.

subject-subject explanation of the way relations form as the complete answer, Buber argues for I-Thou to compliment the I-It explanation. Buber is described by Biemann as a humanist and universal scholar.[13] He was concerned about the manner in which social life is created and maintained. The creation of social life is at the heart of inclusive practices. Communities are judged by their capacity to support all through inclusive approaches. "The concepts of I-Thou clarify his argument that there is never a single I. We are always in response to something or someone and the someone may be personal or spiritual. He uses the device I-Thou and I-It to demonstrate in word forms the constant connection that exists. I-Thou differs from I-It in that it is not bound by the constraints of chronological time and Euclidean space. I-Thou lacks defined boundaries and is thus about wonder and difference."[14]

Buber also explains how I-Thou is not an object that can be summoned and will appear in response to desire. When there is a sudden recognition of time and space within the moment of I-Thou, and a belief that I-Thou will be kept as an object, it vanishes. I-Thou cannot be tightly held as a thing outside you. In terms of I-Thou, Buber explains it this way:

> Nothing is present ... except this one being, but it implicates the whole world. Measure and comparison have disappeared; it lies with yourself how much of the immeasurable becomes a reality for you. These meetings are not organized to make the world, but each is a sign of world order. They are not linked up with one another, but each assures you of your solidarity with the world. The world which appears to you in this way is unreliable, for it takes on a continually new appearance; you cannot hold it to its word. It has no density, for everything in it penetrates everything else; no duration, for it comes even when it is not summoned, and vanishes when it is tightly held."[15]

"It stirs the depth of you." This stirring to the depths is referred to by Buber as "soul of my soul."[16] He suggests I-Thou can be even more than this phrase indicates and creates opportunities of spiritual responsiveness unlike any other times. This is achieved through a freedom from time, space, and boundaries. I-Thou explains a more complete state that can uphold all involved. In terms of inclusive practices it can go much further than I-It or either of Hegel's explanations of subject-object and subject-subject. The set rules and requirements designed for ensuring inclusive practices can

13. Biemann, *Martin Buber Reader*, 1–3.
14. Buber, *I and Thou*, 49.
15. Ibid.
16. Ibid.

be taken further through an understanding of I-Thou. All involved share a sense being together, not in a forced, required way, rather all are upheld, encouraged, and complete.

Buber makes specific reference to issues of time. He states clearly that I-Thou is "your present." He explains that these are times of being fully present in a way that holds all their possibilities and makes the past and the future included, makes them present. There is no need or opportunity to be thinking about the next event or about the sadness of the loss of the present.[17] Once these intellectual activities transpire, the I-Thou has become I-It. The move of the I-Thou into I-It enables time to become on object that can be experienced and used. Buber explains that this is always the fate of I-Thou and must happen, but once this happens there is no longer any present. This means that while many productive aspects of inclusion will happen during the expected times of I-It, it is the remarkable, unexpected circumstances of I-Thou that will change everything. Suddenly, all can sense a difference, a feeling, of being complete and included. Relations flourish and it can be hard to know why.

I-Thou and I-It are not in competition, but work to complement each other. I-It can become I-Thou and can then revert back to I-It. Buber explains that I-Thou allows us to become through relation, but the state of I-It is also necessary. The moves between I-It and I-Thou are happening all the time. Buber's explanation of the states of I-It and I-Thou may appear to argue for clear divisions that can be easily recognized. However, he is clear that this is not the case. He explains these states and the change from one to another as "confusedly entangled."[18] These changes are not logical and orderly. The move from I-Thou to I-It and back again can happen in many different ways. It is difficult to predict such moves and to create, for instance, an I-Thou relation.[19] The expected times of I-It and the social exchange provide a necessary foundation for inclusive practices. Buber's analysis helps us to understand more about times when social exchange moves to a relational moment. Relational times are more enduring, meaningful times with the potential to extend the way inclusive practices are appreciated in a certain setting. Parents who are looking for the right setting for a child that may have specific requirements in terms of their physical abilities will find they are attracted to settings where these relational times happen. The identification and analysis of such times is complex and at the same time very powerful as it stirs the depth of you. Often, families do select educational settings

---

17. Ibid., 26.
18. Ibid., 32.
19. Ibid.

that have these I-Thou aspects, and it will be most evident in their inclusive approaches to all; however, it is hard to explain this to others.

Playing in the In-Between: A Support for Inclusive Practices

The concept of playing in the in-between provides more specific ways to explain the I-Thou of Buber,[20] and how this approach contributes to the process of inclusion in educational settings. Playing in the in-between is also supported by the work of Winnicott,[21] through his concepts of the third zone and unintegration. "The intermediate or third zone is a place of playing and the potential space that involves non-purposive or unintegrated states. The third zone acknowledges the way adults and children draw on their inner world and also the daily physical circumstance."[22]

Playing in the in-between does not focus on each individual recognizing the other and acting in required ways. Relational times of the in-between are different. Those involved are fully present through unknowing, so it is not necessary to act in set ways or to impose required actions on others. The in-between is also about mutuality through love. It is not about independent entities reacting to each other, nor do the entities merge. Both are present and in relation with an absence of social exchange. Playing in the in-between is a concept that explains how relational times go beyond the I-It form of social exchange in a way that can support inclusive practices. It is difficult to provide clear guidelines that will explain when something is the in-between and when it is not; however, an indication may be when those involved are so engrossed that nothing else matters. This type of social analysis cannot teach us how to be part of the in-between but it encourages an openness and trust that promotes inclusion.[23]

"Times of the in-between are moments that bring together everything.... When there is unknowing and complete participation in the present moment, there is a mutuality that is love. It is not about agency and social exchange. It is not a practical social activity related to the development of educational tasks."[24] While the spirit of these ideas is often understood at a deep level, the ideas won't appear as part of the guidelines for inclusive practices. The three elements, being fully present, unknowing, and mutuality through

20. Ibid., 31.
21. Winnicott, *Playing and Reality*.
22. á Beckett, "Imaginative Education," 197.
23. á Beckett, "Playing in the In-Between."
24. á Beckett, "Imaginative Education," 200.

love, combine so that both adults and children can discover new ways of working together through the process of inclusion and this is the time when relations form. When times of relational inclusion unfold then all in the vicinity are upheld, those directly involved and those who observe. This is the time when things can change in a remarkable and positive manner for all.

Being Fully Present

Being fully present is about a wholeness in which all aspects of our being are taken up. "During this wholeness nothing else matters, but at the same time nothing is excluded. The logic of chronological time and Euclidean space and boundaries are not required. It is also about being real, about being relaxed and free of pretence."[25] Complete calling through being fully present means that nothing is left out. What I mean by this is that those involved are called from their separate states, and the physical aspects of the setting also call. The guidelines and policies that support inclusive practices can enable this calling to take place. The call is a moment of change through presence. The complete calling is also explained through mutuality of love, a key idea of playing in the in-between.

Being fully present is also about attention to a single source, and so it can seem that other things are deliberately left out. This is not how it works. All things that could act to distract just don't register and this is not about a lack of care for these things. This means that in the case of a teacher focusing on a child who requires special support to achieve a particular goal, all the other things that could distract are no longer important. It could be argued that this shows a lack of care for other things but this is not the true. "Presence of focus is explained not as exclusion but through care for what is here."[26] There is such care that nothing else is important at that moment.

Ideas about being fully present are explained through Winnicott's[27] concept of unintergration. This concept explains how the things around us that seemed important are no longer needed. In this way they are quite unnecessary and this means we are free of them as distractors. This highlights a vital aspect of inclusion, one that is required if inclusion is to flourish. "All involved can be themselves in relaxed authentic ways. There is a sense of trust in the setting that is secure and dependable and this supports opportunities for unintergration."[28]

25. Ibid.
26. Ibid., 201.
27. Winnicott, *Playing and Reality*.
28. Ibid., 201.

When we are fully present, tension is not evident and things are relaxed. This allows for openness; all is possible. This does not mean that things are haphazard and chaotic; it is more like a holding space. Metcalfe and Game explain the idea this way : "It is not empty or fleshless, and the holder is not a container that holds others like a bowl of peas. Indeed, disrupting this Euclidean space of separate identities, holding consists of a simultaneous holding and being held."[29] This type of holding space describes a setting that is both "structured and dependable in order to be open to new possibilities. Teachers play a crucial role in ensuring that things are relaxed but have direction."[30] These are the times that children are most responsive. They feel supported in this situation and so all in the group are happy to be involved. They will be confident to make suggestions and contribute so that it is not simply another teacher-led activity. Inclusive practices come alive when things are open and relaxed while at the same time structured and dependable.

Another distinctive feature of being fully present is a difference in attitude toward issues of chronological time and Euclidean space and boundaries. While interactions will still be both structured and dependable, considerations of time and space will not be the most dominant factor. Some circumstances require particular attention to time, space, and boundaries; this is a necessary feature in order to complete certain tasks. Hegel's explanation of subjects and their reactions to others in terms of objects is relevant here.[31] This means that the self needs to act on others and not with others. Buber describes this as an I-It circumstance.[32] "Things are compared, defined and understood. [When there is] . . . a lack of focus on chronological time, Euclidean space, and boundaries [there will be a] sense of relaxation and this encourages all to be [inclusive] through being fully present."[33]

Being fully present requires an authentic presence that does not mask the true self. Children are very sensitive to this genuine approach. While many aspects of daily educational programs involve the natural physical world, it is the way teachers present this that requires complete engagement in a real, authentic manner. A teacher can present a planned experience to children, such as opportunities to explore the science topic of floating and sinking, in different ways. It can be well planned with engaging resources suitable for selected age groups; however, if the teacher is not fully present, perhaps there physically but only going through the motions in a superficial way, then there

29. Metcalfe and Game, "Care and Creativity," 72.
30. á Beckett, "Imaginative Education," 201.
31. Hegel, *Phenomenology of Spirit*, 67.
32. Buber, *I and Thou*, 50.
33. á Beckett, "Imaginative Education," 201.

is a lack of authenticity. This teaching situation will be counterproductive for the children. We are all sensitive to a lack of being authentic. Major problems will unfold if teachers lack authenticity while involved in any form of inclusive practice. The teacher and the children may then have difficulty connecting and children may even lose a sense of trust in the situation.

David Steindl-Rast explains the circumstance of being fully present as times when the domination of social exchange is changed by gentle, authentic, grace-filled ways of being.[34] He explains how life can become saturated and overfilled with information while at the same time lacking in meaning. Being fully present can encourage all to be more relaxed, more open to times of the in-between, times when relational inclusion can support both children and staff.

Being fully present has so far included ideas about wholeness of being and encouragement to be fully focused while at the same time relaxed and authentic. Unknowing is the next aspect of the in-between, as unknowing allows us a way into being fully present. Unknowing is free of the domination of social exchange and expectations that can limit possibilities. This is vital in providing programs that are truly inclusive.

Unknowing

Unknowing is central to the concept of playing in the in-between. This is the way that teachers and children can be part of new learning, where all share and discover together. Social exchange and set goals are not needed and yet many valuable things unfold. This is a more open way of learning and it supports inclusive practices designed to ensure that all children have access to equal opportunities. Great things transpire. Unknowing opens the door to being fully present, all are confident and trust one another and the setting. The social exchange requirement of acting in certain ways and meeting specific objectives is useful in other situations. Much can be learned during times of social exchange; however, relational moments that change everything require more open ways of being and are nurtured through a state of unknowing.

Mutuality Through Love

Mutuality through love is the third aspect that explains playing in the in-between. This involves an open generosity that is part of the holding space

---

34. Steindl-Rast, *Music of Silence*, 121.

described by Metcalfe and Game.[35] This is about being open and whole. "This love is also about the tenderness of the face-to-face and a dwelling that is free from the busyness of social life. All these aspects are not different forms or levels of love but the one love."[36] Buber[37] and Metcalfe and Game[38] explain how love is not just about a type of behavior that can be prescribed. If this happens it is a limited form of love. Mutuality through love is more open and more complete as it is at the core of the way relations form. Buber explains this relational love through his detailed explanation of I-Thou.[39] This love is different to the love of I-It that is about desire of the I. This mutuality through love, found by many in educational settings, encourages all to be inclusive, caring, and whole.

Conclusion: Relational Inclusion

Playing in the in-between in the ways that have been detailed can promote opportunities for relational inclusion in educational settings. This means that the foundational practices, polices, and guides that currently provide for inclusion can go further through authentic personal loving ways of being. These are the times that seem to appear from nowhere and make such an impact. When those directly involved are fully present then things are allowed to take their own course. Those observing will also become involved just through watching and may be changed through their observations of relational times. Things are different when relations form.

Times of relational inclusion cannot assume an automatic place in educational settings. This is explained by Buber when he states that "it comes even when it is not summoned, and vanishes when it is tightly held."[40] Although relational times cannot be assumed, staff can be alerted to the difference between the many times of expected social exchange and the other times when those involved are fully present and part of unknowing and mutuality through love. The potential for times of relational inclusion is always there. Being sensitive to this and open to the possibilities can change everything.

---

35. Metcalfe and Game, "Care and Creativity," 72.
36. á Beckett, "Imaginative Education," 203.
37. Buber, *I and Thou*, 28–29.
38. Metcalfe and Game, *Teachers Who Change Lives*.
39. Buber, *I and Thou*.
40. Buber, *I and Thou*, 49.

Reflection Questions

1. What sort of responses do you have to the theories and ideas of Hegel and Buber, and do their ideas remind you of any teaching situations?
2. In what ways do the examples of social exchange and relational times described here relate to examples you have been part of in educational settings?
3. Can you link examples of social exchange and relational times to issues of inclusion in educational settings?
4. Take time to reflect on the three elements of playing in the in-between, as outlined in this chapter. Have you observed or been part of playing in the in-between? In what ways could this idea support positive outcomes in educational settings in terms of inclusion?

Bibliography

à Beckett, Cynthia. "Imaginative Education Explored Through the Concept of Playing in the In-Between." In *Imagination in Educational Theory and Practice: A Many-Sided Vision*, edited by Thomas William Nielsen, Robert Fitzgerald, and Mark Fettes, 191–209. Newcastle upon Tyne: Cambridge Scholars, 2010.

———. "Playing in the In-Between: Implications for Early Childhood Education of New Views of Social Relations." PhD diss., University of New South Wales, 2007.

Biemann, Asher, ed. *The Martin Buber Reader: Essential Writings*. New York: Palgrave Macmillan, 2002.

Buber, Martin. *I and Thou*. 2nd ed. Translated by Ronald G. Smith. Edinburgh: T. & T. Clark, 1958.

Hegel, Georg Wilhelm Friedrich. *Phenomenology of Spirit*. Translated by A. V. Miller. Oxford: Oxford University Press, 1977.

Metcalfe, Andrew, and Ann Game. "Care and Creativity." *Australian Psychologist* 36 (2001) 70–74.

———. "Everyday Presences." *Cultural Studies* 18 (2004) 350–62.

———. *The Mystery of Everyday Life*. Sydney: Federation Press, 2002.

———. *Teachers Who Change Lives*. Melbourne: Melbourne University Press, 2006.

Steindl-Rast, David. *Music of Silence: A Sacred Journey through the Hours of the Day*. New York: HarperSanFrancisco, 1996.

United Nations General Assembly. "Universal Declaration of Human Rights." December 10, 1948. http://www.un-documents.net/a3r217a.htm.

Van Manen, Max. *Researching the Lived Experience: Human Science for an Action Sensitive Pedagogy*. 2nd ed. London, ON: Althouse, 1997.

———. *The Tact of Teaching: The Meaning of Pedagogical Thoughtfulness*. London, ON: Althouse, 1991.

———. *Writing in the Dark: Phenomenological Studies in Interpretive Inquiry*. London, ON: Althouse, 2002.

Winnicott, Donald. *Playing and Reality*. New York: Routledge Classics, 2005.

General Index

Aboriginal children, separation from parents, xxii
abstract thinking, 61
academic locker room talk, 106–8
academic skimming, as a fallacious claim, 131
academics, problems with free speech, 101
acceptance, as conditional, 78
accomplishments, enhancing the teacher's classroom authority, 228
"achievement gap," as a major concern, 21
additional support needs
    children having, 23
    qualifications for teachers of pupils with, 25
adherence to religion, decreasing with education, 309–10
administrators and teachers, remaining at school to help the community, 280
adult issues, introducing to a younger audience, 328
adversarial space, classroom as, 40
adversity, success in the face of, 161
age, of a teacher, 228
agrarian society, churches' desire for, 45
Alberta, funding alternative educational programs, 123
analogs, as the basis of cultural colonization, 59
anchoring instruction, 156

Anglophone school boards, in Quebec, 123
anonymous bullying, 164
anthropomorphic worldview, of the non-Western learner, 294
anti-Christian bias, in typical universities, 113
antideterminism, as one of Florian's "three areas," 32
anti-oppressive lesson and unit plans, 15
anxiety, experiencing, 185
appreciation, children receiving, 78
apprenticeship of the hand, 32
apprenticeship of the head, 32
artistic practice, family pedagogy working as, 14
assertiveness, building individual, 170
assimilation, never in the spirit of unity, 258
attention deficit hyperactivity disorder (ADHD), 184
attitudes, changing, 31
Australian Consensus Centre, 101
authentic inclusion, xxix
authentic presence, 346
authenticity, 77, 347
authoritarian classrooms, 220
authoritarian management, 169
authoritative style, of management, 168
authority, of teachers, 216–29
autism, 184, 185
automaticity, done to a level of, 150
autonomous individual, no such entity as, 55

autonomous life, creating grounds for, 254
autonomy
    contributing to an effective school, 128
    language and, 55–56

banking model of learnng, 15
barriers
    to effective learning, 287
    removing for exceptional learners, 145–46
basic necessary conditions, for teaching, 217, 223
basic trust, 75
Bateson, Gregory, 54
BC Education Plan, xxin11
Becoming Human (Vanier), 241
behavior, ceasing to be regulated by Christian principle, 335
being fully present, 345–47
being-seen-by-others, 78
belief in yourself, 327
beliefs, tolerating, 253
beliefs and values, discussions about, 234
believers, accepting, 265
believing, teachers developing new ways of, 30
belongingness, for all learners, 209
Bernard of Clairvaux, 94
best practice, for learning support, 27
"betweenness," 210
Bhabba, Homi, 89
Bible, using to teach children, 46
The Bible, Disability and the Church: A New Vision of the People of God (Young), 207n38
bibliotherapy, teachers employing, 175
bilingual nation, Canada's status as, 123
biography, dealing with social justice and civil unrest, 331
biological origins, preoccupation with, 208
biosemiotics, emerging field of, 54
black family pedagogy, learning, 11
body, providing support, 75
books, mirroring society, 321

boundaries, between included and excluded, 314
boundary maintenance, 222
boys, aspiring to be cowboys, 42
Brandeis University, 101
British Columbia
    independent schools in, 124
    public and independent enrollment comparison (2005–15), 125
British Columbia School Act, 131–32
Buber, Martin, 340
bullying
    culture of, 168–69
    effects of, 164–65
    factors associated with, 165–72
    fostering students' resilience to, 161
    interventions for, 172–73
    school level prevention and response, 166–68
    as a systemic and persistent problem, 162–65
bureaucratic educational values, compared to cultural and faith values, 132
bystanders, prevention efforts needing to address, 171

Caldecott winners, social connotations of, 321
Canada
    educational choice important to families in, 121
    numerous groups practicing living traditions, 91n50
Canadian diversity, 138
Canadian Jewish Congress, 316
Canadian Secular Alliance, 308
capitalism, 239
Cardus Education Survey, 136
care, as a source of authority, 224
care foundation, priority over the liberty foundation, 105
career, choosing over marriage, 277
Cascade of Alternative Placements (CAP), 149
categories (taxonomies), of the relationship between religion and science, 288–94

Catholic schools, 123, 128
Cathy's story, 143–44
certification, 224
champions, 191–92
Champions for Community Mental Wellness website, 181
chaos theory, 327–28
Character Development Initiative, 311, 314–15
charisma, not necessary for teachers, 221
charter schools, in Alberta, 123
Child and Youth Mental Health (CYMH) office, 184–85, 184n8
childhood, disappearing for children, 333
children
  effect on educators, 69
  grouping according to abilities, disabilities, 23
  at higher risk of being bullied, 163
  liking only when they "behave," 78
children's picture books, 260–63, 320–35
children's stories, examining, 335
"choice" aspect, of education, 124
choice in education
  benefits of, 121–38
  empowering individuals, 136–37
  freedom given by, 137
Christian childhood, 42
Christian churches, laying the foundations for instruction in new schools in Canada, 38
Christian discourse, as Canadian educational thought, 46
Christian educators, 45, 46
Christian faith, considering in Indigenous education courses, 41–42
Christian higher education, 103, 113–14
Christian missionaries, setting up schools for Indigenous peoples, 39
Christian teachers, coming to western Canada from Ontario, 38
Christianity
  effect on Indigenous children's education, 37
  inspired the formation of public schools, 41
  legacy for modern schools and their practices, 46
chumminess, with students, 217
church and schoolhouse, as fortifications of modern Canada, 45
church and state, separation of, 13
citizenship education, as incomplete without Christianity, 45
civic identity, fostering a shared, 252
civic responsibility, 135–36
civilized life, way to, 38
classical liberalism, followers of, 53
classical tolerance
  accepting and including the value and worth of every person, 251
  acknowledging identity and epistemological differences, 250
  appearing to be out of date and unnecessary, 264
  authentic understanding as critically important, 263
  as the bedrock of free, democratic, and just societies, 251
  encouraging critical thinking, dialogue, and debate, 257
  framework of, 250
  implementing a comprehensive application of, 268
  intolerant to harmful behaviors, 255
  judging some ideas as better than others, 265
  misunderstanding of as self-refuting, 255
  necessary for individuals and democratic societies to flourish, 252
  not intrinsically good, 254
  not mutually exclusive from respect, 256
  paradox of, 265
  potential for practicing, 262
  premises of, 251–52

classical tolerance (*continued*)
   promoting learning and justice, 256
   promoting value and respect of persons, 256–57
   reinforcing the ideals of democracy, 267
   requiring egalitarian approach toward persons, 265
   returning to, 259
   understanding epistemological diversity, 264
   welcoming disagreement, 266
classroom authority, 217, 218, 219–20
classroom culture and climate, teachers establishing, 168
classroom discipline scenarios, 112
classroom *ethos*, 220, 225
classroom management, 169, 217, 220
classroom teachers, providing assistance to student teachers, 273
classrooms
   embracing all in the learning process, xxviii
   embracing classical tolerance in, 264
   as open locations, 209
closeness, turning toward someone deepened by, 76
coalescence view, 293
"The Coddling of the American Mind," 111
coercive sanctions, 219
"cognitive ableism," 202n18
cognitive assimilation and imperialism, 37
cohort 1:1970–1979, 322–23
cohort 2:1980–1989, 323–25
cohort 3:1990–1999, 325–28
cohort 4:2000–2009, 328–31
cohort 5:2010–2016, 331–33
cold start, teachers doing a, 227
Collaborative and Proactive Solutions, 188
collaborative strategic reading process, 157
Collapse: How Societies Choose to Fail or Succeed (Diamond), 54
command (or coercion) and consent, distinction between, 219
commitment, to a person, xxix
common epistemology, identified as a threat to democracy, 313
common vision, between home and school, 135
communitarian cultures and religions, as not individualistic, 254
communities
   of learners, creating, 156
   of learning in Japan, 281
   perception of acceptance by peers in, 148
   successful schools becoming, 133
community resources, knowing, 194
community-centric approach, to education, 209–10
comparative ethnographic narrative, in doctoral research, 272
compartment view, 292
competitive environments, resulting in winners and losers, 22
complementary view, 293
complete calling, through being fully present, 345
complete involvement, projecting, 226
Compromising Scholarship (Yancey), 110
Comte, Auguste, 243
conceptual anchor, 156
confirmation view, 290
conflict view, 289, 292
conformity, compared to courage for independence, 78
consciousness, 341
consent
   concept of, 218
   earning over time, 228
   of students, 225
conservative academics, 105
conservative and libertarian students, 109
conservative ideological positions, presenting, 107
conservative students, experiencing discrimination, 107

conservative views, lack of in universities, 106
conservative voters, prioritizing moral foundations, 104
conservatives, moral prioritizations pattern of, 105
constructionist (social/political) solution, for learning deficiencies, 200
constructivist paradigm of learning, committing to, xxi
consumerism, 239
contact view, 289–90
content knowledge, insufficient to improve practice in schools, 30
contrast view, 289, 292, 293
conversations
  engaging in real world, 334
  highlighting different levels of human interaction, 249–55
cooperative learning, 156–57, 170
coproduction, 133–34
corporate university culture, mismatch with radical progressive ideology, 109
counsel, command distinguished from, 219
courts
  as adjudicators of epistemology, 304–6
  linked religion with abuses of educational power, 316
critical identity, learners forming, 94
critical narrative analysis, 7
critical reflection, 62
critical thinking
  aiding students, 255
  application of, 82
  developing, 233
  encouraging humility, 88
  practiced alongside learners, 94
  as predominantly pragmatic and scientific, 87
  as smashing down old ways of thinking, 83
  as a transformative experience for learners, 95
  as a UNESCO mantra, 52
  uses of, 93
critical thinking models, 92
cultural assumptions, underlying interpretations of progress, 53
cultural commons, 60
cultural filters, xxvi
cultural identities, xxxi
cultural liturgies, 108–9, 113
cultural patterns, 64
cultural pluralism, as reality, xx
cultural practices, understanding as ecologies, 54
cultural worldview, 323
cultural/ecological differences, between the spoken and printed word, 61
culturally sensitive education, 48
curriculum
  developing toward an understanding of family, 16
  focusing on the lived cultural ecologies of students, 58
  modification or differentiation of, 28–29
customer loyalty, 225
cyberbullying, 162

daily life, routines of, 340
daily planners, detailing incidents in, 193
Dalai Lama, 235
Dasein, 70, 74
Dawkins, Richard, 243, 288
de Botton, Alan, 243
Dead Poets Society, 222
deaf children, as exceptions, 144
deep learning, requiring humility, xxv
deep root metaphors, 55
deficit learners, persons of difference as, 204
Deficit Theory, 203n23
demographics, affecting classroom ecologies, 153
despair, wisdom and ego integrity versus, 152
determinist (hereditary/genetics) solution, for learning deficiencies, 200

deterministic approach, to learning anomalies, 201
Developmental Delay Theory, 203n23
Dewey, John, 85–87, 93, 198n3, 258
dialogic approach, of family pedagogy, 7
dialogical ability, 73
dialogical encounter, 14
difference and diversity, celebrating and embracing, 241
differences
  making a difference, 55–56, 62
  related chiefly to "looks," 260–61
  related to activities and behaviors, 262
"differences in kind" approach, 203
differentiating instruction, 156
difficulties in learning, 24–25
disagreement, classical tolerance always entailing, 265n69
disciplines, insufficient critical thinking across, 110
discrepancy, between intention and effect in education, 70
discrimination, excluding persons of difference, 202
diverse children, building upon the knowledge of, 3
diverse viewpoints, respect for and willingness to entertain, 96
diversity
  adding to the vast richness of existence, 241
  described, xix–xx
  distorted, superficial-level view of, 261
  experiencing, xxi
  importance of in educational policy, xx
  providing opportunity for development of self-recognition, 199
diversity recognition, examples of, xx
Diversity Week, University of Queensland celebrating, xxxi
"doing," new ways of, 30
dominant discourses, 145, 155
dominant secularism, default position of, 241

double reflection, 341
double-bind thinking, Bateson's concept of, 60
dual audience, in cohort 4, 330
duties, exciting to children, 79

"early childhood settings," 338
ecological conceptual framework, as not ethnocentric, 58
ecological crisis, impacting people's daily lives, 53
ecological intelligence, 54–55, 61–63
ecological sustaining patterns of living, introducing students to, 60–61
ecological systems, culture as, 62
ecological thinking, key characteristics of, 58
ecologically informed paradigm, 51–64
ecologies, 55, 56
ecology of languaging processes, 59
education
  embedded in traditions and ceremonies of learning, 92
  fitting the individual to perform as a member of the state, 43
  goals of, xxvii
  hospitable approach to, 209
  including a risk, 70
  inequality in, xix
  linked with modernity, 310
  as a matter of provincial jurisdiction, 302
  as more than knowledge acquisition, 70–71
  as not a one-sided event, 79–80
  as only an offer, 69
  plannability and predictability in, 70
  power of, 21
  purpose of, xxvi
  as religious practice, 312
  as a religious practice, 313
  requiring meaningful inclusion, 92–93
  as stimulation and enrichment of the soul, 45
  as subjective and situational, 79
  two-fold process of, 44

as an unfolding development (*entwicklung*), 71–72
unfortunate features of today's, 84
Education for All (EFA) initiative, from the United Nations, xix, 20
education professionals, being alert to abuses of power, 316
education reforms, ecologically informed paradigm about, 51–64
education students, steering toward reason, logic, and scientific evidence, 83
education system, knowing your, 189–90
educational choice
    current status in Canada (2015), 122–25
    providing an appreciable benefit to taxpayers in British Columbia, 126
educational literature, taxonomies from, 289
educational opportunities, promoting the understanding of everyone's historical difference, 209
educational process
    multiple ways of knowing in, 313–14
    ownership of resting with multiple epistemologies, 311
educational reforms
    addressing social and eco-justice within an ecological paradigm, 58–63
    assumed to lead social progress, 53
educational rights, as one of Florian's "three areas," 32
educational settings, 338, 340
educational state, in Canada, 37–38
educational system
    exceptional learners navigating through, 206
    representing the imposition of state power, 212
    teaching about various perspectives, 242
educators
    building a foundation of trust and respect with a parent, 193
    considering children holistically, 16
    development of inclusive, 142–43
    including multiple perspectives in the learning process, 91
    influencing children, 69
    looking for critical learning spaces, 267
    as not perfect, 71
    providing support, 75
    respect for diverse viewpoints, 96
effective learning, barriers to, 287
effective teacher induction, as critical, 274
effective teaching, essential elements to, 281
ego integrity, versus despair, 152
elementary or primary education, 338–39
Eliot, T. S., 335
elitism, independent schools promoting, 130
emotions, self-regulation of, 189
empathy, building, 170
empirical experience, 89n35
Employee Family Assistance Program, 184
end of education, as a continuum of relational possibilities, 209
enrollment trends, providing insights into the appeal of choice, 124–25
environmental and social supports, range of, 167–68
environmental commons, 60–61
epistemological context, limitations of, 315
epistemological diversity, xxn10
    as the focus of much concern and examination, 303
    importance of, 262
    reasons for the importance of, 301–2
    school categories and regulation of, 303
epistemological exclusion, example of, xxii, xxiv–xxv

epistemological inclusion, xxii, xxiii, xxiv, xxvi
epistemological inclusion and awareness, concerned with "how I understand reality," 260
epistemological-based inclusion, 251
epistemological-based tolerance, 267
epistemology (characteristics of inquiry and knowledge), 217, 289, 310, 313
epistemology and epistemological diversity, setting the parameters for inclusion, 301
epistemology and religion, nexus of, 302
Equity in Education Tax Credit (EETC), 307
ethics, superseding epistemology, 253
ethnographic methodology, exploring and identifying family pedagogy, 7
Euclidean space of separate identities, disrupting, 346
European Agency on the Development of Special Needs Education, 22–23
excellence in education, including character development, 315
exceptional learners
　agency replaced by a matrix of social and environmental relationships, 204
　defining the personhood of, 204
　definitions and categorizations relating to, 197n2–98n2
　expected to accept either intervention or exclusion, 206
　"fitting" into the preexisting educational community, 201
　identity of, 200
　in a minority position between strangers and friends, 197
　needing extraordinary intervention, 145
　putting on display or keeping out of sight/site, 202
　reaction to the distress of, 208
　as a relation of power relative to normal learners, 201
　representing a "bad choice" or an opportunity missed, 207
　unable to form an identity independent from the self, 201
exceptionality, 143–46, 200
exclusion
　examples of, xxii
　history of, 237–41
　politics of, 207
　public debate on ethics of, 207n36
existence, meaning of, 67
existential analysis and logotherapy, 66–68
existential education
　aims of, 67, 80
　characteristics of, 79–80
　human image in, 72–73
　implications of, 68
　offering support, space, and protection to children, 74–76
　as a self-worth and meaning-oriented education, 66
existential life, leading, 67
existential meaning, possible here and now, 79
existential philosophy, 67
experimental model of disability, 206
expertise, kinds of, 224
extroverts, teachers as, 221
Ezra Jack Keats Foundation website, 260

fairness, as a source of authority, 224
faith
　everyone having, 238
　in family, 11
　in God, 11, 13
faith-based education, segregating students based on their parents' religious worldview, 308
faith-based schools
　as forces of fragmentation, 307–8
　providing a safe space, 316
　religion and education as intertwined, 311–12
faith-informed discourse, 36–48
faith-informed responses

origins of, 36
  as part of educational discourse, 41
faith-informed teachers' practices, with children, 36
false dichotomies, 88, 264
families
  connecting to services and to other families, 190
  helping children cope with the effects of bullying, 167–68
  listening to, 194
  as primary sources, 15
  social role of changing, 333
  support from, 11–12
family histories, role in shaping knowledge, 3
"Family Life Education," primary school teacher of, 5
family night, as a positive experience, 6
family pedagogy
  absent from teacher education curriculum, 4
  described, 3
  implications of, 14
  potential of, 8
  reclaiming as a topic of inclusion for teacher education, 3–16
  review of relevant literature on, 4–7
  of struggle and hope, 8
Family Pedagogy (Pedagogika Rodziny), 4–5
family/parent involvement, types of, 3–4
fault line, over epistemology, 313
fear, leading to intolerance, 259
Feminism and Disability (Hillyer), 207n37
field of activity, for children, 79
first fundamental motivation, dealing with Dasein, 74–76
First Nations peoples, 239, 240, 311
first-year teachers, provided with extensive support and assistance in Japan, 274
focus, explained as care for what is here, 345
foods-and-festivals approach, 261–62, 263

force, connecting to the word "power," 216
foreign culture, extended time in, 282
Foresight family pedagogy, providing evidence of de facto desegregation, 8
fourth fundamental motivation, connection to other people and to the world, 78–79
Francophone school board, in each province, 123
Frankl, Viktor, 66–67, 244
Free Appropriate Public Education (FAPE), 149
free society, safeguarding, 256
free speech, as harmful to some students, 105
freedom
  experienced in a choice environment, 137
  personhood as the source of, 73
freedom of choice
  countering with two faiths, 11
  Foresight family's response to, 8
  information regarding, 7
  as not free, 9–11
freshman academy, in ninth grade, 167
friendships, protecting against victimization, 170
Fukushima nuclear plant, teachers carrying out extended duties near, 280
full inclusion (FI), 141–43
  derived from principles of normalization, 146
  factors influencing positive outcomes of, 149
function of education, as understanding, xxvi–xxvii
fundamental beliefs, every person having, 257
fundamental motivations, from a pedagogical perspective, 74–79
fundamental trust, 75
fundamental value, experiencing, 77
funding, of schools in British Columbia, 125–26
future, children learning for, 79

gender inclusion, theme of, 325
General Teaching Council for
    Scotland, 25
Getting it Right for Every Child, 27
gist, getting, 157
global awareness, developing, 241
God and Man at Yale, 113
"good parent," qualities of a, 6
gospel music, central to worship, 13–14
government funding, of independent
    schools, 138
grade level transitions, 167
graduation rates, of students in
    Washington, DC, 137
graphic novel picture book, 331
Greer, Germaine, 101

Habermas, Jürgen, 243
heart knowledge and commitment, to
    a person, xxix
Hegel, Georg Wilhelm Friedrich,
    198n3, 339
"helping" careers, graduates of
    independent schools tending to
    choose, 138
heroic teacher, myth of, 222–23
"Heterodox Academy"
    (heterodoxacademy.org), 106
heterogeneous society, preparing
    young people for, 267
"hidden curriculum," concept of, 107
hidden moral curriculum, 108–9
higher academic achievement, strongly
    correlated to choice, 122
higher education, ideological diversity
    and, 100–103
higher education of parents, effect on
    public schools, 130
Hiro-sensei (mid-career teacher),
    tribute to, 279–81
historical difference, 200, 211
holding space, 346, 347–48
home environments, ameliorating the
    effects of school stress, 168
home-based parent involvement
    (H-BPI), 4
home-schooling, as an option, 123

homogeneity, abandoning the
    expectation of, 93
homogenous entities, schools as,
    257–59
homogenous student identity,
    encouraging, 83
homosocial groupings, 38
hospitable act, teaching and learning
    as, 92–94
hospitality, education premised on,
    209–10
hosts
    educators acting as good, 92
    schools acting as, xxix
human attachment, good effects of
    secure, 190
human being, essence of, 72
human image, in existential education,
    72–73
human worth, increasing, xxvii
humans, participating in rituals, 244
humble confidence, projecting
    presence, 226
humility, 316

I am I (Fitzpatrick), 262
"I Have a Dream" (speech), 235
ideal learner, 203–4, 205
ideas, marginalized or silenced, 102
ideas and beliefs, attempts to ignore or
    control, xxx
identity, as form, 330
identity and culture, questions
    regarding, 321
identity diversity, xxn10
identity inclusion, xxii–xxiii, xxiv
    concerned with the question of
        "who am I," 260
    responding to, xxvi
identity-based inclusion, 251
identity-based tolerance, 267
ideological biases, of institutions, 113
ideological diversity, 100–103, 106, 113
ideological inclusion, xxiv
ideological perspective, becoming an
    educational imperative, 158
ignorance, manifesting fear, 259
I-It

becoming I-Thou, 343
circumstances, 346
interactions, 340
imaginative preferences, theme of, 325
immigrants, carrying deep religious convictions, 264
imposition, 339
in difference, (re)cognizing our own self, 209
inalienable human rights, inclusion about, 338
inclusion
   according to Hegel and Buber, 339–44
   as current paradigm for service delivery, 146
   demands for, 239
   described, xix
   difficult to achieve for children with additional support, 24
   genesis and goals of, 141
   honoring diversity, xxix
   implementing, xxi
   international context of, 20–24
   as a priority for educational settings in many countries, 338
   purpose of, xxvii–xxviii
   requiring double reflection and recognition of the other, 341
   as a series of issues and problems, 206
   themes common to definitions of, 142
   threatening teachers' identity, 31
inclusion and diversity, value of, 241–43
inclusion policies, implementation of as uneven, 24
inclusive classrooms, critical dimensions of successful, 156
inclusive critical thinking model, 94
inclusive education system, in British Columbia, 142
inclusive learning and perspectives, cavity of, xxxii
Inclusive Practice Project (IPP), 19, 32, 33
inclusive practices
   coming alive when things are open and relaxed, 346
   developing, 19–33
   rules and requirements designed for ensuring, 342–43
inclusive praxis, 154–57
inclusive schools, encouraging greater diversity, xxiii
inclusivity, as an important value in education, 301
independent or private schools, as an option, 123
independent persons, 66, 70
Independent School Act, in British Columbia, 125
independent schools
   academic performance higher in, 130
   conferring a financial benefit on a province, 126
   contributing to egalitarianism, 138
   as generally government regulated, 124
   high-ranking, 122
   offering alternative approaches to teaching, 124
independently constructing, a story, 325
indifference, to the historical uniqueness of others, 209
Indigenous content, avoiding as religious knowledge, 40
Indigenous cultures, ecological intelligence of, 54
Indigenous education, 36
Indigenous knowledge, 40, 41
Indigenous languages and musical instruments, inclusion of, xx
Indigenous learning, moved to the background at school, 47
Indigenous peoples
   beliefs perceived as inferior, 37
   public schooling of, 238
   traditionally relied on storytelling, 271
Indigenous worldviews, conflicting with (Western) science, 294

individual(s)
  as the basic social unit, 51
  finding their own path toward self-discovery, 205
  freedom of, 55
  as normal or abnormal, 144
individual emancipation, 325
individual freedom, understanding, 56
individual intelligence, compared to ecological, 61
individual liberty, not an absolute good for all people, 254
individual self, educators building up, 198
individual sports, fostering, 175
individualism, 56, 153, 205
individualization, 28–29
Individualized Education Plan (IEP) meeting, 189
"individualized learning," xxiii
individual-level response and intervention, 172–75
Individuals with Disabilities Education Act (IDEA), 149
induction practices, in Japan for teachers, 273
induction program, adding more to the burden of first-year teachers, 273
informed guides, on the path of life, 79
initial teacher education, 32, 112
institutions
  moral priorities of, 105
  for the treatment of exceptional persons, 147
instruction, engaging all learners, 169
intellectual disability, 201
intellectual diversity. *See* ideological diversity
intelligence, varieties of, 145
Intelligence Quotient Test (IQT), 204
interactive relationships, naming as ecologies, 63
intergenerational lessons, for teacher education in desegregated school settings, 15

Interim Report of the Truth and Reconciliation Commission, 240
intermediate or third zone, 344
International Covenant on Economic, Social, and Cultural Rights, ratified by Canada in 1976, 127
interpersonal comparisons, humans making, 145
interventionist strategies, marginalizing exceptional individuals, 207n38
interventions
  for bullies, 172–73
  for victims, 174–75
intolerance
  of movements of the Right, 109
  as necessary and right, 254–55
"inviting school success," 154
inviting schools, 154–55
IQ, as a valid measure of normalcy, 145
Isaiah, 235
Islamic educational epistemology, based on "revelation" and intuition, 314
Issues in Indigenous Education class, 36
It, creating for the I a necessary finite quality, 340
I-Thou
  Buber's explanations of, 341–42
  explanation of, 348
  moving into I-It, 343
Jackman, Martha, 307
Japan, teacher acculturation, 272–74
Jesuit University of Philosophy and Education Ignatianum, 5
"just" treatment, of a child, 77
justification, allowing him/herself to be as he/she is, 77
K-12 education, "hidden curriculum" in, 107
kankei (inter-relationships), 274, 281, 282
kazuna (bonds), 281, 282
kids, doing as well as they can, 188
kindergarten, refusal and resistance to, 183–87
King, Martin Luther, Jr., 235
Kirk, Samuel A., 201

kizuki (with-it-ness), 274, 281–82
kizuna (bonds), 274
knowledge
    categories of legitimate, 88
    coming in many different forms, 86
    compartmentalizing and privileging types of, xxvii
    compartmentalizing as scientific or not, 95
    construction of boundaries between forms of, 302
    level required for critical thinking, 233
    marginalization of, 52–58
knowledge acquisition, education as more than, 70–71
knowledge and belief, historical development of, 296–97
knowledge economy, rise of, 22
Kojima-sensei, insights from a veteran teacher in Japan, 277–79

Längle, Alfried, 73, 74
language
    as a conduit in a sender/receiver process of communication, 56–57
    of liberalism, 53, 57
    as metaphorical, 55
    processes hiding and illuminating changes, 58
    sanitization of, 241
LASAR project website, 295n41
law, discussion of the problem of ideological diversity, 112–13
laws of science, as irrevocable, 288
leaders, leading by consent, 225n18
learners
    children reconceptualized as, 16
    including all traditions, 93
Learning about Science and Religion (LASAR) research project, 295
learning demand, relationship between science and religion requiring, 292
learning disabilities (LD)
    Kirk coined the term, 201
    students with bullied, 163

learning for all, as one of Florian's "three areas," 32
learning for life theme, 322–23
learning from others, xxv–xxvi
    faith in, 13
learning spirit, nourishing, 39–40
learning styles, 221
learning support teachers, 27
Least Restrictive Environment (LRE), 149
legitimacy, 225
lesson study, success of Japanese education and, 281
Levinas, Emmanuel, 93
LGBT students, separate schools addressing the needs of, 311
liberalism
    central value of, 55
    claiming to speak in a secular voice, 302
    as a context-free metaphor, 52–53
    permeating every aspect of daily life, 62
    traditions of, 51
liberals, assuming that everyone shares their political views, 106
libertarian liberals, 53
libertarians, 104, 105
liberty, 108
life
    as more serious, 331
    as not feasible and not plannable, 69–70
life stories, sharing, 334
"linguistic hospitality," 210n49
literacy skills, 320, 320n3
literary value of words, on the wane, 328
literary vocabulary, simple or sparse, 333
literature, fostering emotional healing and growth, 175
living traditions
    importance of, 90–92
    of Māori people, 91
local history, family pedagogy restoring the importance of, 14
logical positivists, 89n35

logical reasoning, 89n35
logotherapy, 67
Long Walk to Freedom (Mandela), 235
long-term interventions, for victims of bullying, 174
Lost at School (Greene), 189
love, not just about a type of behavior that can be prescribed, 348
LRE experience, providing for students, 154

Mackay Report, 304, 316
mainstream educational reform initiatives, as both a facilitator and a barrier, 23
Māori people, of New Zealand, 91
map/territory disconnect, Bateson's observation about, 56–57
Marcuse, Herbert, 103
marginalization
　avoiding opportunities for, 171
　of knowledge, 52–58
marginalized learners, 198, 212
marginalized teachers, 212
market liberalism, 51–52
Marsden, George, 86
meaninglessness, Jean-Paul Sartre on, 244
mechanistic worldview, of Western learners, 294
medical model, 205n27
medicine, "hidden curriculum" in, 107
Memorandum 112, 305
mental and physical disabilities
　isolating people with, 241–42
　killing persons with, 147
mental health
　challenges, 188–94
　disorders, 188
　education and, 181–95
　educators developing awareness about, 182
　services for victims of bullying, 175
　victims of bullying having problems, 165
"mental retardation," predominant psychological theories, 203n23
mentors, 273

mentorship, 272
metafictive traits, 330
metaphorical language systems, 56
metaphors, 59, 151
metaphysics (characteristics of reality), 289
method acting, 226n21
military force, 219
Mill, John Stuart, 256, 313
Millennium Development Goals, of the UN, 20
"mini-schools," within larger public schools, 124
Ministry of Education academic credits, private schools granting, 311
misconceptions, schools correcting, 251
"miseducation," imperiling public life, 259
missionaries
　set up schools for Indigenous peoples, 39
　sought guidance from Christian education scholars, 42
　worked to replace Indigenous knowledge, 37
mixed outcome, 287
mobile occupations, abandoning, 38
monistic worldview, 294
Montana
　decentralized school system, 128
　students doing better, 129
moral authority, 225
moral foundations theory (MFT), 103–4
moral lesson, 322–23
moral priorities, applying to individuals, 105
moral psychology, 103
"mother-blaming," shame of, 207n37
motivational interviewing, 173
multicultural days, xxxi, 257
multiculturalism
　in British Columbia, xxixn45–xxxn45
　embracing, 327
　during a time of Trudeauian idealism, 152
multiple intelligences, 156, 221

multitier system of supports (MTSS), 146
mutuality of love, complete calling explained through, 345
mutuality through love, explaining playing in the in-between, 347–48
Myers Briggs type indicator, 221
mystical/spiritual knowledge, from Indigenous peoples, 88
mythopoeic narratives, of cultures, 63

narrative approaches, acceptance of, 272
narrative pedagogies
    interest in, 271–72
    relating to Japanese cultural practices, 274
"national strength," teaching in public schools, 43
Native Canadians, education gap, xxx
Native spirituality, rich in ceremony, story, and teachings, 240
natural science, limited access to personhood, 73
natural systems, study of, 54
nature of science (NOS), teaching students about, 285–86
negative peer relationships, predicting bullying, 170
negative relation, to the other, 339
neurodiversity, 155
neutral stance, amidst a sea of beliefs and values, 234
No Child Left Behind (NCLB), 149
"no platforming," 100–101, 105
nonprogressive views, student harm arising from exposure to, 102
nonprogressive voices, call for an increase in, 110
nonscientific traditions, 84n8, 90–91
normalization, 146, 211
The Normalization Principle (Wolfensberger), 148
Northwest Territories, Board of Education, 38
no-school-no-food lesson, 9
no-tolerance policies, widely implemented, 254

novice teachers, tied to a lesson plan, 150
nuanced Black Family (n-BFP), 3
nuclear radiation, threat of, 280

Oberlin College, 109
'old' and 'new,' dichotomy of, 88
old knowledge, content becoming, 40
"old ways of thinking," perception of, 82–84
On Liberty (Mill), 256
one-to-one teaching, of students with learning difficulties, 29
one-way pedagogical exchanges, leading to stagnation, 273
online curriculum to students at home, 123
online parent engagement resource, for educators, 193
Ontario, schools in, 302–6
Ontario public education
    politics of inclusion in, 301–16
    regulation of religion and religious diversity in, 302
    separate and private schools in, 310–13
open-minded and nonjudgmental, being, 194
open-mindedness, encouraging, 95
openness, to others' ways of thinking, 95
operating grants, for independent schools, 124
opinions, importance of minority, 256
oppressed family needs, for legitimate authority, 15
Oppressed Family Pedagogy (OFP), 3, 8, 9–14
oppression, 8
oral cultures, perpetuating misconceptions and prejudices, 61
organic moral order, sabotaging, 219
"origins," aspect of, 288
the Other
    being treated as, 282
    differences communicated in the behavior of, 62–63

the Other (*continued*)
   engaging with, 241
   learning from and about, 94
   as an object, 339, 340
   relationship with, 56–58
   unconditional responsibility to, 93
Ottawa Christian School, 312–13
Ottawa Islamic School (OIS), 312
outcomes, dependent on underlying knowledge, 287
outside the box, thinking, 274

parameters, defining schools and school systems, 314
parent consultation, requirement for, 193
parental involvement, 135, 193–94
parental satisfaction, with schools they selected, 121–22
parenting practices, 169
parents
   of children who have bullied, 173
   choosing privately funded schools, 307
   communicating with, 192–94
   educational options for school-aged children, 123
   enabling the Dasein of the child, 70
   having a choice in educational experiences of their children, 133
   of victims, 175
passion, about the subject projecting presence, 226
passive aggressive, child as, 186
passive approaches, to classroom management, 169
passive coping, 174
pastiche personality, construction of, 331
patience, exhibiting, 194
pedagogical expertise, 224
pedagogical pet, exceptional learner as, 206
pedagogies of desire, 108–9
pedagogy
   at home, 15
   "specialisms" of, 5

peer collaboration, engaging, 13
peer relationships, fostering positive, 170
peer tutoring, 157
peer victimization, experiencing, 162
peers
   as more aware of bullying than teachers, 171
   volunteering as friends and advocates for vulnerable children, 175
people
   of difference, 205
   learning from each other, 112
   as more important than beliefs, 253
perception, of ownership and responsibility accompanying choice, 137
perfectionists, putting themselves under pressure, 71
permission, consent implying, 218
perpetrators, of bullying at risk, 165
personal meaning, 79
personal practical knowledge, 271
personal values, 76–77
"personalized learning," xxiii
personhood
   crucial test of, 199
   described, 72–73
   recognition of, xxiii–xxiv
persons, self-formation of, 69
Perspectives on the Ideas of Gregory Bateson, Ecological Intelligence, and Educational Reforms (Larson), 54
philosophical and educational literature, on the relationship between religion and science, 289–92
philosophical literature, taxonomies from, 289, 290–91
physical and social environment, minimizing opportunities for bullying, 171
physical bullying, 162
physical posture, revealing degree of engagement, 226
picture books
   change over time in, 322–33

functions of, 321
grouped into cohorts according to decades, 322
playing in the in-between, 338, 344–48
pluralism, in society, 153
pluralistic approach to education, arguments for, 126
pluralistic classrooms, opportunities for inclusive practices, xxvii–xxviii
point of view, learners having, 94
political centralization, school as the weapon of, 211
political discursive innovation, countering the messages of, 10
political diversity. *See* ideological diversity
political ideologies, prioritizing moral foundations, 104
"poor teacher," motivated to improve, 278
"position of the heart," neglecting, 313–14
positive niche construction, 155
positive peer relationships, classrooms promoting, 169
positive school climate, 169
positivistic epistemology, 89
postmodern books, 327, 333
postmodern story, introduced, 325
"Post-Partisan Social Psychology" website, 106
post-school outcomes, for children who bully, 165
power
    of the classroom teacher, 216
    use of, undermining the teacher's authority, 219
power imbalance, between the perpetrator and the victim, 162
practices, ensuring inclusive, 340
pragmatic critical thinking, 84
pragmatic method in education, 86
pragmatism, in the context of higher education, 84
praxis, referring to a habitual act or performance, 150
predicting, 157

A Preface to Moral Sentiments (Smith), 52
preferred intelligences, using, 156
preparation, as a source of authority, 224
presence, of teachers, 225–26
preservice teachers
    considering faith-informed practices, 42
    exploring educational experiences from faith locations, 41
    studying family pedagogy, 6–7
print, fostering abstract thinking and reinforcing reliance upon sight, 61–62
private and faith-based schools, as inherently harmful to the social fabric, 307
private property, ownership of, 52–58
private schools, 310
    more likely to be integrated, 136
    more likely to promote tolerance, voting, and social involvement, 136
    out of step with a modern diverse society, 307
    presence within a public school district having positive impact, 136–37
    status of, 311
    surveys of achievements, 311n22
    tending to be more successful than public schools, 128
professional boundaries, teachers maintaining, 222
professional development
    on classical tolerance in the classroom, 267
    of teachers, 154–55
Professional Graduate Diploma of Education (PGDE), reform of, 19, 32
professional learning, "doing" as an essential element of, 30
progressive educational model, of John Dewey, 198n3
progressive moral curriculum, hidden, 107, 108

progressive voters, prioritizing moral foundations, 104
progressives, moral prioritizations pattern of, 105
progressivism, as an educational model, 85
prosocial skills, teaching, 148
prosperity, as the sole conscious aim, 335
protection, 75, 76
Protestant Christian religious indoctrination, replacing, 304
Protestant press, discussing secularization of schools, 42–43
Protestantism, 37, 309
provinces, each maintaining a Department of Education, 123
psychometric approach to intelligence, in Western cultures, 145
psychotherapeutic treatment, "spiritual" deficit in, 68
psychotherapy, reductionism of, 67
public discussions, painting "religious types" as opposing change or being anti-choice, 238
public education, designed to deliver good citizens, 303
public educators, developing curriculum to include First Nations peoples, 240
public funding mechanism, Ontario included separate schools in, 310
Public School Act, appearing to reflect diversity, xxx
public schools
    Character Development Initiative as mandatory, 315
    compared to independent schools, 122
    conducting on strictly secular and nonsectarian principles, xxx
    excising Christianity and faith as foundations of learning, 44–45
    knowing appropriate in, 304–5
    language of secular rationality in, 303
    operating in an environment muddied by rules, 128
    as an option, 123
    performance improved by competition from Catholic schools, 137
    worldview inclusion in, 233–46
public sector, building social capital in, 134
public spaces
    limiting the reach of religion into, 308
    making available in higher education, 91

quantitative definitions, predisposition toward, 204
questions, ultimate and existential central to the human situation, 244

radical progressive students, demands of, 109
Rand, Ayn, 52–53
rational knowledge, versus irrational belief, 286
rational science, triumph over religious "delusion," 286
rational/critical thinking, 51, 56
rationality, different traditions of, 90
reactive coping, 174
reading
    becoming less shared, 328
    with children, 320
reason, operating in different disciplines, 296
reciprocal acknowledgement, 341
reciprocity, 210
recognition
    of a child, 77–78
    turning into a subject-subject process, 341
recognition and assertion, tension between, 341
reel teachers, misconception induced by, 220–21
refugees, resistance to integration, 264

reinforced outcome, 287
relational bullying, 162
relational inclusion, 348
relational times, 343, 344
relationships, children requiring, 76
religion
    beliefs and values linked to, 234
    coming to the West on the backs of immigrants, 263
    confining to private space, 309
    identification with extremist, reactionary discrimination, 308
    as an important social fault line, 302
    knowledge from, 88
    as more comprehensive category of human knowing, 313
    often linked with "illiberal" modes of educational thought and practices, 302
    as poisoning everything, 236
    as a private matter, 308
    raising important epistemological questions, 302
    referendum on role of in public education, 307
    replacing the authoritative voice of, 153
    separated from education, 305
    as a source of harm, 306–10
    as too controversial, 240
religion and education, existing in distinct and separate epistemological worlds, 306–7
"Religion of Humanity" (Comte), 243
religiosity, relationship with length of time spent in school, 310
religious beliefs, influence on the learning of science, 286
religious communities, almost complete absence of persons of difference from, 207n38
religious content, teaching in a dispassionate and nondevotional manner, 40
religious differences, eliminating, 238
religious faith, 13
religious illiteracy, disquieting, 236–37
"Religious Information and Moral Development" (Mackay Report), 304
religious knowledge and awareness, coming from outside the public school system, 236
religious minorities
    challenging Protestant Christian school opening exercises and religious instruction, 304
    in interaction with state actors, 306
religious perspectives, leading to distortion, 242
religious schools, hateful or discriminatory messages espoused by, 308
religious traditions, awareness of rich stories, parables, and teachings of, 237
religious voices, purging the public square of, 238
religious worldview
    continuing to influence human thought and action today, 246
    developed language to deal with life and death, 243
    lack of knowledge and awareness of, 236
Report of the Commission on Private Schools, 315
"Repressive Tolerance" (Marcuse), 103
reputation, of a teacher, 228
residential schools system, 239, 250–51
resilience, building, 111, 161–76
resources, for science educators, 294–97
respect, 251, 252, 257
respectful recognition, from others, 78
response to interventions (RTI), 145–46
responses, to differences which make a difference, 56
Rice, Condoleeza, 101
rituals, 243–44
Roman Catholic church, role in education, 312
Roman Catholic separate schools identifying parents as the key stakeholders, 312

Roman Catholic separate schools (*continued*)
    included in the Character Development Initiative, 311
    Ontario's funding of, 305
root metaphors, 57–58, 59

The Sacred Project of American Sociology (Smith), 110
Miss Sakaguchi (novice teacher), narrative of, 274–77
Same, Same but Different (Kostecki-Shaw), 261
Sandridge Independent Secular School, in Australia, xxvi
Sartre, Jean-Paul, 244
scapegoats, using "marked" individuals as, 210n48
The School and Society (Dewey), 85
school categories, 303, 311
school level transitions, 167
school policies, against bullying and violence, 166
school shootings, bullying and, 165
school systems
    perpetuating existing inequalities and intergenerational underachievement, 21
    smaller achieving better academic results, 128
school-based mentors, in Japan, 273
school-based parent involvement (S-BPI), 4
schools
    as accessible, open, inclusive, and welcoming, 250
    as homogenous entities, 257–59
    not available in some parts of the world, 20
    responsible for giving children knowledge needed for life in modern Canada, 43
"schools for all," developing, 21
schools of choice, 138
schools-within-schools models, 167
School-Wide Positive Behavior Support (SWPBS), 166

school-wide prevention programs, 166
science
    conflicting with religion, 236
    development of resulting in a Western tradition, 293
    growing out of an attempt to get closer to God, 297
    as just one type of knowledge, 89n35
    operating within traditional frameworks of assumption, 89
    supported by religion, 290
science and religion
    individuals employing both trying to understand the world, 288
    one-dimensional view of the relationship between, 286
    positions of the view of the relationship between, 289
    in the science classroom, 296
science class, outcomes from any given, 287
science education, nature of science and religion in, 285–97
science educators
    challenges facing, 287–94
    implications for, 294–97
Science-Religion Self-Identification Inventory (SRSII), 296
scientific approach, epistemologies besides only, 88
scientific definition of mission and identity, advocated by Dewey, 86
scientific discourse, of so called twenty-first century education, 87
scientific knowledge, as complex, 89
scientific method, Dewey and, 85
scientific reasoning, epistemological bias toward, 304
scientific skill and observation, stressing, 331
scientism, affirming, 244
Scotland, not all children in school, 21
Scottish Teacher Education Committee (STEC), 25
screening, the exceptional learner, 207

second fundamental motivation, revolving around the question of value, 76–77
secondary teachers, describing themselves as "a learnng support teacher," 26
secular progressive inclusivity, 308
secular society, insisting on neutrality yet teaching little about religious worldviews, 240
secular university, becoming increasingly marginal to American society, 263
secularism, as not religiously neutral, 305
self, needing to act on others and not with others, 346
self-acceptance, 75
self-actualization, 199
self-authorization, 226–28
self-determined history, reliance on, 199
self-efficacy, predicting behavior, 168
self-formation, 69, 72
self-knowledge, 199
self-regulation, 189
self-sacrifice, 92
self-worth, 68, 78
semiotic systems, 54
Sendai Earthquake, 279
sense of humor, 221
separate schools, 303, 310–11
separation, of people because of beliefs and identity, xxii
services, families involved with for mental health challenges, 187
shared responsibility, for children who face difficulties, 28
shared telling, story as, 325
short-term interventions, for victims of bullying, 174
Shulman, Lee, 31–32
sibling relationships, significant to child resilience, 167–68
siblings, providing support, 75
sink or swim, beginning teachers left to in Canada and the United States, 272

sink or swim metaphor, having no equivalent in Japanese teacher education, 274
skills deficit, displaying, 88
social and cultural remediation, legitimized behind a veil of scientific neutrality, 207
social and personality psychology, lack of political diversity in, 110
social capital, coproduction and trust as components of, 134–35
social connotations, of Caldecott winners, 321
Social Darwinian thinking, role in Nazi Germany, 57
social exchange, 343, 347
social function, of picture books, 320
social impact, 333
social intelligence, fostering, 174
social justice liberalism, 51–52
social justice liberals, 53
social life, creation of at the heart of inclusive practices, 342
social practices, of the hidden progressive moral curriculum, 108
social psychology, bias and discrimination by progressives in, 110
Social Role Valorization (SRV), 148
social skills
 instruction by teachers, 170
 teaching to victims of bullying, 174
social spiritism, interest in, 328
social workers, needing to deal with many upsetting situations, 111
socialization
 of Japan's teachers, 273
 of student life at universities, 109
societies, dominated by particular worldviews, 239
socioecological approach, to resilience, 161
socioeconomic status, effect on public schools, 130
sociology, lack of ideological diversity, 110–11
sociology of education, goal of, 153

"soul of my soul," 342
sources, of truth and certainty, 244
space
  children needing sufficient, 75
  creating where a lot of ideas are presented, 112
  first fundamental motivation focusing on, 76
"speaking for," replacing reciprocity with, 210
special education, 145–46, 212
special education needs (SEN), 26
special education systems, developing, 22
special education teacher, becoming in the UK, 26
special education view, "classic," 23
special educators, transition planning for, 167
special needs students, in independent schools, 131
special needs teachers, 31
specific learning disabilities (SLDs), 157
spiritual knowing, referred to as intuition, 314
spiritual responsiveness, creating opportunities of, 342
spirituality
  affecting learning, 41–42
  becoming less prominent in reading material, 328
  of the human being, 68
  of persons involved in education, 69–73
sponsor teacher, providing inspiration, 277
standardized measurements of diversity, identifying a pathological condition, 204
standardized questionnaire, identifying the range of views held by students on science and religion, 296
"standards-based" reforms, 22
state control, over epistemological diversity in public institutions, 314

Steps to an Ecology of Mind (Bateson), 54
stereotypical discriminatory ideas, about the role of women, 307
stories
  influencing young readers, 320–21
  providing a way to learn, 334
  as shared telling, 325
story form and audience, changing, 327
storytellers, 271, 316
strategic learning, 157
strategic reading process, 157
strengths, focusing on, 155
structural contexts, for children, 78–79
student difficulties, with the nature of scientific knowledge, 292
student goodwill, 225
student work, assessment of poor quality, 112
students
  awareness of bullying, 172
  becoming friends with, 217
  becoming fully engaged with, 226
  cognitively removed from their families' authority, 47
  commonly perceiving science and religion to be in opposition, 293
  discovering the wide ranging positions scientists have, 293
  listening to, 194
  from non-Western cultures encountering difficulties with science, 293
  rejecting evolution, 288
  requiring an education permeated with classical tolerance, 259
  teaching to seek help, 170–71
  tolerating the behavior of, 267
  understanding as three dimensional people, xxxi
  wanting teachers to be professionals, 222
students with disabilities, segregation of, 147–48
subject-area expertise, 224
subjectivity, of education, 71
subject-object interactions, expected, 339

subject-object model, 341
subject-object relations, 340–41
subject-self-learner, 198
subject-subject process, 341
subsidiarity
    enacting, 138
    principle of, 127–30
Sunday schools, teaching and learning provided in, 47
supernatural phenomena, 288
"superstition," as a term loaded with meaning, 310
support
    children experiencing through the assistance of others, 75
    first fundamental motivation focusing on, 76
"Supporting Meaningful Consultation with Parents," 193, 193n20
sustainability thinking, promoting, 52
Syrian refugees, as religious, 264n66

T_4 Euthanasia Project, in pre-war Nazi Germany, 147
taken-for-granted patterns, of thinking, 65
Tatchell, Peter, 101
Tea Party activists, 53
teacher, in relationship to students, 314
teacher acculturation, in Japan, 272–74, 275, 281
teacher authority, nonessential sources of, 220–23
teacher development courses, focusing on extending knowledge and skills, 29–30
teacher education, areas to reform, 32
teacher education programs
    considering family pedagogy in, 11
    in Japan, 273
    time allocated within to cover issues of inclusion, 25
teacher induction, 273, 274
teacher narratives, of experience, education, and story, 274–81
teacher stories, learning from, 281–82

teacher training, in prevention, identification, and intervention, 168
teachers
    adjusting to Christian practices becoming state practices, 41
    advice on mental health, 187–88
    alternatives for teaching tolerance in schools, 266
    authority of, 216–29
    becoming friends with students, 222
    beginnng, 28
    believing in students, xxviii–xxix
    caring deeply for children, 281
    carrying out extended duties, 280
    of children with support needs, 28
    Christian coming to western Canada, 38
    classroom providing assistance to student teachers, 273
    concerns deriving from increasingly diverse educational communities, 148–49
    developing knowledge and positive attitudes to inclusion, 29
    differentiating instruction to meet the varied needs of their learners, 169
    as enigmatic and mysterious, 222
    first-year in Japan, 274
    as funny, 221
    gaining authority over youngsters, 47
    heading off bullying in their classes, 169
    initial education, 32, 112
    learning support, 26, 27
    marginalized, 212
    myth of heroic, 222–23
    needing to authorize themselves, 227
    needing to be sensitive to the context in which they work, 314
    new, 33
    not promoting any particular kind of worldview or ideology, 240

teachers (*continued*)
    as not social workers, 189
    novice tied to a carefully composed lesson plan, 150
    personality types of, 221
    poor motivated to improve, 278
    preservice, 6–7, 41, 42
    professional development of, 154–55
    qualities of good, 224
    reel, 220–21
    replacing knowledge systems students brought with them, 47
    role in promoting participation and achievement, 19
    role of Japan's, 274
    roles and identities in special education, 26–27
    roles in developing inclusion, 28–31
    in schools of choice enjoying a greater degree of freedom, 137
    special needs, 31
    sponsor providing inspiration, 277
    teaching effective coping strategies, 174
    views of the inclusion task, 24–26
    white, 11
    wide-ranging tasks of, 27
teacher's authority, sources of, 223–28
teacher-to-teacher conversations, 271, 272
teaching
    act of represented by various metaphors, 150
    as a continuous learning process, 276
    permitting ourselves to, 226
teaching philosophy, of learning alongside the students, 278
technology
    as culturally neutral and as the expression of progress, 51
    solving problems, 331
tension, between the spheres of "normal" and "special" education, 200
theological education, long-standing focus on "formation," 113

theology, 113
third fundamental motivation, 77
"the third space," 89–90
third Viennese school of psychotherapy, 67
third zone, 344
"three apprenticeships," 32
time
    Buber's specific references to issues of, 343
    required for relationships, 76
time, space, and boundaries, attention to, 346
times of the in-between, elements of, 344–45
tolerance
    accommodating a misunderstood and false application of, 255
    as the basis of a free society, 256
    children's picture books focused exclusively on teaching, 260
    consisting of a mixture of affirmation, resistance, and celebration, 256
    definition of, 253
    as a dirty word, 252–55
    incorrect understanding of, 266
    limits to, 254
    mutually dependent with respect, 257
    neoclassical classification of, 253
    not included in the four classical virtues or in the three Christian virtues, 250
    not interfering with individual freedom, 254
    as not the ultimate goal, 265
    people demanding its demise, 252
    of a person's behavior while appreciating and respecting the person, 265
    replaced with mutual respect, 252
    respect and, 251
    restrictions to, 256
    upholding a praxis of, 250
    what it should and should not be, 267–68

what teachers need to know about, 249–68
without understanding, 265
top-down hierarchy, in Japanese schooling, 273
top-down legislation, resulting in a kind of alphabet soup, 149
tradition, meaning of, 84n8
traditional bullying, 162
traditional education, portrayed as old and irrelevant, 84
traditional epistemologies, perceived as "unscientific," 87
traditional expectations, giving teachers a kind of authority, 224
traditional knowledge, 89, 95n66
traditions
    described, 82n1
    embracing through critical thinking, 93–94
    judging, 95
    never serving as a substitute for truth, 93
    not depending on the scientific method for validation, 89
    owned by people, 91
    perceiving as an impediment to learning, 82
    providing a normative force holding a society together, 92
    vital for critical thinking, 91
traditions and beliefs, knowledge from fundamental, 88
training people to think, in prescribed ways, 87
transcultural teacher narrative, 271–82
transformative learning, as a UNESCO mantra, 52
transitions, planning for, 167
Treaty of Maastricht (1992), section entitled "Principle of Subsidiarity," 129
"trigger warnings," 101, 111
Trudeauian idealism, 152
trust
    experiences of, 75
    as a by-product of coproduction, 134
    in a secure setting, 345
"turning toward someone," 76
Tutu, Desmond, 244
two perspectives outcome, 287

UN Convention on the Rights of the Child, 127
uncritical critical thinking, in teaching and learning, 82–96
undisturbed outcome, 287
unified scientific outcome, 287
unilateral public education, proponents of, 122
unintergration, Winnicott's concept of, 345
United Church of Canada, 43n25, 44
United Nations Education for All initiative (EFA), 21–22
United Nations Universal Declaration of Human Rights, 126–27
universal civic values, all schools committed to teaching, 132
Universal Declaration of Human Rights, 338
universities
    assumed ideological neutrality of, 113
    concerns about coddling at, 111–12
    modern or typical, 102n14
University of Sydney, student union threatened to deregister student religious groups, 102
university teacher preparation programs, improving, 273
unknowing, central to the concept of playing in the in-between, 347
"upcoming discipline," family pedagogy as, 5
"useful," what is perceived as, 89
"Useless Eaters," euthanized, 147

value claims, of a living tradition, 90
values education, 131–36
values neutral position, providing, 131
Vanier, Jean, 241–42
verbal bullying, 162
victimization, exacerbating communication disabilities, 165

victims
  effects of bullying on, 164
  interventions for, 174–75
victims and bullies, characteristics of, 163–64
view labels, in the proposed empirically oriented taxonomy, 292–93
viewpoint diversity. *See* ideological diversity
vigilance, by teachers, 172
visions of life, 234, 246
vocation, metaphor of teaching as, 150, 151
"Vocation in Theology-based Nursing Theories," 151
vocational efficacy, challenges to, 152
vocational questions, teachers tormenting themselves with, 226–27
vocational satisfaction, potential challenges to, 151–53
vocational thriving, 155
voice, represented more by children, 325
Voltaire, 253

wars, caused by religion, 236
way of knowing, Western science presented as the foremost, 294
ways of life, 234, 246
We Can Get Along Together: A Child's Book of Choices (Payne), 261–62
Western education, systemic inequalities in, xx
Western nations, as increasingly religious, 264n66
Western rationalist epistemologies, 313
Western tradition, of the nature of science, 293
white teachers, not prepared to engage local family pedagogy, 11
Who Should Survive? One of the Choices on Our Conscience, 207n36
whole person, inclusion as a theory recognizing, xxix
wholeness, 345
Widdowson, Francis, 95n66
Williams, Rowan, 288
Wolfensberger, Wolf, 146
wordless books, 325, 327, 331, 333
words
  history of, 57
  revising the meaning of, 55
  understanding as metaphors, 59
work, viewing as a calling, 158
worked example, from a larger ethnographic study, 7–9
world religions, included in the high school program, 304
worldview perspectives (secular and religious), teaching about various, 243
worldviews
  coming to a greater understanding of different, 245
  decrease in knowledge and awareness, 235–36
  defined, 234
  exclusion of First Nations' visions of, 240
  having similar structures, 244
  inclusion in public schooling, 233–46
  teaching about in various subject areas, 245
  unraveling at the edges, 333
  as visions of life and ways of life, 246
wrapping up, 157

youth, connecting to other youth experiencing mental health challenges, 190
Youth in Residence at the Kelty Mental Health Resource Centre, 190

zatsudan (informal teacher-to-teacher conversations), 278
zero-tolerance policies, 254n25
Zine, Jasmin, 313–14, 316